MUGHAL DOCUMENTS
(1526-1627)

MUGHAL DOCUMENTS
(1526-1627)

S.A.I. TIRMIZI

MANOHAR
2025

First published 1989
Reprinted 2024, 2025

ISBN 978-81-85054-71-1 (hardbound)
ISBN 978-81-19953-62-2 (ebook)

Published by
Ajay Kumar Jain *for*
Manohar Publishers & Distributors
4753/23 Ansari Road, Daryaganj
New Delhi 110 002

Printed and bound in India

To

Professor S. Nurul Hasan

PREFACE

It was Leopold Von Ranke, father of modern science of history, who stressed the importance of basing history on genuine and original documents. He established, for the first time, in Germany, 'the Cult of the Document' early in the 19th century. This new cult soon influenced English historiography which in turn affected the writings of the British historians of Mughal India who advocated the use of documents in historical studies.

While V.A. Smith did recognise the importance of official documents, it was W.H. Moreland who emphasised the inestimable value of documents for the agrarian history of India. He observed, "Our knowledge of the form and content of Akbar's charitable grants of land has been materially increased by the discovery of a bundle of old papers preserved by a Parsi family in Gujarat, a locality where one would scarcely have set out to search for Mughal documents; and it is still possible to hope for other discoveries of the same kind. The systematic collection and publication of such documents would furnish material of inestimable value for the future historian, not merely of the agrarian system, but of the whole life of the people of India." (*The Agrarian System of Moslem India*, Delhi, 1929, p. xvii).

Moreland obviously had in mind J.J. Modi's *The Parsees at the Court of Akbar and Dastur Meherjee Rana* (Bombay, 1903) and H.S. Hodivala's *Studies in Parsi History* (Bombay, 1920). How such documents can be used for elucidating specific issues has been demonstrated by Bashirud Din Ahmad's *Faramin-i Salatin* (Delhi, 1926), K.M. Jhaveri's *Imperial Farmans (A.D. 1579 to A.D. 1805) granted to the Ancestors of His Holiness the Tikayat Maharaj* (Bombay, 1928), *Kitab-i Daftar-i Diwani wa Mal wa Mulki-i Sarkar-Alyee* (Hyderabad, 1933), M.S. Commissariat's *Imperial Mughal Farmans in Gujarat* (Bombay, 1940), Abdul Bari Maani's *Asanidus Sanadid* (Ajmer, 1952), Yusuf Hussain Khan's *Selected Documents of Shah Jahan's Reign (1634-1658)* (Hyderabad, 1953), *Selected Waqai of the Deccan (1660-1671)* (Hyderabad, 1953), *Selected Documents of Aurangzeb's Reign (1659-1706 A.D.)* (Hyderabad, 1958), B.N. Goswamy and J.S. Grewal's *The Mughals and the Jogis of*

Jakhbar (Calcutta, 1967), *The Mughals and Sikh Rulers and the Vaishnavas of Pindori* (Calcutta, 1969), K.P. Srivastava's *Mughal Farmans* (Lucknow, 1974), M.Z.A. Shakeb's *Mughal Archives I* (Hyderabad, 1977), S.A.I. Tirmizi's *Edicts from the Mughal Harem* (Delhi, 1979), M.A. Nayeem's, *Mughal Documents: Catalogue of Aurangzeb's Reign 1658-1663 A.D.* Vol. I, Part I, (Hyderabad, 1980), S.A.I. Tirmizi's *Calendar of Acquired Documents (1402-1719)* (New Delhi, 1982) and M.A. Ansari's *Administrative Documents of Mughal India* (Delhi, 1984).

These selections have been published on the obviously sound assumption that documents provide the historians of Mughal India with a most authentic and useful source material. However, these selections are intended to elucidate specific issues or are concerned with specially chosen areas in terms of time and space. The need for an integrated study of Mughal documents cannot, therefore, be over-estimated.

The present publication purports to fulfil this long-felt need to some extent. It contains 350 documents published from time to time till 1980. Calendared and critically edited, they cover the reigns of the first four Mughal emperors and span a period of almost a century. Among others, the documents include: *farmans, soyurghals, hukms, nishans, parwanchas, husbul hukms, hasbul amrs, tumars, ahadnamas, iqrarnamas, bainamas, hibanamas, mahzarnamas, qismatnamas, qabzulwusuls,* etc.

Most of these documents are found on paper with the exception of a few which are written on thick cloth. The language used in a majority of the cases is Persian though there are quite a few instances of bilingual (Persian-Hindi, Persian-Gujarati) and biscriptual (Diwani-Kaithi) documents. What is more significant is the fact that one of the *farmans* of Jahangir bears a portrait each of the Emperor, Prince Khurram, courtiers and Jain monks. Similarly the seal of Khan-i Khanan Munim Khan has a galloping deer engraved in its background. Some of the documents contain many archaic words and expressions which provide data for research to the students of Gujarati and Hindi philologists. They also constitute raw materials for the study of diplomatics and sigillography which are disciplines anciliary to history.

Establishing their authenticity and determining their authorship and dates, wherever necessary, these documents have been calendared and arranged strictly in a chronological order with a five-fold purpose. First, to give a general idea of their nature and contents as also their territorial range; second, to gauge their value for the historiography of Mughal India; third, to point out Turko-Mongol influences on them; fourth, to apply the canons of diplomatics in order to determine their authenticity; and fifth, to enable scholars to delve deep into their contents with a view to their better utilisation.

Before I conclude I should like to offer my thanks to the authorities of the Indian Council of Historical Research for the grant which has made possible the preparation of this volume.

S. A. I. Tirmizi

New Delhi

30th June, 1988

ABBREVIATIONS

AIOC	All India Oriental Conference
AS	Asanidus Sanadid
COR	Calendar of Oriental Records
CDMA	Catalogue of Delhi Museum of Archaeology
CPEUM	Chancellery and Persian Epistolography under the Mughals
DLFMN	Descriptive List of Farmans, Manshurs and Nishans
FS	Faramin-i Salatin
IESHR	Indian Economic and Social History Review
IF	Imperial Farmans
IHC	Indian History Congress
IHRC	Indian Historical Records Commission
IMF	Imperial Mughal Farmans
JBBRAS	Journal of Bombay Branch of Royal Asiatic Society
JBRS	Journal of Bihar Research Society
JIH	Journal of Indian History
JPHS	Journal of Punjab History Society
JUB	Journal of the University of Bombay
MF	Mughal Farmans
MJJ	Mughals and the Jogis of Jakhbbar
NRPR	National Register of Private Records
OCM	Oriental College Magazine
PBMN	Political Biography of a Mughal Noble: Munim Khan-i Khanan
SFSP	Some Farmans Sanads and Parwanas
SII	Studies in Indian Islam
SPH	Studies in Parsi History
PC	Persian Catalogue
TKTB	Tanqihul Kalam fi Tarikhil Bilgiram

CONTENTS

INTRODUCTION

The wheel of the Mughal administration rotated round the person of the *badshash* or emperor who was supposed to be at the head of the society which was theoretically divided, according to Humayun, into three classes viz., (1) *ahl-i daulat* or the governing class comprising the emperor, members of the royal family, the army and the nobility; (2) *ahl-i saadat* or *literati* which included the *ulama* or theologians, *qazis* or judicial functionaries, the *saadat* or descendants of the holy Prophet, men of learning like physicians, poets, writers as also leaders of religious thought and persons of reputed piety and religious devotion; and (3) *ahl-i murad* who catered to the pleasures of the aforementioned two classes and comprised musicians, minstrels and dancing girls.[1] This stratification of the Mughal society is fully reflected in the Mughal chancellery practices which mirror the hierarchical relationship between the classes above referred to. In order to make a comparative study of these practices, it is absolutely essential to find out to what extent the Mughals modelled their chancelleries on the lines of their predecessors in India and the practices prevalent in their own homeland.

2

In ancient India, the *rajasasanas* or royal-edicts were classified into three categories. First, *dana-sasanas* or edicts recording gifts. Second, *prasada-sasanas* or edicts recording various kinds of favours, and third, *jaya-patras* or letters of victory. Revenue-free land grants were usually engraved on durable *tamra-patra* or copper-plates although such documents were sometimes incised even on stones.[2] These *raja-sasanas* were drafted according to the following established procedure: (1) After making a grant of land the king caused the preparation of a *lekha* or document; (2) it was then engraved on copper-plates or written on a piece of cloth; (3) it contained a description of the king and three of his immediate predecessors and of the land granted together with its boundaries and measurement and was endowed with the king's seal, signature and date; (4) a high official was entrusted with the drafting of the charter.[3]

These characteristics are noticeable in some of the royal-edicts that have come down to us in the form of epigraphs commencing from the days of the Mauryas. Such epigraphical records fall into three classes. First, royal-edicts such as the pillar-edicts of Asoka. Second, epigraphs commemorating particular achievements of a monarch in panegyrical *kavyas* or eulogistic *praiasti*. Third, grants in favour of learned Brahmins, religious or deserving institutions or individuals.[4] It is pertinent to point out in this connection that some of the cave-inscriptions belonging to the Ksaharata and Satavahana rulers of the 2nd centruy A.D., were no doubt copies on the cave walls from the original *raja-sasanas* on cloth or copper-plates.[5] The earliest copper-plate charters of the usual type so far discovered come from the southern areas of India and constitute the Prakrit charters of the Pallavas of Kanchi assignable to the middle of the 4th century A.D.[6] A recently discovered copper-plate of Isvararata, ruler of Kathiawar region, appears to belong to the end of the 4th century A.D.[7] In the north, the Dhanaidaha plate dated Gupta year 113/433 A.D. was issued during the reign of Kumaragupta I.[8]

Two centuries later when Hiuen-tsang visited India from 630 to 644 A.D. he found separate custodians of records of the monasteries as well as the State. The latter were collectively called *ni-lo-pi-tu* or *cha.*[9] When the Chinese traveller took leave of Harsha, the King gave him letters of introduction to the princes through whose territories he was to pass on his way to China. These letters were written on fine cotton pieces and sealed with wax.[10] The officer-in-charge of the drafting of documents in Kashmir was called, *pattopadhyaya* who belonged to the *Akshapatala* department or Record Office.[11] Similarly the Cholas maintained an organised Record Office which housed records on palm-leaves. Among the permanent records, there were records of land-rights based on accurate surveys, and registers for demand collection and balance-statements showing the position of receipts, etc.[12]

Kshemendra's *Lokaprakasha* as also *Sukraniti* and *Lekhapaddhati* of anonymous authors have quoted some specimens of different types of documents which were in vogue during early medieval times. The *Sukraniti* refers to the various categories of documents which are tabulated hereunder with their characteristics:

Document	*Characteristics*
Sasanapatra	Document of public-notice and regulation containing king's own signature.
Jayapatra	Document of judgement containing an account of the case or suit brought forward as also arguments for and against.

Ajaapatra	Document entrusting functions to tributary chiefs, officers and governors.
Prajanapatra	Notification informing priests, worshippers, etc., of the rites they have to perform.
Prasadpatra	Document conferring rentfree lands etc., on persons satisfied with their services, valour, etc.
Bhogapatra	Document making gift or conferring rights to enjoyment.
Kardikrit	Charter of right to tribute.
Upaynikrit	Charter of privileges for a certain period.
Bhagalekha	Partition-deed.
Danapatra	Deed of gift which is indestructible and cannot be received back.
Sadipatra	Document containing an account of the things pledged, values received as also of witnesses in the matter of a transaction involving pawn or pledge of movables or immovables.
Satyalekhya	Agreement between two townships pledging to observe *dharma* without fighting with one another.
Samritpatra	Treaty between two kings to observe *dharma* without indulging in fighting.
Rinalekhya	Document of loan containing an account of witnesses framed on receipt of some money on interest.
Suddhipatra	Document of purgation containing an account of witnesses framed after some curse has been worked out or a penance has been duly performed.
Samayikapatra	Business deed framed by individuals after combining their shares of capital for some business concern.
Khesmapatra[13]	Document beginning with obeisance or blessing, and fully explaining the affairs and meant for master, servant or those who were to be served.

Like *Sukraniti*, the *Lekhapaddhati* is anonymous. It was written under the Muzaffarids of Gujarat at the end of the 15th century by some official. The book was composed in mixed Sanskrit as a guide to revenue officers and professional petition and letter-writers. It was evidently meant to be a manual of models of public documents and specimens of official and other correspondence suitable for various occasions. Some of such documents are listed below:

Bhojpatra	Royal charter
Pattala	Imperial edict
Gunpatra	Order of royal favour
Dharmasasanam	Religious grant
Dharmakshram	Religious document
Tamarsasana	Copper plate grant
Rayhundika	Royal bill of exchange
Hastaksham	Receipt
Bhumibikriya-patram	Land sale-deed
Grahanakpatram	Confiscation order
Bibhangampatram	Nullifying deed
Abhayadana	Amnesty deed
Gunakshram	Letter of concession
Prasadpatala	Rent-free land grant deed
Gunakshar	Document for a lease of land
Guptpatala	Deed of permanent lease
Uttrakshrani	Deed granting lands to merchants at a favourable rent
Vayvanarpatala	Deed of debts
Grahaddanakpatra	Deed for mortgaging a house
Adhipatra	Mortgage bond[14]

3

While India had well developed chancellery practices the Turkish conquerors brought with them the Perso-Turkish administrative institutions which had evolved in their own land. They invoked the spirit of the Sasanid Persia and derived ideological vitality and stamina from it. The court of Delhi, in certain respects, became the replica of the Sasanid Court.[15] As a matter of fact the court of Delhi and the court of Ghazna were the co-inheritors of the Sasanid tradition. It is interesting to note that under the Ghaznavids the royal missives were recorded on a special Chinese paper which was dyed with saffron and scented with rose-perfume and solution of ambergris and musk.[16] Another distinction that presupposes the class barrier is reflected not only in the special style but also the nomenclature reserved for the documents of the ruling classes.

The Seljuq administration retained the chief features of the Sasanids. The chancellery worked in two branches under two heads who were designated as the *Sahib-i Diwan-i Rasail* and the *tughrai* respectively. It was the duty of the *tughrai* to inscribe the official documents in curved script and to draw the *tughra* on them. The most important documents which the chancellery issued to various military, civil and religious officials were: (a) the *manshur* (diploma), the *taqlid* (deed of investitures), the *misal* (commission or mandate) and the *fathnama* (proclamation of victory).[17]

The Mongols could not dispense with the organs of administration of their predecessors. The *wazir* of the Mongols had the chief responsibility of issuing the *amsila* with his endorsement. He was assisted by *bitikchis* together with several other scribes.[18] The chief feature of the Mongol chancellery was the introduction of *yarligh* (Mongol *jarligh*) meaning a decree, a general term used for the old *manshur*.[19] Again the Mongol substituted *sozmiz* or *sukhan-i ma* for the Seljuq *tughra* which was a visible symbol for the king's majestic splendour.[20] Ghazan Khan (1295-1304 A.D.) issued *yarligh* to all competent authorities regarding the tax regulations. In this *yarligh* he ordered employment of reliable officers and compilation of tax-schedules and laid down the date for payment.[21]

The Mongol *yarligh* was replaced by *manshur* and *nishan* under the Timurids. The *manshur* of Amir Taimur (1370-1404 A.D.) dated 1 Rajab 801 A.H./9 March 1399 A.D. conveys to Amirzada Pir Muhammad at Shiraz the news of his victory over Sultan Mahmud Tughluq.[22] Shahrukh, son and successor of Timur, sent a communication in response to the petition dated Jumada II 819 A.H./ July 1402 A.D. from Ghiyasud Din Khizr Khan (1399-1421 A.D.) permitting the Timurid Governor of India to cause the *khutba* to be read and the *sikka* to be struck in the name of the Timurid ruler.[23] The *nishan* of Sultan Husain, grandson of Timur, asked Sultan Ghiyasud Din Khizr Khan to send Nurud Din Muhammad al Husaini back to Herat.[24] Sultan Abu Said (1452-67 A.D.) issued a *farman* dated 1463-64 A.D. in favour of Sayyid Shadi and Sayyid Sharful Mulk confirming them as trustees of a shrine.[25]

While the Turkish conquerors were busy consolidating their empire in India, Khurasan itself was subjugated by the Mongols. This resulted in the influx of savants into India where they found haven of peace. The splendour of the court of Khurasan was transferrred to Delhi, Multan and Lakhhauti. The Turkish Sultan's court became an "asylum, refuge, resting place and point of safety."[26] Since many of these immigrants belonged to distinguished governing classes and had a long record of administrative experience, they were readily taken into administration. In these bands of immigrants were many *munshis* who came to India in search of patronage and attached themselves to one court or the other. These *munshis* brought with them the chancellery practices prevalent in their own countries. The advent of these *munshis* stimulated a keen desire for learning chancellery practices among the local people. Amir Khusrau (651-752 A.H./ 1253-1325 A.D.) holds the scholars of India, particularly the *munshis*, in high esteem. He says, "the learned men of Hindustan, especially the immigrants who have settled down in Delhi, surpass all other scholars in their erudition . . . . a *munshi* born and brought up in the cities of Hindustan, especially in Delhi, without much practice, can speak any language in its style and can even, mould the prose and poetry (of that language) and adopt the style of any country he visits."[27]

Amir Khusrau himself composed *Rasailul Ijaz* or *Ijaz-i Khusraui* which is one of the earliest treatises written in India on the art of epistolography and rhetoric. It was completed in 719 A.H./ 1292 A.D.[28] and comprises five *risalas* or treatises. They contain miscellaneous prose pieces including some documents. The first document in chronological order is the *fathnama*[29] or letter of victory dated 5th Shawwal 680 A.H./ 17 January 1282 A.D.[30] and sent to Delhi by Ghiyasud Din Balban after the conquest of Lakhnauti.[31] The second official document in the chronological order is the *farman* proclaiming Alaud Din's accession to the throne.[32] This is followed by *tauqi* or mandate conferring the *iqta* of Maabar on Prince Farid Khan, son of Alaud Din.[33] Next in the chronological order is the *misal* or royal command dated 700 A.H./1300-1301 A.D. assigning the *diha* or village Nasur to Shaikh Shamsud Din,[34] who was appointed *Mutasarrif*.[35] The subsequent document is *farman-i tughra* dated 13 Safar 709 A.H./ 23 July 1309 A.D. and addressed to the merchants of the sea and the ports. It refers to transportation of the gifts and goods of Arabia, Habsha (Ethiopia), Bahrain, Barbar, Maghrib and Syria.[36] A *parwana* dated 30 Rabi I 709 A.H./7 September 1309 A.D. and addressed to the officials of *Ishtinara* or *Mashal Khana* says that Ziaud Daula Sirajud Din who was responsible for lighting in the court was also appointed *shahna* or superintendent in charge of the oil manufacturers and merchants of the metropolis of Delhi.[37] A *farman* dated 716 A.H./ 1316-1317 A.D. confers the Office of the Chief *Qazi* of Delhi, the imperial metropolis, on Abdur Rahman Usman Ashraf. It gives us some idea about the working of the judicial department and duties and functions of a qazi.[38] Another important document is the *arzdasht* or despatch dated 30 Rabi I 702 A.H./22 November 1302 A.D. of the chief slave of *Baha-i Suqi*, the *hakim* of the *khitta* of Nagore addressed to Ziaul Haq wad Din, *sadr-i jahan*. It relates to the complaint brought in the *Diwanul Mazalim* against the highhandedness and misappropriation of Malik Islam, the *Wali*.[39]

The length of some of these documents as also their grand eloquent style cast a shadow of doubt on their genuineness but some scholars tend to accept "the importance of their main themes" because of the substance of their contents, the dates and names of persons and places occurring in them.[40] These scholars seem to have overlooked the fact that the *Rasailul Ijaz* was professedly composed to demonstrate the author's prowess in the field of prose as much to provide instructions for the young literary aspirants of his age. Moreover it was the author's intention to add to the existing nine styles of epistolography a tenth of his own.[41] The author himself makes it plain that he has made ample use of his own fruitful imagination in writing fictitious letters and that of others who had done the same before him and thus had given shape to a book of charm and originality by skilfully editing these single and compound words, short and long phrases and brief and lengthy documents purporting to be official.[42] Whatever the motivation of Khusrau in writing the *Ijaz*, the fact cannot be denied that the nomenclature used by Khusrau for the various categories of documents was obviously modelled after the one already in vogue in his own times.

This is corroborated by his contemporaries. Fakhr-i Mudabbir deals with *ahdnamas* or treaties and refers to the following essentials in this context: (a) all *ahdnamas* should be made in writing; (b) both parties should act upon the treaty; (c) all concerned officers should affix their signatures on it; (d) the treaty should be read out before the parties.[43] Mir Khurd reproduces the *ijazatnamah* dated 22 Rabi I 679 A.H./22 July 1280 A.D. to Shaikh Nizamuddin by his teacher Maulana Kamalud Din Zahid and the *khilafat-namah* dated 22 Zilhijiah 724 A.H./10 December 1324 A.D. by Shaikh Nizamud Din Auliya to his disciple Shamsud Din Yahya.[44]

Contemporaneous with Khusrau was Ainud Din Abdullah Mahru Multani (d.c. 764 A.H./1362 A.D.) whose *Tarassul-i Aynul Mulki*, commonly known as the *Insha i Mahru*, is perhaps the earliest collection of copies of state papers and private documents that have survived the vicissitudes of time. The author was a soldier and statesman of the time of the Khalijis and the Tughluqs. His *Insha* comprises letters and documents written or drafted by the author on different occasions over a number of years. Some of these letters were primarily intended to serve generally as specimens of elegant correspondence as is evident from their vagueness and omission not only of dates but also of names of persons and places. It comprises 134 items in all arranged more or less systematically. First are given the official documents issued by the Central Government and then the author's own letters.[45] The official documents belong to the following categories: (1) *misal*,[46] (2) *manshur*,[47] (3) *ahadnama*, (4) *parwana*, and (5) *arzadasht*.

The *manshur* confers on Prince Fath Khan (1351-76 A.D.) the government of the *iqlim* or clime of Sind and advises the Prince to look after the prosperity of the *riaya* or peasantry, and to ensure contentment of the *hasham* or army. It also admonishes the Prince to show consideration to the *saadat* or descendants of the holy Prophet, *ulama* or theologians, *mashaikh* or mystics and *sulha* or pious men. It instructs the *umara* or nobility, *rais*, rajas, *muqaddams* and residents of the *wilayat* of Sind to render obedience to the *misal* of the Prince as if it is a *farman* issued by the Sultan himself.[48] Another *manshur* addressed to the *karkuns* of the *arsa* of Gujarat confirms as *wajah-i maash* the *takia* attached to the *khanqah-i Kudia* as also adjacent *diha* and the wells in the *shahr* of Nahrawala previously held by the late Shaikh Hajji in favour of Shaikh Abu Bakr Shiabud Din commonly known as Shaikhzada-i Yazdi.[49]

The *misal* of Firuz Shah announces the despatch of forces to Lakhnauti for the suppression of the rebellion of Ilyas Hajji. It assures the *zamindars* comprising *muqaddams, mafruzis, maliks* and the like of the territory between river Kosi and Lakhnauti, that if they proceed to the court, they will be exempted from the payment of *mahsul* of the said *wilayat* for the current year and their *kharaj* and *mahsul* will be fixed for the following year as was the practice during the days of Sultan Shamsud Din.[50] The *arzdasht* dated 11 Safar 763 A.H./ 10 December 1361 A.D. was submitted by Ainud Din to Firuz Shah in respect of *awqaf* in the *wilayat* of Multan. It states that *muhasiba* was made of the land as per instructions of the *Diwan-i Wizarat* and the land was divided into two categories. First, the land earmarked for the upkeep of the mausoleums of the past kings, and second, the land intended for the benefit of the *ulma, mashaikh* and such *amirs* as had brought under plough the dead lands.[51]

Akin to *Munshat-i Mahru* is the *Manazirul Inssha* of Khwaja Imadud Din, commonly known as Mahmud Gavan (d. 886 A.H./1481 A.D.), the celebrated minister of the Bahmanis of the Deccan. It is indeed a veritable *code-in-aid* for the art of *belles lettres* containing at the same time the terms of reference for the epistolographers.[52] The author wrote letters on behalf of his masters and himself to foreign rulers and men of letters. These diplomatic epistles have been collected under the title of *Riyazul Insha*.[53]

4

It is indeed a matter of regret that very few original documents of the Turko-Afghan Sultans of Delhi have come down to us. They are either lying unnoticed in private collections or seem to have succumbed to the ravages of time. There is yet another factor responsible for their destruction. We are told that the royal *farmans* were literally washed off under Balban.[54] This was done obviously for reasons of economy in as much as the quantity of paper produced was not sufficient to cope with the increasing demand. This is perhaps the reason why the edicts of the Turko-Afghan Sultans of Delhi inscribed on stones have survived while those on paper have not come down to us with the exception of a very few pertaining to the Lodis.[55]

The Arabic *fatwa* of the reign of Sultan Alaud Din Alam Shah has come down to us. It was compiled by Ibrahim and dated 849 A.H./1445-46 A.D. It contains instructions to the *qazis* relating to the disposal of cases for which there are no provisions in the Quran or the Hadis.[56] The Persian *parwana* of *Masnad-i Ali* Mahmud Khan Lodi issued to Shaikh Chailda, a descendant of Baba Farid *Ganj-i Shakar*, in 899 A.H./1493 A.D. contains a grant of two villages in the *pargana* of Nindru.[57] The Persian *sanad* dated 25 Rajab 925 A.H./24 July 1519 A.D. purports to be a renewal of a land grant of the reign of Ibrahim Lodi. It contains apparently an order for giving possession of 300 *bighas* of land to Shaikh Hasan, son of Barkhurdar Husain, who had been granted this land in the *mauza* Gonda of *pargana* Sandila, pertaining to the *khalisa* lands, administered by the *Diwan-i Ala*, under the *shiqdari* of Malik Abul Fath. The document is written in *taliq* with transliteration in *Kaithi* script.[58] This Afghan practice of biscriptual document continued under Sher Shah[59] and is discernible in some documents of the early part of the reign of Akbar.

As with the Turko-Afghans so with the Bahmanis, the surviving documents are extremely rare. The authenticity of the Mudhel *farmans* of the Bahmani Sultans of the Deccan has been doubted.[60] However, the *farman* of Firuz Shah Bahmani, housed in the Andhra Pradesh State Archives is genuine. Drafted in the *Diwanul Wizarat*, it is dated 25

Zilqada 808 A.H./14 May 1406 A.D. and bears the royal *tughra* and seal. It makes *wajih inam* grant of land to Maulana Muhammad, *Qazi*, and his descendants of the *qasbas* of Kalyanabad in perpetuity.[61] Similarly the *amr* dated 1 Jumada II 894 A.H./2 May 1489 A.D. addressed to the *karkuns* of *Darul Mulk* Muhammadabad conveys the orders of Sultan Mahmud Shah II Bahmani to the effect that 5250 *bighas* of land in the *mauza* of Malhur, hitherto earmarked as *muqasa* for the sons of Khan Azam Khan, has been acquired for the *khalsa* and assigned for the expenses of the mausoleum of Shah Nimatullah in favour of Amirza Muhibbullah and his descendants, the *mutawallis* of the aforesaid mausoleum. It bears a number of official seals.[62] The undated *misal* bearing the seal of Khwaja Jahan Mahmud Gavan conveys the orders of Mahmud Shah II Bahmani to the same effect.[63] The undated Bahmani grant assigns one *chawar* land as *inam* to Pirzada Ali Shah, resident of the city of Muhammadabad, in perpetuity and exempts him from all cesses. It bears illegible seals as also text in Modi script pertaining to the said grant.[64]

Compared to the Bahmanis, the surviving documents of the Muzaffarids of Gujarat are larger in number. The first such document is a land grant dated 812 A.H./ 1409-10 A.D. It pertains to grant of land for the maintenance of an *imam* and a *muazzin* in one of the mosques built by Sayyid Sikandar, the patron-saint of Mangrol. It refers to grant of land, not assignments of revenue, and stipulates that no *kharaj* paying peasant was to be employed on the land which was granted.[65] Some documents of the reign of Muzaffar II have come down to us. First is a document in Gujarati, executed by Manek Changa, Asdin Mehrwan, Dhayyan Rana, Rana Jamas, Asa Bahram, Manek Behram, Khurshid Chacha, Bahram Sagar, Naiya Rana, Mehrwan and the whole community of the Parsis of Nagmandal (Navsari) on the day of Bahman in the month of Bahman during the reign of Muzaffar II. It assigns 100 palm-trees and 10 *bighas* of *inam* land free from all taxes to Ervad Rana Jeshang.[66] Another document of the reign of Muzaffar II is a sale-deed dated 7 Shawwal 923 A.H./ 23 October 1517 A.D. It was executed by Mali Muhammad Yusuf, *wakil* of *Musammat* Ismat Khatun, daughter of Muhammad Haibatullah and *qaum* (wife) of Malik Jiu Ahmad Khatri, in the court of Tajud Din, *Hakim* of Navsari, regarding 20 *bighas* and 19 *biswas* of *bhatta* land alongwith 40 *tad, khajuri* trees, etc., located in the neighbourhood of Nagmandal (Navsari) and given to her by her husband in lieu of part of her *mehr* sold to Manak Changa Desai for a consideration of 500 *faddiahs*. It bears the seal of the said *Qazi* on the top as also signatures of Mubarak Yusuf and several other witnesses in Gujarati.[67] The third document is an agreement executed and signed by Manek Changa, Asdin Mehrwan, Dhayyan Rana, Khurshid Chacha and others on the day of Bahman in the month of Bahman in Samvat 1576/ 11 January 1519 A.D. It states that 10 *bighas* of land with 100 plam trees growing thereon and situated in Nagmandal (Navsari) will be kept with Ervad Rana Jeshang.[68]

Of the reign of Bahadur Shah a couple of documents have survived. The first such document is a mortgage-deed in Gujarati executed on the day of Bahman in the month of Azar in Samvat 1588/14 November 1531 A.D. It states that Seth Dhayyan Rana borrowed from Adhyaru Rana Jaisang 30 *tankas* in cash, each *tanka* being of the value of sixty *dokdas,* in lieu of which he mortaged the house of Dhayyan Khurshed, situated in Nagmandal, which will be released on the full payment of the said loan. It adds that Seth Dhayyan Rana will make good to Adhyaru Rana Jai Sang all the expenses incurred on repairs of the house. It bears the signatures of Dhayyan Rana as also those of two witnesses, viz., Waccha Pahlam and Asa Bahiram[69]. The second document of the reign of Bahadur Shah is a *taqsimnama* executed on the day of Aban in the month of Bahman in Samvat 1590/19 January 1533 A.D. by Adhyaru Nagoj Rustam and Adhyaru Rana Jaisang to the effect that the dispute between them in respect of the boundaries of the courtyard of their houses has amicably been settled. It is in Gujarati and bears signatures of Nagoj Rustam, Rana Jaisang and others.[70]

Six documents of the reign of Mahmud III are availabe to us. The first document is a sale-deed executed on the day of Khurdad in the month of Mihr in Samvat 1595/23 September 1538 A.D. It states that Seth Dhayyan Rana has sold with the cognisance of *panchkul* to Adhyaru Rana Jaisang in perpetuity the house of Behdin Dhayyan Khurshed Adrav along with the land together with its enclosure and all the furniture therein located in Nagmandal in lieu of 68 *tankas pratabahra* in cash. It is in Gujarati and bears signatures of Dhayyan Rana and several witnesses.[71] The second document is dated the day of Azar in the month of Mihr in Samvat 1600/ 21 September 1543 A.D. It is an agreement executed between Chanda Sahiyar and Adhyaru Mahirvan Padam to the effect that the cost of constructing the wall between their houses, shall be divided equally between them. It is in Gujarati and bears the signatures of Chanda Sahiyar and Mahirvan Padam as also those of witnesses.[72] The third document is dated 30 Safar 952/13 May 1545 A.D. It states that Waman, son of Chaturbhuj, deposed in the court of Muhammad bin Mahmud, *Qazi* of Navsari, that he had sued Mahrvan son of Sayar, son of Kamdin

Tabib for a loan of 700 *faddiahs,* each *faddiah* equal to the old *dogani,* due to his uncle Sodhal, son of Rakha. It adds that after the claim had been heard, the said Mahrvan stated in reply that the said loan had been repaid by the said Sayar in his lifetime to the said Sodhal and the deponent also admitted this fact. It further adds that 110 *faddiahs* which had remained unpaid (on account of interest) were taken in cash from the said Mahrvan by the said deponent who gave up his claim. It bears the seal of the *qazi* on the top as also signatures of witnesses and mark in *Hindwi* of Waman.[73] The fourth document is dated the day Isfandarmaz in the month of Amardad in Samvat 1608/18 July 1551 A.D. It is an agreement executed between Adhyaru Jal Kamdin and Parsi Anjuman which had sent the said Adhyaru Rana to Daman for the performance of Zoroastrian ceremonies. It states that for every *vehva* (marriage with a virgin) and *ghagharana* (marriage between widower and a widow) celebrated in Sanjan and Daman the said Adhyaru Rana shall be paid 12 *faddiahs sadhan* (sic). It adds that Adhyaru Jiva of the Sanjan family shall perform all the ceremonies upto the boundaries of Tarapore while the *Vehvas, ghagharanas* and *afringans* of Monori shall be celebrated by Adhyaru Rana but the fee for muttering the *baj* in Manori shall be taken by Adhyaru Jiva. The document is in Gujarati.[74] The fifth document is dated 5 Jumada II 960/ 1553. It is a *farman* of Mahumd III assigning a sum of 10,60,000 coins for the maintenance of the descendants of Sayyid Sikandar, and the upkeep of his shrine, mosque and staff. The officials are instructed to leave the stipulated amount to the assignee and "to bring to the revenue office, all the surplus and to follow instructions in this respect".[75]

Three documents of the reign of Ahmad III are available to us. The first document is dated 2 Rajab Samvat 1611/3 June 1554 A.D. It is the *hukm* of the *Diwan Shri* of the *shiq* of Navsari and the *Huzur Shri Malikush Sharq* Zainud Din and the *Havaldar* Malik Shri Habib Abdul Halim and Mahan Devdas Kahanan addressed to the *khots* and *talatis* of *mauza* Jalalpur near Navsari. It states that a piece of *bhatta* land was in possession of Adhyaru Hoshang Rana by way of *inam* but during the visit of *Majlis-i Ali* he was dispossessed of the grant owing to the jealousy of his enemies. Consequently the grantee went to the court of the Malik Shri and brought a *parwana* for the restoration of his *inam.* Accordingly the addressees are ordered that the *bhatta* land in question may be given over to him and instructed to obey the order in letter and spirit. The *hukm* is in Gujarati and bears an illegible seal on the top.[76] The second document is dated the day of Aban, the month of Avan in Samvat 1612/23 October

1555 A.D. It is a *taqsimnama* of the property of Rana Jaisang between Dastur Meherji Rana and sons of the latter's brother Rana Hoshang. It states that the property as also debts and liabilities are to be shared half by Meherji and the remaining half by the sons of Hoshang while the old mother of Hoshang is not only to occupy and sleep in that part of Hoshang's house which is on the north-west but also to get 75 old *tankas pratabahra* out of the common funds and is also to be provided with two pairs of *ijar* and four *sadras* every year by the parties jointly. It is in Gujarati and bears the signatures of Mahya Waccha, Jaisang Hoshang, Khurshed Hoshang and Bahman Hoshang.[77] The third document is dated the Zamiyad day, the month of Farvardin in Samvat 1614/7 April 1557 A.D. It is a sale-deed executed in the *amal* of Malikush Sharq Imadul Mulk Rumi in respect of a piece of land measuring seven *majani bighas* equivalent to nine tailors' *gaz*, situated at Hajira sold by the three brothers S/Shree Kadu Rana, Ava Rana and Chayyan Rana to Patel Narsang Manak and Patel Nagoj Manak, both brothers, for a consideration of 61 *tankas pratabahras*, each *tanka* being of the value of 60 *dokdas*. The said land has been sold in perpetuity, excepting the wild date-trees which are already fully grown but the young wild date-trees, mango, tamarind, jujube and babul and all other plants growing on the said land shall belong to the purchaser. It bears the signatures of the vendors as also witnesses.[78] The fourth document is dated the day of Azar, month of Isfandarmaz in Samvat 1622/17 February 1565 A.D. It is an agreement executed by Mahyar Vachcha, Bahman Chanda, Kaikubad Mahiyar, Padam Rustam and other Zoroastrian priests addressed to the Anjuman of Navsari. It states that the priest who practises dishonesty in the share of *bhagar*, appropriates the *farast* of the Behedin, shall be responsible to the Anjuman for the loss. Again he, whose turn it is to perfrom the *baj* ceremony, shall also perform the *khub* in the first *pahar* of the day and finish all the *bajs* by the second *pahar* and shall take the usual allowance as fee for the *baj*. Moreover he shall be guilty before the Anjuman if he be dishonest in the matter of the fees of *srosh*, *siav*, marriage, remarriage, and all such ceremonies. It is in Gujarati and bears the signatures of twenty-four priests.[79]

Two documents of the reign of Muzaffar III have survived. The first document is dated the day Ardibihsht, the month Isfandarmuz and Samvat 1626/11 February 1569 A.D. It is an agreement executed by Mahyar Vachcha, Shapur, Asa, Kaikubad Mahyar and other priests addressed to the Anjuman of Navsari. It states that the priest who begins officiating at the *yacna* ceremony shall not drink *toddy* and he who drinks it shall not hold the *barcam* in his hand. He shall be out of the Barashnum.[80]

5

Against this broad perspective presented in the preceding pages, it is proposed to assess the diplomatic and historical value of 350 documents issued from time to time during the reigns of the first four Mughal emperors of India. These documents fall into two broad categories: *muhavarat* or private epistles and *tauqiat* or public documents. The latter are sub-divided according to the status of the issuing authorities.

Royal Edict

These were the missives issued from the sovereign, queen-consort, queen-mother, prince, princess and as such can be classified as under:

Farman: This term is applied to the royal missive that issued from the sovereign bearing the imperial *tughra* and seal. The first two lines of the *farmans* are always abbreviated in order to distinguish them from ministerial orders wherein all the lines are of equal length.[81]

Manshur: It denotes a royal mandate addressed to a privileged person belonging to the royal family or the ruling class. It forms the subject of congratulations and condolences. During the war of succession at the end of Shahjahan's reign, *manshur* acquired an unprecedented political and administrative significance as an order of Prince Aurangzeb who had become the *de facto* ruler while the monarch and the heir apparent were alive and hostile.[82]

Fathnama: It is a letter of victory composed in grandiloquent style with a view to parade royal prowess. Its purpose is to commemorate the glorious victory. It was a common practice to despatch them to all countries, clans and retainers.[83]

Hukm: The connotation of this term is some what uncertain. It stands for an edict of Queen Mother, or Queen Consort. There are, however, three exceptions to this definition. Babur speaks of his favourite wife Maham Begam's edict as a *farman.*[84] Nur Jahan refers to her edict as a *nishan* in the body of the text though the *tughra* at the top unequivocally calls it a *hukm.*[85] The edict issued by the rebellious Prince Khurram has been designated as *hukum* and *nishan* (115). It was also a privileged order of *Khan-i Khanan* as is borne out by the orders of Bairam Khan(8) and Munim Khan(20) who had the privilege of issuing a *hukm* though they could, as a rule, issue a *parwancha. Hukms* like *farmans* are crowned with *tughra* or *unwan* and their first two lines are abbreviated in order to distinguish them from *parwanchas*.[86] (66).

Nishan: It denotes an order of a prince or princess or wife of a prince and usually bears *tughra*, or *unwan* of the sovereign in addition to that of the grantor as against *hukm* which is crowned by the *tughra* or *unwan* of the grantor only[87] (102).

Official Rescripts

Parwancha/Parwana: It is a corrupt form of *farmancha* or little *farman* and differs from *farman* in two respects. First, it does not possess royal *tughra* and seal. Secondly its first two lines are not abbreviated as is the case with *farmans, hukms* and *nishans*. The *parwanchas* are ministerial patents which tend to support and supplement royal orders.[88]

Sanad: This term, has a very wide application. It signifies confirmation and verification of a previous order of land grant, appointment and commission, any privilege or immunity accorded to the recipient. It may denote a patent, permit, deed, decree or more precisely, a written authority to enjoy a grant of any nature[89] (55).

Hasbul hukm: It is an order issued by the ministers on behalf of the emperor. The *Diwan-i ala* evidently had to deal with orders of importance and sometimes of political significance following in the wake of the *farmans* for the sake of emphasis or additional injunctions[90](28,74).

Hukmnama: It was issued by the authorities at the court and the provinces to verify, confirm and settle previous grants to the beneficiaries of the original grantor, his/her descendants and in all cases on the authority of the previous deeds[91] (39,97).

Qaulnama and *ahadnama:* A *qaulnama* in the form of a preliminary engagement seems to be instrumental to an *ahadnama* or treaty (181).

Tamliknama: It denotes a deed of transfer, whether of gift or conveyance[92] (303).

Mahzarnama: A written collective attestation; a list or roll of persons present[93] (100).

Bainama: It denotes a civil contract in which transfer of ownership in property is made in consideration of price paid or promised or partly paid and partly promised. It was executed under the seal of *mufti* or *qazi*. It generally bears the signatures of the vendor, Amatya and several witnesses[94] (33,34,79).

Hibanama: It is a gift deed regulated by the Muslim Law of alienation in which the property held in proprietary right is conferred on a beneficiary so that he/she may derive a benefit therefrom[95] (87).

Qabzulwusul: It denotes a deed of receipt or acknowledgement of a document acknowledging the receipt of money or other valuables[96] (113).

Chaknama: It specifies a chart detailing area and boundaries of a piece of the assigned land. Every minute detail was registered in the chart with statistics and description of adjoining places. Those who supervised the survey or took part in the execution of the *chak* on the spot included *muqaddam, qanungo, chaudhari, munsif, karkun* and *jarib kash.* The *chak* was sealed by the *qazi* and the official surveyors[97] (140).

Tailqa: It denotes the gist or abridgement of the *yad-dasht* signed by the *waqia-nawis, risaladar, mirarz, darogha* and finally the minister concerned[98] (94).

Hukm-i rahdari: It denotes a transit visa issued by a minister under royal instructions to a foreign traveller or trader or to any servant of the state proceeding on a journey on official business. It is addressed to the officials of every territory through which the bearer had to pass and records the nature of the business[99] (80).

6

In order to determine the authenticity of the various categories of documents referred to earlier, it is absolutely essential to subject them to the beams of the searchlight of diplomatics or critical study of form of documents. It is a usual experience that documents having common place and time of origin tend to conform almost to an identical pattern. It is not possible to subject all the categories of document to the science of diplomatics. However, an attempt has been made to apply these canons to only three categories of *tauqiat*, viz., *farman, hukm* and *nishan* in order to illustrate the broad principles of diplomatics. Normally such document consists of two parts, viz., recto and verso.

Recto: It is usually divided into three distinct parts, viz., (a) Preamble (b) Notification and (c) Conclusion. There are various subdivisions and not all the parts mentioned are necessarily found in every document.

Preamble: It comprises (i) *sarnama* (superscription) (ii) validation, (iii) marks of honour. *Sarnama* which usually constitutes invocation to God either by name or sacramental formula or through a symbolic letter. Usually a document begins with one of the names of God as a token of blessing or benediction. The most agreeable device has been to conjoin the third person singular *Huwa* (He, i.e., God) with such epithets describing the divine attributes as may be in consonance with the text.

The *farmans* of the reigns of Babur and Humayun as also those of the earlier period of Akbar bear the invocation *Huwal Ghani* (He is Independent). This invocation appears on the Mughal *farmans* upto 984 A.H./ 1576 A.D. It seems to have been replaced by *Huwal Akbar* or He is Great which was in vogue till 992 A.H./ 1584 A.D. This was substituted by *Allahu Akbar* (God is Great) by Akbar. This last formula held ground throughout the reigns of Jahangir and Shah Jahan[98] but was subsequently given up by Aurangzeb soon after his accession. He adopted some time about 1072 A.H./ 1662 A.D. the formula *Bismillahhir Rahmannir Rahim* (I begin in the name of God, the Merciful, the Compassionate). The Queen Mothers and Queen Consorts always employed the invocation of the reigning king in their *hukms*. This is also generally true of the *nishans* of princes and princesses though some deviations have been noticed as detailed hereunder :

Prince/Princess	*Sarnama*
Shuja	Bismillahhir-Rahmannir-Rahim
Jahan Ara	do
Nadira Banu	(a) do
	(b) Huwal Qadir

Validation: In *farmans, hukms* and *nishans* there are two instruments of validation, viz., (a) *Muhr* (seal) and (b) *Tughra.*

Muhr: Underneath the *sarnama* and to the right is affixed the royal seal as an instrument of authentication. Babur employed round lineal seal in his *soyurghal*. This seal contains the name of the emperor in the central ring with those of his ancestors upto Timur in five outer circles round about. Similarly the *farman* of Humayun, making a *madad-i maash* grant has been validated by a round lineal seal of the emperor[100] Abul Fazl refers to five kinds of seals used for different purposes in the reign of Akbar (1) *Uzuk* round small seal used for authenticating *farman-i sabti;* (2) *Muhr-i Kalan* or large lineal seal into which the name of Akbar and those of his ancestors upto Timur, were engraved. It was used for letters to foreign kings and later on for all purposes; (3) Square seal used for all other orders besides the *farman-i sabti*. It has the legend *Allahu Akbar jalla jalalahu* (God is Great, exalted be His glory); (4) *Mihrabi* niche-shaped seal employed for judicial transactions. It contains the following verse around the name of the king:

Rasti mujib-i raza-i khuda ast;
Kas na didam ke gum shud az rah-i rast.
Uprightness is the means of pleasing God;
I saw none lost in the straight path.

(5) A separate seal was used for all matters connected with the harem.[101] In the beginning of his reign Jahangir had a round dynastic seal but later on he got engraved a square lineal seal and this pattern was more or less followed by Shah Jahan and Aurangzeb.

The *hukms* and *nishans* are validated by the seals of Queen Mothers and Queen Consorts and princesses respectively. They usually contain legends which include the titles of the owner along with the appellations of the father, husband or son followed by the year of engraving.

Tughra and Unwan: Just beneath the *sarnama* appears either *tughra* or *unwan. Farmans* as also *hukms of* Queen Consorts and *nishans* of princes and princesses are crowned by *tughras and unwans.* The *nishans* invariably bear two *tughras,* one each of the princc/princess and the reigning monarch.[102]

Tughras are employed not only to validate the documents but also to display the majestic splendour of the issuing authority whose name and titles are elaborately drawn in an ornamental style of calligraphy wherein letters are interwoven and the uprights marshalled in a processional rhythm. The *tughras* are usually designed in a square or rectangle drawn with *shanjarf* or vermilion or liquid gold. A comparative study of the *tughras and unwans* furnishes interesting data for the study of Mughal titles.

Marks of Honour: Underneath the *tughra* and above the notification sometimes appear the following marks of honour which were established as a tradition according to the rank of the addressee and the extent of favour desired to be bestowed upon him. First, by putting signature in addition to the official seal. Second, by adding a line or two at the top in his own hand. Sometimes the emperor wrote the whole of the *farman* in his own hand in respect of important matters and third, by impressing the *punja-i mubarak* or the royal palm on the *farman.* The mark of the *punja* was supposed to be the highest distinction. In the nineth year of the reign of Jahangir, the Rana of Udaipur demanded the royal *punja* as a condition of the treaty into which be entered after his defeat at the hands of Prince Khurram and the condition was complied with.[103]

NOTIFICATION: It constitutes the main part of the document and consists of (a) *khitab* or address and (b) purpose. Most of the administrative orders, viz., *farman-i mulki wa mali, farman-i bayazi* and even *farman-i rahdari* open with *khitab.* The notifications of *farmans* do not have any specific or common openings but in most of the cases they begin with the formula such as *chun ba arz-i muqaddas rasid* (it has been brought to the august notice).

Purpose: It briefly explains the motive in issuing the edict. This is followed by exposition of the particular circumstances involved. The promulgator is not mentioned by name in the body of the text. Even his/her deceased forebears are alluded to by their posthumous titles some of which are mentioned hereunder:

Emperor	*Posthumous Title*
Babur	*Firdaus makani*
Humayun	*Jannat ashyani*
Akbar	*Arsh ashyani*
Jahangir	*Jannat makani*
Shah Jahan	*Firdaus ashyani*
Aurangzeb	*Khuld makani*[104]

The purpose ends with the promulgator or donor firmly declaring his/her motive by such words as *bayad* or it is incumbent. This clause is the vital core of the edict inasmuch as it is a legal decree of promulgation.

CONCLUSION: It consists of (a) *takid* and *tahdid* (b) Date of promulgation. *Takid* denotes an emphasis and *tahdid* indicates threat of responsibility for the royal decree. The local officials under the threat of responsibility are required to execute the imperial edict accordingly and recognise the legal possession as decreed. The *takid* and *tahdid* in the royal edicts take the form of tautological and synonymous phraseology.

Date: The date given at the end of the edict is that of issue. The form in which dates are given is of particular importance in determining its provenance and authenticity. Wide variety of practices were followed at different times. Babur and Humayun followed the lunar Hijra calendar. It was Akbar who introduced the solar Ilahi era in 992 A.H./1584-85 A.D. but is was calculated from the year which commenced on 11 March 1556 A.D. It continued to be in force till the death of Jahangir. Shah Jahan favoured the old lunar era but allowed the solar months to be supplemented to the date entries. Aurangzeb permitted its use only in the revenue registers.[105] The use of lunar calendar was inconvenient both to the tax-collector and tax-payer because of its non-concurrence with the harvests. This was perhaps the reason why most of the Mughal emperors from Akbar onwards used the Turkish duodenary solar cycle particularly in their revenue documents. Every year of this cycle is named after an animal and the name is always followed by the Turkish word *il* meaning an year.

Verso: The *verso* of some of the edicts contains *zimn* or resume of the elaborate procedure through which it passed at different stages. It reflects the technical exposition of the office routine adopted in drafting of the edict. Two *Waqia-nawis* or diary writers were in continuous attendance and recorded all that happened or was said. The next day the *waqia* or diary duly corrected by the concerned official was laid before the emperor for approval. Thereafter each item was copied separately and given to those who were affected by the emperor's remarks. It was countersigned by the *parwanchi, mir arz* and *risaladar* or person who brought the matter before the emperor. In this form the record was called a *yad-dasht* or memorandum. It was then handed over to the copyist who kept the *yad-dasht* and made a proper abridgement of it. It was signed and sealed by the *waqia-nawis*, the *risaladar*, the *mir arz* and the *daroghah*. This document was called a *taliqa*[106] (94).

The procedure detailed above is reflected in the *zimn* or resume of some of the edicts. The *zimn* includes the following details:

Yad-dasht: It contains the day, date and year of the *waqia* recorded in the *risala* of so and so, the *chauki* of so and so, by such and such *waqia-nawis* during his *naubat* or the diary-day to the effect that the facts of the assignee or the grantee were submitted to the emperor and the order was passed to the effect that the resume of the text on the *recto* was recorded verbatim as per the *tasdiq-i yad-dasht*.

Shrah (endorsement). The *yad-dasht* is followed by endorsement by all the concerned officials. Each official used formulary peculiar to his office.

Nishanis (marks): The *pishdasts* (Personal Assistants) and *mutasaddis* (clerks) of the departments made hieroglyphic entries on the margin of the *zimn* indicated by peculiar formulary or abbreviation peculiar to his department. If there was any slip of pen or any mistake the same was corrected and the abbreviation *sad* (correct) was endorsed by the office concerned. If any fraud was detected or any word of the text was struck off, the same was amended and the *muhr-i adam tabdil* was affixed at the top of the document. This served as a safeguard against forgery and malpractice.[107]

It is significant to note that in the *sharh* each official used formulary peculiar to his office as detailed below :

Official	Endorsement	Translation
Pishdast-i Diwan	*sabt shud*	It has been recorded

Pishadast-i Khan saman	*ittalatualaih*	I have been informed
Pishdast-i Bakshi	*waqaftualaih*	I have been intimated(62)

This formulary appears to have been part of official terminology of the day. Each of these was peculiar to some departmental head or his personal assistant and was a sort of pass-word which was perfectly understood by his colleagues who at once understood through what hands or officials this particular document had passed.

7

Most of these documents by their very nature are concerned with administrative problems but some of them do throw revealing light on political affairs. Akbar's last days were rendered unhappy by grief and anguish because Prince Salim rose in rebellion against Akbar and set himself up as an independent king at Allahabad. By Mihr 45 Ilahi/ Septemebr 1600 A.D. he started issuing *farmans* from his court at Allahabad. In September 1600 A.D. Akbar sent Salima Sultan Begam who wielded great influence on her step son. She wrote from Allahabad that Salim was willing to submit but the death of Gulbadan Begam on 7 February 1603 A.D. delayed the successful consummation of the diplomatic parleys. In the meanwhile on 1 Isfandarmaz, 47 Ilahi/9 February 1603 A.D. Salim issued an edict which has been designated as *hukm* in the *unwan* but as *farman* in the text. The seal impressed on this edict gives the title of the rebellious prince as *Abul Muzaffar Sultan Salim Badshah Ghazi* (115).

This indicates that till February 1603 A.D. Salim had not given up his rebellious designs. In the following month Salima Sultan Begam wrote to Akbar that she had cleaned the stain of savagery and suspicion from the heart of the prince and that she would soon bring him to the court.[108] The reconciliation thus effected between father and son was temporary in as much as Salim again proceeded to Allahabad and began to act in a highly objectionable manner. However, when all the rival claimants to the throne were removed, Salim became reconciled to his father who confined him for sometime before pardoning him in November 1604 A.D.

Soon afterwards Akbar passed away and Salim ascended the throne with the title of Nurud Din Muhammad Jahangir Badshah Ghazi in 1605 A.D. It was during his reign that the first English and Dutch factories were established at Surat in 1612 A.D. and 1616 A.D. respectively. Muqarrab

Khan, the Mughal Governor of Surat, seems to be aware of the fact that the English and the Dutch came to India under the cloak of merchants to conquer the lands therein (181). This also applied to the Portuguese who had already established themselves at Goa, Daman and Diu. In 1613 A.D. they seized, in the vicinity of Surat, four Mughal ships which carried a huge treasure. Provoked by this incident, the Mughal forces besieged Daman and arrested most of the Portuguese living in the Mughal empire. Even Fr. Jerome Xavier was put in the custody of Muqarrab Khan. The hostilities came to an end with the treaty of peace concluded on 7 June 1605 A.D. between Muqarrab Khan and Goncal Pinto da Fonseca by virtue of the powers delegated to them by their respective constituent powers. The main terms of this treaty were as follows: (1) Neither of the two powers would ask for any compensation for the losses incurred in the war. However, out of the goods left by the Portuguese in the Mughal territory, Jahangir would be allowed to take 70,000 Xerafins as compensation for the coal which was taken from the ship that had come from Mecca and the residue of the said goods would be returned to their owners; (2) the two powers would neither engage in any trade with the said nations. Nor would they shelter them in their ports; (3) the Portuguese Viceroy would grant for two years only two passes for two ships to go from Surat to Mecca free of duties in addition to the usual pass which was given every year regularly for one ship to make the said voyage. Moreover the Portuguese would also give two passes to two ships free of duties to go from Surat to Hurmuz; (4) the two powers would not give shelter to the Malabaris in their respective dominions; (5) the King of Portugal would retain his right intact in the customs of Diu as well as any other vessels that were accustomed to sail with cargoes by the gulf of Cambay (181).

8

More significant is the light these documents shed on the social conditions of the period covered by them. In an age noted for its uncompromising religious intolerance in Europe, Akbar displayed abundant catholicity. This is fully reflected in his policy of *Sulh-i Kul* or Universal Peace. The Jangam Bari Math in *qasba* Benares enjoyed the favours of Akbar. This *math* had been associated with the followers of the Shaivite sect. Malik Arjun Jangam was the hereditary title held by the head priest of this Math who was always the eldest son of the family. He collected all the offerings made to the Badshah (saint) and other gains from different quarters and distributed them among all the *faqirs* of the sect (65). In 973

A.H./1565-66 A.D. Akbar confirmed Malik Arjun Jangam in possession of 480 *bighas* of culturable land previously held by him as *madad-i maash* (19). The Jangams and Rajpur Dev owned a *gumbad* or dome each in Prayag and Arail in addition to a garden. When the Jangams complained to Akbar that the inhabitants of these two places harassed them in one way or the other, the Emperor addressed a *farman* in Zilqada 982 A.H./ February-March, 1575 A.D. to the *hakim, shiqdar, gumashta* and *mutasaddis* to take action in such a way that the miscreants found no opportunity to disturb the Jangams (35). Similarly in the reign of Jahangir the Jangams brought to the notice of the authorities that Nazir Beg, resident of Benares, had been interfering with their *math* without any justification. Consequently Asad Khan Mamuri, issued a *husbul hukm* to the concerned officials to ensure that Nazir Beg did not interfere with the *math* (210).

As with the Jangams of Benares so with the Vallabhacharya of Gokul, Akbar and Jahangir were equally magnanimous. The Vallabhacharya was called *Marifatagah* (Knower of Divine Mysteries) by Akbar(45). Bithaleshwar, second son of Vallabhacharya, who resided in Gokul, was recipient of a number of favours from Akbar. On 3 Safar 989 A.H./9 March, 1581 A.D. Akbar ordered his officials to allow the cows of Bithaleshwar to graze anywhere in the *khalisa* or *jagir* lands without any obstruction or molestation whatsoever (58). The cows of Govardnan were allowed to graze in the *chiragah* or medow of the village of Savi near Mathura. On 11 Mubarram 987 A.H./20 November 1588 A.D. Khan-i Khanan issued a *hukm* to the officials of *pargana* Aao asking them neither to cause any obstructions to the grazing of the cows nor should they be bothered for *qurq* and *gaushumari* in as much as the village in question has been given in grant for this very purpose (77).

If cow is considered sacred by the Brahmins, peacock is held in great veneration by them. It is supposed to be a vehicle of Saraswati, goddess of learning. It was perhaps to respect these sentiments of the Brahmins that on 11 Khurdad 38 Ilahi/22 May 1593 A.D. Akbar issued a *farman* from Lahore notifying prohibition of *shikar* or hunting and *zibah* or slaughtering of peacock in the vicinity of *pargana* Mathura, *sahar*, Mangotah. This *farman* was issued under the *risalah* of Abul Fazl (89).

Similarly, the Jains were recipients of Mughal favours. In the reign of Akbar, Hiravijaya Suri was the supreme pontiff of the Svetambar Jain sect. Born in Palanpur in 1526 A.D. he was made Archarge in 1559 A.D. In 991 A.H./1583 A.D. Akbar invited him to Fatehpur Sikri to expound the tenets of Jainism in the *Ibadatkhana* and honoured him with the title of

Jagatguru. It was at the instance of this *Jagatguru* that Akbar issued instructions to the officials of Malwa, Akbarabad, Lahore, Multan, Gujarat to the effect that no one might kill any animals during the twelve days of *Paryushana* on the hills of Siddhachal, Girnar, Taranga, Keshrinath and Abu, all situated in Gujarat, and the hill of Samat Shikhar *alias* Parsnath in Bengal alongwith all the *kothis* or firms and the temples below these hills as also all other places of pilgrimage of the Jain Svetambar sect through out the empire (68). In 1608 A.D. Jahangir instructed his officers not to interfere with the houses of the disciples of Vijayasena Suri, Vijayadeva Suri and Nandivijaya. He also ordered that no taxes should be demanded from the pilgrims, visiting the *tirtha* at Shatrunjaya. He also prohibited slaughter of animals throughout the empire on Sundays and Thursdays every week, on the new moon day every month as also on the *Nauroz* and on the anniversary day of his coronation (132). Udayahan Sha led a Jain deputation to the court of Jahangir. This deputation, comprising Vivekharsha, Parmanand and others, was introduced to Jahangir by Raja Ram Das. Subsequently Jahangir issued instructions to the effect that no one should be allowed to slaughter animals during the *Paryushana* festival and that the defaulters should be dealt with sternly (136). In July 1616 A.D. when Jahangir was at Ajmer, the *chelas* or desciples of Bajidev (Vijayadeva) Suri and Nandji Suri waited upon the emperor who was convinced of their *Yazdanparasti* or Divine worship and issued instructions to the officers of the empire not to interfere with or obstruct in any way the religious practices of this *jamat* or community so as to enable them to continue to pray for the permanence of the holy empire as also for the augmentation of the royal dignity (188).

As with the Jain monks, Akbar and Jahangir were benevolent with the Jesuit fathers also. The Jesuit Mission under Fr. Jerome Xavier was despatched from Goa to the Mughal court. It reached Lahore on 5 May 1595 A.D. and was accorded a gracious reception at the court, Akbar gave them permission to build a church at Lahore and also to baptise at Cambay. Subsequently when the Jesuits desired to build a church at Cambay, Akbar issued instructions on 25 Farwardin, Ilahi 42/4 April 1597 A.D. to the concerned officers not to stand in their way in building a holy church of Jesus and to engage themselves in their own worship (101).

Similarly in 1612 A.D. Jahangir issued a *farman* instructing the officials of Gujarat to the effect that no obstruction should be caused to the Firangi Padris who had been permitted to construct an *igriz* or chapel at Ahmedabad for their worship and prayer (150). Subsequently in 1615 A.D. it was brought to the notice of Jahangir that some English men were staying in the Padri's house located at Jawhariwad in Ahmedabad. Jahangir, therefore, instructed the *mutasaddis* of Ahmedabad to accommodate the English men somewhere else and thereafter not to allow any one to enter the Padri's house without proper permission as the doors of the *nazul* house were shut throughout the empire (183). In 1626 A.D. Jahangir issued a *farman* exempting a Christian cemetery from all taxes (301).

Equally favoured were the Parsis (Zoroastrians) *mobids*. Dastur Mehrji or Mahyar Rana, popularly known as Mahrvaid, was a leading *mobid* or Zoroastrian theologian from Navsari in the reign of Akbar, who came in contact with them during the seige of Surat in 1573 A.D. It was in response to Akbar's invitation that Mehrji accompanied the emperor to Agra. He became a principal physician *(tabib)* and a leading teacher in Zoroastrian lore at the imperial court. The eminent services rendered by him to the Zoroastrian creed at the Mughal court justly won him the gratitude of his coreligionists who formally recognised him as their head. This honourable position he held till his death in 1591 A.D. (57). It is significant to note that in one of the documents Mehrji has been referred to as *mutiul Islam* or submissive to Islam and as such could not be taken as *zimmi* or protected subject liable to payment of *jizya* (62). The *hukm* issued under instructions of Akbar in 1566 A.D. exempts the *muzarian* of Qazi Alam who had been granted *madad-i maash* land in *mauza* Sarwarpur, *tappa* Maipur (20).

This religious tolerance is also reflected in the subsistence grants made by the Mughals. By these grants the emperor alineated his right to collect the land revenue and other taxes for the life time of the grantee in perpetuity. Such grants were known as *madad-i maash, aima, milk, amlak, muafi, rozina, wazifa*. The department charged with looking after these grants was presided over by *Sadr* or *Sadrus Sudur* at the imperial court. Such grants lapsed on the death of the grantee. Part or whole of the grant was confirmed in favour of the legal heirs of the deceased only on their making a petition (127).

The *ahl i sadat* or the pious and the learned were dependent on the *ahl- i daulat* or the ruling class for their means of livelihood which they obtained in the form of subsistence grants. Such grants, according to Abul Fazl, were meant for four classes of persons: (1) men of learning; (2) religious devotees; (3) persons of noble lineage who, out of ignorance, could not take to any employment and (4) destitute persons without the capacity for obtaining livelihood.[109]

The recipients of such grants generally belonged to the orthodox class and as such constituted a bastion of conservatism to a large extent. The interests of this class were naturally affected when Akbar began to build a new theoretical basis for his imperial sovereignty by embarking on the policy of religious tolerance and matrimonial alliances with the martial Rajputs. The Rajput consorts in the harem gained such an ascendancy on Akbar that he abstained from everything which they thought repugnant to their nature. It was probably in pursuance of this new policy that Akbar extended the benefits of the subsistence grants to the different communities of his non-Muslim subjects as well, though there are solitary instances of Hindu divines enjoying such benefits before the inauguration of the policy of religious tolerance.

In 973 A.H./1565 A.D. Akbar confirmed Malik Arjun Jangam of Benares in the possession of 480 *bighas* of cultivated land previously held by him as *madad-i maash* (19). Similarly he granted two hundred *bighas* of land as *inam* in village Bhoa *pargana* Pathan, *sarkar* Punjab on 25 Jumada I 979 A.H./15 October 1571 A.D. to Jogi Udant Nath (61). He exempted Pachchumal from *jizya* and the temples at Shoram from taxes (40). In a *farman* dated 8 Ramazan 987 A.H./ 29 October 1579 A.D. Akbar empowered people of different castes to manage their affairs in accordance with their own customs (50). Maryam Makani, Hamida Banu Begam, mother of Akbar, issued a *hukm* on 1 Ramazan 989 A.H./29 September, 1581 A.D. instructing the officials of the *pargana* Mahaban, *sarkar* Agra to allow the cows of Bitleshwar, *zunnardar*, to graze anywhere in the *Khalsa* and *jagir* lands and to ensure that they were neither obstructed nor molested (60). On 16 Rabi II 1012 A.H./13 September 1603 A.D. Akbar issued a *farman* asking the officers to hand over possession of 100 *bighas* of land located in *mauza* Gobindpur, *pargana* Chausa to Basudeo Misr as *madad-i maash* and not to demand any land revenue or tax from him (117). Following the policy of his father Jahangir too gave *madad-i maash* grants to the Hindus. On 17 Azar 1 Ilahi/29 November 1606 A.D. he issued a *farman* instructing the officials to hand over possession of 200 *bighas* of land as *madad-i maash* to Jogi Surat Nath in *Pargana* Pathan *sarkar* Punjab (126). Subsequently when Surat Nath passed away the same grant was made over to Thannath and other *chelas* of the deceased in 1614 A.D. (166). On 14 Khurdad 9 Ilahi/ 25 May 1614 A.D. Jahangir granted *mauza* Phukkar (Pushkar) by way of *inam* to the *zunnardars*, *pujaris* and *purohits* (164).

Like the Jains, and the Christians, the Parsis were also recipient of subsistence grants from Akbar and Jahangir. In 1609 A.D. Jahangir granted a piece of land measuring 6 *bighas* as *inam* to the *Firangis*. Out of these 6 *bighas* 3 *bighas* were earmarked for construction of a cemetery and a garden (134). On 21 Muharram 989 A.H./25 February 1581 A.D. Bairam, son of Qilij, instructed the officials that Dastur Mehr Tabib had been granted one *aul* of *mazru* and three *auls* of *uftada* land as *wazifa* in *qasba* Navsari as he had no means of subsistence. He directed them to leave 109 khajuri trees, pertaining to his *milk* in his possession and not to cause any harassment whatsoever so as to enable him to devote himself with a tranquility in praying for the permanence of the empire (57). In 991 A.H./1583 A.D. Dastur Mehr Tabib was confirmed in the grant of his *wazifa* to the tune of 3 *dokdas* from the *mandvi* of Gandvi and 10 *dokdas* from the *mandvi* of Navsari per diem (66). Four years later on 3 Rabi II 995 A.H./ 3 March 1587 A.D. Abul Qasim, *Diwan* of Gujarat, issued a *hasbul hukm* to the effect that Dastur Mehr Tabib was assigned 5 Muradi *dokdas* out of 13 *dokdas*, previously fixed and directed the officials to pay to the grantee the said sum every day out of the *wujuh* of the *mandvi* of *qasba* Navsari (74). When Dastur Mehr Tabib passed away in 1591 A.D. his son, Dastur Kaikobad, commonly known as Qaim or Kamdin, went to the imperial court for securing renewal of the grants and impressed the emperor so favourably that the latter made an addition of 100 *bighas* to the original grant (83). On 10 Isfandarmaz 40 Ilahi/19 February 1596 A.D., Akbar conferred 300 *bighas* of land alongwith *tad* and *khurma* trees in *qasba* Navsari as *madad-i maash* on Dastur Kaikobad (94) Fazil, *Mir Adl* under Jahangir, confirmed Qaim (Dastur Kaikobad) in possession of his land alongwith the trees on 7 Isfandarmaz 21 Julus/15 February 1627 A.D. (317).

Nor were the Muslim *makhadim* ignored. In consequence of interference of the *amils* of the *khalisa* and *jagirdars*, the makhadim were put to trouble and harassment. Akbar, therefore, issued a *farman* on 27 Rabi II 986 A.H./3 July 1578 A.D. to the *karoris*, *jagirdars* and *mutasaddis* of the empire to the effect that they should assign tracts of land as *madad-i maash* to the *makhadim* in a few villages in a *pargana* independent of the *khalisa* and *jagir* land. This was to be done in such a way that the land in a village was assigned to *makhadim* in separate plots with well-defined boundaries. If the land thus assigned in a particular village was not sufficient to cover the *madad-i maash* to the *makhadim* in that *pargana*, land in another village was to be assigned on the same principle as stated above till the entire land was assigned to the *makhadim* in that *pargana* as *madad-i maash*. Each of the *makhadim* was required to build a house, a *chaupal*, a garden, a mosque, etc., in the village wherein he was assigned *madad-i maash* land. If the *makhadim* resided in one *pargana* and the *madad-i maash* land was assigned to him in another *pargana*, he should not be allowed to take possession of the assigned land till he produced a new *sanad*, but if a person left a *pargana* voluntarily without any pressure and settled down in the *pargana* wherein the *madad-i maash* had been assigned to him, his claim should be recognised. The officers were directed to carry out these instructions faithfully and submit an audited *tumar* of each *pargana* to the emperor as early as possible (46).

The *makhadim* were thus obliged to settle in villages where they were required to build mosques and *chaupals*. While mosque was meant for congregational prayers, *chaupal* was the place where the village community assembled for conducting public business. Akbar thus used *makhadim* for social purposes but earlier Sher Shah had made it obligatory for them to undertake regular practice in archery to counteract malefactors creating disturbances. They were also required to co-operate with the government officials in punishing malefactors as also in collecting revenue (332). The *makhadim* were thus not mere parasites but served social and administrative purposes under Sher Shah and Akbar.

Jahangir, however, looked upon the *makhadim* as "an Army of Prayers"[110] and employed them as apologists and propagandists of his empire. In this Army of Prayers organised by Jahangir, were included a number of women irrespective of caste and creed. Immediately after ascending the throne, Jahangir asked *Hajji* Koka, foster-sister of his father, to bring to him such women as deserved to be presented with land and money.[111] It is, therefore, not surprising to find a large number of *madad-i maash* grants made by Jahangir to women. Some of such grants are given in a chronological order in the following table:

Date	*Grantee*	*Grant*	*Location*	*Reference*
1610-11 A.D.	Bibi Joola Koochi	150 *bighas*	*pargana* Haveli Hajipur, *sarkar* Hajipur, *suba* Bihar	144
1612 A.D	Aisha and Zainab	400 *bighas*	*pargana* Chand, *sarkar* Rohtas *suba* Bihar	151

28 December 1612 A.D.	Bega, widow of Rahman Beg	60 *bighas*	*pargana Haveli* Hajipur *sarkar* Hajipur *suba* Bihar	153
8 September 1613 A.D.	Nuru and her sons	100 *bighas*	*mauza* Devhan *pargana* Amrdha *sarkar* Sambhal	157
11 June 1615 A.D.	Firuz Khatun, widow of Mahmud	50 *bighas*	*pargana* Suket	182
15 July 1617 A.D.	Ajmeri, Bazi *Kalawant* and their mother	(a) 30 *bighas* (b) 2 seers of grain per diem	*mauza* Kaiter	199
16 November 1617 A.D.	Sandal and others	100 *bighas*	*pargana* Fakharpur *sarkar* Bahraich	201
16 October 1618 A.D.	Zohra and others	200 *bighas*	*pargana* Fakharpur *sarkar* Bahraich	214
25 July 1615 A.D.	Zainab and others	50 *bighas*	*pargana* Dariabad *sarkar* Lucknow	222
July-August 1619 A.D.	Samdan	30 *bighas*	*pargana* Siddar *sarkar* Lucknow	223
1620-21 A.D.	Raj Gosain and others	200 *bighas*	*pargana* Fakharpur, *sarkar* Bahraich	242
21 July, 1621 A.D.	(a) Daulat Bakht, widow	40 *bighas*	*suba* Ajmer	248

	of Shaikh Hajji			
	(b) Nirma, widow of Hasan	40 *bighas*		
	(c) Jeo, widow of Allahadad	40 *bighas*		
	(d) Alam Khatun, widow of Ibrahim	30 *bighas*		

Besides the needy widows and orphans, *madad-i maash* grants were also made to meet the expenses of mosques, *khanqahs, roshnai* and *langar* at Sufi shrines (97, 106, 212). Sometimes such grants comprised six villages including as many as 4,57,700 *bighas* of land (212). It should be noted in this connection that the *madad-i maash* grants included two categories of land, viz., *mazru* or cultivated and *uftada* or culturable waste. Under Akbar the standing rule was to give half the area of the grant in land already cultivated and the other half in culturable waste and if the latter was not available the area of the grant was to be reduced by one-fourth (61). Whenever the *madad-i maash* grantee passed away, half of the grant was usually conferred on the heirs of the deceased (215).

Apart from the *madad-i maash,* the documents contain interesting data in respect of the social conditions of the period they deal with. What strikes one most is the fact that the Mughal governing class was status conscious to such an extent that it made fine distinction even in the nomenclature and form of the documents issued from the chancelleries. In fact the wheel of the state revolved round the person of the emperor who was supposed to be at the head of the society. Next to the emperor, the position of primacy was enjoyed by the royal family which included queen-mother, queen-consort, queens, princes and princesses. The Mughal harem enjoyed considerable prestige but neither the queens nor the princesses could wield the sceptre. Notwithstanding this handicap, Maham Begam, wife of Babur, enjoyed exalted position and was allowed to sit by the side of her husband on the throne of Delhi. It is interesting to note in this connection that when Humayun offered to marry Hamida Banu, she is reported to have first refused to consider the proposal of a person who occupied too elevated a social position for her own rank and observed, "I would rather marry a man whose lapel I can hold than one whose pedestal I can not reach." After her marriage she enjoyed the title of *Maryam Makani* and stood by Humayun through thick and thin. She used to issue *hukms* confirming the *farmans* issued by her son, Akbar. It was through the efforts of Hamida Banu and Gulbadan, sister of Humayun, that reconciliation was brought about between Akbar and Salim when the latter rebelled against his father in 1601. A.D. [112]

The Mughal harem consisted of both Muslim and non-Muslim queens. If Humayun's Muslim consort enjoyed the coveted title of *Maryam Makani* Akbar's Rajput empress had the honorific of *Maryam-Zamani*. Similarly Jahangir's Rajput consort enjoyed the title of *Jagat Gosaini* or Gosaini of the world. The death of *Jagat Gosaini* and retirement of *Maryam Zamani* led to the decline of the Rajput influence in the Mughal harem. Subsequently the marriage of Jahangir with Mihrunnisa, afterwards called Nur Jahan, resulted in the preponderance of the Khurasani influence in the Mughal harem. [113]

Jahangir reposed great confidence in Nur Jahan who enjoyed a number of privileges. In 1622 A.D. she was allowed to have her drums and orchestra sounded after those of the emperor. She sometimes sat in the *jharokha* and dictated orders to the officers. The *hukms* bearing her seal and coins struck in her name, have survived the ravages of time. While the theory of Nur Jahan Junta has rightly been disputed, it is difficult to deny the fact of her ascendancy during the last five years of Jahangir's reign when she actively participated in the politics of her time as is evident from a number of *hukms* issued by her. [114]

Immediately below the royal family came the *umara* or nobility which was not a feudal type of organisation based on the principles of rights and duties as was the case in the West. The Mughal monarch created an aristocracy of talents and competence at his will by granting *mansabs* and conferring titles. The status of a noble rested on the *mansab* he occupied, the revenue assignment he held and the title he enjoyed. These distinctions were highly coveted and jealously guarded. The Mongol title *Khan* appears to have been most popular among the Mughal nobility. [115]

Under the Mughals the titles of nobility acquired new dimensions. "The King" observes Manucci, "confers these names (by which the nobles were known) either as a mark of distinction and of the esteem he holds them in by reasons of their services, or else from friendship and liking. These lords (nobles) acquire more wealth as well as more titles that is to say, when any new title is given to them, their allowance is augmented." [116] It was not easy to acquire such titles as they required heavy payment and maintenance of great display. *Mir Khan* had to present Rs.1,00,000 to Shah Jahan for the mere addition of letter *alif* to his title which consequently became *Amir Khan* or chief of the chiefs. [117]

Some of the coveted titles under the Mughals were *Khan-i Khanan, Khan- i Zaman, Khan-i Dauran, Amirul Umara, Sadr-i Jahan, Masihuz Zaman,* etc. It is significant to note in this connection that the Mughals continued the use of the Mongol title of *Khan,* but they never conferred on their nobles the title of *Malik,* so common among their predecessors, the Afghans. They, however, had no hesitation in adopting the *Daulah*-ending titles which were current in the Deccan. It was under Jahangir that *Jang*-ending titles came into fashion.[118] Some specimens of *Mulk*-ending, *Daulah*-ending and *Jang*-ending titles are given below:

Burhanul Mulk	*Itimadud Daulah*	*Fath Jang*
Mutamidul Mulk	*Asafud Daulah*	*Salabat Jang*
Umdatul Mulk	Rukhud Daulah	Firuz Jang

Mughal nobility included a number of Hindus who rose to some of the highest offices of the state. They were awarded Sanskrit and Persian titles as given below:

Emperor	*Noble*	*Title*
Akbar	Raja Bhagwan Das	*Amirul Umara*
	Raja Man Singh	*Mirza Raja*
	Raja Todarmal	*Mutamidud Daulah*
		Umdatul Mulk
Jahangir	Bir Bahadur	*Maharaja*
	Nand Vijaya	*Khush Fahm*
	Jagannath	*Maha Kavrai*
	Bhau Singh	*Mirza Raja*
	Bikramajit	*Jag Raj*
	Pitambar Das	*Ray Rayan*
	Anup Singh	*Sinhdalan*[119]

Less privileged than the governing class was the religious class comprising Muslim *ulama* and *makhadim, Hindu zunnardars* and *Gosains,* Jain *Acharyas,* Christian *Padris* and Zoroastrian *Dasturs.* It was from amongst the *ulama* that *Sadrus-sudur, qaziul quzat, Shaikhul Islam, mir adl, mufti, khatib, hafiz, qazis,* etc., were recruited. Cases against high handedness of provincial *Qazi's* were heard by Governors and decided in consultation with the *makhadim* (26) above referred. Maulana Ibrahim Sanduqvi and his son Ismail Sanduqvi held the office of *Hafiz* or Reciter of the holy Quran at the shrine of Khwaja Muinud Din Chishti at Ajmer (175).

By virtue of the *madad-i maash* grants the *makhadim* penetrated into the countryside. These unofficial apologists and propagandists of the empire constituted pockets of influence in the rural areas. They also operated through the *khanqahs* and Sufi shrines which were visited by members of all communities without any distinction of caste and creed. The shrine of Khwaja Muinud Din Chishti was in particular an object of special reverence under the Mughals and this sentiment was fully exploited by the *mutawallis* and *mujawirs* who were responsible for the upkeep of the shrine. Apart from a large number of *madad-i maash* grant made to them, Akbar confirmed the office of *Roshnai chiragh* or lighting the lamp in favour of Alam who was supplied with one *maund* of oil for this purpose (36). The *nuzurat* or offerings made to the shrine were deposited in the *qindil* and were divided among the *mujawirs* (172). More often than not these *mujawirs* quarrelled among themselves over the distribution of *nuzurat* collected from the pilgrims. In 992 A.H./1584 A.D. they were summoned to the *Adalat-i Alia* or Supreme Court at Fathpur. Subsequently they agreed to the shares as laid down in the *sanad* issued under the seal of Tajud Din al-Husaini (69).

Equally exercised were the *purohits* of Pushkar over the distribution of the offerings made to their temples. When the two sections of the *zunnardars* of Pushkar quarrelled over their share in the charities, Jahangir cancelled the grant of the village of Pushkar made to them earlier but soon afterwards on 12 May 1617 A.D. he restored the grant and instructed the *zunnardars* that the pilgrims visiting Pushkar would be at liberty to choose their *purohits* from either of the two sects and whatever they gave in charity would not be objected to by anyone of them. However if the offerings were made to the two sects collectively, every share-holder should get his share fixed for him. They were also asked to avoid any quarrel in the said village on the issue of grazing of cows and warned them that if they repeated their misconduct they would be imprisoned in the fort (197).

The Shaivite Jangams of Benares, the Vaishnavite Vallabhacharyas of Gokul, the Svetember Jain pontifs, the Jesuit Fathers and Parsi *Hirbeds* and *Mobeds*, were leaders of their respective religious sects and exercised considerable influence on their followers.

Next to the religious class came the domestics and slaves who constituted a familiar feature of every respectable household. The criterion for the selection of female slaves has been somewhat humourously suggested by a Mughal noble: Buy a Khurasani woman for her capacity for nursing children, a Persian woman for the pleasures of her company, and a Transoxianian woman for thrashing her as a warning for the other two.[120]

The data in respect of the masses are very meagre. The plight of the Muslim masses was more or less the same as that of the Hindu masses. Most of the Muslim masses were converts from Hinduism and as such could not give up their caste distinctions and exclusiveness. Some of the documents do refer to *muzarian* or cultivators and *riaya* or peasants but they occupy peripheral position in the status-ridden society. In 1610 A.D. the *ganwars* of village Papri Khurd complained to Nawwab Muzaffar Khan Niyazi, *Hakim* of *pargana* Shamsabad that Miran Sayyid Mustafa had usurped the village which belonged to them. The *Hakim*, therefore, appointed *amins* to inquire into the matter. Miran Sayyid Mustafa submitted the relevant documents and after further evidence it was found that the claim of the *ganwars* was false. The suit was, therefore, dismissed (142).

The masses and the classes congregated at the shrines of reputed Sufi saints. The prince and the peasant thronged to the shrine of Khwaja Muinud Din Chishti at Ajmer. Soon after conquering Chittor in 975 A.H./ 1567 A.D. Akbar travelled all the distance from Agra to Ajmer on foot to pay a visit to the shrine of Khwaja Muinud Din Chishti in fulfilment of the vow he had taken before launching the Mewar campaign. Two years later, after the birth of Prince Salim he again made his famous pilgrimage to Ajmer on foot. From 1570 A.D. to 1580 A.D. Akbar visited Ajmer almost every year but after 1580 A.D. he never went there though he lived till 1605 A.D.[121]

Jahangir made Ajmer headquarters of his operations against Mewar and stayed there from 1613 A.D. to 1616 A.D.[121] These royal visits to the shrine of Khwaja Muinud Din Chishti made a deep impression on the minds of the people. People thronged to his shrine without any distinction of caste and creed. They made *nazr* at the time of *sartarashi* or shaving the head. This was synonymous with *mundan* which connotes a ceremony performed on children among both Hindus and Muslims soon after their birth. The *urs* or death anniversary ceremonies of the saint were attended by members of all communities and thereby subscribed to the principles of universal love the saint had preached and practised in his lifetime. This created a sense of unity in their thinking which tended to break some of the social and religious barriers and paved the way for emotional integration.

Not far from the shrine of Khwaja Muinud Din Chishti is located Pushkar which was visited by multitudes of Vaishnavite Hindu pilgrims. Equally sacred to the Shaivite Hindus were the Jangambari *math* at Benares (19) and the *mahants dera* at Narot (114). Yet another holy place for the Hindus was Gokul where cows considered sacred by the Hindus were allowed to graze freely anywhere in the *khalisa* lands (58). While the Hindus practised *ahimsa* or non-violence all over the land, the Jains were kind to all animate objects. They looked upon their killing with abhorrence and revulsion. In order to respect these sentiments Akbar and Jahangir had prohibited killing of animals at the sacred places of the Jains during the twelve days of *Paryushana* festival (68) and the defaulters were dealt with sternly (136).

The Parsis observed various ceremonies which were mostly associated with their *Agiary* or fire-temple and *Anjuman*. *Sarosh* was the ceremony performed in honour of the dead during the first three days (48). In 1579 A.D. the Parsis of Navsari executed an agreement with their *Anjuman*. This agreement stipulated that all matters relating to the *Agiary* were entrusted to Meherji Rana. The priests concerned were to bring the *dokdas* which might fall to their share for the *sarosh* and sacred bath. No one was to take the *dokdas* and if any one did so he was deemed a defaulter before the *Anjuman* (48, 51). In 1589 A.D. Meherja Rana sent a *Hirbed* or priest to Diu with *Barashnum* or bundle of sacred twigs to perform religious rites (81). The religious matters of the Parsis were decided at the meetings of the *Anjuman* in which the priests participated (105).

Besides marriage and remarriage the following ceremonies were performed at the *Agiary*: (a) *Sarosh:* The ceremony was performed in honour of the dead during the first three days. (48); (b) *Navsa:* The sacred bath given every third day during the *Barashnum* ceremony lasting for nine days (51); (c) *Ghagharana:* It was a marriage between widow and widower (139). For performing these ceremonies and rituals the priests got the following fees: (a) *Siav:* The consecrated clothes which were presented to the priests as a part of their fees (51); (b) *Sanjana:* The fees of the ceremonies falling to the lot of the priests who had gone to Navsari from Sanjan with the sacred fire (51); (c) *Bhagar:* Share of the fee falling to the lot of the original priests of Navsari (51).

9

Equally important are the data contained in these documents in respect of economic conditions. India being an agricultural country the majority of its people lived in villages. The leading economic feature of these villages was production mainly for purposes of local consumption. The land provided fodder for the animals and food for men. In the agrarian system of Mughal India *muzari* or cultivator obviously had an important duty. He was required to till the land and pay a share of the products to the State. The intermediaries constantly endeavoured to discover and appropriate what the cultivator endeavoured to retain and conceal. The only redeeming feature of this situation was the risk of losing cultivators which set some limits to the extractions of the intermediaries. This contest between the intermediaries and the peasantry was obviously detrimental to economic development.

The land was divided into two categories, viz., *uftada* or culturable waste and *mazru* or cultivated. The latter was further divided into two kinds, viz., *khud kashta* or personally cultivated and *raiyat kashta* or peasant cultivated (38). In accordance with the seasonal division of the agricultural year, the assessment was separately made for the *kharif* or autumn harvest and *rabi* or spring harvest. The amount assessed was called *jama* as against *hasil* or amount collected.

The alienation from the peasant of his surplus produce took largely the form of *mal* or land revenue exacted on behalf of the state. Besides *mal* there were a number of other taxes, known as *lawazim- i sultani* or royal perquisites which, in Akbar's time, became *mutalibal- sultani* (4, 109). However, there were *mutawajihat* (1). These were subsequently replaced by *wujuhat* which were divided into *jihat* or imposts on manufactures of respectable kind and *sairjihat* or market transit dues (118).

There were in addition, exactions and perquisites appropriated by officials and *zamindars* and as such were excluded from the *jama*. The perquisites were known as *faruat, abwab- i malba* and *ikhrajat*. *Baghat* was a tax levied from orchards which constituted, after land revenue, a major object of taxation. Akbar and Jahangir tried to abolish this tax, but it was reimposed in the reign of Aurangzeb. In Gujarat revenue also accrued from the sea. Navsari and Gandvi on the western sea-board were the *mandvis* or warehouses (66). Qilij Muhammad Khan was the *Mir- i Mal* of the *mandvi* of Navsari in 991 A.H./1583 A.D. (66).

The internal trade was carried on through the well protected highways which were manned by customs officers. In 997 A.H./1589 A.D. Abdur Rahim *Khan- i Khanan* issued a *hukm- i rahdari* to the custom officers, ferrymen and husband-men on the road from Jalalabad to Kabul prohibited them from demanding any toll from Ali Koka and his companions who were deputed to Kabul on some state business (80). In 1592 A.D. Akbar abolished custom duty on cattle, grain, flourmills, etc., but horses, elephants, camels, sheep, goats, armour and silk-cloth were excluded from this exemption. Officials were instructed not to interfere with the affairs of artisans, merchants and others under the pretext of realising toll or duty. When it was brought to the notice of Akbar that custom duties were exacted from the people on some highways, in bazars and markets, he issued instructions to appoint spies to bring to book the defaulters and directed the tax collectors to execute requisite bonds to be forwarded to the imperial court (84). In 1614 A.D. Jahangir instructed Rai Suraj Singh to safeguard the highways (170). Eleven years later Shantidas Jawahari, the celebrated Jain magnate of Ahmedabad, was placed under the protection of Asaf Khan, *Wakil* of the empire (316).

What is more interesting is the light these documents shed on the prices of land, residential-houses and precious stones as indicated in the following table:

Property	*Size*	*Value*	*Site*	*Year/ A.D.*	*Reference*
Land	20 *bighas* including fruit trees water-channel, tanks and *takabs*	100 *tanka i* Adli	*Qasba* Bilgiram	1542	334
Residential land	Per gaz	35 *jital i siyah* Islam Shahi	do	1550	338
Milki and *khoti* land	4 *biswas*	12 silver *tankas*	do	1556	339
Residential house	Single storey	47000 *tankas*	Ahmedabad	1573	33
Land	4 *biswas*	15 *tankas*	*Mauza* Kahjari district Bahraich	1579	49
Necklace	12 marwarids weighing 6 *mashas* and 6½ *rattis*	Rs. 48/-	Danta	1618	209
		Mahmudis			
Land	12 *bighas*	525	Baroda (Gujarat)	1619	229
Land	2 *bighas*	Rs. 3/-	Sandila	1621	251

The Mughals had inherited different measures of land from their predecessors. The Indian *gaz* or yard has had a very chequered history. It was Sikandar Lodi who introduced *gaz- i Sikandari* which was equal to 30-36 inches of the present measure. It remained official standard till the 31 or 33 *Julus* of Akbar when it was replaced by the *gaz- i Ilahi* (86). It should be noted in this connection that prior to 19 *Julus*, *jarib- i san* or hemp-rope was used as a measure of length. It consisted of 56 *gazs*. When wet, it used to decrease in length. In order to obviate this short-coming, Akbar introduced *tanab- i bans* or bamboo-rod which measured 60 *gaz*. A *bigah* by the new measure was larger than the one by the old. In order to convert the old *bigah* into the new a reduction of 13 or 13.02 per cent was made (61).

Besides introducing the *gaz- i Ilahi* the Mughals imposed standard currency on all the regions that came under their sway but certain regions continued to honour local currencies inherited from previous regimes although it was no longer uttered by the imperial mints. In Gujarat *tanka pratabhara* and *Mahmudi* continued to be used at Navsari even after the conquest of Gujarat by Akbar. *Pratabhara* is a corrupted form of Pratap *varaha*, the name of a medieval coin which was further corrupted by the Portuguese to *Par dao d' ouri*. It seems to be identical with the silver coin, *Muzaffari* which was equal to 3/5 of a rupee. *Dokdas* were also current in Navsari and in 982 A.H./1574 A.D., 60 *dokdas* were equal to one *tanka pratabhara* of old stamp (34). In the beginning of the 17th century the value of a *Mahmudi* was about 2/5 of a rupee but tended to rise perhaps owing to the cessation of its minting under the Mughals who encouraged use of *rupya* or rupee for purposes of administration and commerce.

10

From what has been stated above it is evident that the Mughals modelled their documentary practices after those prevalent in their homeland as also after those followed by their predecessors in India. The *sarnama or the tughra*, or the *nishan* is affixed on the obverse and the endorsements made on the reverse of these documents indicate the normal procedure followed by the court officials before they were issued and thus provide an insight into what may be called the departmental machinery of the Mughal chancellery in the preparation and promulgation of these documents. The technical details connected with drafting of these documents are also of considerable interest to the students of diplomatics and deserve careful study. In their preambles these documents constantly refer to the grants made in previous regimes. The reigning rulers formally respected the commitments made by their predecessors. By their very nature most of these documents are mainly concerned with administrative problems but some of them do shed revealing light on the political, social and economic conditions of the period they deal with. These documents mirror the status-ridden society of their age. The nomenclature reserved for the documents of the governing class presupposes the class barriers. This is corroborated by the fact that the bulk of the documents are concerned with *ahl-i daulat* or governing class, *ahl-i sadat* or ecclesiastical class, *ahl-i murad* or catering class. Some documents do refer to *muzarian* or cultivators and *riaya* or peasants but they occupied a peripheral position in the status-ridden society. In the agrarian society of Mughal India *muzari* was required to till the land and pay a share of the produce to the intermediary. The intermediaries constantly endeavoured to appropriate, through various taxes, cesses and perquisites what the cultivators endeavoured to retain and conceal. This contest between the cultivators and the intermediaries was obviously detrimental to economic development. The plight of the Muslim masses was more or less the same as that of the Hindu masses. Most of the Muslim masses were converts from Hinduism and as such could not give up their caste distinctions and exclusiveness. The Hindu and Muslim masses thronged to the Sufi shrines. The *urs* ceremonies at such shrines were attended by the princes and the peasants without any social and religious inhibitions and subscribed to the principles of universal love and compassion the saint had preached in his life time. This created a sense of unity in their thinking that tended to break some of the social and religious barriers which separated them. Besides the Sufi shrine the imperial court created favourable conditions for the development of social and cultural affinities between different communities. As a matter of fact Akbar had embarked upon a policy of religious tolerance. He was influenced to some extent by the peculiar Jain doctrines of *ahimsa* or non-violence. This was partly the result of the magnetic personalities of the pontiffs which the Jains produced at that time. This policy was also determined by the fact that the Jains at that time formed a small but active, wealthy and influential class among the loyal subjects.

NOTES

1. K.M. Ashraf, *Life and Conditions of the People of Hindustan* (New Delhi, 1970), p. 82.
2. D.C. Sircar, *Indian Epigraphy* (Delhi, 1965) p. 102.

3. *Ibid.*, pp. 105-06.
4. *Ibid.*, pp. 3-4.
5. *Proceedings of the Indian History Congress* (1940), p.52.
6. Sircar, *op. cit.*, p. 107.
7. *Epigraphia-Indica,* XXXIII, p. 303.
8. Sircar, *op. cit.*, p. 107.
9. *On Yuan Chwang's Travels in India, 629-645 A.D.* T. Watters (London, 1904-05), p. 154.
10. S.N. Sen, *India Through Chinese Eyes* (1956) p. 125.
11. George Buhler, *Indian Palaeography* (New Delhi, 1980) p. 121.
12. K.A. Nilakanta Sastri, *The Colas* (Madras, 1975) p. 469.
13. *The Sukraniti*, ed. Benoy Kumar Sarkar (New Delhi, 1973) pp. 91-92.
14. *Lekhapaddhati* ed., Chimanlal Dalal and Gajanan. K. Shrigodekar (Baroda, 1925) p. VII.
15. Ziaud Din Barani, *Tarikh- i Firuz Shahi* (Calcutta, 1891) p. 25.
16. Momin Mohiuddin, *The Chancellery and Persian Epistotography under the Mughals* (Calcutta, 1971) p. 2.
17. Ibid., pp. 4-5.
18. Ata Malik Juvayni, *Tarikh-i Jahan Gushai* tr. J.A. Boyles (Manchester, 1958) II p. 605.
19. A.K.S. Lambton, *Landlords and Pesants in Persia* (Oxford, 1953) p. 99.
20. V.V. Barthold, *Four Studies in the History of Central Asia (Leiden, 1958)* p. 178.
21. *Ibid.*, pp. 153, 163.
22. Abdul Hossein Navai, *Asnad wa Makatibat- i Tarikh- i Iran* (Tehran, 1977) pp. 68-73.
23. *Ibid.*, pp. 143-145.
24. *Ibid.*, pp. 388-89.
25. *Catalogue of the Delhi Museum of Archaeology Red Fort* (Calcutta, 1926) S. No. G. 28 p. 27.
26. Minhaj Siraj, *Tabaqat-i Nasiri,* Vol. I, tr. C. Raverty (London, 1881), pp. 598-99.
27. Wahid Mirza, *The Life and Works of Amir Khusrau* (Delhi, 1974), p. 160.
28. Amir Khusrau, *Ijaz-i Khusraui* (Lucknow, 1875-76) V. p. 167.
29. The *Fathnamas* were composed in grandiloquent style to parade the royal prowess before the world. Barani, *op. cit.* p. 361.
30. Prof. K.A. Nizami has taken this *fathnama* to be a private essay rather than an official document on the ground that Barani has referred to the official despatch of the victory by Malik Qiwamud Din Dabir and that Khusrau was too young at the time to be entrusted with such a responsible task *Some Aspects of Religion and Politics in the Thirteenth Century* (Aligarh 1961), p. 341. It may be noted that Khusrau at that time was 31 years old.
31. Amir Khusrau, *op. cit.*, Ijaz V. pp. 5-13.
32. *Ibid.*, IV, pp. 104-19.
33. *Ibid.*, III, pp. 119-41.
34. *Ibid.*, II, pp. 17
35. *Ibid.*, pp. 18
36. *Ibid.*, IV, pp. 41-44.
37. *Ibid.*, II, pp. 19-20.
38. *Ibid.*, II, pp. 4-17.
39. *Ibid.*, II, pp. 21-25.
40. S.H. Askari, 'Material of Historical Interest in Ijaz i Khusravi' *in Medieval India - A*

Miscellany (Delhi, 1969).

41. Amir Khusrau, *op. cit.*, Ijaz, I. 53.
42. *Ibid.*, IV, p. 22.
43. Fakhr-i Mudabbir *Adabul harb washshajaah* (rotograph Aligarh Muslim University), ff. 59a-59b.
44. Mir Khurd, *Siyarul Auliya* (Delhi, 1302 A.H.) pp. 104-05 and 209-31.
45. Ainud Din Mahru, *Inshah-i Mahru*, ed., Shaikh Abdur Rashid (Lahore, 1965), p.1.
46. The *misal* and the *manshur* appeared under the Ghaznavids and these were among the principal mandates during the Turkish period. The *manshur* was a diploma of approbation conferred on religious authorities or the clergy as a token of reverence accorded to them by the Sultans. The *nishan* appeared under the Tughluqs as a proclamation of ordinance. *Insha-i Mahru in Journal of Asiatic Society of Bengal* (1923).
47. *Ibid.*
48. Ainud Din, *op. cit.*, pp. 2-8.
49. *Ibid.*, pp. 14-15.
50. *Ibid.*, pp. 15-17.
51. *Ibid.*, pp. 37-39.
52. Momin, *op. cit.*, p. 243.
53. Imadud Din Mahmud Khweja Jehan, *Riyazul Insha*, ed., Shaikh Chand (Hyderabad, 1948).
54. Barani, *op. cit.*, p. 64.
55. A.B.M. Habibullah has given a brief note on the Baran *farman* of Muizzud Din Muhammad bin Sam Ghori. (*The Foundation of Muslim Rule in India*, Allahabad, 1971, p. 367). Dr. Agha Mahdi Hasan has given summary translation of the *farman* of Muhammad bin Tughlaq (*The Tughlaq Dynasty*, New Delhi, 1976 p. 363) and Maulavi Bashirud Din Ahmad has reproduced the texts of some of the documents of the Turkish Sultans (Maulavi Bashirud Din Ahmad *Faramin-i Salatin-i* Delhi. 1926) but their genuineness cannot be asserted beyond doubt till their originals or facsimiles are examined.
56. Indian Museum, Calcutta, No. 49; *Proceedings of the Indian Historical Records Commission*, XXIX, pt. I., 1953.
57. Mahmud Ahmad Abbasi, *Tazkiratul Kiram, alias Tarikh-i Amroha* (Delhi), p. 34.
58. Mohammed Shafi, 'Three Old Documents' in *Proceedings of the Idara-i Maarif- i Islami*, (Lahore, 1936), pp. 283-85.
59. For details please see Appendix I.
60. B.A. Saletore, 'Mughal Farmans' in *New Indian Antiquary II* (April, 1939).
61. Yusuf Husain Khan, *Farmans and Sanads of the Deccan Sultans* (Hyderabad, 1963), pp. 1-2.
62. *Ibid.*, p. 4.
63. *Ibid.*, p. 3.
64. *Ibid.*, p. 4.
65. I.H. Qureshi, 'The Documents Relating to the Nature of Religious Assignments in the Sultanate of Gujarat' in *Indian Historical Records Commission*, XXI, (1944), pp. 61-62.
66. J.J. Modi, *The Parsees at the Court of Akbar* in *Contributions on Akbar and Parsees* ed., B.P. Ambashtya (Patna, 1976). pp. 158-60.
67. S.H. Hodivala, *Studies in Parsi History* (Bombay, 1930), pp. 155-61.
68. J.J. Modi, 'The Parsees at the Court of Akbar and Dastur Meherji Rana' *in Journal of*

Bombay Branch of the Royal Asiatic Society, XXI, 1904, pp. 227-29.

69. Hodivala, *op. cit.*, p. 194.
70. *Ibid.*, pp. 202-204.
71. *Ibid.*, pp. 198-200.
72. *Ibid.*, p. 242.
73. *Ibid.*, pp. 162-64
74. *Ibid.*, pp. 227-28.
75. Qureshi, *op. cit.*, *IHRC*, XXI, pp. 61-62.
76. Hodivala, *op. cit.*, pp. 207-08.
77. *Ibid.*, pp. 211-12.
78. *Ibid.*, pp. 245-46.
79. *Journal of the Bombay Branch of the Royal Asiatic Society*, XXI (1900-1903), pp. 220-21.
80. *Ibid.*, p. 223.
81. S.A.I. Tirmizi, 'Medieval Indian Diplomatics' (MID), Presidential Address, *Proceedings of the Indian History Congress 43rd Session*, (Kurukshetra, 1982), pp. 228.
82. *Ibid.*
83. Zahirudin Muhammad Babur, *'Baburnamah* I, tr. by A.S. Beveridge, (New Delhi, 1979) p. 319.
84. *Ibid.*, II, p. 630.
85 - 88. Tirmizi, *op. cit.*, MID, pp. 228-29.
89. Momin, *op. cit.*, 86.
90. Ali Muhammad Khan, *Mirat-i Ahmadi* I, ed. Syed Navab Ali (Baroda, 1927) pp. 247-83.
91. Momin *op. cit.*, p. 89.
92. H.H. Wilson, *Glossary of Judicial and Revenue Terms* (New Delhi, 1855) p. 507.
93. *Ibid.*, p. 321.
94- 95. Momin, *op. cit.*, pp. 114-117.
96. Wilson, *op. cit.*, p 244.
97. Momin, *op. cit.*, pp. 91-92.
98. Ibn Hasan, *Central Structure of the Mughal Empire* (New Delhi, 1970) p. 94.
99. Momin, *op. cit.*, p. 97.
100. S.A.I. Tirmizi *Miscellany of Medieval India*, (Delhi, 1986) p. 9.
101. Abul Fazl, *op. cit.*, *Ain*, pp 270-75.
102. *Ibid.*, pp. XVII-XIX
103. Jahangir, *Tuzuk- i Jahangiri*, tr. Rogers and Beveridge (New Delhi 1978), p. 134.
104. S.A.I. Tirmizi, *Index to Titles* (Calcutta, 1979) p. ix.
105. L.V.S. Bendry *Tarikh- i Ilahi* (Poona, 1933) p 18.
106. Ishtiaq Husain Qureshi, *The Administration of the Mughal Empire*. (Patna, 1979) p. 81.
107. Tirmizi, *op. cit.*, MIM, p. 14.
108. A.L. Srivastva, *Akbar- the Great* (Lucknow 1975). p. 472.
109. Abul Fazl *op. cit.*, *Ain* I, p. 278.
110. Jahangir *Tuzuk- i Jahangiri* I. II, Alexander Rogers and Henry Reverdige (Delhi 1968) p. 10.
111. Jahangir *op. cit.*, I, p. 46.
112 - 114. S.A.I. Tirmizi, *Edicts from the Mughal Harem* (New Delhi, 1979) p. x-xiii, 41.
115. Tirmizi, *op. cit.*, IT p. xii.

116. Nicholao Manuchi, *Storia Do Mongor* (1653-1708) II. *tr*. W. Irvine (London, 1907) p. 369.
117. Saqi Mustaid Khan. *Maasir-i Alamgiri* tr. J.N. Sarkar (Calcutta, 1947), p. 290.
118. Tirmizi, *op. cit.*, IT p xii.
119. *Ibid.*, pp. xiv-xv.
120. Abul Fazl, *op. cit.*, *Ain* I. p. 346.
121. S.A.I. Tirmizi, *Ajmer Through Inscriptions* (Delhi, 1968) p. 12.

BABUR (1526-1530)

13 Zilqada, 933 A.H./11 August 1527 A.D.

1. Farman[1] of Babur[2] addressed to the revenue officials, confirms the grant of *mauza*[3] Sahrgul Pindori (sic)[4] *pargana*[5] Vatala,[6] yielding revenue of 5,000 *tanka-i siyah*[7] per annum in favour of Jalal,[8] *Qazi*[9] of the said *pargana* as *suyurghal.*[10] Instructs officials not to harass the grantees on account of *mutawajjihat,*[11] *malujihat*[12] and asks them not to demand fresh *farman* or *parwancha*[13] every year.

On the top of the document are (a) *sarnama*[14] *Huwal Ghani*[15] (b) *Unwan*[16] *farman- i* Zahirud Din Muhammad Babur *Badshah*[17] *Ghazi*[18] and (c) round dynastic seal[19]. On the reverse are endorsements of the officials and the round seal of Zainud Din Khwafi,[20] the great *dastur*[21] and *sadr.*[22] (*IHRC*, XXXXVI, Pt. II. 1951, pp. 51-52).

8 Rabi I, 934 A.H./2 December 1527 A.D.

2. *Farman* of Babur addressed to the *diwans*[1] of Muhammad Sultan Bahadur[2], confirms village Auhadpur,[3] *tappa*[4] Haveli,[5] *qasba*[6] Fathpur Sandi[7] with *jama* of 800 *tanka-i siyah* and 250 *bighas*[9] of land in the vicinity of the said *qasba* in favour of *Qazi* Abdud Daim,[10] son of Ilhadad. The grantee is to realize the *hasil*[11] thereof as before and enjoy it as *madad-i maash*[12]. He is not to be troubled on account of *mal, jihat, ikhrajat*[13] and *dhonka sali,*[14] or *passi.* (*TKTB*, p. 144, *IESHR*, IV, 1967, p. 220).

Rajab, 936 A.H./25 March 1530 A.D.

3. Sale-deed executed by Maulana Fathullah Abdullah and Piyare, sons of Ahmad, in favour of Miran Sayyid Nizamud Din for selling the right of *milk*[1] *khoti* over 20 *biswas*[2] of land in village Papri khurd,[3] *tappa* Haveli, *khitta*[4] Shamsabad[5] at a price of 700 current *tanka-i Adl Sikandari*[6] and in consideration of annual payment of 300 *tankas.*

The document bears *tughra* of *Qazi* Ismail as also signatures of the witnesses. (*IESHR*, IV, 1967 pp.220-21).

Muharram 937 A.H./July-August 1530 A.D.

4. *Farman* of Babur addressed to the *amirs,*[1] *wazirs*[2], *shiqdars*[3] and *mutasaddis*[4] of *sarkar*[5] Tatarkhan[6], etc., confirming *Qazi* Abdul Halim,

son of *Qazi* Abdus Samad, and his brothers in possession of the land and *wazifa*[7] previously granted to them by the *sanad*[8] of the Sultan Ibrahim[9] and the *tauqi*[10] of Sultan Sikandar[11], instructs them not to bother them with *taufir*[12], *ushr*[13], *daroghana*[14] and *shiqdarana*[15] and to exempt them from the payment of *mal, jihat, ikhrajat* and all the *takalif-i diwani* and *lavazim-i-sultani*[16]. Asks them not to harass the grantees by demanding fresh *farman* and *parwancha* and to honour the *tauqi* when it reaches them. The *farman* was issued from the capital of Agra. (*OCM, May 1933, p. 119*).

HUMAYUN (1530-39 and 1554-56)

15 Muharram, 938 A.H. / 29 August 1531 A.D.

5. Sale-deed executed by Bibi Shukir, daughter of Salar Tharu and wife of Salar Sulaiman, in favour of *Qazi* Abdud Daim, son of Ilhadad for selling 16 out of 20 *biswas* "known and reputed as *milk* and *khoti*" of village Sharafuddinpur[1], together with cultivated land of village Shaikhanpur[2], *qasba* Bilgram[3] for 450 *tanka-i-Adli.*[4]. The vendor transfers her rights including *milk* of trees, fruits, water-channels, tanks, *takab*[5] etc., but excluding mosque and graves. The village is bounded on the east by the river Akrandi and *pargana Malanwa*[6], on the south by village Bochanpur[7] and on the north by village Ka(n) dharlya[8]. (*IESHR*, IV 1967, pp. 221-227).

6. Undated *farman* of Humayun addressed to Sayyid Muhammad Nasirud Din Rizwi, asking him to reach Delhi to be honoured with the royal favours in recognition of his services in the battle with Sher Khan[1] when he received 35 wounds. (*IHRC*, XXIX, Pt.I, 1953, p. 96).

24 Zulqada, 964, A.H./18 September 1557 A.D.

7. Judgement of the Arbitrator. A complaint is brought to the *Diwan-i-Shara*[1] of *qasba* Bilgram by Mubarak, son of Yusuf, on his own behalf and on behalf of the co-sharers, that all the 20 *biswas* ("known and reputed as *milk* and *khoti*") of land in village Dhauli[2], *qasba* Bilgram, was their rightful property by inheritance and purchase. He alleges that Bhoraj, son of Dhanun, has unsurped the land in question and requests that its possession be restored to them. In reply to this complaint, Bhoraj produced sale-deeds for 8 *biswas* and 5 *biswansis*[3] only saying sale-deeds for the remaining land were lost. Both the parties agreed to appoint Miran Sayyid Abdun Nabi Piyara as *hakam* to give his verdict. After perusal of the case, the arbitrator admitted Bhoraj's claim to 8 *biswas* and 5 *biswansis* only and asked him to withdraw his possession from the remaining 11 *biswas* and 15 *biswansis* of land and handed over its possession to the complainant. Both the parties agreed to abide by the decree of the arbitrator. It bears the seal of *Qazi* Sadrud Din and signature of witnesses. (*IESHR*, IV, 1967, pp. 223-224).

AKBAR (1556-1605)

7 September 1558 A.D.

8. *Hukm*[1] of Bairam Khan[2] addressed to the officials of Allahabad (Prayag), directs them to deliver possession of 1,500 *bighas* of land situated in *qasba* Payag[3] to Sayyid Abdul Qadir as *muafi* grant after measuring, consolidating and demarcating it. Orders them not to press him for a renewed *sanad* every year. On top there is a *tughra* of Akbar which is closely followed by the name of Bairam Khan. There are seals of Akbar and Bairam Khan as well. (*SI*, XV, No.1, January 1978, pp. 43-44).

Muhrram, 966 A.H./October- November 1558 A.D.

9. *Hukm* of Bairam Khan granting 200 *bighas* of land to Shaikh Gadabanda for maintenance. It bears Bairam Khan's seal. (*IHRC*, XII, 161.)

Rabi II, 966 A.H./January- February 1559 A.D.

10. *Farman* of Akbar addressed to the officials *of sarkar* Sambhal, granting 400 *bighas* of land in village Bawanipur[1], *khitta*[2] Sambhal, to Shaikh Buddan and Shaikh Ahmad. On the top it bears *unwan* of Jalalud Din Muhammad Akbar *Badshah Ghazi* as also a seal of Akbar. There is neither a *tughra* nor endorsement on the back which bears some seals of the officials including that of Bairam Khan. (*AIOC*, X. 1940. pp. 466-67).

12 Jumada I, 967 A.H./10 February 1560 A.D.

11. *Parwana* of Sayyid Alam Husaini[1] and Sayyid Ikrami Mubarak addressed to the *chaudharis*[2], *muqaddams*,[3] and *qanungos*[4] of *qasba* Ajmer[5]. confirms the grant measuring 20 *bighas* of land along with 2 wells by way of *inam*[6] in the name of Shaikh Qutban[7], *khadim* of the shrine of Khwaja Muinud Din Chishti[8], who has been enjoying it for long and directs the officials not to harass the grantee for *wujuh*[9]. The Persian text is followed by the *Kaithi* version. There is a round seal each of Sayyid Alam Hussaini and Sayyid Ikrami Mubarak on the right-hand margin at the end. (*AS*, pp. 11-14).

Shaban, Julus 5/967 A.H./April- May, 1560 A.D.

12. *Farman* of Akbar addressed to the *hukkam*[1], *ummal*[2], etc. of Ajmer, intimates them that the office of *tauliyat*[3], has been conferred upon

Shaikh Hussain[4] *sajjadanashin*[5] of the shrine of Khwaja Muinud Din Chishti. States that the said *mutawali*[6] will look after the *langar*[7], distribute the income assigned to him, pay 15,000 *tanka-i Muradi*[8] to his mother, give fixed shares to the *mujawirs*[9] avoiding all conflict and dispute in the division of the proceeds. Directs the officials not to charge any tax on the grant, nor to demand a fresh *farman* from him every year. It bears the seal of Akbar on the top. (*FS*, 2-3)

967 A.H./1559-60 A.D.

13. *Farman*[1] of Akbar granting a few hundred *bighas* of revenue free land to a family of Sayyids of *sarkar* Lakhnau[1]. It also refers to the *sanad* of Sher Khan. It bears the *sarnama* 'Huwal Ghani' a *tughra* and a round seal of Akbar on the top. (*MF*. I. p. 3).

Julus 4/1559-1560 A.D.

14. *Farmam* of Akbar confirming Sayyid Abdul Qadir Rizawi in possession of the land, *haveli*[1] and garden which were granted to his father, Sayyid Muhammad Nasirud Din Rizawi, in recognition of his services in the battle with Sher Khan Afghan. (*IHRC*, XXIX. Pt. I, 1953, p. 96).

25 Shaban, 968 A.H./11 May 1561 A.D.

15. *Parwana* addressed to *jagirdars*[1], Mubarak Khan Jalal Sharwani, *Munsif*[2] Haider Miyan, *Shiqdar* of *pargana* Sandila, and other officers. Informs them that land in village Mahrepur of the said *pargana* has been assigned to Shaikh ..... as *madad-i maash* where he should take up his residence and spend his time in meditation and prayers. Orders them to measure, demarcate and consolidate the land and deliver possession thereof to the grantee who should not be bothered for any tax or cess. (*COR*. II. p. 11.)

Zilaqada, 969 A.H./July-August 1562 A.D.

16. *Farman* of Akbar addressed to the *wakils* of the *hakim* of Ajmer[2], orders them not to allow any one to bury the dead in the land adjoining the *maqbara*[3] of Khwaja Muinud Din Chishti without permission of Khwaja Husain, descendant of Khwaja Muinud Din Chishti. It bears seal on the top. (*FS*. pp. 1-2).

1562 A.D.[1]

17. *Hukm* of (Munim Khan) *Khan-i Khanan*[2], states that the details of the hereditary *jagir* assigned to the *qanungo* of *pargana*[3] Khargon[4] by the former rulers have been made known to the Emperor who has confirmed the rights of revenue collection in favour of the said *qanungo*. Instructs the officers and servants[5] of the said *pargana* to treat the orders of the said *qanungo* as those emanating from government[6]. The *hukm* bears a seal with the legend *'Khan-i Khanan Banda-i Shah-i-Akbar'*[7]. In the background a galloping deer is engraved. (*IHC*. XXX. 1968, pp. 183-85).

***Jumada I, 971* A.H./*December 1563-January 1564* A.D.**

18. *Farman* of Akbar addressed to the *qazis, jagirdars* and *ummal* of *pargana* Bilgram, informs them that the *maliks*[1] of some newly cultivated land of the said *pargana* have petitioned to be allowed to sell their land held in *milk* or to give it on lease for cultivation and realise their share of *malikana*[2]. Orders are, therefore, issued that they should follow what is prescribed in the *fatwas*[3] and not to put any restraint on the petitioners for any reason not sanctioned by the *shariat*[4], and not to allow anyone to violate the *shariat*. (*IESHR*, IV, 1967, p. 225).

973 A.H.[1]/*1565-66* A.D.

19. *Farman* of Akbar addressed to the *diwans amils*[2], *chaudhuris*, and *qanungos* of *sarkar* Haveli Benares[3], confirms Arjun Jangam[4] in possession of 480 *bighas* of cultivated land previously held by him as *madad-i maash* in the *mahal*[5] of the said *sarkar*. Asks them (addresees) to hand over possession of the land to the grantee and instructs them not to demand *malujihat, ikhrajat* and the *awarizat*[6] like *qunlugha*[7] and *peshkash*[8]. It bears the *sarnama 'Huwal Ghani'* on the top and a seal dated 971 A.H. on the back. (*IHRC*, XLTV, 1976. p. 206).

***Safar 974* A.H./*August-September 1566* A.D.**

20. *Hukm* of *Khan-i Khanan* Muhammad Munim Khan, granting 20 *bighas* of cultivable and 50 *bighas* of fallow land in village Sarwarpur[1], *tappa* Maipur[2] as *madad-i maash* to *Qazi* Alam from the beginning of the *kharif* of *Pars-yil*[4] so that he may acquire the revenue thereof and utilise it for his maintenance. The *hukm* issued by the order of Akbar enjoins upon the *hakims, diwans* amils and other officials of *pargana* Bhojpur[5], *sarkar Darul Khilafa*[6] Agra[7], to exempt the grantee and his *muzarian*[8] from payment of *malujihat, wujujat, sairikhrajat*[9] and all the demands of the *diwani* such as *qunlugha, peshkash, savi*[10], *jaribana*[11], *zabitana*[12], *muhrana*[13], *saddoi-i qanungoi, takrar-i zarat*[15], *harjkharch*[16], *wajuh*[17], *jizya*[18], *muhtarifa*[19], *taughana*, etc. Asks the officials not to allow Tahir Koka and Dost Muhammad to occupy that land. It bears the *unwan hukm-*

i Muhammad Munim *mulaqqab Khan-i Khanan''*. (*PBMN*, pp. 96-97, *IESHR*, IV, I, pp. 223-24).

976 A.H./1568-69 A.D.

21. *Farman* of Akbar, addressed to the officials of *pargana* Amroha[1] *sarkar*[2] Sambhal[2], informs them that 300 *bighas* of land situated in village Khanpur[3], *pargana* Amroha, *sarkar* Sambhal, have been granted to Shams Khan as *madad-i maash*. Orders them to deliver possession of the land to the grantee and demand no tax whatsoever from him. (*CDMA*, p. 31).

1568 A.D.[1]

22. *Farman* of Akbar addressed to the *hukkam, diwans, ummal,* and *mutasaddis*, etc., informs them that Nabera[2], a part of Chitoor[3], yielding a *jama* of one lakh of *tanka- i Muradi* has been granted to Shaikh Husain, by way of *suyurghal*. Orders the officials to hand over possession of the *mauza*[4] to the *gumashtas*[5] of the grantee and not to demand *malujihat, ikhrajat,* etc. from him. Nor should they ask him to produce a renewed *farman* and *parwancha* every year. (*FS*,.p. 1).

977 A.H.[1]/1569 A.D.

23. *Farman* of Akbar granting village Savai[2], part of Naraina[3], under Sambhar[4] administration, to Khwaja Husain, as *madad-i maash*. It bears the seal and *tughra* of Akbar. This *farman* is torn and no date of writing is available. The name of the addressee is also missing. (*IHC*, XIII, p. 251).

Rabi II, 978 A.H./September 1570 A.D.

24. *Farman* of Akbar addressed to *Umdatul Mulk*[1] Nizamud Din Muhammad Qasim Khan[2] and Tardi Beg Sultan[3], states that Malla (Mali), *muqaddam* of village Khandarya, *pargana* Bilgram, has attended and complained that one Abdus Samad has usurped the *muqaddami*[4] of the said village. If this be true both the officials should bring together the parties and forbid any illegal encroachment. In case no settlement is arrived at, the parties should be sent to the *Diwani-i Ala* for consideration of the matter. (*IESER*, IV, 1967. p. 226).

29 Rabi II, 978 A.H./30 September 1570 A.D.

25. *Farman* of Akbar appointing *Qazi* Nizam[1] to the office of *Qanungo* of Bijnor[2], and stating that the appointee's duties would be to collect

revenue, encourage ryots, and look after the welfare of the people in general. It bears the seal of the Emperor. (*IHRC*, XII. p. 165).

15 Jumada I, 978 A.H./15 October 1570 A.D.

26. Decree on a dispute. Mali, son of Anki, and Parshad, son of Karam (Party A) asserted on production of an imperial order that "all the 20 *biswas* of land in village Khandarya has been seized unjustly by *Qazi* Abdus Samad, son of *Qazi* Kamal (Party B). Thereupon Muhammad Khan and Tardi Beg Sultan along with the *makhadim*[1] collected in the *Jama Masjid*[2] to hear and enquire into the above complaint. Parshad son of Nala, appeared on his behalf and on behalf of the co-sharers, and described as *muqaddams* of villages Barauni[3], Khadkanian[4] and Bhadnaur[5] (Party C).

Party A claimed 3 *biswas* and Party B, 17 *biswas*. Evidence of the parties was heard and the documents produced by them were gone through. After investigation it was decided that the complaint of Party A was baseless and the *makhadim* recognised the claim of Party B.

The Decree bears a number of seals including that of Tardi Beg Sultan and a number of signatures in Persian and Devnagiri characters of those present. (*IESHR*, IV, 1967, pp. 226-228).

Rajab 978 A.H./November-December 1570 A.D.

27. *Farman* of Akbar addressed to the *chaudharis* and *qanungos* of *sarkar* Bijagarh[1], informs them that the *mauzas* and *mahals* lying within the jurisdiction of *sarkar* Bijagarh have been placed under the control of Muhammad Khan who has always been in the vanguard of the imperial army.

It bears the seal of Akbar. (*IHC*, XXX, 1969, pp. 374-75).

978. A.H./1570-71 A.D.

28. *Hasbul hukm*[1] of Shihabud Din Ahmad Khan Hasani[2] addressed to *chaudharis, jagirdars, qanungos,* etc., states that the emperor has sent *dasturul amal*[3] to *sarkar* Bijagarh and Muhammad Khan has been empowered to decide all the pending cases relating to revenue of the said *sarkar*.

On the top is written, in black ink, the *unwan* "*Farman-i Jalalud Din Muhammad Akbar Badshah Ghazi*". It is a bilingual document, in Persian and Hindi, and bears, the seal of Shihabud Din Ahmad Khan Hasani. On the reverse is an endorsement and an illegible seal. (*IHC*, XXI, 1969, pp. 271-72).

22 Shaban 979 A.H./9 January 1572 A.D.

29. *Farman* of Akbar addressed to Habibullah Kamal[1], holder of *pargana* Gopamau in *tuyul*[2], states that the Emperor has been informed that a sum of 8,311 *tankas* has been actually taken on the orders of Khwaja[3] Mahmud and Sulaiman[4], agents of the *Mutamidul Mulk* Tardi Sultan and Afzal Sultan[5], from the pious and honest *Qazi* Kamal, the *Qazi* of *pargana* Bilgram, and his brothers. Orders him to enquire into the matter and take necessary steps to refund the amount to the persons concerned.

It bears the *sarnama 'Huwal Ghani'* and the seal of Akbar on top. There are seven other seals on the reverse. (*IHRC*, XXII, 1945, pp. 33-4) ; *IESHR*, IV, 1967, p. 229, Doc. p. 13).

979 A.H./1571-72 A.D.

30. *Farman* of Akbar ordering reinstatement of *Qazi* Kamal, who was illegally dismissed, on his office of the *Qazi* of Gopamau and compensating him in cash. (*IRRC*, XXV, p. 113).

Ruz[1] Ormuzd[2], mah[3] Shahriwar[4], Samvat 1629/4 Rabi II, 980 A.H./14 August 1572 A.D.

31. An agreement executed and signed by Manochaher, Bahman, Nagoj. Manek, Nausherwan Changa, Rustam Jamshad[5] and others of Navsari[6] addressed to Mahyar Vachcha[7] during the regime of Qilij Muhammad Khan[8] states that 10 *bighas* of land with 50 palm and 100 date-trees, situated at Pipalia[9], will be maintained as *inam* year to year, free from all taxes. (*JBBRAS*, XXI, 1900-03, pp. 224-25).

980 A.H./1572-73 A.D.

32. *Farman* of Akbar granting a piece of land in village Gobri[1], part of Bahraich in Lucknow. (*IHC*, 1938, p. 60).

Ramazan 981 A.H./December 1573-January 1574 A.D.

33. Sale-deed executed in the Court of Justice of the chief city of Ahmadabad[1], in the presence of *Qazi*, officers of the Momins and the officers of *Qazi* Imadud Din by Bhoja bin Devdas bin Gopal in respect of a single-storey house consisting of three rooms and bounded on the east by Government offices, on the west by the house of Kashya bin Bajya and on the north by the house of Rai Dagu Agnihotri. The vendor has declared that he is the sole proprietor of the house in question and no one else has any share or right in the said house. The vendor has agreed to sell the house for 47,000 *takas*[2], and this amount has been paid in full by the vendee, Vishnu bin Jadu bin Bora and that complete possession of the house has been given to the vendee. All these facts have been testified by Bhavan bin Kesu bin Ratan and Ramji bin Nayan Veerjanki.

It bears signatures of the vendor and Muhammad Jalaluddin. The document is bilingual, in Persian and Sanskrit, and is written on a thick piece of cloth. There are names of Aziz Koka[3], Qazi Mir Ahmad, Amatya[4] Suri and Treasurer Shaikh Mundi. (*IHRC*, XXX).

Ruz Khurdad, mah Tir Samvat 1631/2 Rabi 982 A.H./22 June, 1574 A.D.

34. A sale-deed[3] is executed by Bai Pomi, wife of Gardi[4] Asdin, and Vura Shapur Asdin in respect of a house sold to Ervad Padam Mahiyar[5] for a sum of 13 *tankas Pratabahra*[6], of old stamp, each *tanka* of the value of 60 *dokdas*[7], under the *amal*[8] of Qilij Muhammad Khan when Darwesh Muhammad held office at Nagmandal[9].

It bears signatures of the vendors, Bai Pomi and Shapur Asdin, as also of the witnesses. (*SPH*, pp. 249-50).

Zilqada, 982 A.H./February-March 1575 A.D.

35. *Farman* of Akbar addressed to the *gumashtas* of *hakim* and *shiqdar* and *mutasaddis* of *qasba* Prayag and Arail[1] informs them that Rajpur Dev and the associates of Jangam, residents of the said *qasba*, own two *gumbads*[2], one in Prayag and the other in Arail, in addition to a garden. They have complained that some inhabitants of the area are harassing them in one way or another. Orders the addressees to take necessary action in such a way that the miscreants find no opportunity to disturb them. (*IHRC*, XLIV, p. 209).

982 A.H./1574-75 A.D.

36. *Farman* of Akbar addressed to the *karoris*[1], *shiqdars* and *karkuns*[2] of *pargana* Sambhar confirms the office of *Roshanai Chiragh*[3] of the mausoleum of Khwaja Muinud Din Chishti in favour of Alam as heretofore and orders them to supply one maund[4] of oil to the person concerned for the purpose and not to ask him for a fresh *farman* every year.

It bears the *sarnama* "*Huwal Ghani*" as well as a round *uzuk*[5] seal of the Emperor on top. On the reverse is the *parwancha* of Shaikh Abdun Nabi[6], *Sadr*. Of the seals of the officials, only that of Asaf Khan[7] is in a sound condition. (*AS*, pp. 3-5).

16 Muharram 983 A.H./27 April 1575 A.D.

37. *Farman* of Akbar granting 1085 *bighas* of land near Delhi to Nizamud Din and others as *madad-i maash*. It bears the seal of Akbar. (*IHRC*, XII, p. 161).

23 Rabi I, 983 A.H./2 July 1575 A.D.

38. *Farman* of Akbar addressed to the officials of *pargana* Haveli[1], *sarkar* Kara[2], *suba* Allahabad, says that 700 *bighas* of land had been granted as *madad-i maash* in *pargana* Haveli, *sarkar* Kara, *suba* Allahabad to Sayyid Faridud Din Muhammad Danishmand, son of Sayyid Ashraf, in the year 967 A.H./1559-60 A.D. On the death of the grantee, the said grant had lapsed to the *Khalisa Sharifa*[3]. Orders that the land be delivered to Sayyid Abdul Hayy, Sayyid Abdun Nabi, Sayyid Shah Muhammad and Sayyid Abdus Sami, brothers and sons of the deceased who waited upon the Emperor and brought forth the justification of their title to the grant in question. Adds that 30 *bighas* of land recovered from Shaikh Alladeh of village Dilawarpur[4], has been granted to Sayyid Yusuf Qadiri and his sons as *madad-i maash*, making the total grant of 730 *bighas* of land of which 500 *bighas* were *khudkashta*[5] and 230 *bighas* were *raiyat kashta*.[6] Instructs the officials concerned to deliver possession of the land to the grantees and not to demand any tax from them nor to ask for a renewed *sanad* every year.

It bears the seal of attestation of *Qazi* Abdus Sami[7]. (*MF*, I, pp. 5-6).

15 Ramazan 983 A.H./18 December 1575 A.D.

39. *Hukumnama*[1] of *Khan-i Jahan* Husain Quli Khan Bahadur[2] addressed to the *gumashtas* of the *jagirdars* and the administrators of *pargana* Banahra[3], *sarkar* Monghyr[4], *suba* Bihar, informs them that Miran Sayyid Ali Muhammad[5] had been granted 2,500 *bighas* of land in village Sultanpur[6] in the said *pargana* by way of *madad-i maash* in the past. Confirms the said grant in the name of the grantee after verification by *Qazi* Yaqub[7] and the *qanungos*. Orders them to deliver possession of the land in question to the grantee from the beginning of *kharif* of *Sichqan-il* after measuring, demarcating and consolidating it and not to bother him for such dues as *qunlugha, sadri, jaribana, peshkash, muhtarifa*, etc., nor to insist on a renewed *sanad* every year.

It bears the seal of *Khan-i Jahan* Husain Quli Khan Bahadur. (*IHRC*, XXVI, Pt. II, pp. 2-3, JBRS, XLIII, pp. 215-16).

8 Shawwal 983 A.H./10 January 1576 A.D.

40. *Farman* of Akbar addressed to Pachchumal, *chaudhari* of Shorman,[1] communicates exemption of *jizya* and other taxes on temples. (*NRPR*, p. 199).

C.983 A.H./1575-76 A.D.

41. *Farman* of Akbar addressed to the *hakims, karories, amils, mutasaddis*, etc., of Ajmer, intimates that Sayyid Fathullah[2] has been assigned the same duties as he used to perform heretofore and advises them not to harass him on any score and to show every consideration and favour to him. It bears the *sarnama* '*Huwal Ghani*' and a round seal with the legend '*Allahu Akbar*' on the top. On the reverse the *zimn* refers to *Umdatul Mulk* Nizamuddin Muhammad Qasim Khan. (*AS*, pp. 9-10).

29 Safar 984 A.H./28 May 1576 A.D.

42. *Farman* of Akbar addressed to the *karori* s states that *mauza* Nadila[1], *pargana* Haveli[2] *Hazrat*[3] Ajmer has been bestowed upon Shaikh Fathullah and his brothers as usual by way of *madad-i maash* as also to meet the *urs*[4] expenses. Directs them not to bother the grantees for *taufir*. Nor should he ask for fresh *farman* and *parwancha* every year. Instructs the *maqaddams, riaya*[5] and *muzarian* of the said village to render their accounts to the grantees from harvest to harvest every year.

It bears the *sarnama* '*Huwal Ghani*' and a round uzuk seal of the Emperor on top[6]. (*AS*, pp. 5-8: *DLFMN*, p. 69, *NRPR*, I, Pt. II, 51).

Ruz Mihr[1], mah Amardad[2], Vikram Samvat, 1633 Jumada I, 984 A.H./ 28 July, 1576 A.D.

43. Sale-deed[3] executed at Nagmandal under the *amal* of Qilij Muhammad Khan, regarding sale to Adhyaru Meherji Vachcha[4] in perpetuity for the *pratabahrd tankas* which had been given to Patel Khurshed Chadha in cash by Meherji Vachcha by way of loan.

It bears the signatures of Patel Khurshed, the vendor, as well as of several witnesses. (*SPH*, pp. 217-18).

984 A.H./1576-77 A.D.

44. *Farman* of Akbar addressed to the Shar(sic)ullah granting him 100 *bighas* of land in *pargana* Jalalpur[1] Mulkhan, *sarkar* Manikpur[2] *suba* Allahabad, as *madad-i maash*. (*NRPR*, VI, p. 116).

29 Jumada II, 983 A.H./13 September 1577 A.D.

45. *Farman* of Akbar addressed to the officials of the empire orders them not to harass Vithaldas[1] of *qasba* Gokul[2], a well-wisher of the empire, as also his relations and retainers. Instructs them not to demand any cess from them.

It bears the *sarnama* '*Huwal Ghani*' and the seal of Akbar on the top. (*IF*, No.I; *NRPR*, I, Pt. II, 75).

27 Rabi II, 986 A.H./3 July, 1578 A.D.

46. *Farman* of Akbar addressed to the *karoris, jagirdars* and *mutasaddis* of the empire states that in consequence of the interference of the *amils* of the *khalisa* and the *jagirdars,* the *makhadim* are put to trouble and inconvenience. Orders that from the beginning of the *kharif* of the *Pars-il,* the aforesaid officials should assign tracts of land as *madad-i maash* to the holy persons in a few villages in a *pargana* independent of the *khalisa* and *jagir* lands. This should be done in such a way that the land in a village be assigned to *makhadim* in separate plots with well defined boundaries. If the land assigned in a particular village is not sufficient to cover the *madad-i maash* to the *makhadim* in that *pargana,* land in another village should be assigned on the same principle as stated above till the entire land is assigned to the *makhadim* in that *paragana* as *madad-i maash.* Each of the *makhadim* should build a mosque, a house, a *chaupal*[1], a garden, etc. in the village in that *pargana.* If a person resides in one *pargana* and the *madad-i-maash* land has been assigned to him in another *pargana*, he should not be allowed to take possession of the assigned land till he produces a new *sanad.* But if a person leaves a *pargana* voluntarily without any pressure and settles down in *pargana* where *madad-i maash* land has been assigned to him, his claim should be recognised. The officials, therefore are directed to carry out these instructions faithfully and submit an audited *tumar*[2] of each *pargana* to the Emperor as early as possible. It bears the *sarnama* '*Huwal Akbar*'[3]. On the back are two seals, one of which is of Abdun Nabi. (*MF*, I, p. 7; *COR*, II, p. 7).

29 Shaban 986 A.H./31 October, 1578 A.D.

47. Sale-deed executed by Hashmat Raut, *muqaddam* of village Mamrazpur[1], *pargana* Bisara[2], for the sale of 400 *bighas* of land, situated in village Mamrazpur along with *muqaddami* for an earnest amount of Rs. 55 only in favour of Hazrat Murshid Jala *Risaldar*[3]. It bears the seal of the *Qazi.* (*SESP*, p. 104).

Roz Bad 1, mah Tir Vikram Samvat 1635/12 March 1579 A.D.

48. Agreement executed by the Parsis of Navsari and addressed to the *anjuman* thereat, stipulates that when they perform *sarosh*, the priest in turn will give the sacred bath after seeking permission of Meherji Rana. Persons, entitled in turn, shall bring the *dokdas* which may fall to their share for the *sarosh* and sacred bath. No one else shall take them, and if any one does so, he will be a defaulter before the *anjuman*. He who performs the *sarosh* and gives the sacred bath, must first ask Meherji Vachcha, or if he does so without asking him, he shall be a wrong doer before the *anjuman*.

It bears signatures of thirteen executants including Mobed Khurshed, Chandra Kaka, Padam Rustam, Bahram Jang, Dhampal Kamdin, Bahman Hoshang, etc. (*JBRAS*, XXI, 1903, p. 216).

Rabi II, 987 A.H./May-June 1579 A.D.

49. Sale-deed executed by Muhammad Mahmud and Bibi Baghi, daughter of Farid Ataullah, in respect of a piece of land measuring four *biswas* situated in *mauza* Kahjari[1] sold for a sum of 15 *tankas* and specifying the boundaries of the land in the *mauza*.

It bears signatures of the vendors. (*COR*, II, p. 60).

8 Ramazan, 987 A.H./29 October 1579 A.D.

50. *Farman* of Akbar addressed to Pachchumal, *chaudhari* of Shoram, district Muzaffarnagar, empowering people of different castes to manage their affairs in accordance with their own customs. (*NRPR*, p. 200).

Ruz Mihr, mah Dai[1] Vikram Samvat 1636/9 Zilqada, 987 A.H./28 December 1579 A.D.

51. Agreement executed by the priests, Padam Rustam, Kaikobad Mahiyar[2], Chandna Kaka and others addressed to the *Anjuman* of Navsari, stipulates that all the matters relating to the income of the *Agiary*[3], marriage, re-marriage, *sarosh*, *siav*[4], *sanjana*[5], *nav-so*,[6] *bhagar*[7] are entrusted to Ervad Meherji Vachcha. He who contravenes the agreement or does anything else in connection with the *agiary* without the permission of Ervad Meherji Vachcha, shall be debarred for one year from his share. He who fraudulently or dishonestly receives any fees, shall have to give two for every *dokda* which he receives. This agreement is given to Ervad Meherji Vachcha and will remain with him and he who breaks this agreement will be a wrong-doer before the *Anjuman*.

It is signed by twenty persons. (*JBRAS*, XXI, 1900-03, pp. 218-19).

987 A.H./1579-80 A.D.

52. *Farman* of Akbar addressed to the officials, says that 50 *bighas* of land has been granted as *madad-i maash* to Shaikh Sadullah and others in *sarkar*...out of the *khalisa* land. Orders the officials to release the land to the grantees without asking them for any tax whatsoever. Nor should they press for renewal of the *farman* every year.

It bears the *sarnama* '*Huwal Akbar*', *tughra* and small round seal of Akbar on the top. On the reverse is an endorsement with six seals which could not be deciphered. (*HF*, I, p. 9).

20 Muharram 988 A.H./7 March 1580 A.D.

53. *Farman* of Akbar addressed to the officials, grants as *madad-i maash* 1,000 bighas of cultivable lamd situated in *pargana* Jhajjar[1], *sarkar* Delhi, to the *mujawirs* of the shrine of *Makhdum* Majdud Din *Hajji*.[2] The *mujawirs* have inherited it from their predecessors and are authorised to collect the proceeds thereof from year to year. Formerly this grant comprised 700 *bighas* of land only. The officers are directed not to disturb the grantees in any way.

It bears a round seal and *tughra* of Akbar on the top. (*IHRC*, XXXV, Pt. II, pp. 60-61).

8 Shawwal 988 A.H./16 November 1580 A.D.

54. *Parwana* issued by Imadud Din *bin* Jalalud Din Ilahi to *Qazi* Imadud Din, informs him that Shaikh Hashim, son of Shaikh Fathullah, *mujawir* of the *rauza*[1] of Khwaja Muinud Din Chishti complained to the Emperor that Mansur *mujawir* has picked up quarrel on division of *nuzurat*[2]. The Emperor has ordered that the complaint of the said *mujawir* be looked into and the division of the *nuzurat* be effected in such a way that there be no room for any dispute in this regard in future.

The seal of Imadud Din is given on the top in the left hand margin with the remark, "the subject is according to the original." (*AS*, pp. 14-15).

15 Shawwal, 988 A.H./23 November 1580 A.D.

55. *Sanad* of *Sadrus Sudur* addressed to the *shiqdar*, accountants, headman and *qanungos* of *pargana* Sandila, says that Shaikh Gadai[1], son of Shaikh Raju, has a large family without any means of support. Confirms him in the grant of land measuring 25 *bighas* and 14 *biswas* of the cultivated and fallow land situated in *pargana* Sandila as heretofore.

Orders the said officials to measure, demarcate and consolidate the land and deliver possession thereof to the Shaikh from the beginning of the autumn harvest of the crocodile year 988 A.H./1579-80 A.D. and not to harass him on any ground whatsoever.

It bears an illegible seal and details of the grant. (*CPEUM*, p. 142).

1580 A.D.

56. *Sanad* of Akbar addressed to *Qazi* Sayyid Imamud Din purporting to know how the offerings of the *dargah* at Ajmer are distributed among the *khadims*[1]. (*NRPRI*, Pt. II, p. 52).

21 Muharram 989 A.H./25 February 1581. A.D.

57. *Parwancha* addressed to the *amils, mutasaddis, desais*[1] and *qanungos* of *qasba* Navsari informs them that Parsi Mehr Tabib[2], who has no means of subsistence, has been granted one *aul*[3] of cultivated and three *auls* of culturable waste and *wazifa*[4] in *qasba* Navsari. Orders them to measure, demarcate and consolidate the land and hand over possession to the grantee and cause him no harassment on any ground whatsoever so that having tilled it according to his ability, he may spend the proceeds thereof in providing the means of subsistence and devote himself, with a tranquil mind, in praying for the permanence of His Majesty's powerful kingdom. Directs that 109 *khajur*[5] trees pertaining to his *milk* should be left in his possession.

It bears the invocation '*Huwa*' on the top and the seal of Bairam, son of Qilij. On the reverse there are a few official endorsements and two seals, one of them being that of Malik Husain. It passed through the *risala*[6] of Rai Bhawani Das *Mustaufi*[7]. (*SPH*, pp. 172-74).

3 Safar, 989 A.H./9 March 1581 A.D.

58. *Farman* of Akbar addressed to the officials, says that the cows of Vithal Rai, a Brahmin by caste, should be allowed to graze anywhere in the *khalisa* or *jagir* lands and nobody should obstruct or molest them. Vithal Rai may reside in Gokul peacefully and comfortably.

It bears the *sarnama* '*Huwal Akbar*' and the seal of Akbar with the legend *Allahu Akbar*[A] on the top. (*IF*, No.III; *NRPR*, I, Pt. II. p. 76).

3 Rajab, 989 A.H./3 August 1581 A.D.

59. *Hukm* of Malik Muazzam, an official of Akbar, addressed to Pachchumal, *chaudhari* of Shoram, declares that only the eldest man of a caste can be appointed as head of a *panchayat*(sic). (*NRPR*, p. 200).

***Ramazan 989* A.H./*29 September 1581* A.D.**

60. *Hukm* of Hamida Banu Begam[1] addressed to the *karoris* and diligent officers of *pargana* Mahaban[2] *sarkar* of *Darul Khilafa*, Agra, informs them that in pursuance of the Imperial *farman* the cows of Bithleshar, *zunnardar*[3], be allowed to graze anywhere in the *khalisa* or *jagir* land and no one should obstruct or molest them. It is incumbent upon them to obey the orders and act accordingly. It bears the *sarnama* '*Huwal Akbar*' and the seal of Hamida Bano Begam on the top. (*IF*, III).

***14 Shawwal 989* A.H./*11 November 1581* A.D.**

61. *Farman* of Akbar addressed to the *karoris*, *amils* and *jagirdars* of *pargana* Pathan[1], *sarkar* Punjab[2], informs that two hundred *bighas* of *mazru*[3] *and uftada*[4] land measured by *jarib-i san* which is equal to one hundred and seventy *bighas* by *tanab-i bans*[5], situated in *mauza* Boh[6] of the said *pargana* was granted to *Jogi* Udwant Nath[7] by way of *inam* as usual. Out of this fifty *bighas* of land are submerged under water and as such fifty bighas of waste land should be given to the grantee in lieu thereof. The said officials, threfore, are ordered to measure, demarcate and consolidate the land and hand it over to the grantee who should not be harassed for payment of any tax. The grant is free from all taxes and no new *farman* or *parwancha* should be demanded from him every year. It bears the seal of Akbar on top. (*MJJ*, p. 51-52).

***Zilqada 989* A.H.[1] /*November-December 1581* A.D.**

62. *Parwana* of Muhammad Qilij Khan addressed to the *shiqdar* and *amils* of *qasba* Navasari, informs them that Mehr Tabib Parsi *Mutiul Islam*[2] had been granted one piece of *uftada* land in the vicinity of *qasba* Navsari as *madad-i maash* in the days gone by and the same is renewed and confirmed in his name as usual. Orders the said officials to measure, demarcate and consolidate the said fallow land and deliver possession thereof to the grantee who may till the land without any obstruction. It bears the *sarnama* "*Huwa*" on the top and a seal of Muhammad Qilij Khan bearing the year 976 A.H. On the reverse there are two illegible seals and the following endorsements: 1. *sabt shud* or It has been recorded ; 2. *Ittalatu alaih* or I have been informed; 3. *Waqaftu alaih* or I have been intimated.[3] (*SPH*, pp. 169-70).

1581 A.D.[1]

63. *Farman* of Akbar addressed to the *muqaddams*, *mutasaddis*, *karoris*, ryots and *muzaris* of *sarkar* Tirhut[2], says that Ajit[3], brother of Gopal Das[4],

Mutiul Islam, *Qanungo* and *Chaudhari* of the said *sarkar* waited on the Emperor and stated that offices of *qanungo* and *chaudhari* of the said *sarkar* were assigned to Gopal Das, who rendered meritorious services by ameliorating the condition of the ryots. Having been convinced of the fact, it is hereby ordered that the offices of *Qanungo* and *Chaudhari* of the said *sarkar* be restored to Gopal Das as usual. He is authorised to realise from the ryots the *rusum-i chaudharai* at 1 *tanka* per *bigha* and *rusum-i qanungoi* at ¼ *tanka* per *bigha*, totalling 1¼ *tankas* per *bigha* and support himself by this income. The addressees are ordered to regard Gopal Das as the official *chaudhari* and *qanungo* and obey him faithfully, paying the said *rusum* regularly. It bears a seal on the top. On the back is an endorsement. The names of Mubarizud Din *Khan-i Jahan*, *Qazi* Nizamud Din and Bhagwan Das are given. (*IHRC*, XXXVI, Pt. II, pp. 90-91).

21 Shaban, 990 A.H./10 September 1582 A.D.

64. Sale-deed executed by Dhir, son of Khattu, *Muqaddam* of village Jakhneli[1], in favour of Miran Sayyid, son of Rasul, for selling, two *biswas* of *muqaddami* with cultivated land, in village Jakhneli, *tappa* Saunek[2], *pargana* Shamsabad, for 400 *tanka-i Muradi*. The land which the vender inherited from his ancestors also includes an orchard, a pond, trees, a well, etc. (*IESHR*, IV, 1967, p. 229).

Pre-1582 A.D.[1]

65. Attestation certifies that nearly 178 *bighas* of land are in possession of Malik Arjun Jangam of Benaras. In all the *sanads* the name, Malik Arjun, is written. Now when Rai Baruna *karori* was investigating the holdings of *aima*, he was very much surprised to find that in all the documents of the earlier rulers and that of the officers of the Emperor, the name Malik Arjun Jangam was mentioned. The body of Jangams explained that in their sect the elder, who became the successor of Arjun, being the *mutawalli*, was called Malik Arjun who collected all the offerings of the Badshah (saint) and other gains from different quarters and distributed them among the *faqirs*[2] of the sect. As the *Qazi*, the *Mufti*[3], the citizens and the followers have testified that they (officers) had left the above mentioned land in possession of Malik Arjun Jangam according to the instructions of the *farman* these few lines have been written as testimony so that it may be relied upon. It bears an illegible seal and the *surnama* '*Huwal Akbar*'. (*IHRC*, XLIV, pp. 207-08).

25 Zilhijja 991 A.H./30 December 1583 A.D.

66. *Parwancha* of Qilij Khan, *Mir-i Mal*[1], addressed to Fath Khan, says that a sum of 13 *dokdas* was conferred upon Mehr *Tabib*, and his offspring long ago by way of *wazifa*. Orders the addressee to continue the same to the grantees as usual, paying every day three *dokdas* from the *mandvi*[2] of Gandevi[3] and ten *dokdas* from the *mandvi* of Navsari. The addressee should obtain *qabzul wulsul*[4] and he will be given credit for the sum in the accounts on presenting the receipt. It bears the seal of Qilij Khan, *Mir-i Mal*. On the reverse are some official endorsements and some seals of the officials : Tajud Din, son of Khwaja Hasan, Qutb Khan, Muhammad Lutfullah, etc. (*SPH.* pp. 180-82).

5 Sudi Phagun 1641 Samvat/20 February 1584 A.D.

67. *Sanad* of Raja Mukand Ram Sen for the grant of a piece of forest tract in village Ekda[1], *tappa* Bahgawan[2], *pargana* Powakhali[3] in the name of Sant Das Gosain as *bishunprit*[4]. It bears the seal of Raja Mukand Ram Sen. (*SFSP*, 81, *IHRC*, XXXIV, Pt. I. Exhibits. p. 99).

7 Jumada II, 992 A.H./6 June 1584 A.D.

68. *Farman* of Akbar addressed to the Governors, *Jagirdars* and officials of Malwa, Akbarabad[1], Lahore[2], Multan[3], Ahmadabad, etc., says that the Emperor having heard of the holiness and penance of Hirvijaya Suri[4], the Acharya[5] of the Jain[6] Svetambar[7] sect, summoned him to his court to expound the tenets of Jainism. The Emperor honoured him with the title of *Jagat Guru*[8]. At the time of his departure the *Acharya* made a request that the hills of Siddhachal[9], Girhar[10], Taranga[11], Keshrinath[12], and Abu[13], all situated in Gujarat, and the five hills of Rajgir[14], and the hill of Samat Shikhar *alias* Parsnanath[15], in Bengal, along with all the *kothis*[16], and temples below these hills, as also all other places of pilgrimage of the Jain Svetambar community throughout the empire, should be handed over to the Jains so that no one might kill any animal on those hills or near those temples during the 12 days of the *Paryushana*[17] festival which takes place in the month of *Bhadrapad*[18]. The Emporor has given his consent to this request and has bestowed all these hills and temples on Hirvijaya Suri. It is a beautiful document with its borders decorated and has the *tughra* of Akbar on the top. (*JUB*, IX pp. 9-10).

Rajab 992 A.H./June-July 1584 A.D.

69. Agreement regarding division of *nuzurat* among the *khadims* of the shrine of Khwaja Muinud Din Chishti. It is agreed that the *nuzurat* should be divided among the *mujawirs* according to past practice as follows:

Alam, Abdul Karim, Abda and their brothers and Shaikh Bakhsh	1½ share
Miyan Shaikh Hashim, son of late Shaikh Farthullah along with *gul*[1] and *post*[2]	½ share
Shaikh Ibrahim, Shaikh Bhowan, Jamal Shah, Shaikh Ibrahim and their brothers	1 share
Shaikh Mansur and his party	1 share
Shaikh Qutban and others	1 share
Shaikh Bhikan etc. and their brothers	1 share

The names of Shaikh Kamal, Shaikh Taj Muhammad, Shaikh Mansur, Shaikh Farid, Shaikh Bakhsh, etc. appear at the end of the *sanad.*

In the margin of the *sanad*, it is stated that Shaikh Kamal bin Daniyal[3], Taj Muhammad bin Farid, Shaikh Mansur bin Shaikh Darya, Shaikh Ismail bin Sultan, Shaikh Bakhsh bin Ibrahim, Shaikh Avjha bin Shaikh Sulaiman Mattha, Shaikh Farid bin Qutban, Shaikh Ibrahim bin Chandan, the *mujawirs* of the holy shrine gathered together and attended the *Adalat-i-Aliya*[4] at Fathpur[5] and agreed to the terms laid down in the body of the *sanad.* There is a seal of Tajud Din al-Husaini on the right-hand margin. This endorsement is dated *Shaban* 992 A.H./July-August 1584 A.D. (*AS*, pp. 15-19).

2 Shaban 992 A.H./30 July 1584 A.D.

70. *Farman* of Akbar addressed to the officials informs them that grant of land measuring 30 *bighas* situated in *pargana* Siddhaur[1], *sarkar* Lucknow has been conferred upon Sayyid Alam and Sayyid Hayy as *madad-i maash.* The grant has been made out of the *khalisa* land. Orders the officials to measure the land with *tanab-i bans*, consolidate it and deliver possession thereof to the grantees and not to realise any tax from them. It bears the invocation '*Allahu Akbar*'[2] a *tughra* and a round seal of Akbar on the top. On the back of the document is a *yad-dasht*[3], prepared in the *risala* of *Hakim* Abul Fath[4], Chauki[5] of Shaikh Abul Fazl[6] and the *waqia nawisi*[7] of Lal Gopal. There are several seals but none is fully decipherable. (*MF*, I, 10, *IHRC.* XXXIV Pt. I, Exhibits 113).

15 Rajab 993 A.H./3 July, 1585 A.D.

71. *Farman* of Akbar addressed to *chaudharis, muqaddams, qanungos*, royots and *muzaris* of *pargana* Bhatner[1], *sarkar* Hissar Firoza[2], informs them that Rai Rai Singh[3] has been granted the said *pargana* from the beginning of *Kharif* of Takhaqui-il[4], 993 A.H. in exchange for Lakhipur[5], *pargana* Dibalpur[6], in the *sarkar* of the Punjab on the dismissal of Mir Ziaud Din and others. Orders them to furnish to him complete account of land revenue and other civil dues from crop to crop and from year to year honestly and regularly and present themselves for expedition when called upon to do so. It bears the *sarnama* '*Allahu Akbar*' and a seal of Akbar on the top. (*DLFMN*, p. 1).

22 Safar, 994 A.H./2 Febuary 1586 A.D.

72. Sale-deed executed by Narain, Asa, Ahan, Lakhan, Lakhmi, Zautan and others in respect of village Jarha[1] including a well and gardens situated in *pargana* Sandila sold to Miyan Amman, son of Roshan, for a sum of Rs. 160. It is a true copy certified by Muhammad Saidud Din Ahmad, son of *Qazi* Muhammad Nasir and bears the seal of *Qazi* Abdur Razzaq and signatures of twenty-one witnesses. (*COR*, II, pp. 60-61).

22 Ramazan 994 A.H./27 August 1586 A.D.

73. *Sanad* of Pahar Singh, son of Man Dhata Rai for the grant of 10 *kuroh*[1] of rent-free land situated in village Bhusahi Buzurg[2], *pargana* Samaisa[3], *sarkar* Hajipur[4], *suba* Bihar, in the name of Hazrat Shah Kabir Muhammad for his livelihood and *nazr* to Hazrat Pir Dastigir Shaikh Abdul Qadir Jilani[5]. (*SFSP*, p. 126).

3. Rabi II 995 A.H./ 3 March 1587 A.D.

74. *Hasbul hukm* addressed to the *mutasaddis* of *mandvi* of *qasba* Navsari, says that the *wazifa* of Mehr Tabib Parsi was previously fixed at 13 *dokdas* by virtue of the former *parwanchas*. Out of the said sum, five *Muradi dokdas* are assigned to him. Now on the basis of this *hasbul hukm*, the said officials are to pay the said sum to him every day out of the *wujuh* of the *mandvi* so that he may devote himself in praying for the permanence of His Majesty's dominion. It bears the invocation, "*Huwa*" on the top. On the reverse there is a seal of Abul Qasim[1], son of Ahmad, and the following endorsements: (a) *Ittalatu alaih* dated 27 Zilqada, 994 A.H./ 16 November 1585. (b) *Ruju shud* dated 28 Rabi I, 995 A.H. (26 February 1587). (c) *Muttalatu* dated *3 Rabi* II, 995 A.H. (3 March, 1587) and (d) *Ba daftar rasid* dated 28 Rabi II, 995 A.H./28 March 1587 A.D. (*SPH*, pp. 183-84).

1 Jumada II 995 A.H./29 April, 1587 A.D.

75. *Sanad* of Imadul Mulk to Farid Nagori and Manohar *Qanungo*, informs them that a piece of land measuring 240 *bighas* and 4 *biswas*, situated in *mauza* Nadila, *pargana* Haveli of *Hazrat* Ajmer, has been allotted to Shaikh Ismail, *mujawir*, as his share. Orders them to demarcate and consolidate the land in the presence of Shaikh Taj Muhammad and his brother, Abda and hand it over to the assignee so that he may cultivate the land and enjoy the produce thereof. The invocation "*Allahu Akbar*" and a round seal of Imadul Mulk are given on the top. Another round seal of Nad-i Ali is given at the bottom on the right hand margin. (*AS*, pp. 19-20; *NRPR*, I, Pt. II, p. 52).

1587 A.D.[1]

76. *Farman* of Akbar addressed to Rai Rai Singh says that the Emperor left Lahore[2] about a year earlier. It was settled that the addressee would either proceed to the Deccan or join the royal camp, but nothing has been done so far and for the last three years or so the addressee has been behaving in the same manner. If he is unable to do any work, he should state it clearly so that the Emperor may exempt him from service or give that province in *jagir* to someone else. Adds that he should take necessary steps to escort Sobha Mal and Jamna Mal to the royal court.(*DLFHN*, p. 16).

Ruz Azar[1]***, mah Azar***[2]***, Ilahi 33/11 Muharram, 997 A.H./20 November 1588 A.D.***

77. *Hukm of Khan-i Khanan* Mirza Khan Bahadur[3] *Sipah Salar*[4] to the officials of *pargana* Aao[5], informs them that there is a *chiragah*[6] in the villages of Savi[7], etc, where the cows of Goverdhan[8] graze. Orders them not to cause any obstruction to the grazing of the cows there on account of *quruq*[9] and *gaushumari*[10] as the villages in question have been given in grant for this very purpose. They are further advised not to demand fresh *parwancha* from the owners every year on any pretext. They should act according to the sublime order and take action accordingly. It bears the invocation '*Allahu Akbar*' on the top. On the reverse are given seals of *Khan-i Khanan* and others with endorsements. (*IF*, III A).

1588 A.D.[1]

78. *Farman* of Akbar addressed to the Raja[2] of Rajauri[3] conferring on him the title of *Mirza*. (*NRPR*, 37).

8 Rabi I, 997 A.H./15 January 1589 A.D.

79. *Bainama* executed by Imam Ali, *Musammat* Begi Sultan and *Musammat* Shamso respectively son, daughter and widow of Mir Darwesh

Muhammad, the *tarbuzfarosh*[1] in respect of a *haveli* sold to Miyan Shaikh Taj Muhammed son of Shaikh Farid, *mujawir* for a sum of Rs. 30 in the presence of Miyan Shaikh Hasan, son of Ali and 16 others. The *haveli* consists of 1 *riwaq*[2] with 2 terraced *kothris*[3], four houses of which two are covered by *kolu*. It is bounded on the east by the house of Miran, son of Shaikh Muhammad, on the west partly by the *haveli* of Shaikh Daulat Kashmiri and partly by the hill, on the north by the house of Allah Bakhsh, son of Manjhu *safed-baf*[4], and on the south by the wall of the fort. It bears the round seal of Abdur Rahim, *Mufti*. (*AS*, pp. 20-22; *NRPR*, I Pt. II. p. 52).

27 Shawwal, 997 A.H./29 August 1589 A.D.

80. *Hukm-i*[1] *Rahdari*[2] of *Khan-i Khanan* Abdur Rahim Khan to customs officers, ferry-men and husbandmen on the road from Jalalabad[3] to Kabul[4], prohibits them from demanding any toll from one Ali Koka and his companions who are reported to have been deputed to Kabul on some state business. It bears the invocation, '*Allahu Akbar*' and below it the *unwan* '*Hukm-i Khan-i Khanan* Mirza Khan Bahadur *Sipahsalar*' and the seal of *Khan-i Khanan* on the top. (*AIOC*, X, p. 467).

Mah Asar Samvat 1646/November-December 1589 A.D.

81. Letter from Asdin to the *Bahadins*[1] of Diu[2], says that he and three others had sat together in the *Agiary*, where it was declared that all the *Bahadins* of Diu wanted a *hirbed*[3] with *barashnum*[4], to go there and perform the *afringan*[5] for the peace of the dead in addition to the *baj* and *gehsarna*[7] rites. On hearing this Ervad Meherji Rana agreed and hastened to send such a priest to perform the religious rites. Adds that he is a wise and worthy man, capable of doing all what is required for their religion. His services may be continued. (*JBBRAS*, XXI, pp. 230-31).

10 Rabi II, 998 A.H./6 February 1590 A.D.

82. *Sanad* issued in favour of Abdud Daim and Abdul Khaliq, sons of Shaikh Ismail *mujawirs*, who are engaged in the study of *ulum-i din*[1] authorising them to draw *wazifa* at the rate of two *tanka-i Muradi* per diem per head out of the *wazifa* fixed for Abdus Sattar, *Hafiz*[2], who has left for his heavenly abode. It bears the invocation '*Allahu Akbar*' on top and two round seals of Imadul Mulk and Nad-i Ali on the right-hand margin. (*AS*, pp. 22-23: *NRPR*, I. Pt II. p. 52).

***1591** A.D.*[1]

83. *Farman* of Akbar addressed to the officials of the empire grants 100 *bighas* of land as *madad-i maash* to *Dastur* Kaikobad, son of *Dastur* Mahyar, who is already in possession of 200 *bighas* of land. (*JUB*, IX. p. 21).

***7 Ardibihisht Ilahi 37/17 April 1592** A.D.*

84. *Farman*[1] of Akbar addressed to Rai Rai Singh informs him that custom duty on cattle, grain, flour-mills, etc., has been abolished and the royal orders have already been issued in this regard. However horses, elephants, camels, sheep, goats, armour and silk-cloth are excluded from the aforesaid exemption. Adds that none should interfere with the affairs of merchants, artisans and others under the pretext of realising toll or duty. Orders to raise a small sum of money for watch and ward have also been revoked. The Emperor however feels pained to know that some imprudent persons are exacting custom duty from people on some highways in bazars and markets. Orders the addressee to keep strict watch over individuals in the territory under his jurisdiction and appoint spies to bring to book the defaulters who dare realise custom duty contrary to the orders. Further directs the addressee that the tax collectors should execute bonds in this regard to be sent to the court. It bears the invocation '*Allahu Akbar*' and the seal of Akbar at the top. (*DLFMN*, pp. 2-3).

***12 Ramazan 1000** A.H.**/12 June 1592** A.D.*

85. *Bainama* executed by the five sons of Muhammad....Habibullah, Jamal, Fazlullah, Husain, Jalal and their widowed mother in respect of two *koluposh* houses located in Jhalra[1] sold to Shaikh Chandan, son of Shaikh Chand *mujawir* for a consideration of Rs.11 in the presence of Shaikh Taj Muhammad, Sayyid Wajihud Din, Abdul Qadir, Shaikh Ismail, son of Sultan, Miyan Abdul Karim, son of Munis, and others. The boundaries of the houses are as folows:

East	...	Thoroughfare
West	...	House of Faridu *faqir*
North	...	Mosque of Maqsud Ali and *nala*[2]
South	...	Road leading to *takia*[3] of Najmud Din (AS, p. 23).

***2. Shawwal 1000** A.H.**/2 July 1592** A.D.*

86. *Farman* of Akbar recalls the earlier *farman* dismissing *Qazi* Kamal from the *Qazat* of *pargana* Bilgram and in lieu thereof grants 200 *bighas* of cultivated land as *madad-i maash.* There upon Kamal appeared before the Emperor and it was ordered that if *Umdatul Mulk* Shaham Khan Jalayar, *Jagirdar* of *pargana* Bilgram, considered him honest and sincere, he should be reinstated with a grant of 150 *bighas* of land as *madad-i maash.* Shaham Khan having so certified, Kamal is now reinstated as *Qazi* of that place and he and his sons are allowed to hold 150 *bighas* of land, to be measured by *gaz-i Ilahi*[1], as *madad-i maash* with effect from *kharif Lui-il.*[2] The present and future *jagirdars, karoris, aimma*[3], etc., are ordered to recognise him as *Qazi*, measure the said area of land and deliver it to him. They are not to demand from him land revenue or other cesses. (*IESHR*, IV, 1967, pp. 229-30).

***c 1000* A.H./*1591-92* A.D.[1]**

87. *Hibanama*[2] executed in respect of a *haveli* made of stone and consisting of *chahardiwari*[3], a house and a *suffa*[4], etc., situated in the city of Ajmer, which is gifted to Taj Muhammad, *mujawir* of the *astana*[5] of *Hazrat Qutbul Aqtab.* He has been given possession of the said *haveli* and he may use it as he thinks best. No one is permitted to harass him or his dependants in any way or demand rent therefor. In the margin it is stated that whenever the Emperor visits Ajmer and stays there, the executor of the *hiba nama* will have every right to stay in the said *haveli* as long as the Emperor stays in Ajmer. It bears the round seal of Sayyid Abdur Rahim. (*AS*, pp. 25-26).

***Rabi II, 1001* A.H./*December 1592-January 1593* A.D.**

88. *Parwana* addressed to the *mutasaddis, chaudharis, qanungos,* and *muqaddams* of *pargana* Aimi[1], *sarkar* Lucknow informs them that out of the *khalisa* land situated in Jasmalpur[2], three hundred thirty nine *bighas* were granted to *Shaikhul Islam* Abu Bakr as *madad-i maash.* A dispute has now cropped up about the land in question. Intimates that Khwaja Muhammad Mirak has been directed to measure and demarcate the land in question in close co-operation with the addressees and hand over possession thereof to the grantee. It bears an illegible seal. (*COR*, II, pp. 32-33).

***11 Khurdad, Ilahi 38/22 May 1593* A.D.**

89. *Farman* of Akbar addressed to the *karoris* and *jagirdars* of *parganas* Mathura[1], Sahar[2], Mangotah[3] and Od, notifies that in future *zibah*[4] and *shikar*[5] of peacocks[6] in the neighbourhood of these *parganas* will be strictly forbidden[7] and that there should be no obstruction to the grazing of cows. The officials are, therefore, ordered to enforce these orders within their jurisdiction very strictly and should not allow anyone to defy them. It bears the invocation '*Allahu Akbar*' and the seal of Akbar on top. It was drafted at the capital Lahore. On the back is the endorsement to the effect that it passed through the *risala* of Abul Fazl[8] and the *waqia-nawisi* of Khwaja Hatim. It bears the lineal[9] seal of the Akbar. (*IF*, IVA; *NRPR*, I. Pt. II, p. 76).

1003 A.H./1594-95 A.D.

90. *Parwana* of Rahmat Khan, an official of Akbar, addressed to Shaikh Alaud Din and other *mutasaddis* of *pargana* Hisampur[1], orders them to deliver possession of 170 *bighas* of land situated in village Kasraula[2] to Mir Sayyid Ghiyasud Din. On the reverse is an endorsement to the effect that it was sent to the *risala* of Shaikh Faizi. (*COR*, I, p. 78).

30 Tir Ilahi 40/12 July 1595 A.D.

91. *Farman* of Akbar addressed to Rai Rai Singh states that the Emperor is shocked at the inaction[1] of the Rai who is still staying in his territory while the Emperor's son has already proceeded to a foreign land and has besieged it for a long time. Due to his inaction the royal army has been reduced to a critical situation. Orders him to proceed immediately on pilgrimage to any *tirath*[2] of his own choice and hand over the charge of the town and the territories to the men of Dalpat[3].

P.S. In the margin advises the Rai either to proceed to the court along with the *ahadis*[4] or hand over all his elephants to Shah Muhammad, the *ahadi*, and himself proceed to any *tirath*. It bears the invocation '*Allahu Akbar*' and a seal of Akbar on the top. (*DIFMN*, p. 5).

19 Rabi I, 1004 A.H./13 November 1595 A.D.

92. *Sanad* affirming that Muhammad Halim on his own behalf and on behalf of his brothers, Khwaja Abdullah and Khwaja Shah, sons of Khwaja Hasan, is assigned 20 *bighas* of land, measured with bamboo *jarib* in proprietory right as *madad-i maash* and that Shaikh Ruknud Din, Shaikh Ahmad, Abdul Qadir and others have been assigned 9 *bighas* of land as *muafi*. The grantees are entitled to appropriate the produce of 29 *bighas* for their expenses. The document bears signatures of five witnesses. (*COR*, II, p. 31).

Ruz Bahman, ... /mah Dai 1595 A.D.[1]

93. *Maktub* of Nausherwan[2] addressed from Lahore to his mother, Bai Dhanai in Navsari, states that the writer is glad to know from the letter of Adhyaru Rustam that the Bai has been married. Says that Kikaji[3] will be sent to her later on. Kaka Meherji[4] has done a great deal of service to him. Night and day, hungry and thirsty, he was in attendance upon the Padshah (Akbar) and obtained Kikaji's release from prison. Gives a shop, a meadow and a garden to him as a gift. Requests his mother to deliver possession of the shop, garden, etc., to Bai Kiki wife of Kaikobad and dismiss the *bania*[5] who has opened a shop there, telling him that the shop has been given as a gift to her and that he must pay the rent to Adhyaru Kaka's family and obtain a receipt therefor from Mahrnosh Kaka. Asks her not to worry about expenses and go on inquiring about Bai Pomi, Bai Makai and Hansisi. Enquires how much the marriage ceremony has cost. Assures her that Kikaji will pay all the debts. Offers his *namaskar*[6] to his aunts, Jasi, Shahijan, Hira and Mahlan. (*SPH*, pp. 221-22).

10 Isfandarmaz[1]***, Ilahi 40/19 February 1596 A.D.***

94. *Farman* of Akbar addressed to the *hukkam, ummal, karoris, jagirdars* of *qasba* Navsari, *sarkar* Surat[2], informs them that grant of land measuring three hundred *bighas* by *gaz-i Ilahi* situated in *qasba* Navsari has been conferred upon Kaikobad Parsi, son of Mahyar Dastur Meherji Rana along with the *tar*[3] and *khurma*[4] trees theron with effect from the *kharif* harvest of *Qui-il*[5] as *madad-i maash.* Instructs the said officials to measure and consolidate the land and hand over possession thereof to the grantee. Directs them not to disturb or interfere with the said grant for government dues like *qunlugha, peshkash, jaribana, zabitana, muhrana, daroghana, muhassalana*[6], *deh-nimi*[7] *sad-doi qanungoi,* etc., and not to ask for a renewed *farman* and *parwancha* every year. It bears the invocation '*Allahu Akbar*' and a seal of Akbar on the top. On the reverse is given a *taliqa*[8] dated 13 *Aban*[9], *Ilahi* 40 giving details of the grant. It has been endorsed in the *risala* and *chauki* of Allami Shaikh Abul Fazl and *waqia nawisi* of Maazud Din Husain. There are seals of *Khan-i Khanan*[10], Mirza Koka, Nazr Ali bin Husain and Kamalud Din Husain, etc. (*JBRAS*, XXI, p. 163-74).

22 Isfandarmaz, Ilahi 40/3 March 1596 A.D.

95. *Farman* of Akbar to Rai Rai Singh states that the Emperor is much surprised to know that the addressee is still in the territory of Jaitore[1]. Asks him whether this is due to illness or excessive drinking or on account of the insinuations of Bhatiani[2] or Tujia[3], the slave. If he is tired of work, he should state it clearly so that he might be replaced by his son. Deputes Mohan Das to report the real position to the Emperor. If the Rai is keen to proceed on the Deccan expedition, he is welcome to do so, otherwise, he should proceed to Malwa and wait at Ujjain till the arrival of the Mughal army there and should do what he has been ordered to do. It bears the invocation '*Allahu Akbar*' and the seal of Akbar on top. (*DLFMN*, p. 4).

5 Arbihisht Ilahi 41/14 April 1596 A.D.

96. *Farman* of Akbar addressed to the *chaudharis*, headmen, *qanungos*, ryots and cultivators of *pargana* Niryad[1] informs them that *pargana* Niryad is bestowed upon Rai Rai Singh by way of *jagir* in exchange for the *parganas* of Tahara[2], Qasur[3] and Atgarh[4] from the beginning of the *kharif* of *Bichi-il*[5]. Directs the addressees to look upon him as their *jagirdar* and pay him all dues punctually and regularly. It bears the seal of Akbar on top. (*DLFMN*, p. 6).

1 Shawwal 1011 Fasli/1004 A.H./19 May, 1596 A.D.

97. *Hukmnama* of an official of Akbar addressed to the subordinate officials informs them that 10 *bighas* of rent-free land situated in village Bhusahi Buzurg, *pargana* Saraisa, *sarkar* Hajipur, *suba* Bihar have been granted to Shah Muhammad Kabir and his sons as *madad-i maash* as also to meet the expenses of the mosque, *khanqah* and the needy. Orders them to take necessary action accordingly. It bears an illegible seal. (*SFSP*, p. 126).

22 Aban, Ilahi[1] 41/4 November 1596 A.D.

98. *Farman* of Akbar addressed to the *hakims*, *amils*, *karoris and jagirdars* of *pargana* Pathan says that Udwant Nath had been granted two hundred *bighas* of land in *pargana* Pathan as *inam*. Shaikh Abul Fazl proposed seventy-eight *bighas* of land, whereas Miran Sadr-i Jahan[2] recommended one hundred *bighas* of land by *gaz-i Ilahi*. Acting upon the said recommendation, the Emperor has ordered that Udwant Nath and others may be granted one hundred *bighas* of land in the old *mahal* as *madad-i maash*., The officials should measure and consolidate the land and deliver possession thereof to the grantee who should not be asked to pay any tax like *qunlugha, peshkash, jaribana, deh-nimi, sad-doi, qanungoi*, etc. Nor should they be compelled to produce a renewed *farman* and *parwancha* every year. It bears the invocation '*Allahu*

Akbar' the *tughra* and the lineal seal of Akbar on the top. On the reverse is *a zimn* dated 22 *Aban* 41 *Ilahi*, touching on the details of the grant. It passed through the *risala* of *Sadr-i Jahan*, the *chauki* of Raidas Kachchwaha[3] and *waqia nawisi* of Fazil *Munshi*. Details of the division of the land among the grantees are also given. There are several seals of the officials including that of Mirza Aziz Koka. (*MJJ*, pp. 59, 61, 63).

26 Zilqada 1004 A.H./12 July 1596 A.D.

99. Document of Shaikh Ahmad, *Sadr-i Jahan*[1], Jamali, Abdul Qadir and others to Miyan Hamid, assign voluntarily and without any pressure 9 *bighas* of land out of the 29 *bighas* owned by them as *madad-i maash* to the grantee (Miyan Hamid) for his subsistence. The grantee will recognise their proprietary right in the land and they will stick to the agreement as long as they own the said land. The document bears the invocation '*Allahu Akbar*' and the signatures of ten witnesses. (*COR*, II. pp. 31-32).

1005 A.H.[1]/1596 A.D.

100. *Mahzarnama*[2] issued by Sadiq Muhammad Khan[3] to the people of Navsari says that on 26th *Rabi* II, 1005 (1596 A.D.) a person, named Kaikobad, son of Mihryar, a Parsi, brought a *farman* of Akbar in the court of *Shar-i Sharif*[4] of the Navsari and Khawaja Mirza Jan, *Shiqdar* of the said *qasba*, with the request that the grant of 200 *bighas* of land with *tar* and *khurma* trees growing thereon, situated in the vicinity of Navsari, previously held by Mihryar as *madad-i maash*, should be continued to him. Accordingly in order to ascertain the facts and figures of the grant in question the Khwaja called a meeting of *karkuns* the *gumashta-i shumari*[5], *riaya* and *muqaddams* of the said *qasba*. They ascertained all the facts and measured the land. They found that in the previous year the grantee did not derive any income therefrom as the land was submerged in water. Those who knew the correct position of the matter put down their signatures on it so that it might be a trustworthy document. Accordingly, several persons like Abdul Karim, Nur Muhammad, Muhammad Abdur Razzaq, Govind Narain, Nana Jadav, Kuka Nanak, etc., in all 17 persons put their signatures on the *mahzar*. It bears the invocation '*Allahu Akbar*' on the top. (*JBBRAS*, XXI, pp. 207-12).

25 Farward in Ilahi 42/4 April 1597 A.D.

101. *Farman* of Akbar addressed to the Officer-in-Charge of the city of Kambayat[1] states that the *padris*[2] of the holy church of Jesus[3] desire to build a house of prayer in Kambayat. Orders him not to stand in their way so that they may build a church and engage themselves in their own worship[4]. It bears the seal and *tughra* of Akbar on top. (*JPHS*, V. No.1. pp. 10-11; *JUB*, IX, p. 22).

29 Azar, Ilahi 42/10 December 1597 A.D.

102. *Nishan*[1] of Prince Salim[2] addressed to Rai Rai Singh asks him to proceed to the aid of *Khan-i Khanan*[3] so that he may recommend the addressee to the Emperor for the grant of 'Military Standard'. Further asks him to send as many *cheetas*[4] as possible to him (Prince). For the present he should despatch the *cheeta*, Nilkanth by name, which he has in his possession, to the court with Bita, the *ahadi*, who is carrying a gift of *farghul*[5] for the addressee. It bears the invocation '*Allahu Akbar*' and the seal of Prince Salim on the top. (*DLFMN*, p. 8).

9 Dai, 42/20 December 1597 A.D.

103. *Farman* of Akbar addressed to the *jagirdars* of Gujarat etc., informs them that the Emperor has forgiven the wrongs of Rai Rai Singh and has restored to him the *jagir* of Junagadh[1] and other districts. Orders the *jagirdars* etc., to hand over the aforesaid districts to the deputies of the Rai. The tenants are advised to pay the revenues to the Rai regularly. There is a seal on the top. (*DLFMN*, p. 7).

15 Shahriwar, Ilahi 43/28 August 1598 A.D.

104. *Farman* of Akbar addressed to Rai Rai Singh informs him that his representation has been given due consideration and weight and the *farmans* regarding Rawal Ham and Rawal Bara have been sent to him accordingly. If he is satisfied with their conduct and behaviour and if they are prepared to make amends for what they have done in the past, he should give them *farmans* and assure them of the royal kindness and favours. It bears the invocation '*Allahu Akbar*' and the seal of Akbar on the top. (*DLFMN*, p. 9).

Ruz Khurdad, mah Dai Vikram Samvat 1655/22 December 1598 A.D.

105. Agreement[1] between the *Anjuman* of Navsari and the priests who assembled there and agreed to the following. Whosoever allots the shares of the *bhagar* shall, after giving his due to the holder of the *baj*, take as his fixed shares, only 5 rotis[2], 1 *polis*[3], 5 *daruns*[4] and 9 *karole*[5]. Whosoever takes more shall be punished as an offender by the *Anjuman*. No one shall take away anything from the *frasast*[6] after the *baj* is muttered. When the *daruns* for the *chashni* arrive and the general *chashni* ceremony has been gone through, he (performer of the ceremony) should take, besides his customary share of the *chashni*, only 15 *daruns*[7] for his labour, but he shall take nothing more. Secondly, if there is any business relating to the *Agiary*, it must be done after seeking permission from Ervad[8] Hirji, son of Dastur Shri Meherji Vachcha. If Ervad Hirji is not present, the other brother should be asked for orders before it is done. It bears signatures of the witnesses, one of the important witnesses being Hoshang Asha[10]. (*SPH*, pp. 230-32).

19 Shawwal Ilahi 44/1007 A.H./5 May 1599 A.D.

106. *Parwana* of an official of Akbar to the subordinate officials informs them about the grant of 10 *bighas* of rent-free land situated in village Bhusahi Buzurg, *pargana* Saraisa, *sarkar* Hajipur, *suba* Bihar in the name of Muhammad Kabir to meet the expenses of the *khanqah* and the *mosque*. Orders them to take necessary action. It bears an illegible seal. (*SFSP*, p. 127).

11 Shahriwar Ilahi 44/ 12 Safar 1008 A.H./24 August 1599 A.D.

107. *Farman* of Akbar to Rai Rai Singh says that though he (addressee) had agreed to serve under his son, Prince Murad[1] and to send his son and grandson to the court he should not break the journey at any place. Warns him not to be negligent in any way. It bears the seal on the top. (*DLFMN*. p. 10).

18 Tir Ilahi 45/ 17 Zilhijja 1008 A.H./29 June 1600 A.D.

108. *Farman* of Akbar to Rai Rai Singh intimates that the Emperor has arrived at Burhanpur[1] and that the fort of Asirgarh[2] has been besieged by the imperial troops. Adds that Prince Salim is engaged in repelling the *Rana*[3] and Prince Daniyal[4] is laying siege to Ahmadnagar[5] fort. Is surprised to note that he (addressee) had left Ahmedabad about a year back and has not yet crossed Mahumdabad[6]. If he proceeds thus, why should he not return to his own *jagir?* It bears the seal of Akbar on the top. (*DLFMN*, p. 11).

Mihr Ilahi 45/September-October 1600 A.D.

109. *Farman* of Sultan[1] Salim addressed to the *amils, jagirdars,* and *karoris* of *pargana* Haveli Banaras confirms 178 *bighas* of land as *madad-i maash* in the said *pargana* in favour of Malik Arjun Mal Jangam. Orders the addressees to leave the land in possession of the grantee and not to bother him for any tax like *qunlugha, peshkash, savri,* *deh-nimi, gaushumari, sad-doi shikar*[2] and *begar, takrar-i zarat, ikhrajat* and *awarizat* like *takalif-i diwani* and *mutalibat-i sultani*. It bears the seal of Sultan Salim on the top. On the back are impressed seven seals which are not legible. It was issued under the *risala* of Shaikh Ahmad, the *Sadr*. (*IHRC*, Vol. XLIV, p. 208).

3 Aban 45, 6 Rabi II 1009 A.H./15 October 1600 A.D.

110. *Farman* of Akbar addressed to the *chaudharis*, *qanungos*, ryots and cultivators of *sarkar* Nagore[1] informs them that *sarkar* Nagore and other places have been assigned to Rai Rai Singh as *jagir* from the beginning of the autumn of the *Sichqan-il* on the transfer of Madho Singh[2] and others. Orders them (addressees) to look upon him (Rai Rai Singh) as their *jagirdar* and to pay him all dues regularly from crop to crop and from year to year without fail. It bears the invocation '*Allahu Akbar*' and the seal of Akbar on the top. (*DLFMN*, p. 12).

1009 A.H./1600-1601 A.D.

111. *Hukm* of Sultan Salim issued by Raghu Koka addressed to the agents and administrators of *pargana* Kahalgaon[1], *sarkar* Monghyr, *suba* Bihar[2], states that the grant of 190 *bighas* of land, situated in village Usthoo[3] as *madad-i maash* to Sayyid Mir, son of Sayyid Ali Muhammad, is duly verified by Mir *Sadr-i Jahan*. Orders the officials to allow the grantee to retain the land in question and not to disturb him in any way. It bears the seal of Raghu Koka. (*IHRC*, XXBI, Pt. II. p. 3; *JBRS*, XLIII, p. 216).

Azar, Ilahi 47/16 November 1602 A.D.

112. *Farman* of Sultan Salim addressed to Rai Rai Singh says that a certain ruby being brought by a jeweller for Salim was unknowingly bought by the addressee. Orders him to hand over the said ruby to Lal Miyan[1] who will pay the price for it. Sends *khilat* of silk by way of gift. It bears the invocation '*Allahu Akbar*' and seal of Salim on the top. (*DLFMN*, p. 13).

9 Rajab 1011 A.H./13 December 1602 A.D.

113. *Qabzul Wusul* executed by Muhammad Masum *Chaudhari* for Rs.15 paid to Fathullah *alias* Mal, merchant, son of Shaikh Shihabud Din in receipt of the sale price of land for residential purposes. It bears an illegible seal. (*COR*, II, p. 76).

Post 1011 A.H./1602-1603 A.D.[1]

114. *Parwana* of Jamil[2] addressed to the *gumashtas* states that Tan Nath[3], Ban Nath Jogi[4], etc., are in possession of 200 *bighas* of land situated in Narot[5], *pargana* Pathan by virtue of the *farman* of the Emperor. The *gumashtas* of this quarter and others are warned not to harass or molest the said *faqirs* on any ground whatsoever. It bears the invocation '*Allahu Akbar*' and the seal of Jamil on the right-hand margin. (*MJJ*, p. 103).

1 Isfandarmaz, Ilahi 47/Ramazan 1011 A.H./9 February 1603 A.D.

115. *Farman*[1] of Sultan Salim addressed to the *hukkam, ummal, jagirdars* and *karoris* of *pargana* Sadarpur[2], *sarkar* Khairabad[3], informs them that 240 *bighas* of land by *gaz-i Ilahi* situated in *pargana* Sadarpur, *sarkar* Khairabad have been granted as *madad-i maash* to Shaikh Idris and seven others from the beginning of *kharif* of *Parsil*. The officials are ordered to measure, demarcate and consolidate the land and hand over possession thereof to the grantees. Further directs them not to realise any cess, viz., *qunlugha, peshkash, savi, deh-nimi, muqaddami, gaushumari, sad-doi qanungoi*, and other dues like *hissa-i resasad*[4], *shikar, begar, takrar-i samrat*. They are exempted from all *takalif-i diwani* and *matalibat -i sultani*. They should not insist upon *sabt-i harsala*[5] after *tashkhis-i chak* nor should they ask the grantees to produce afresh a *farman and parwancha* every year. It bears the invocation. '*Ya Malik ul Mulk*'[7] and the round seal of Sultan Salim[8] on top. The *unwan* reads '*Hukm-i jaahan Mata-i Abul Muzaffar Sultan Salim Badshah Ghazi*'[9] There is no *tughra* of the Emperor Akbar.[10] On the reverse there is a *zimn* giving details of the grant. The *farman* was issued under the *chauki* of Lal Beg[11], *risala* of Shaikh Nurullah and *waqianawisi* of Abdus Salim. There are five round seals of which those of Nurullah, Aqibat Mahmud and Muinud Din are legible. An endorsement in the margin has ben made by *Umdat ul Mulk Ruknus Sultanat Sharif Khan.*[13] (*IC*, XLVII, No.2, pp. 121-24, *MF*, pp. 13-14).

1 Farwardin Ilahi 48/ 11 March 1603 A.D.

116. *Farman* of Sultan Salim addressed to the *chaudharis, qanungos, mutasaddis, jagirdars,* and *karoris* of *sarkar* Hajipur, *suba* Bihar states that Kamalud Din, son of Mir Sayyid Muhammad, has been granted land in a village in the said *sarkar* as *madad-i maash*. Orders them to satisfy the grantee and not to act against his suggestions and advice. Warns them not to allow any interference with the said grant. It bears the seal of Sultan

Salim. (*IHRC*, XXVI, Pt. II, p. 3; *JBRS*, XLIII, p. 218).

***16 Rabi us sani*[1] *1012* A.H./*13 September 1603* A.D.**

117. *Farman* of Akbar addressed to the officials orders them to hand over possession of 100 *bighas* of land, situated in village Gobindpur[2], *pargana* Chausa[3], to Basudeo Misr as *madad-i maash* and not to demand land revenue or tax from him. (*SFSP*, p. 70).

***2 Mihr*[1], *48 Ilahi/15 September 1603* A.D.**

118. *Farman* of Akbar addressed to the *hukkam, ummal, jagirdars* and *karoris* of *qasba Navsari, sarkar* Surat, intimates them that grant of land measuring 300 *bighas* by *gaz-i Ilahi*, alongwith *tar* and *khurma* trees, situated in the said *qasba,* had been conferred upon Kaikubad, Parsi, son of Mahyar, from the *kharif* crop of *Qui-il* as *madad-i maash*. Orders the said officials to hand over possession of the land to the grantee as usual and refund the entire produce thereof received during the past and current year to the grantee. Further, they are directed not to bother him for *malujihat, ikhrajat,* and *sair jihat* like *qunlugha, peshkash, jaribana, zabitana, muhrana, daroghana, muhassalana, deh-nimi, sad-doi qanun-goi, takrar-i zarat, zakat ul jihati*[2], *zabt-i harsala* after *tashkhis-i chak,* all *takalif-il diwani* and *ikhrajat-i sultani*[3] from him nor to ask him to produce a renewed *farman* or *parwancha* every year. It bears the invocation '*Allahu Akbar*' and the lineal seal of Akbar on the top. On the reverse is the *zimn* giving details of the grant with a *yad-dasht* dated 2 *Mihr, Ilahi* 48, endorsement of *Madar ul Mahham* Asaf Khan, the *chauki* of *Bakhshi-ul Mulk* Khwaja Fathullah[5] and *Waqia nawisi* of Muhammad Shafi. There are a number of seals, prominent among them being of Fathullah, Asaf Khan and Al-Husaini *Sadr-i Jahan*. (*JBBRAS*, XXI, pp. 189-93).

***1 Isfandarmaz Ilahi 48/9 February 1604* A.D.**

119. *Hukm of Khan-i Khanan* Mirza Khan Bahadur *Sipah Salar* addressed to the *mutasaddis* of *qasba* Navsari, *pargana* Tulari[1], states that His Majesty had issued a *farman* in respect of the *wazifdars* of *suba* Gujarat to the effect that half of the *madad-i maash* land should be released to the grantees. Consequently half of the land, i.e., 150 *bighas* out of 300 *bighas*, in *mauza* Tavri, *pargana Tulari*, were released to Kaikubad in Navsari as *madad-i maash*. Now the aforesaid person has brought a fresh *farman* from His Majesty to the effect that the land for the *madad-i maash* to Kaikubad, measuring 300 *bighas* should be given to him in full, with the *khurma* trees thereon and that the grantee should not be harassed for *malujihat*, *sair jihat* and *takalif-i diwani*, nor should there be any other obstacle in his way. In compliance with the orders of His Majesty, the said officials are directed to take necessary action in the matter. It bears the invocation *'Allahu Akbar'* on the top. On the reverse is the *zimn* giving details of the grant under the *taliqa* of Mirza Hasan Ali Beg[4], and seals of Mirza Abdul Malik, *Diwan*, helper to the *Sadr*, and Khwaja Muhammad Maasum, *Mir Bakhshi*. (*JBBRAS*, XXI, pp. 202-04).

***16 Ardibihisht, Ilahi 49/25 April 1604* A.D.**

120. *Farman* of Akbar addressed to Rai Rai Singh orders the addressee to take all possible steps to look after the children and relations of Shams Khan, who are living in *pargana* Jhunjunu[1] so that Shams Khan, who is a loyal servant, may discharge his duties at the court peacefully and efficiently. It bears the seal of Akbar at the top. (*DLFMN*, p.14).

***21 Khurdad Ilahi 49/31 May 1604* A.D.**

121. *Farman* of Akbar addressed to the *chaudharis*, *qanungos*, headmen, tenants and cultivators of Shamsabad states that the *pargana* Shamsabad has been partitioned into two. One continues to be called Shamsabad as before while the other has been named Nurpur. The villages lying on this side of the river Ganges will comprise the *pargana* of Nurpur[1], while those on the opposite bank will pertain to the *pargana* of Shamsabad. Both of them have been assigned to Rai Rai Singh Rathor as *jagir*. The officials should make entry of the *jagir* in their records and allow no alteration, modification or curtailment therein. The addressees are advised to look upon Rai Rai Singh as *jagirdar* of the two *parganas* and pay all the dues to him without any hesitation. It bears the invocation '*Allahu Akbar*' and seal of Akbar at the top. (*DLFMN*, p.15).

***2 Amardad Ilahi 49/14 July 1604* A.D.**

122. *Farman* of Sultan Salim addressed to the *hukkam*, *ummal*, *jagirdars*, *karoris*, etc., informs them that two hundred *bighas* of land, measured by *gaz-i Ilahi*, situated in *pargana* Bari, *sarkar* Lucknow, have been granted to Shaikh Alimullah as *madad-i maash* from the beginning of *kharif* of *Lui-il*. The officials concerned are ordered to measure, demarcate and consolidate the land and hand over possession thereof to the grantee who should not be asked to pay any tax like *malujihat*, *ikhrajat* and *awarizat*, viz., *qunlugha*, *peshkash*, *deh-nimi*, *muqaddami*, *sad-doi qanungoi hissa-i rasasad*, *shikar*, *begar*, *zabt-i harsala*, *takalif-i diwani* and *matalibat-*

i sultani. Nor should he be harassed for the production of a renewed *farman* or *parwana* every year. It bears the invocation '*Allahu Akbar*' and *tughra* and seal of Sultan Salim on top. On the reverse is recorded a *zimn* dated 23 Mihr, 49 *Ilahi*, giving details of the grant. Written under the *waqia nawisi* of Ibrahim Beg, and it bears the seal of Aminul Mulk. (*FS*, pp.40-41).

5 Jumada II, 1014 A.H./8 October 1605 A.D.

123. *Nishan* of *Hazrat-i ala*[1] *Shahzada-i alamiyan*[2] (Prince Salim) addressed to the officials of the empire states that 1,562 *bighas* and 13 *biswas* of cultivated and fallow land have been granted to Mir Sayyid Ahmad as *madad-i maash* in pursuance of the imperial *farman* and the *parwana* of Khwajagi Fathullah. Directs them to fix the boundaries of the aforesaid land according to the *chaknama* of the *karoris*. It bears the *sarnama* '*Allahu Akbar*' and four illegible seals. (*COR*, II, p. 33, *IHRC* XXIX, Pt.I. 1953, Exhibits, 162).

29 Mihr, Ilahi 50/11 October 1605 A.D.

124. *Nishan* of Prince Salim addressed to Rai Rai Singh[1] informs the addressee that the Emperor has grown very weak and imbecile. Asks him to reach the court without delay. It bears the seal of the Prince at the top. (*DLFMN*, p. 17).

JAHANGIR (1605-1627)

30 Tir Ilahi[1] 1/15 Rabi I, 1015/11 July 1606

125. *Farman* of Jahangir addressed to the *hukkam, ummal, jagirdars*, and *karoris* of *pargana* Kathuah[2], *sarkar* Punjab, states that 10 *bighas* of land situated in *mauza* Naroli Sanga[3], *pargana* Kathuah, *tappa* Parol[4], *sarkar* Punjab had been granted to Chandar Nath Jogi[5] as *madad-i maash* and entered in the *daftar*[6] on 29 Shaban, 986 A.H./31 October 1578 A.D. The grantee having died, his *chela*[7], Bhandar Nath[8], and others waited on the Emperor and apprised him of the facts. Consequently, orders are issued to the effect that the said land should be granted to Bhandar Nath as *madad-i maash* from the beginning of *kharif* of *Yunt-il*[9]. The officials are accordingly instructed to measure and consolidate the land and hand over its possession to the grantees. It is further ordered that the grantees may not be bothered for imposts like *malujihat, ikhrajat, awarizat, qunlugha, peshkash, savri, deh-nimi, muqaddami, qanungoi sad-doi, gau-shumari, hissa-i rasasad shikar, begar, jalkar*[10], *bankar*[11], *muhtarifa, baghat*[12], *takrar-i zarat, zabt-i harsala* after *tashkhis-i chak.* Nor should they demand from him fresh *farman* or *parwancha* every year.

It bears the invocation '*Allahu Akbar*' and *tughra* and lineal seal of Jahangir on the top. On the reverse is an endorsement giving details of the grant. It passed through the *risala* of Miran *Sadr-i Jahan, Marifat*[13] of Khwaja Muhammad Momin, *chauki* of Keshav a Maru[14] and *waqianawisi* of Khwaja Ali Naqi. There are seals and endorsements of Itmadud Daulah and others. (*MJJ*, pp.79-88.)

17 Azar, Ilahi 1/8 Shaban, 1015 A.H./21 November 1606 A.D.

126. *Farman* of Jahangir addressed to the *hukkam, ummal, jagirdars* and *karoris* of *pargana* Pathan, *sarkar* Punjab states that 200 *bighas* of land, measured by *gaz-i Ilahi*, situated in the said *pargana* had been granted to Surat Nath Jogi by way of *madad-i maash.* The grantee has now waited on the Emperor and submitted that the land in question remains submerged under water due to the frequency of floods. The imperial orders are hereby issued to the effect that he may be granted waste land in lieu thereof in the same *mahal* or elsewhere from the beginning of *kharif* of *Yunt-il* as *madad-i maash.* The officials are, thereof, ordered to measure and consolidate the land and deliver possession thereof to the grantee and different taxes like *qunlugha, peshkash, savri, deh-nimi, muqaddami,* *sad-doi qanungoi, hissa-i resasad, shikar, begar, takrar-i zarat* and *zabt-i harsala* after *tashkhis-i chak* and all the *takalif-i diwani* and *matalibat-i-Sultani*, etc., may not be demanded from him. Nor should he be asked to produce a renewed *farman* or *parwancha* every year. It bears the invocation '*Allahu Akbar*' and seal and *tughra* of Jahangir on the top. On the reverse is an endorsement with the seals of Itimadud Daulah, *Sadr-i Jahan* Al-Husaini, Abdur Razzaq[1] and others. (*MJJ*, pp. 95,96,98,99).

22 Farwardin, Ilahi 2/13 Zilhijja 1015 A.H./1 April 1607 A.D.

127. Copy of *farman* addressed to *jagirdars, karoris*, etc. of *pargana* Haveli[1], *sarkar* Kara, informs them that by the *farman* dated *Jumada* 1,984 A.H., Akbar had granted 3,207 *bighas*, 2,727 *bighas*, 1,714 *bighas* and 19 *biswas* to Sayyid Matha and others as *madad-i maash* in *pargana* Haveli, *sarkar* Kara. On the death of Sayyid Matha and a few others the grants had been discontinued. Now Sayyid Abul Khair, Sayyid Mustafa and other heirs of the late grantees have waited on the Emperor and pleaded for their rights and stated that they had no other source of livelihood. The royal orders have been issued to the effect that 750 *bighas* of land out of the said grants have been granted to the said grantees. Orders the aforesaid officials to measure and demarcate the land and deliver its possession to the grantees, and not to demand any tax or ask the grantees for a renewed *farman* or *parwancha* every year. On the reverse of the document is a *yad-dasht* endorsed by the *sadarat* of *Sadr-i Jahan, chauki* of Ram Das Kachchwaha, and *marifat* of Khwaja Muhammad Momin and the *waqia nawisi* of Masud. Statement of the division of the land among the various shareholders is also given. There is an attestation seal of *Qazi* Muinud Din. (*MF*, I, pp.16-17).

28 Farwardin, Ilahi 2/19 Zilhijja 1015 A.H./7 April 1607 A.D.

128. *Farman* of Jahangir addressed to Rai Rai Singh acknowledges receipt of his letter through his *wakil* and is highly gratified to learn that the addressee is proceeding to the court along with his relations and members of his family. When he reaches Lahore[1], he should leave his sons and relations there and personally proceed, with as many men as possible, to the court where he will be honoured with special favours. Sends his personal shawl as gift for him. It bears the seal of Jahangir on the top. (*DLFMN*, p.19).

1 Khurdad, 2 Julus 25 Muharram, 1016 A.H./12 May 1607 A.D.

129. *Farman*[1] of Jahangir addressed to Jan Beg[2] appoints him as *faujdar*

of Baroda[3] in *suba* Gujarat and intimates him of the duties and functions he will have to perform. Enjoins him to administer the country well, root out disagreeable and seditious elements and endeavour to encourage and promote cultivation and inhabitation.

It bears the seal and *tughra* of the Emperor. (*NRPR*, VI.pl: *IHRC*, XXXV, Pt.I, Exhibits, p.142).

1 Aban, 2 Ilahi Jumada II-Rajab 1016 A.H./October-November 1607 A.D.

130. *Farman* of Jahangir to Rai Rai Singh states that he has learnt that the addressee has led an expedition against Dalpat for his rough and rude manners towards the addressee and has besieged him[2]. Orders him to despatch his representation again detailing the facts therein so that the imperial troops may be sent to punish him in such a way as to serve as a warning to all. Has deputed Bahaud Daulah to bring him to the court. It bears seal of Jahangir on the top. (*DLFMN*, pp. 20-21).

1607 A.D.

131. *Sanad* . . . . addressed to Maulana Bhikaji, *Khatib*, grants him an allowance for lamp-oil. It bears seal of Muhammad Ahmad, *qazi* of Baroda. (*PC*. pp. 2-3).

3 Ilahi/1608 A.D.

132. *Farman* of Jahangir addressed to Governors, officials and *jagirdars* of *suba* Gujarat, orders them not to allow anyone, without permission of the authorities, to enter or put up in the temples and the *dharamsalas*[1] of the Jain community, which are under the control of Vijayasena Suri[2], Vijayadeva Suri[3] and Nandivijaya[4]. Further, directs them to see that none interferes with the houses of the disciples of these leaders and no tax is demanded from pilgrims visiting the *tirtha* of Shatrunjaya[5]. Lastly there should be no slaughter of animals throughout the empire on Sundays and Thursdays of every week, the new moon day of every month, on the *Nauroz*[6] and on the anniversary of His Majesty's accession. Nor should anyone indulge in hunting and fishing or catching of birds. This *farman* was issued by the Emperor in compliance with the request of Yatis Vivekharsha[7] and Parmar[8]. (*JUB*, IX, pp. 10-11).

Pre-1016 A.H./1608-1609 A.D.

133. *Farman* of Jahangir acknowledges acceptance of the *peshkash* offered by Jan Beg. It bears the seal of the Emperor. (*IHRC*, XXIX, Pt.I. 1953, Exhibits, p. 174, *NRPR*, VI, p. 19).

2 Aban, Ilahi, 4/26 Rajab 1018 A.H./15 October 1609 A.D.

134. *Farman* of Jahangir addressed to *karoris* and *jagirdars* of the empire, states that out of a piece of land measuring *6 bighas*, 3 *biswas*, situated in Agra, are granted to the *Farangis* from the *kharif* of the year *Takhaqui-il* by way of *inam* for purpose of construction of a garden and a cemetery[1]. The officials are hereby ordered to deliver possession of the land to the grantees and not to ask them any tax like *qunlugha, peshkash, jaribana, zabitana, muhrana daroghana, muhassilana, sad-doi qanun-goi,* etc. They are further directed not to demand a renewed *farman* or *parwancha* from them every year. It bears the seal and *tughra* of Jahangir. On the reverse are official endorsements in Persian and Marathi with three seals of the officials. (*JPHS*, V.I pp. 12-13).

7 Farwardin, Ilahi 5/17 March 1610 A.D.

135. *Farman* of Jahangir addressed to Rai Rai Singh sends a private robe for the addressee through his *khawas*, Sarang Dev[1], and informs him that on accomplishing the expedition successfully, he will be duly honoured with royal favours on the recommendation of the Prince. It bears the seal of Jahangir on the top. (*DLFMN*, p.23).

26 Farwardin, Ilahi 5/5 April 1610 A.D.

136. *Farman* of Jahangir addressed to the officials of the empire states that a Jain deputation led by Udayaharsh[1], has been introduced to the Emperor by Raja Ram Das, with the request to prohibit slaughter of animals during the holy days of the Paryushana festival. His Majesty, therefore, orders the officials that none should be allowed to slaughter animals during the said festival and that the defaulter should be dealt with sternly. It contains the portraits of Jahangir, Prince Khurram[2], some courtiers and monks. (*JUB*, IX. p. 11; *IHRC*, XVII, Exhibits. p.4).

4 Amardad 5 Julus/6 Jumada I, 1019 A.H./ 17 July 1610 A.D.

137. *Farman* of Jahangir addressed to the officials, agents, *jagirdars*, *karoris*, etc., says that Mir Sayyid Muhammad Pir Damaria[1] had been granted land measuring 3,500 *bighas* in the *pargana* and *sarkar* of Hajipur by virtue of the *farman* of Akbar. The said Mir having died, his son, Mir Sayyid Yahya, came and waited on the Emperor. Being fully convinced of his rights and claims, it was decided that 1,000 *bighas* of

land measured by *gaz-i Ilahi* should be granted as *madad-i maash* to the Mir and his mother from the beginning of *kharif Ilan-il* in the old *mahals* and in village Nagra[2], Haveli Patna[3]. Orders them (addressees) to deliver possession of the land to the grantee and not to bother him for such dues as *qunlugha, peshkash, jaribana, zabitana, muhrana, daroghana, muhassilana, begar, shikar, deh-nimi, muqaddami, sad-doi qanungoi* and dues and shares of bazaars and *muthtarifa, jalkar, bankar, baghat*, etc. Nor should they insist on a renewed *sanad* every year. It bears the seal and *tughra* of Jahangir. On the reverse are given several endorsements by the officials like Khwaja Jahan *Bakhshiul Mulk,*[4] *Wazir* Itimadud Daulah[5], Khwaja Abul Hasan *Madarul Maham*[6], Khwaja Nizamud Din Ahmad, *Diwan*. From the endorsements, it is evident that the Mir's mother was to be granted 700 *bighas* of land. (*IHRC*, Vol. XXVI. Pt. II. pp. 3-4).

4 Shahriwar, 5 Julus/17 August 1610 A.D.

138. *Farman* of Jahangir addressed to the *hukkam, ummal, jagirdars* and *karoris*, informs them that 4,200 *bighas* of land under cultivation and 2,690 bighas of fallow land, situated in *mauza* Nadila, *pargana* Haveli Ajmer[1], is confirmed in the name of Shaikh Hashim, son of Shaikh Fathullah, Shaikh Ismail, son of Taj Muhammad, and others. The said grant had been previously enjoyed by late Shaikh Fathullah and his brothers. Out of this grant, 1,000 *bighas* of land is earmarked to meet the expenses of *urs* and the remaining 5,890 *bighas* are reserved as *madad-i maash* for the grantees. Orders them not to harass the grantees for any dues whatsoever on account of *qunlugha, peshkash, jaribana, zabitana, muhrana, daroghana, muhassilana, begar, shikar, deh-nimi, muqaddami, sad-doi qanungoi* and *zabt*, from year to year. Advises them also not to insist on a fresh *farman* or *parwancha* every year. It bears the *tughra* and seal of the Emperor in addition to the invocation '*Allahu Akbar*' on the top. The reverse of the *farman* bears the following endorsements.

Sharah: The grant, measuring 6,890 *bighas* of land, is made to meet the expenses of *urs* of Hazrat Qutbul Aqtab and also as *madad-i maash* allowance to Shaikh Hashim and others in compliance with the *yad dasht* dated 30 *Khurdad/Ilahi* 5, 27 *Rabi* I, 1019 A.H. 10 June 1610 A.D. Prepared in the *risala* of Asaf Khan, in the *chauki* of Mustafa Khan[2] and *waqia nawisi* of Beg Muhammed, the orders of the Emperor are to be carried out when the *tumar* bearing the seals of Hasan Beg, *Diwan* of *suba* Ajmer, and Khwaja Ahmad, *Mutawalli*, reaches the *daftar*. The number of the beneficiaries of the grant is given as 26. (*AS*, pp. 30-36: *NRPR*, I, Pt. II. p. 51, *DLFMN*, p. 69).

***Ruz Ram*[1], *Sahriwar 1667* v.s./ *August-September 1610* A.D.**

139. Sale-deed executed under the *amal* of Abul Hasan, *hawala* of Khwaja Nizam[2] and *shiq* of Mirak Mahmud Sharif in the presence of five persons of good family to the effect that Adhyaru Kuka Bahman, Nariman Kaka Hasani[3], Bai Hansi, wife of Mobed and Bai Chayyin, wife of Mihiravan, hereby vend the incorporeal right of the fees of thirty marriages in lieu of 45 Changizkhani *chhapris*[4] which were paid by vendee, Ervad Mihirivan Kaikobad to the *Diwan* of the Government on their behalf at their request to make up the deficiency in the revenue for the year 1667 *Samvat*. By a former document dated *ormuz mah Sahriwar, Samvat* 1664, the four vendors referred to above had sold to the vendee the fees of 23 marriages out of which fees for a marriage and *ghagharanas*[5] had been received by the vendee. The vendee is entitled to the fee of 14 other marriages also. So, in all 58 marriages are due to him. He shall celebrate and receive the fees of altogether 58 marriage *vivah*[6] *jamnas* (?) and *ghagharanas*. They have hereby sold their four shares jointly to the vendee and no one will interfere until he has celebrated and received fees of all of them. It bears signatures of the four vendors and several witnesses. *(SPH*, pp. 252-53).

***14 Ramazan, 1019* A.H./*20 November 1610* A.D.**

140. *Chaknama* of land in villages Darapur[1], Muhammadpur[2] and Hasanpur Madho[3] states that a grant of land measuring 520 *bighas* situated in villages Darapur, Muhammadpur and Hasanpur Madho, *pargana* Mallawan, *sarkar* Lucknow, had been granted as *madad-i maash* to Shaikh Habibullah and his brothers. The officials bearing ill will and grudge towards the Shaikh resumed his land situated in village Darapur and included it in the *khalisa*. The Shaikh submitted repeated representations to the *Amirul Umara* who issued *parwanas*, but nothing came out. The Shaikh has again submitted his petition for justice and restoration of his land to him. Accordingly a *parwana* has been issued to Miyan Mir Khan, the *Faujdar* and *Amin* of the said *pargana* to the effect that he should separate the original grant from the *khalisa* land and hand it over to the said grantee. Thereupon Miyan Farhat Khan, *Munsif*, Adam Khan, *Shiqudar* and Kayastha *Karkun* .... accompanied by *chaudharis* and *qaunungos* were sent to measure the land and deliver its possession to the grantee. The officers segregated 86 *bighas* of land from village Darapur, included in the *khalisa* and handed over its possession to the Shaikh and his brothers. After the conclusion of the Mallawari campaign, when Mir Khan was camping in Bangarpur[4], the *muqaddam* of village

Darapur misrepresented to him that the *chak* of the Shaikh was correct and was not less in area, so the additional land given to him is in excess. Thereupon Mir Khan again deputed Farhat Khan, *Munsif* Miyan Adam Khan, *Shiqdar*, *chaudharis*, *muqaddams* and *qanungos*. They again visited the land in dispute and measured the *chak* of Darapur measuring 275 *bighas* and 10 *biswas* by *gaz-i Ilahi*. 76 *bighas* and 16 *biswas* by *gaz-i Ilahi* were handed over to the Shaikh and his brothers respectively; and 60 *bighas* by *gaz-i Ilahi* from village Madhopur[5] were confirmed as of old. It bears the signatures and seals of Mir Khan, Adam Khan, *Shiqdar* and Dindas *Karkun*. It also bears signatures of *chaudharis*, *muqaddams* and *qanungos* in Hindi, as also seals of Shaikh Abdul Wahid, Shaikh Abdus Samad and others. (*CORI*, p.1).

22 Shawwal 1019 A.H./ 28 December 1610 A.D.

141. *Sanad* of an official of Jahangir for the grant of 200 *bighas* of land situated in village Shahbaspur, *pargana* Saraisa, *sarkar* Hajipur, *suba* Bihar in the name of Shaikh Ibrahim as *madad-i maash*. It bears an illegible seal. *(SFSP*, p.125).

25 Shawwal 1019 A.H./31 December 1610. A.D.

142. Judgement on a dispute. The *ganwars*[1] of village Papri Busurg brought a complaint before Nawab Muzaffar Khan Niyazi, *Hakim* of *pargana* Shamsabad, that Miran Sayyid Mustafa has usurped village Papri Khurd, which belonged to the complainants from the time of their ancestors. The Miran denied the allegations and asserted that Kachhis[2] and Chamars[3] were holders of the village. They sold it to the *shaikhzadas*, viz., Fathullah, Abdullah and Piyare, sons of Maulana Ahmad, son of Farid. The *shaikhzadas* mortgaged their possession with Bannu, *baqqal*[4] of village Addi Turk (?), and then after redeeming it, sold it to the defendant's father, Mir Sayyid Nizam from whom the defendant inherited it. The present complainants once before put up the same claim, but it proved false. Thereupon the *Hakim* ordered Miyan Firuz Khan, Maulana Fahim Khwaja, Krishandas, *Diwan* Shaikh Abdul Wahid *Munshi*, Shaikh Farid and Narayandas, *Khushnawis*[5] as *amins* to inquire into the matter. Miran Sayyid Mustafa submitted the sale-deed and the judgement of *Qazi* Sadrud Din along with the mortgage-deed contracted with Bannu. After further evidence, it was decided that the complaint of the *ganwars* was false and the suit was dismissed. *(IESHR*, Vol. IV, March 1967, pp. 231-32).

***1610** A.D.*

143. *Farman* of Jahangir addressed to Hajji Muhammed regarding grant of land. *(DLFMN*, p. 70).

***5 Julus 1011 Fasli/ 1610-11** A.D.*

144. *Farman* of Jahangir addressed to officials states that *Musammat* Bibi Joola Koochi has been granted land measuring 150 *bighas* situated in *pargana* Haveli Hajipur, *sarkar* Hajipur, *suba* Bihar as *madad-i maash.* Orders the officials concerned to deliver possession of the land to the grantee and demand no tax from her. It bears seal and *tughra* of Jahangir.(*SFSP*, p. 15).

***22 Farwardin, Ilahi 6/27 Muharram 1020** A.H./ **1 April 1611** A.D.*

145. *Parwana* of...addressed to the *gumashtas* of *karoris* and *jagirdars* of *pargana* Mallawan, *sarkar* Lucknow, states that grant of land measuring 170 *bighas* situated in the said *pargana* was made to *Qazi* Bayazid, *Qazi* Muhammad, *Mutawalli. Maulana* Abdul Jalil and Abdul Fath by way of *madad-i maash*, in accordance with the *farman* dated the 29 *Rabi* II 983 A.H./8 July 1575. The said persons having died, Shaikh Abdul Hakim, Shaikh Ismail, Shaikh Habib, Khairullah, Abdul Jalil, etc, have preferred their claims and as such the grant is confirmed in their names. *(CORI*, pp. 2-3).

***2 Amardad Ilahi 6/14Jumada I, 1020** A.H./**15 July 1611** A.D.*

146. *Farman* of Jahangir addressed to the officials states that *Musammat* Alam Khatun is granted 65 *bighas* of land situated in village Jagdishpur, *pargana* Chirand[2]. *sarkar* Saran[3], *suba* Bihar, as *madad-i maash*. The officials are directed not to demand any tax whatsoever from the grantee as the land is rent-free. *(SFSP*, p.8).

***22 Amardad, Ilahi 6/4 Jumada II, 1020** A.H./**4 August 1611** A.D.*

147. *Farman* of Jahangir addressed to the officials informs them that Shaikh Allahdad and others have been granted land measuring 380 *bighas* situated in village Paranpur[1], *pargana* Haveli[2], *sarkar* Bahraich as *madad-i maash*. The officials are directed to measure and demarcate the said land and hand over its possession to the said grantees. Further, they are reminded that the grant is free from all taxes and that they should not ask for a renewed *farman* or *parwancha* every year. It bears the *sarnama 'Allahu Akbar'* on the top. On the reverse is a *yad dasht* prepared and endorsed in the *sadarat* of *Sadr-i Jahan*, *chauki* of Naqib Khan, *Marifat* of Khwaja Nizamud Din Ahmad and *waqia nawisi* of Inamullah. Details of the grant of land allocated to each grantee are specified with location. It bears seal of *Qazi* Usman. *(MFI.* p. 18).

4 Ramazan, 1020 A.H./31 October 1611, A.D.

148. *Sanad* for 140 *bighas* of land granted to Shaikh Chandan, *khadim* of the *rauza* of Khwaja Muinud Din Chishti by way of *madad-i maash.* The *chaudharis* and *qanungos* are hereby directed to confirm the land in the name of the grantee who has been in possession of it by virtue of the earlier *sanads*. He has the necessary documents in his possession. It bears the invocation '*Allahu Akbar*' on the top and the round seal of Asaf Khan on the right-hand margin. *(AS,* p. 148, *NRPR,* I p. 53).

14 Zilhijja, 1020 A.H./7 February 1612. A.D.

149. *Sanad* directing the *mutasaddis* of the *mazar* of Khwaja Muinud Din Chishti to see that Shaikh Hashim, along with his sons, and Shaikh Ismail, along with his brothers, draw half a maund of grain from the *langar* and one seer of oil for the lamp everyday without any objection and obstruction. It bears the invocation '*Allahu Akbar*' and a round seal of Ahmad-al Hajji *Khadimul fuqra* on the right hand margin. *(AS,* p. 148).

20 Mihr, Ilahi 7/16 Shaban 1021 A.H./2 October 1612 A.D.

150. *Farman* of Jahangir addressed to the *hukkam, ummal* and *mutasaddis* of *suba* Gujarat intimates that the *Firangi Padris* at Ahmadabad have been permitted to construct an *igriz*[1] there for worship and prayer. Orders them not to cause any obstruction to them. It bears the invocation '*Allahu Akbar*', seal and *tughra* of Jahangir on the top. On the reverse, there is an endorsement to the effect that it passed through the *risala* of Itimadud Daulah and *naubat-i waqa* of Muhammad Husain Shukr Allah. There is a small seal, also. *(JPHS,* V.I. pp. 17-18: *JUB,* IX, pp. 22-23).

Azar, Ilahi, 7/Ramazan-Shawwal 1021 A.H./November-December 1612 A.D.

151. *Farman* of Jahangir addressed to the officials says that 400 *bighas* of land situated in *pargana* Chaund[1], *sarkar* Rohtas[2], *suba* Bihar, have been granted to *Musammat* Aisha and *Musammat* Zainab by way of *madad-i maash.* As the land is rent-free grantees should not be asked to pay any tax whatsoever. It bears a number of illegible seals. *(SFSP,* p. 3).

24 Azar, Ilahi 7/5 December 1612

152. Copy of the *farman* of Jahangir addressed to the *hukkam, diwans, ummal* and *mutasaddis* of *suba* Ajmer, informs them that the *tauliyat* of the *mazar* of Khwaja Muinud Din Chishti has been conferred upon Shaikh Husain[1], great grandson of the holy saint. Orders the said officials to regard him as a *mutawalli* of the said shrine and pay him due regard. *Umdatal Mulk Madarul Mahham* Murtaza Khan[2] is enjoined upon to post a writer with the *mutawalli* who may be paid his share in the property left by his ancestors as well as his share in the *roshnai* and *urs*. It bears *tughra* and seal of Jahangir on the top. On the reverse is the *yad dasht* dated 24 *Azar, Ilahi* 7/17 *Jumada* II, 1021 A.H. prepared in the *risala* of Murtaza Khan. There are four seals, one of them being of Muazzamul Mulk. (*FS* pp. 3-4).

17 *Dai, Ilahi, 7 Zilaqada, 1021 A.H. /28 December 1612 A.D.*

153. *Farman* of Jahangir addressed to the officials states that 60 *bighas* of land situated in *pargana* Haveli Hajipur, *sarkar* Hajipur, *suba* Bihar, has been conferred upon *Musammat* Bega *Kooch* Rahman Beg, as *madad-i maash*. Orders the officials concerned to deliver possession of the land to the grantee and not to ask her to pay land revenue and other taxes. It bears a number of illegible seals. (*SFSP*, p. 15).

Post 1612 A.D.[1]

154. *Farman* of Jahangir addressed to Rai Suraj Singh, *zamindar* of Bikaner, informs him that as Mansur, Bhatti and others rebels of Lakhi Jungle are committing depredations. Nizamud Din Asaf Khan is hereby ordered to punish the rebels and establish peace and order in those *parganas* and *mahals*. Has also deputed Alif Khan there to extirpate the insurgents. Asks him to render all possible help to Alif Khan. It bears the invocation '*Allahu Akbar*' and the seal of the writer on the top. (*DLFMN*,. p. 71).

1613-14 A.D.[1]

155. *Farman* of Jahangir addressed to Rai Suraj Singh, son of Rai Rai Singh, informs him that Dalpat has waited on the Emperor and as such the addressee should not stay there any longer but proceed to the court immediately. It bears seal of Jahangir on the top. (*DLFMN*. p, 22).

20 April, 1613 A.D.

156. *Farman* of Jahangir conferring the office of *chaudhari* and *qanungo* on Bhattanand for the *parganas* of Bagwan[1], Jahangirpur[2], Ukhra[3], Nadia[4], etc. *(IHRC,* V. Exhibits, p.155).

25 Shahriwar, Ilahi, 8/3 Shaban, 1022 A.H./8 September 1613. A.D.

157. *Farman* of Jahangir addressed to the officials informs them that *Musammat* Nuru and her sons have been granted 100 *bighas* of land situated in village Devhari[1], *pargana* Amrdha[2], *sarkar* Sambhal, as *madad-i maash.* Orders them to measure and consolidate the land and hand over its possession to the grantees. They are directed not to levy any tax on them and not to ask for a renewed *sanad* every year. It bears the invocation '*Allahu Akbar*', a square seal and *tughra* of Jahangir on the top. On the reverse is given *yad dasht* prepared in the *risala* of Tatar Khan[3] and *waqia nawisi* of Askari Mamuri. There are three seals of Sayyid Ahmad and others. (*MFI,* p.19).

1022 A.H./1613-14 A.D.

158. *Farman* of Jahangir addressed to the officials, informs them that a piece of land measuring 115 *bighas* situated in *pargana* Siddhaur, *sarkar* Lucknow, has been bestowed upon Sayyid Ubaidullah and others as *madad-i maash.* They are ordered to measure and consolidate the land and deliver its possession to the grantees. No tax is to be demanded from them. It bears the invocation '*Allahu Akbar*', and *tughra* and square seal of Jahangir on the top. On the reverse is a *yad dasht* endorsed in the *chauki* of Naqib Khan[1], and the *waqia nawisi* of Nimat Ali Khan. There are five seals which are illegible. Division of the land among the grantees has also been indicated. (*MF*, I, p. 21; *IHRC*, XXXI (1), p.168).

2 Bahman, Ilahi 8/11 January 1614 A.D.

159. *Farman* of Jahangir addressed to Rai Suraj Singh states that the Emperor is much pleased to know of the defeat of Dalpat and capture of his elephants. Sends a robe through Jamal Muhammad who will bestow upon him all the captured elephants. Advises him to guard the culprit until he reaches the court in fetters. It bears the invocation '*Allahu Akbar*' and seal of Jahangir on the top. *(DLFMN,* p. 24).

15 Farwardin, Ilahi 9/25 March 1614 A.D.

160. *Nishan* of Prince Khurram addressed to Rai Suraj Singh states that there was dispute regarding the boundary line of the *parganas* of Sirsa and Bhatner some time back. The dispute has now been settled since the son of Rai Bharat Chand, accompanied by Sundar Das, the tax-collector of Sirsa, defined and demarcated the boundary line in the presence of the people there. The son of Rai Bharat Chand has recovered the revenue of the land situated in *pargana* Sirsa from Bhara Jaya and Bahadur Jaya who had seized the said land. The revenue thus realised has been handed over to Sundar Das, *karori* of Sirsa. As the said *pargana* has been conferred upon him (addressee) in *jagir*, it is his duty to collect the revenue of the land from the persons referred to above and deposit it with Nauroz Beg, the *karori* of Sirsa. Now all the government dues are to be recovered from them. It bears the seal of Prince Khurram. (*DLFMN*, p. 25).

6 Ardibihisht, Ilahi 9/16 April 1614 A.D.

161. *Farman* of Jahangir addressed to Rai Suraj Singh states that before the receipt of the addressee's representation, Raja Man Singh (Kachwaha[1]) had been ordered to hand over the sons of Dalpat to the royal court. Has also come to know that he (addressee) has in his custody seven of the ladies of Dalpat's harem. Orders him (addressee) to send all of them along with the younger daughter of Dalpat to the royal court without any delay. It bears seal of Jahangir on the top. (*DLFMN*, p. 26).

27 Ardibihisht, Ilahi, 9/6 Rabi II, 1023 A.H./6 May 1614 A.D.

162. *Farman* of Jahangir addressed to the *hukkam, ummal, jagirdars* and *karoris*, intimates that 46 *bighas* of land situated behind Osari in the suburbs of Ajmer city, has been granted as *madad-i maash* to Sayyid Khubullah, Sayyid Karamullah, etc. Orders them to measure and consolidate the land and hand it over to the grantees and not to exact any dues from them on account of *qunlugha, peshkash, jaribana, zabitana, muhrana, muhassilana, daroghana, begar, shikar, deh-nimi, muqaddami, sad-doi qanungoi* and *zabt* from year to year. Advises them also not to ask them for renewed *farman* and *parwancha* every year. It bears the invocation *'Allahu Akbar'* and *tughra* and seal of the Emperor on the top. The reverse bears the following endorsements: The grant is made in the name of Sayyid Khubullah and Sayyid Karamullah as *madad-i maash* in compliance with the *yad dasht* dated 5 *Farwardin* corresponding to 14 *Safar* 1023 A.H./26 March 1614 A.D. prepared in the *chauki* of ... in the *risala* of Abid Khan[1] and *waqia nawisi* of Ishaq Harvi in consideration of the representation made by Sayyid Khubullah to His Majesty. The names of the beneficiaries of the grant with the statement of land granted to each of them are also given. (*AS*, pp. 37-39; *DLFMN*, p. 69, *NRPR*, I. Pt. II, p. 53).

1 Khurdad, Ilahi 9/12 May 1614 A.D.

163. *Farman* of Jahangir addressed to Rai Suraj Singh says that a large number of tenants and cultivators of *pargana* Narmar have complained to the royal court that Raghunath Rathor, Sudarshan, Gokal Das, Bhagwan, Qawi Afghan, and Husain Qaim Khani have seized 2 villages of their territory and have realised 24,00,000 of *dams* and are bent upon plundering and killing them. Orders him (addressee) to look into the matter and inflict severe punishment on the culprits, restoring the villages and the misappropriated money to the genuine owners and rehabilitating the tenants and peasants in their places. It bears the seal of Jahangir on the top. (*DLFMN*, p. 27).

14 Khurdad[1], Ilahi, 9/25 May 1614 A.D.

164. Copy of the *farman* of Jahangir addressed to the *jagirdars* and *karoris* of *sarkar* Ajmer states that *mauza* Phukkar[2] was granted to the *zunnardars* by way of *inam*. It was also ordered that Khwaja Sri Rang, Rai Mai Das, Rai Ram Chand and Mikand Das should divide the land in the ṣaid *mauza* among the *zunnardars* according to their respective shares as indicated in the *qismatnama*[3] detailed below:

Sons of Kalyan (sic) ..., Tirath, *purohit*[4] and *zumardaran,* and Dama and other *pujaris*[5].

It bears the invocation *'Allahu Akbar'* on the top. On the back is given a *yad dasht,* prepared and endorsed in the *chauki* of Asaf Khan, *risala* of Ani Rai Singh[6] and *waqia nawisi* of Badiuz Zaman. *(ASI,* p. 140, *DLFMN*, p. 69).

6 Tir, Ilahi, 9/17 June 1614 A.D.

165. *Farman* of Jahangir addressed to the officials informs them that about 40 *bighas* of land situated in *pargana* Parchhiyar[1], *sarkar* Saharanpur[2], has been granted as *madad-i maash* to Shaikh Muhammad, son of Shaikh Husain, and his sons. They (addressees) are ordered to measure and consolidate the land and deliver its possession to the grantees. They are also directed not to demand any tax from them nor to ask for a renewed *farman* or *parwancha* from them. It bears the *sarnama 'Allahu Akbar'* and *tughra* and a square seal of Jahangir on the top. On the reverse is given an endorsement with seven seals which are not legible. (*MF*, I. p. 20).

27 Tir, Ilahi, 9/10 Jumada II, 1023 A.H./8 July 1614 A.D.

166. *Parwana*[1] of Itimadud Daulah addressed to the *gumashtas* of *jagirdars* and *karoris* of *pargana* Pathan states that 200 *bighas* of land situated in the *pargana* had been granted to Surat Nath in accordance with the *farman* of the Emperor. Surat Nath has died. The same grant is now bestowed upon Tan Nath and other *jogis, chelas* of the deceased *jogi*, as *madad-i maash* from the beginning of *kharif* of *Pars-il.* Orders the addressee to measure and consolidate the land and deliver its possession to the grantees. It bears the invocation *'Allahu Akbar'* and the seal of Itimadud Daulah on the top. On the reverse is a *zimn* endorsing the grant. (*NJJ*, pp. 107-108).

5 Amardad, Ilahi 9 Jumada II, 1023 A.H./18 July, 1614 A.D.

167. *Farman* of Jahangir to Rai Suraj Singh states that the Emperor has come to know that Gokul, Sudarshan, Raghunath and other rebels have realised a sum of Rs. 30,000 as the imperial money, from Dalpat and plundered the inhabitants of *pargana* Lunian, depopulating the villages far and wide. Consequently orders have been issued to Hashim Beg Khushti[1] to inflict suitable punishment on the rebels. Orders him (addressee) to cooperate with him (Hashim Beg Khushti) in chastising and expelling the rebels and recovering from them the imperial money and dues of the people so that they may not be able to repeat their heinous activities, and agriculture and trade may prosper. It bears the seal of Jahangir on the top. (*DLFMN*, p. 28).

31 Amardad, (Ilahi) 9/17 Rajab 1023 A.H../13 August 1614 A.D.

168. *Farman* of Jahangir addressed to Rai Suraj Singh states that he has learnt that Keshu Baluch has recently severely chastised and punished Chandra Bhan, a notorious thief, robber and rebel who has fled and entered his (addressee's) territory. Orders him (addressee) to depute such persons as may pursue him until he is captured or expelled from those territories. It bears the invocation *'Allahu Akbar'* and the seal of Jahangir on the top. (*DLFMN*, p. 29).

4 Mihr, Ilahi 9/22 Shaban 1023 A.H./17 September 1614 A.D.

169. *Parwana* of Itimadud Daulah addressed to the officials of *pargana* Hisampur, *sarkar* Bahraich, directs them to restore 250 *bighas* of land in village Kasraula to *Musammat* Bibi Khunza Jahan, *Musammat* Bibi Shaha and others. (*COR*, I. p. 79).

4 Mihr, Ilahi 9/22 Shaban 1023 A.H./17 September 1614 A.D.

170. *Farman* of Jahangir addressed to Rai Suraj Singh, orders him to present Mehta Lakhmi Chand in the royal court immediately. Appreciates the services rendered by him (addressee) in managing the thoroughfares so successfully and hopes that he would make still greater efforts to stipulate and inhabit the places and safeguard the thoroughfares. It bears the invocation '*Allahu Akbar*' and the seal of Jahangir on the top. (*DLFMN*, p. 30).

2 Aban, Ilahi 9/21 Ramazan 1023 A.H. 15 October 1614 A.D.

171. *Farman* of Jahangir addressed to Rai Suraj Singh orders him to send the property of Dalpat through his trustworthy servants to the Royal Court. Further asks him to release Dalpat's men from prison as Dalpat has been dealt with severely. It bears the invocation '*Allahu Akbar*' and the seal of Jahangir on the top. (*DLFMN*, p. 31).

5 Aban, Ilahi 9/24 Ramazan 1023 A.H./18 October 1614 A.D.

172. *Farman* of Jahangir to the officials states that the *nuzurat* of the *rauza* of Khwaja Muinud Din Chishti which were deposited in the *qindil*[1] were divided into 5½ shares as follows: children of Masud, 1½ share; children of Bahlol, 1 share; children of Ibrahim, 1 share, and children of Thaka, 2 shares. The *nazr* at the time of *sar-tarashi*[2] etc., was enjoyed exclusively by Masud. As the offsprings of Bahlol were in large number, their share was comparatively lesser. In view of this fact the Emperor has issued orders that in future the *nuzurat* of *qindil* would be divided into six shares as follows: Hashim and other sons of Masud, 1½ shares as usual; Sayyid Ismail, Sayyid Abdul Hayy, Abdul Majid, Matha, Hassan, etc., sons of Bahlol 2 shares; children of Thaka, 2 shares; and children of Ibrahim ½ share, and the *nazr* from the *mahal-i sartarashi* will be enjoyed exclusively by the children of Masud as usual. Orders them (addressees) to see that this arrangement is not disturbed in any way and no one usurps the right and share of others. It bears a round seal and *tughra* of Jahangir on the top. On the reverse is given a *yad dasht* dated 28 *Shahriwar Ilahi* 9/25 *Shaban* 1023 A.H./30 September 1614 A.D., prepared and endorsed in the *risala* of Itimadud Daulah, in the *chauki* of Khwaja Ibrahim Husain and *waqia nawisi* of Askari Mamuri, touching on the details of the grant mentioned above. Statement of the grantees with their respective shares is also given. (*AS*, pp. 108-110; *NRPR*, I. Pt. II. p. 52; *DLFMN*, p. 69).

24 Mihr, Ilahi 9/7 October 1614 A.D.[1]

173. *Farman* of Jahangir addressed to the *hukkam, ummal, jagirdars, karoris,* etc., informs them that 36 *bighas* of land, situated in *mauza*

Kania, have been granted to Hajji Muhammad, son of Allahdad, resident of Ajmer by way of *madad-i maash* from the beginning of *kharif, Tawishaqan-il*. Orders them (addressees) to measure and consolidate the land and deliver the possession thereof to the grantee and not to bother him for any cess like *qunlugha, peshkash, jaribana, zabitana, muhrana, muhassilana, daroghana, begar, shikar, deh-nimi, sad-doi qanungoi*, etc. Further directs them not to ask for a renewed *farman* and *parwanha* from the grantee. It bears the invocation '*Allahu Akbar*', and a square seal and a *tughra* of Jahangir on the top. On the back of the *farman* is a *yaddasht* dated 24 *Mihr, Ilahi* 9 *Ramazan* 1024 A.H./7 December 1614, prepared and endorsed in the *risala* of Miran Sayyid Ahmad Qadiri, *chauki* of Iradat Khan and *waqianawisi* of . . . . giving details of the grant mentioned above. (*AS*, pp. 146-47).

Aban Julus 9/Ramazan-Shawwal 1023 A.H./October-November 1614 A.D.

174. *Farman* of Jahangir addressed to *hukkam, ummal, jagirdars, karoris*, etc., states that 210 *bighas* of land situated in *pargana* Laharpur, *sarkar* Khairabad, has been conferred upon Lala Misr, and others from the beginning of *kharif* as *madad-i maash*. The officials are ordered to measure and consolidate the land and hand over its possession to the grantees. They are further directed not to realise any tax like *qunlugha, peshkash, jaribana, zabitana, muhrana, begar, deh-nimi, muqaddami, sad-doi qanungoi, zabt-i harsala* after *tashkhis* and *chak* and *takrar-i zarat* from them, nor to ask for a renewed *farman* and *parwancha* from them every year. (*FS*, p. 45).

1 Dai, Ilahi 9/20 Zilqada 1023 A.H./12 December 1614 A.D.

175. *Parwana* of Itimadud Daulah addressed to the *mutasaddis* of the *rauza* of Khwaja Muinud Din Chishti says that the office of reciting the holy Quran in the morning at the *rauza* has been held for long by Maulana Ibrahim Sanduqi and his son, Hafiz Ismail and that they have been occupying a *hurja*[1] in the *rauza* for generations. Orders that the office and possession of the *hujra* by the persons concerned should not be disturbed in any way by the *khadims* of the shrine. It bears the invocation '*Allahu Akbar*' on the top and a round seal of Itimadud Daulah at the bottom on the right-hand margin. (*AS*, p. 149; *NRPR*, Pt. I. 757).

1023 A.H./1614-15 A.D.

176. *Sanad-i Sadaratul ulliyatul aliya* addressed to the agents of *karoris*, and *jagirdars* of *pargana* Batala, *suba Lahore* informs them that the wife of Shaikh Qutb, a chaste and pious lady, has been granted 60 *bighas* of land by virtue of the *farman* dated the 7 *Khurdad, Ilahi* 13 as *madad-i maash* from the beginning of the spring harvest of the horse year. Orders the officials to measure, demarcate and consolidate the land in question and hand over possession thereof to the grantee. Further directs them not to molest and harass the grantee for any tax, nor to demand from her any *farman* or *parwancha* from year to year. It bears the *saranama* '*Allahu Akbar*' and seal of Sayyid Ahmad Haqq, the *Sadrus Suddur*. (*CPEM*. p. 143).

9 julus/1023-24 A.H./1614-15 A.D.

177. *Farman* of Jahangir regarding grant of land in *pargana* Kakori[1]. (*IHC*. 1938. Exhibition, p. 60).

9 Mah . . . , Julus 9/1023-24 A.H./1614-15 A.D.

178. *Hukm of . . . addressed to the gumashtas* of *jagirdars* and *karoris* of *pargana* Hasanpur, *sarkar* Bahraich, informs them that a piece of land measuring 25 *bighas*, situated in the said *pargana*, has been conferred upon *Musammat* Bibi Fatima and others as *madad-i maash* from the beginning of *kharif* in accordance with the *farman* dated 14 *Dai, Julus* 9. Orders the officials to measure, demarcate and consolidate the piece of land and deliver possession thereof to the grantees. Further, they are directed not to molest or harass the grantees for any reason whatsoever. It bears the *sarnama 'Allahu Akbar'* and an illegible seal. (*COR*, II pp. 33-34).

9 Bahman, Ilahi 9/27 Zilhijja 1023 A.H./18 January 1615 A.D.

179. *Farman* of Jahangir addressed to Rai Suraj Singh states that he has sent Har Ram, *khawas* to summon him. Orders him to set out for the royal court along with the *khawas* immediately. Further, asks him to depute his men to recover the sum of Rs. 30,000 from Gokul, Sudarshan and others, on Dalpat's account. It bears the seal of Jahangir on the top. (*DLFMN*, p. 32).

5 Farwardin, Ilahi, 10/24 Safar 1024 A.H./15 March 1615 A.D.

180. *Farman* of Jahangir addressed to *hukkam, ummal, jagirdars* and *karoris* says that Deorai[1] and Somalpur[2] villages in *pargana* Ajmer, were granted as *madad-i maash* to the *mujawirs* of the *mazar* of Miran Sayyid Husain *khing Sawar*[3] and also to meet the expenses of *urs, roshnai*, etc. The *mutasaddis* of the said *rauza* were subsequently ordered to resume and include the said grant in the *khalisa* from *Rabi* of *Pars-il.* On the representation of the *mujawirs,* the Emperor is pleased to grant them 4,308 *bighas* of land in the said villages from the beginning of *Rabi* of *Pars-il* as *madad-i maash* as also to meet the expenses of *urs* and *roshnai.* Orders the addressee to hand over the possession of the land to them and make no demand upon them for any dues like *qunlugha, peshkash, jaribana, zabitana, muhrana, muhassilana, daroghana, begar, shikar, deh-nimi, muqaddami, sad-doi qanungoi,* etc., nor should they ask them to produce a renewed *farman* and *parwancha* every year. It bears a square seal and a *tughra* of Jahangir on top. On the reverse is given a *yaddasht* dated 3 *Zilqada* 1023 A.H./5 December 1614 A.D. prepared and endorsed in the *risala* of Itimadud Daulah, *chauki* of Iradat Khan[4] and *waqianawisi* of Ahmad Isfahani, furnishing details of the grant referred to above. Statement of the piece of land earmarked for the grantees, *urs,* and *roshnai* is given with seals of the officials. *(AS.* pp. 127-36).

7 June 1615 A.D.

181. Articles of the Treaty of Peace between the subjects of Jahangir and the Portuguese signed by Nawab Mucanebxhan[1] and Goncalo Pinto da Fonseca, by virtue of the powers delegated to them by their Lords. Whereas the British and the Dutch came to India under the cloak of merchants to settle there and to conquer lands therein and whereas the said Ambassadors of Peace have settled that Jahangir and the Portuguese Viceroy of India, will not engage in any trade with the said nations, or neither will they be sheltered in their ports, nor be supplied with provisions, the Viceroy and his successors will be obliged to banish them out from the sea of Gujarat within a period of three months from the day they arrive and if they even capture Surat, the Mughal Emperor permits the Portuguese to fight and drive them out and he will give all necessary help; the British who are living in the dominion of the Mughal Empire will leave by way of Masulipatam[2] with their property.

Item No. I: The Mughal Emperor and the Portuguese will not ask for any compensation for the losses incurred in the war, nor will they be debarred from moving freely and trade in the territories of the two powers. The Mughal Emperor will release all the Portuguese prisoners who are found in his dominion and have not embraced Islam. The

Viceroy will also set at liberty all the subjects of the Mughal Emperor, who have not become Christians.

Item No. II: Out of the goods left by the subjects of the King of Portugal in the territory of the Mughal Emperor, the Mughal Emperor will be allowed to take 70,000 Xerafins[3] as compensation for the coral which was taken from the ship that had come from Mecca and the residue of the said goods will be returned to their owners.

Item No. III: The Viceroy of India will grant for two years only two passes for two ships to go from Surat to Mecca free of duties in addition to the usual pass which is given every year regularly for one ship to make the said voyage. Two passes will also be given for two ships free of duties to go from Surat to Ormuz[4]. The Viceroy will give one keel of an empty ship in compensation for one burnt at Goga.[5]

Item No. IV: The Malavares (Malabaris) who are pirates, will not be given shelter in the ports of the two powers and those who enter will be arrested and handed over by each of the two Powers.

Item No. V: The King of Portugal will retain his right in fact, as enjoyed by him heretofore, in the customs of Diu[6] as well as any other vessels that are accustomed to sail with cargoes by the Gulf of Cambay. The treaty was sealed and signed by the two Powers on the 7th June 1615 Jero Xavier[7] Pinto da Fonseca. (*IHRC,* IX. pp. 78-80).

31 Khurdad, Ilahi 10/24 Jumada I, 1024 A.H./11 June, 1615 A.D.

182. *Farman* of Jahangir addressed to the *hukkam, ummal, jagirdars, karoris,* etc. of the empire, informs them that fifty *bighas,* of land, situated in *pargana* Suket, have been granted to *Musammat* Firuz Khatun, wife of Mahmud, and her sons as *madad-i maash,* from the beginning of *kharif of Tawishaqan-il.* Orders the officials to measure, demarcate and consolidate the land and deliver it to the grantees and not to realise any tax like *qunlugha, peshkash, jaribana, muhassilana, muhrana, begar, shikar, deh-nimi, muqaddami, sad-doi qanungoi,* etc., from them. Nor should they demand a renewed *farman* and *parwana* from them every year. On the back is the seal of Itimadud Daulah. (*FS,* pp. 47-48: *CIMA,* p.27).

19 Mihr, Ilahi 10/19 Ramazan 1024 A.H./2 October. 1615 A.D.

183. *Farman* of Jahangir addressed to the *mutasaddis* of *suba* Ahmadabad says that the Englishmen are staying in the house of the *Padris* situated in *muhalla* Jawahari Wada with their consent. As the doors of the *nazul*[1] house are shut throughout the empire, it is hereby ordered that the

Englishmen may be accommodated in another *muhalla* and the house of the *Padris* may be evacuated and left in their possession and hereafter they (authorities) should not allow any one to enter the Padris house without proper permission. It bears the *sarnama 'Allahu Akbar'* as also seal and *tughra* of Jahangir on the top. (*JPHS*, V, I, p. 19; *JUB* IX, p. 23).

26 Ramazan, 1024 A.H./9 October 1615 A.D.

184. *Sanad* of Salim Lodi, official of Jahangir, addressed to the officials of *pargana* Hisampur, *sarkar* Bahraich, confirms Miran Sayyid Alaud Din in the grant of village Kasraula in the said *pargana*, originally granted by Akbar, as *madad-i maash*. (*COR*, I. p. 79).

1615 A.D.

185. *Sanad* of the *Qazi* of Baroda addressed to Maulana Bhikaji, *Khatib*. grants him 40 *bighas* of land near village Savad. (*PC* pp. 2-3).

10th Julus 1024-25 A.H./1615-16 A.D.

186. *Farman* of Jahangir grants Lasoora to Miran Sayyid Mahmud, who brought three treasures from Baghdad.[1] (*IHRC*, XI. Exhibits, p. 258).

Pre-1616 A.D.[1]

187. *Hukmnama* of *Khan-i Khanan* addressed to Rai Suraj Singh, asks him to stay in the Deccan and wait for fresh orders. It bears seal of *Khan-i Khanan*. (*DLFMN*, p. 72).

2 Amardad, Ilahi 11/10 Rajab 1025 A.H./14 July 1616 A.D.

188. *Farman* of Jahangir to the officers states that Bikha Harkhe[1], Jayanand Jati, Chela of Baji Dev (Vijayadeva) Suri and Nandji waited on the Emperor in the *ghusalkhana*[2] at Ajmer with the request for a *farman* in favour of the monks of the Jain *jamat*[3] who are virtuous and their only job is the worship and adoration of God. Convinced of their piety and holiness, the *farman* is hereby issued to the effect that the officers, functionaries, *jagirdars*, *mutasaddis* and the administrators of the empire should not interfere with or obstruct in any way the practices of this *jamat*, and should allow them to attend to their worship and devotion and *yazdan parasti*[4] with perfect peace of mind so that they may continue to pray for the permanence of the holy empire as also for the augmentation of the royal dignity. It bears the seal and *tughra* of Jahangir on top. On the back is a *yad dasht* dated 24 *Bahman, Ilahi* 10/24 *Muharram* 1025 A.H. 13 February 1616 prepared under the *chauki* of Khwaja Ibrahim Husain through the mediation of Azmat Khan and *waqia nawisi* of Abdul Wasay. It bears the *sharh* of Itimad-Daulah and Diyanat Khan[5]. There are two small seals of Asaf Khan and Banmali Ram Rai on the margin of the *farman*. (*INFG*, pp. 26-29; *JUB* IX 16-29).

2 Amardad, Ilahi 11/10 Rajab 1025 A.H./14 July 1616 A.D.

189. *Nishan* of Prince Khurram addressed to Rai Suraj Singh informs that his representation has duly reached the Emperor and assures him of royal favours. It bears the invocation *'Allahu Akbar'* and the seal of Prince Khurram on the top. (*DLFMN*, p. 34).

10 Amardad Ilahi 11/18 Rajab 1025 A.H./22 July 1616 A.D.

190. *Farman* of Emperor Jahangir addressed to the *hukkam, ummal, jagirdars* and *karoris* informs them that Shaikh Farid, son of Shaikh Qutb, *mujawir*, resident of Ajmer, and his sons have been assigned 300 *bighas* of land from *kharifTawishaqan-il* out of 560 *bighas* held by them heretofore in the village assigned to the shrine of Khwaja Muinud Din Chishti by way of *madad-i maash*. Orders them to measure and consolidate the said land and hand over the same to the grantees and directs them not to demand any dues like *qunlugha, peshkash, jaribana, muhrana, muhassilana, zabitana, daroghana, begar, shikar, deh-nimi, sad-doi qanungoi*, etc. from them. Further, advises them not to demand a fresh *farman* and *parwancha* from them every year. It bears a seal and *tughra* on the top. On the reverse is given *yaddasht* dated 14 *Bahman Ilahi* 11/ *Muharram* 1024 A.H./13 February 1616, prepared in the *risala* of Miran Sayyid Ahmad Qadiri, in the *chauki* of Azmat Khan and *waqianawisi* of . . . . Details of the land along with the grantees are recorded. A seal of *Qazi* Zuhurullah is also given. (*AS*, *pp*. 70-71 *DLFMS*, p.70).

1 Shahriwar Ilahi 11/1025 A.H./13 August 1616 A.D.

191. *Farman* of Jahangir grants 30 *bighas* of land in *pargana* Panipat to Adar Banu for maintenance. It bears the *tughra* and seal of the Emperor. (*IHRC*, XIII. p. 162).

28 Mihr, 11 Ilahi 9 Shawwal/1025 A.H./10 October 1616 A.D.

192. *Farman* of Jahangir addressed to the *hukkam, ummal* and *jagirdars*, informs them of the grant of land measuring 400 *bighas* in the names of Shaikh Ahmad and his brothers, situated in the villages of the shrine. Orders them neither to bother the grantees for any cess nor to demand fresh *farman* and *parwancha* from them every year. It bears the *tughra* and seal of the Emperor as well as the invocation *'Allahu Akbar'* on the top. On the reverse are given four seals, two of them being of Sayyid Ahmad Qadiri and Abul Hasan Tarkhan while the remaining two are illegible. (*AS*, pp. 20-41; *DIFMN*, p. 69).

10, Azar Ilahi, 11/22 Zilqada, 1025 A.H./21 November 1616 A.D.

193. *Farman* of Jahangir addressed to *hukkam, ummal, jagirdars* and *karoris* states that in response to the representation made to the Emperor 130 *bighas* of land situated in villages of the *rauza* has been granted to *Musammat* Bibi Jan and others by way of *madad-i maash*. Orders the officials to measure and consolidate the land and to hand it over to the grantees. Advises them not to demand any cess whatsoever from them, nor to insist on a fresh *farman* and *parwancha* every year. *Sarnama 'Allahu Akbar'* and the seal and *tughra* of the Emperor are given on the top. It bears the following endorsements on the reverse: The grant is made to her and others in compliance with the *yaddasht* dated 24 Isfandarmaz, 9/13 February 1615 A.D., prepared in the *chauki* of Khwaja Ibrahim Husain, in the *risala* of Sayyid Ahmad Qadiri and in the *waqianawisi* of.....(*AS*, pp. 42-43; *DLFMN*, p. 69).

1616 A.D.

194. *Farman* of Jahangir addressed to Shaikh Ahmad grants him a piece of land in Nandla for his maintenance and support. (*DLFMN*, p. 69; *NRPR* I(1) p. 59).

1616 A.D.

195. *Farman* of Jahangir addressed to Hajji Muhammad confers grant of a piece of land on him as *madad-i maash*. (*NRPR* ,I Pt. II. p. 59).

5 Isfandarmaz Ilahi, 11/16 Safar 1026 A.H./13 February 1617 A.D.

196. *Nishan* of Prince Khurram addressed to Rai Suraj Singh informs him that fresh orders to call him will be issued when the Prince encamps at Burhanpur and hopes that he will discharge his duties at the *thana* carefully and whole-heartedly. It bears the invocation *'Allahu Akbar'* and the seal of Prince Khurram on the top. (*DLFMN*, p.33).

2 Khurdad, Ilahi, 12/16 Jumada I, 1026 A.H./13 May 1617 A.D.

197. *Farman* of Jahangir addressed to the *hukkam, ummal, jagirdars* and *karoris* states that he has learnt that *mauza* Phukkar is inhabited by two *qaums* of *zunnardars* and the said village was granted to both of them. As

there was a dispute between them regarding its division, the grant was cancelled. It is now ordered that the Hindu pilgrims performing pilgrimage to Phukkar will be at liberty to choose their *purohit* from either of the two *qaums* and whatever they give in charity will not be objected to by any one of them. If alms are given separately to each of the two sects, it will be the duty of each sect to divide them among themselves and if the alms are made to both the sects collectively, every shareholder should get his share fixed for him. Further, they are advised to avoid any sort of quarrel or dispute in the said village on the issue of grazing cows. If they repeat their misconduct, they will be considered guilty and will be imprisoned in the fort. It is also ordered that *mauza* Phukkar, *pargana* Haveli Ajmer, is regranted as *madad-i maash* from the beginning of *Ilan-il* to the *zunnardars* of Phukkar. Orders them (addressees) to give possession of the said village to the grantees and not to demand any cess like *qunlugha, peshkash, jaribana, zafitana, muhassilana, muhrana, daroghana, begar, shikar, deh-nimi, muqaddami, sad-doi qanungoi*, etc., from them. Nor should they ask them to produce renewed *farman* and a *parwancha* every year. It bears the invocation *'Allahu Akbar'* a square seal and a *tughra* of Jahangir on the top. On the reverse is given a *yaddasht* dated 30 *Azar, Ilahi 11*, corresponding to 11 *Zilhijja* 1025 A.H./ 21 December 1616 A.D. prepared and endorsed in the *chauki* of Mustafa Khan, *risala* of Abhay Rai Singh, and *waqianawisi* of Muhammad Habib Shukrullah, touching on the details of the grant mentioned above. (*AS*, pp. 142-43; *DLFMN*, p. 70).

22 Khurdad, Ilahi 12/6 Jumada II, 1026 A.H./1 June 1617 A.D.

198. *Nishan* of the Prince Khurram addressed to Rai Suraj Singh informs him that *pargana* Pahlodi[1] which has now been annexed to the royal estates and included in the *khalisa mahals* is committed to the charge and care of the addressee. Orders him to direct his men and agents not to interfere with the said *pargana* and its villages. It bears the invocation *'Allahu Akbar'* and the seal of Prince Khurram on the top. (*DLFMN*, p. 35.).

3 Amardad, Ilahi 12/21 Rajaf, 1026 A.H./15 July 1617 A.D.

199. *Farman* of Jahangir addressed to the *hukkam* informs them that a grant of land measuring 30 *bighas* situated in village Kaiter[1] has been made to Ajmeri, Bazaid *Kalawant* and their mother. In addition to this grant, an allowance of two seers of grain per diem has also been allotted to them from the shrine. (*AS* , p. 147; *DLFMN*, p. 70).

1 Shahriwar, Ilahi 12/21 Shaban, 1026 A.H./ 14 August 1617 A.D.

200. *Parwana* of Itimadud Daulah to the *mutasaddis* of the *mazar*[1] of Khwaja Muinud Din Chishti informs them that Inayatullah and Akram Ali, sons of Abdur Rahman, were granted 4 seers of grain by way of *rozina*[2] from the *langarkhana* of the said *mazar* from the beginning of *kharif Ilan-il* in compliance with the *farman* of Emperor Jahangir. Orders them to continue payment of the said allowance to the grantees every day as usual and not to harass them for a fresh *farman* or *parwancha* every year. It bears the invocation '*Allahu Akbar*' on the top and a round seal of Itimadud Daulah on the right-hand margin. (*AS*, p. 150).

5 Azar, Ilahi 12/27 Zilqada, 1026 A.H./16 November 1617 A.D.

201. *Farman* of Jahangir addressed to the *gumashtas* of *jagirdars* and *karoris* of *pargana* Fakharpur, *sarkar* Bahraich, intimates that 100 *bighas* of land situated in the said *pargana* have been granted to *Musammat* Bibi Sandal[2] and others as *madad-i maash*. One-fourth of this land is cultivable and three-fourth culturable but lying fallow from the beginning of the *kharif*. Orders the officials to measure, demarcate and consolidate the land and hand over its possession to the grantees. Further, they are directed not to molest or harass the grantees on any ground whatsoever. It bears the *sarnama*, '*Allahu Akbar*' and the seal of Jahangir. There are seals of Sabir Ali and Hajji Koka. (*COR*, II, p. 34).

10 Azar, Ilahi 12/2 Zilhijja, 1026 A.H./21 November 1617 A.D.

202. *Hukm* of Nur Jahan addressed to Rai Suraj Singh states that Sultan Singh Rathor who is in addressee's service, owes some money to Kishan Das and his son, Baroman, the Treasurer of Nur Jahan. Orders the addressee to pay off the said debt to Kishan Das and Baroman from his own estate and to realise the same from his (Rathor's) salary. It bears the invocation '*Allahu Akbar*', and the seal of Nur Jahan on the top. (*DLFMN*, p. 38).

15 Zilhijja, 1026 A.H./4 December 1617 A.D.

203. *Nishan* of Prince Khurram addressed to Rai Suraj Singh states that the Emperor is fully satisfied with his services and convinced of his loyalty as expressed by him (addressee) in his letter addressed to Wazir Khan[1]. Hopes that he (addressee) will be more earnest and eager in his attachment to the Emperor. Assures him that as a reward for his devotion, sense of duty and services rendered by him, he will be loaded with favours like his father very shortly. It bears the *sarnama 'Allahu Akbar'* and the seal of Prince Khurram on the top. (*DLFMN*, p. 37).

13 Dai, Ilahi 12/6 Muharram, 1027 A.H./ 24 December 1617 A.D.

204. *Nishan* of Prince Khurram addressed to Rai Suraj Singh states that he has learnt from the petitions of the *karori* and the *faujdar* of *pargana* Tahara that the tenants of some of the villages of the said *pargana* have migrated to the villages of *pargana* Bhatinda. Adds that the agents there have not surrendered them to the *karori* and the *faujdar* of *pargana* Tahara. Orders him to take such steps that the said agents do not detain a single individual of *pargana* Tahara. It bears the invocation *'Allahu Akbar'* and the seal of Prince Khurram on the top. (*DLFMN*, p. 36).

9 Bahman, Ilahi 12/1 Safar, 1027 A.H./18 January 1618 A.D.

205. *Farman* of Jahangir addressed to the officials states that Shaikh Bhikkan and his sons have been favoured with grant of land measuring 20 *bighas* situated in *pargana* Haveli Hajipur, *sarkar* Hajipur, *suba* Bihar as *madad-i maash*. Orders the officials to deliver possession of the land to the grantees and demand no tax whatsoever from them. It bears a number of illegible seals. (*SFSP*, p. 15).

Post-17 Bahman, Ilahi 12/26 January 1618 A.D.[1]

206. *Farman* of Jahangir addressed to *hukkam, ummal, jagirdars* and *karoris* says that three villages comprising 27,910 *bighas* of land had been granted as *madad-i maash* to Shaikh Kamal, son of Sultan, and others, in all 229 *mujawirs* of the *maqbara*[2] of Khwaja Muinud Din Chishti, and every share holder hold his share by virtue of the division made by Hasan Beg[3]. Now when the Emperor paid a visit to Ajmer, out of the said grantees only 198 persons holding 25,450 *bighas* of land waited on the Emperor. Thereupon the Emperor ordered that 5,161 *bighas* of land should be left to the grantees and the rest be taken over. Thirdly, some persons holding 1,306 *bighas* of land did not come to wait on the Emperor. The grantees who had waited on the Emperor and accompanied him as far as Mandu, apprised him of their miserable condition. They told him that a large number of them depended upon this land only. The Emperor, thereupon, ordered that the grantees who had waited on the Emperor and held land by virtue of the *qismat* made by Hasan Beg, should be given over half of the land and the rest be taken over from them and those who had not waited on the Emperor should be granted no land. It was further ordered that the land now granted and situated in the two villages of Bir[4], *viz.*, Haveli Ajmer and Kankiniadas[5] *pargana* Bandhan Sundari[6], *sarkar* Ajmer, would be first examined and assessed by Mir Fathullah, *Mutwalli*, in the company of Shaikh Husain and Ram Das *Bakhshi* of Ajmer. Thereafter the land would be divided into respective shares and given over to each grantee from the beginning of *rabi Bichi-il*. Shaikh Kamal, son of Sultan would get 55 *bighas* of land as his share. It was also ordered that when a grantee passed away his descendants would get half of the land and the remaining half would lapse to the Government. Orders them to obey the orders strictly and not to realise anything from the grantees by way of *qunlugha, peshkash, jaribana, muhassilana, zabitana, muhrana, daroghana, begar, shikar, deh-nimi, muqaddami, sad-doi qanungoi*, etc., nor to demand a fresh *farman* and a *parwancha* every year. There is a seal and *tughra* of Jahangir on the top. On the reverse is given a *yad dasht* dated 17 *Bahman, Ilahi* 12, correspoinding to 8 *Safar* 1027 A.H./5 February 1618 A.D. prepared and endorsed in the *risala* of Sayyid Ahmad Qadiri, in the *chauki* of Mutamid Khan[7] and *waqia nawisi* of Abdul Karim, furnishing details of the aforesaid grant. Statement of the land granted to and taken over from the grantees is also given along with the names of the grantees. (*AS*, pp. 105-107).

28 Bahman, Ilahi 12/2 February 1618 A.D.

207. *Farman* of Emperor Jahangir addressed to the *hukkum, ummal, jagirdars* and *karoris* says that the villages comprising 27,310 *bighas* of land had been granted as *madad-i maash* to Sayyid Firuz and others in all 229 *mujawirs* of the *maqbara* of Khwaja Muinud Din Chishti and every one of the grantees held his share in his possession in accordance with the division made by Hasan Beg. Other details are the same as given in No. 206 above. It bears *yad dasht* dated 27 *Isfandarmaz* 12/16 March 1618 A.D. prepared in the *chauki* of Aqil Khan[1] *risala* of Sayyid Ahmad Qadiri and *waqia nawisi* of Abdul Wasay giving details of the grant mentioned above. Statement of the land granted to each *mujawir* is also given. There is a seal of Qazi Abdun Nabi. (*AS*, pp. 84-87).

Ardibihisht, Julus 13/14 April 1618 A.D.

208. *Farman* of Jahangir addressed to the *hukam, ummal, jagirdars* and *karoris* says that the three villages comprising 27,310 *bighas* of land were granted as *madad-i maash* to Shaikh Ali and others in all 229 *mujawirs* of the *maqbara* of Khawaja Muinud Din Chishti and every grantee was in possession of his share according to the division effected by Hasan

Beg. Other details are the same as given in 206 above. It bears *yad dasht* dated 18 *Dai, Ilahi* 12/2 January 1618 A.D. duly entered in the *risala* of Miran Sayyid Ahmad Qadiri, *chauki* of Inayat Khan[1] and *waqia nawisi* of Abdul Karim, touching on the details of the grant mentioned above. Statement of the land granted to and taken over from the grantees is also given. (*AS*, pp. 92-96).

24 Shaban, 1027 A.H./17 August 1618 A.D.

209. *Sanad* stating that Gujar[1] of *muuza* Danta[2] had found a necklace of 12 *marwarids*[3] weighing 6 *mashas*[4] 6½ *rattis*[5] in his village. The necklace after being tested by Rasa *sarraf*[6], son of Sadhu, and other goldsmiths, was sold through Abdul Qaim, *mujawir,* to Sardul for Rs. 48 which was paid to the Gujar. It bears the invocation '*Allahu Akbar*' on top and four seals of Khwaja Husain, *Qazi* Nizamud Din and others in the right hand margin. It also bears signatures of Shaikh Bahlol, Abdur Rahim and Shaikh Farid as witnessess. (*AS*, p. 150).

13 Ramazan, 1027 A.H./4 September 1618 A.D.

210. *Hasbulhukm* stating that the *mutasaddis* of *pargana* Muhammadabad *alias* Benares, *suba* Allahabad, should know that Arjun Mal Jangam and others, inhabitants of *qasba* Benares, have stated that they own a building in the said *qasba* and that a person called Nazir Beg, resident of the same place, has been interfering with the said building for long without any justification. The officials concerned are ordered to look into the matter at once and to see that Nazir Beg does not interfere with the building in any way. Adds that the building should be restored to the owners, if seized by him (Nazir Beg). There is a seal of Asad Khan[1] on the right hand margin. (*IHRC, I-IV*, p. 209).

26 Shahriwar, Ilahi 13/28 Ramazan, 1027 A.H./ 8 September 1618 A.D.

211. *Farman* of Jahangir addressed to the *wazirs, amirs, hukkam, mutasaddis,* etc, informs them that the offices of *zamindari* and *chaudhari* of *tappas* Barari, Dewra, etc., excluding *nankar*[1] of *pargana* Kahalgaon, *sarkar* Monghyr, *suba* Bihar, are conferred on Hira Nand son of Madusudan[2], *zunnardar,* and his descendants from the *kharif* of *Tawishaqan-il.* He will attend to his duties and by his good behaviour will keep the ryots and tenants happy and pleased and will endeavour to increase population and improve cultivation. Every year he will forward a statement of his office and a report of his work under the seal and signature of the *qanungos* through the *Diwan* of the Province. Directs them not to harass him in any way or demand from him a fresh *sanad* every year. It bears the *tughra* and seal of Emperor Jahangir on the top. On the reverse is recorded the *zimn* giving details of the grant. (*IHRC,* XVIII, pp. 190-191).

Post-16 Mihr, Ilahi 13/29 September 1618 A.D.

212. *Farman* of Jahangir addressed to the *hukkam, ummal, jagirdars* and *kororis* of Ajmer states that villages comprising 4,57,000 *bighas* of land yielding annual income of Rs. 9050 were granted as *waqf* to the shrine of Khwaja Muinud Din Chishti in pursuance of the *yad dasht* dated 19 *Amardad, Ilahi* 8/30 July 1613 A.D. The proceeds accuring from the said villages had been partitioned into three shares, the first share was reserved for *Urs* and *roshnai*[2], the second share was earmarked for the support and maintenance of Shaikh Husain, descendant of Khwaja Muinud Din Chishti, and the third share was meant for *fuqra*[3] and *takiadars*[4]. When the Emperor visited Ajmer those *faqirs* who held 3,230 *bighas* of land and 7 *maunds* and 6 *asar*[5] of grain did not appear before him. The Emperor, therefore, ordered discontinuation of their grants. Most of the *faqirs* and *takiadars*, who accompanied the Emperor from Ajmer to Mandu apprised the Emperor that those deprived of their grants had no other source of livelihood except the land, grain and *langar* assigned to them on behalf of the *rauza*. Orders were, accordingly, issued that those who had waited on the Emperor at Ajmer and had been granted land and grain from the *langar*, were allowed to retain half by virtue of the *yad dasht*. It was also ordered that the heirs of the grantees too should be given half the share in land and grain from the *langar*. The officials concerned, therefore, are directed to measure, demarcate and consolidate the land and hand it over to each one of these as also the grain from the *langar*, without fail. The grantees should not be bothered for the payment of various cesses like *qunlugha, peshkash, jaribana, muhassilana, zabitana, muhrana, daroghana, begar, shikar, deh-nimi, muqaddami, sad-doi qanungoi*, etc. nor should they be asked to produce a renewed *farman* and *parwancha* every year. It bears a square seal and *tughra* of Jahangir on top. On the back is the *yad dasht* dated 16 *Mihr, Ilahi* 13/10 October 1613 A.D. prepared in the *chauki* of Aqil Khan, *risala* of Sayyid Qadiri and *waqia nawisi* of Shaikh Abdur Rahim, furnishing details of the grant. (*FS*, pp. 4-8).

24 Mihr, Ilahi 13/27 Shawwal, 1027 A.H. 7 October 1618. A.D.

213. *Farman* of Jahangir addressed to Raja Jai Singh[1] advises him to send the news regularly to the royal court without fail. Assures him of all the royal favours. It bears the *sarnama 'Allahu Akbar'* and *tughra* of Jahangir on the top. (*JIH*, XXXVI, Pts. 1-3, p. 263).

3 Aban, Julus 13/15 October 1618 A.D.

214. *Parwana* of Sayyid Ahmad, *Sadr*, addressed to the officials of *pargana* Fakharpur, *sarkar* Bahraich, states that in pursuance of the *farman* of Jahangir dated the 12 *Amardad*, 13 *Julus*, it is hereby ordered that the officials should measure, demarcate and consolidate 200 *bighas* of land situated in the said *pargana* and deliver possession thereof to *Musammat* Zohra and others. It bears seals of Hajji Koka and Sabir Ali, officials of Jahangir. (*COR*, I, p. 86).

17 Azar, Ilahi 13/21 Zilhijja, 1027 A.H./29 November 1618 A.D.

215. *Parwana* of an official of Jahangir to the subordinate officials states that *Musammat* Bega Khan (sic) who was granted 60 *bighas* of land in *pargana* Haveli Hajipur as *madad-i maash* in accordance with the *farman* of Jahangir has died. Now the grant to the extent of 30 *bighas* of land situated in village Dhankhti, *pargana* Hajipur, is conferred on the heirs of the deceased *Musammat* as *madad-i maash*. Orders them to take necessary action accordingly. It bears illegible seals with signatures. (*SFSP*, p. 111).

1618 A.D.

216. *Sanad* of the *suba* of Gujarat addressed to Maulana Bhikaji, *Khatib*, states that 48 *bighas* of land situated near village Savad are granted to him (addressee) for his maintenance. It bears the seals of Safdar Khan, Sayyid Ahmad Qadiri, Abul Hasan Itimadud Daulah, Sabir Ali and Manohar Das, officials of Jahangir. (*PC*, pp. 2-3).

8 Isfandarmaz, Ilahi 13/11 Rabi 1 1028 A.H./16 February 1619 A.D.

217. *Farman* of Jahangir addressed to the officials states that 170 *bighas* of land situated in *pargana* Sadarpur, *sarkar* Khairabad, have been granted to Shaikh Abul Faiz and others as *madad-i maash*. They are directed to deliver possession of the land to the grantees after measuring and consolidating it. Further, they are ordered not to demand any tax. Nor should they demand renewed *sanad* from them. It bears the invocation '*Allahu Akbar*' and a *tughra* of Jahangir on the top. On the reverse is the *yad dasht* prepared and endorsed in the *risala* of Sayyid Ahmad Qadiri, *chauki* of Tatar Khan and *waqia nawisi* of Fazlullah. There are seven seals of different officials, one of them being of Sayyid Ahmad Qadiri. Statement of the division of land among the grantees is also given. (*MF.*, p. 22; *IHRC*, XXXII, Exhibits p. 99).

Ruz Rashn, 18 Isfandarmaz, Ilahi 13/ 2 February 1619 A.D.

218. *Farman* of Jahangir addressed to the *hukkam, ummal, jagirdars, karoris*, etc., of *sarkar* Surat states that one hundred *bighas* of land situated in *qasba* Navsari *sarkar* Surat have been conferred on *Mulla* Jamasp and *Mulla* Hoshang and their sons as *madad-i maash* from the beginning of *rabi* harvest, *Qui-il*. Orders the said officers to measure, consolidate and demarcate the land and hand over its possession to the grantees and not to harass or molest them for any tax like *qunlugha, peshkash, jaribana, muhassilana, zabitana, muhrana, daroghana, be-gar, shikar, deh-nimi, muqaddami sad-doi qanungoi*, etc., and all civil dues and imperial obligations. Further, they are directed not to demand a renewed *sanad* from them every year. It bears the *sarnama 'Allahu Akbar'* and a seal and a *tughra* of Jahangir on the top. On the reverse is the *yad dasht* dated the 13 *Azar julus* 13 corresponding to 16 *Zilhijja*, having been submitted through the *risala* of Sayyid Ahmad Qadiri and *waqia nawisi* of Muhammad Baqar stating that the two grantees have presented themselves before the Emperor and offered four *phials* of *itr* and Rs. 100 as *peshkash* on 2 *Shahriwar, Julus* 13 and that they have been favoured with the said grant. There are some seals of the officers of the state. (*JBRAS*, No. LXXI, Vol. XXV, 1917-18, pp. 422-436; *JUB*, IX, p. 21; *FS*, pp. 45-47).

4 Ardibihisht, Ilahi 14/9 Jumada I 1028 A.H./14 April 1619 A.D.

219. *Farman* of Jahangir addressed to the *hukkam, ummal, jagirdars* and *karoris* informs that 500 *bighas* of land were granted to Sayyid Mansur, *mujawir*, resident of Ajmer, as *madad-i maash*. As the grantee in question has waited on the Emperor and convinced him of his rights, the Emperor has added 200 *bighas* of land lying fallow in *mauza* Bir to the grant already held by him thus making a total of 700 *bighas* of land. This will be in force from the beginning of *Ilan-il*. Orders them (addressees) to measure and consolidate the land and deliver its possession to Sayyid Mansur and his sons and not to demand anything from them by way of *qunlugha, peshkash, jaribana, zabitana, muhrana, muhassilana, dar-oghana, begar, shikar, deh-nimi, muqaddami, sad-doi qanungoi*, etc. Nor should they demand a fresh *farman* and a *parwancha* from them every year. It bears a square seal and a *tughra* of Jahangir on the top. On the reverse is given a *yad dasht* dated 16 *Mihargan Ilahi*, 11/25 *Ramazan* 1025 A.H./9 October 1616 A.D., prepared and endorsed in the *risala* of Miran Sayyid Ahmad Qadiri in the *chauki* of Khwaja Ibrahim Husain[1] and *waqia nawisi* of Abdul Wasay touching on the details of the grant. (*AS*, pp. 116-117; *DLFMN*, p. 70).

27 Ardibahisht, Julus 14/2 Jumada II 1028 A.H./7 May 1619 A.D.

220. *Farman* of Jahangir to the *hukkam, ummal, jagirdars* and *karoris* states that three villages comprising 27,314 *bighas* of land were granted as *madad-i maash* to Sayyid Matha and others, in all 229 *mujawirs* of the *rauza* of Khwaja Muinud Din Chishti and every one of the grantees had his share in his possession. Other details are the same as in No. 206 above. It bears a *yad dasht* dated 8 *Dai, Ilahi* 11, corresponding to *Zilhijja* 1026 A.H./30 December 1616 A.D., prepared and endorsed in the *risala* of Sayyid Ahmad Qadiri, in the *chauki* of Itibar Khan, and *waqia nawisi* of Muhammad Zahid, touching on the details of the grant mentioned above. Statement of land granted to and taken over from the grantees is also given along with the names of the grantees. (*AS*, pp. 118-124; *DLFMN*, p. 70).

10 Amardad, Ilahi 14/20 Shaban, 1028 A.H./23 July 1619 A.D.

221. *Farman* of Jahangir addressed to the officials informs them that *Musammat* Bibi Shana and her sons have been granted land situated in *pargana* Dera[1], *sarkar* Lucknow, as *madad-i maash*. They are ordered to release the land to the grantees, after measuring, demarcating and consolidating it. Furthermore, the officials are instructed not to realise any tax and demand a renewed *farman* or *parwana* from them every year. It bears a *tughra* and a square seal of Jahangir on the top. On the reverse is the *yad dasht* prepared and endorsed in the *risala* of Hajji Koka, *chauki* of Tatar Khan and *waqia nawisi* of Muhammad Miran. There are seven seals of Sayyid Ahmad, Itimadud Daulah, Sabir Ali, Ram Rai, etc. It is recorded in the *zimn* that the grant has been made at the initiative of Nur Jahan[2]. (*MF*, I, p. 25).

12 Amardad, Ilahi 14/22 Shaban, 1028 A.H./23 July 1619 A.D.

222. *Farman* of Jahangir addressed to the officials states that *Musammat* Zainab and others have been granted 50 *bighas* of land situated in *pargana* Daryabad[1], *sarkar* Lucknow, as *madad-i maash*. They are ordered to deliver possession of the land to the grantees after measuring, demarcating and consolidating it. The grant is free from all taxes, and no renewed *farman* is to be demanded from the grantees every year. It bears a *tughra* and a square seal of Jahangir on the top. On the reverse is the *yad dasht*, prepared and endorsed in the *risala* of Hajji Koka, *chauki* of Mutamid Khan and *waqia nawisi* of Abdul Karim. There are seven seals of different officials. Details of the divisions of land among the grantees is also given. In the *zimn* there is a reference to Nawwab Mahd uliyya[2] indicating that the grant has been made at the initiative of Nur Jahan. (*MF*, I, p. 24).

Amardad, Ilahi 14/Shaban-Ramazan 1028 A.H./July-August 1619 A.D.

223. *Farman* of Jahangir addressed to the officials states that *Musammat* Samdan has been granted land measuring 30 *bighas* situated in *pargana* Siddhaur, *sarkar* Lucknow, as *madad-i maash*. The officials concerned should measure, demarcate and consolidate the land and deliver its possession to the grantee in question. No tax is to be levied and no fresh *farman* or *parwancha* be demanded from the grantee every year. It bears the *sarnama 'Allahu Akbar'* as also a *tughra* and a square seal of Jahangir on the top. On the reverse is the *yad dasht* prepared and endorsed in the *risala* of Hajji Koka, *chauki* of Mutamid Khan and *waqia nawisi* of Abdul Karim. There are six seals of Sabir Ali, Ram Rai, Itimadud Daulah and others. The endorsement refers to the good offices of Nur Jahan Begam sought by the grantees. (*MF*, I, pp. 28-29).

2 Shahriwar, Ilahi 14/14 Ramazan, 1028 A.H./15 August 1619 A.D.

224. *Hukm* of Nur Jahan addressed to Ganga Bai states that a village, belonging to Udai Singh, son of Dalpat Singh, have been attached, Haya and Mohan have been done to death and their relatives confined. An attestation signed by a body of people and sealed by Hashim and Muhammad Naqi has been submitted to the Royal Court. Orders her (addressee) to release all the relations of Haya and Mohan from confinement and send them to the Royal Court. Adds that she should avoid going near the said village. It bears the invocation '*Allahu Akbar*' and the seal of Nur Jahan on the top. (*DLFMN*, p. 39).

6 Shahriwar, Ilahi 14/18 Ramazan, 1028 A.H./19 August 1619 A.D.

225. *Nishan* of Prince Khurram addressed to Muqarrab Khan states that Sayyid Mir Muhyud Din had been granted 1,000 *bighas* of land in village Sipara[1], *pargana* Sanda[2], as *madad-i maash*. Has now learnt that Jahangir Quli Khan[3] had, in lieu of the said land, allotted as *madad-i maash* land situated in village Jalalpur, *pargana* Saraisa, to the said Mir and his son.

It is hereby ordered that in accordance with the *sanad* of Jahangir Quli Khan those lands should be treated as genuine and approved and the same may be given to the grantees. It bears the seal of Prince Khurram. On the reverse is given the name of Afzal Khan[4]. (*IHRC*, XXVI, p. 51 *JBRS*, XL III, p. 219).

15 Azar, Julus 14/29th Zilhijja, 1028 A.H./27 November 1619 A.D.

226. *Hukm* of (Itimadud Daulah) addressed to the *gumashtas* of *jagirdars* and *karoris* of *pargana* Fakhrapur, *sarkar* Bahraich, informs them that a grant of land measuring 100 *bighas* by *gaz-i Ilahi* situated in the said *pargana* has been bestowed upon *Musammat* Bibi Sandal and others as *madad-i maash* from the beginning of the *kharif* crop. Directs the officials concerned to measure, demarcate and consolidate the land and hand over its possession to the grantees who should enjoy the proceeds thereof without any obstruction or molestation. It bears the *sarnama* '*Allahu Akbar*' and the seal of Itimadud Daulah. (*COR*, II, pp. 34-35).

3 Dai, Ilahi 14/17 Muharram, 1029 A.H./14 December 1619 A.D.

227. *Farman* of Jahangir addressed to the *hukkam, ummal, jagirdars* and *karoris*, informs them that three villages comprising 27,310 *bighas* of land were granted as *madad-i maash* to Sayyid Ismail and others, in all 229 *mujawirs* of the *maqbara* of Khwaja Muinud Din Chishti and each of the grantees held the land in his possession according to the division made by Hasan Beg. Other details are the same given in No. 206 above. It bears a seal and *tughra* of Jahangir on the top. On the reverse is given a *yad dasht* dated 1 *Tir, Ilahi* 13/28 *Jumada* II, 1027/22 June, 1618 A.D. prepared in the *risala* of Miran Sayyid Ahmad Qadiri, *chauki* of Itibar Khan and *waqia nawisi* of Muhammad Zahid Harvi, touching on the details of the grant referred to above. A statement of land granted and resumed is also given. (*AS*, pp. 73-77; *DLFMN*, p. 70).

6 Dai, Ilahi 14/20 Muharram, 1029 A.H./17 December 1619 A.D.

228. *Farman* of Jahangir addressed to the *hukkam, ummal, jagirdars* and *karoris* states that three villages comprising 27,310 *bighas* of land had been granted to Bahlol and others, in all 299 *mujawirs* of the *maqbara* of Khwaja Muinud Din Chishti by way of *madad-i maash* and in accordance with the division effected by Hasan Beg. Other details are the same as given in No. 206 above. It bears a seal and a *tughra* of Jahangir on top. On the reverse is given a *yad dasht* dated 27 *Isfandarmaz* 12/19 *Rabi* I 1027 A.H./17 March 1618 A.D., prepared in the *chauki* of Aqil Khan, *risala* of Sayyid Ahmad Qadiri and *waqia nawisi* of Abdul Wasay giving details of the land mentioned above. A statement of the land granted and resumed is also given with the names of the grantees. (*AS*, pp. 79-83; *DLFMN*, p. 70).

***1619* A.D.**

229. Conveyance deed executed by Sayyid Azmatullah, son of Buzurg, in favour of Mirza Yaqub Sulaiman and Bibi Khairun Nisa of Baroda in respect of 10 *bighas* of land for 525 *Mahmudis*. (*PC*, pp. 4-5).

14 Julus/1028-29 A.H./1619-1620 A.D.

230. *Farman* of Jahangir addressed to the officials states that *Musammat* Des and others have been granted land measuring 115 *bighas* situated in *pargana* Siddhaur *sarkar* Lucknow as *madad-i maash*. They are ordered to deliver possession of the land to the grantees after measuring, demarcating and consolidating it. The grant is free from all taxes and as such no land revenue and imperial levies may be demanded. It bears a *tughra* and a square seal of Jahangir on the top. On the reverse is the *yad dasht*, prepared and endorsed in the *risala* of Hajji Koka, *chauki* of Tatar Khan and the *waqia nawisi* of Muhammad Momin. There are three seals of different officials. (*MF*, I, p. 27).

.... Ilahi 14/1619-20 A.D.

231. *Sanad* of Itimadud Daulah addressed to the *gumashtas* of the *jagirdars* and *karoris* of *pargana* Ajmer informs them that by virtue of the imperial *farman*, Sayyid Mahmud, son of Sayyid Abdus Samad, and other brothers of Sayyid Chand along with their sons have been granted 160 *bighas* of land in the *mauzas* assigned to the *rauza* of Khwaja Muinud Din Chishti by way of *madad-i maash* from the beginning of *Ilan-il*. Orders them to measure and consolidate the land and deliver its possession to the grantees. It bears the *sarnama* '*Allahu Akbar*' on the top and details of distribution of the land are also given. A round seal of Itimadud Daulah is impressed on the right-hand margin. (*AS*, p. 153; *NRPR*, I(2), p. 58).

11 .... 1029 A.H./1619-20 A.D.

232. *Chakbast*[1] communicating compliance with the *farman* of Jahangir dated 2 .... 1021 A.H./1612-13 A.D. It bears illegible seals. (*SFSP*, p. 112.)

Ilahi . . . . /1620 A.D.[1]

233. *Farman* of Jahangir addressed to the *mutasaddis* and *jagirdars* of *pargana* Kasmar[2] , *sarkar* Saran, *suba* Bihar states that Narain and Bhowal, sons of Nalo Tirhutia, residents of *pargana* Kasmar appeared in the court and complained that the *jagirdars* and *chaudharis* took money from them for fishing in the *Hauz* Kakrail and other *nalas*. Instructs the addressees to stop demanding money from them and to provide necessary relief. (*SFSP*, p. 8).

22 Farwardin, Ilahi 15/31 March 1620 A.D.

234. *Hasbul Hukm* of the reign of Jahangir addressed to the officials states that Narain and Bhowal, residents of *pargana* Kasmar, *sarkar* Saran, are hereby granted the right of fishing in *Hauz* Kakrail and other *nalas* in *pargana* Kasmar. They are exempted from all cesses and other dues. Orders the officials concerned not to harass the said persons in any way. (*SFSP*, p. 42).

4 Ardibihisht, Ilahi 15/20 Jumada I, 1029 A.H./13 April 1620 A.D.

235. *Farman* of Jahangir addressed to the *hukkam, ummal, jagirdars* and *karoris* informs them that the three villages comprising 27,310 *bighas* of land were asigned as *madad-i maash* to Sayyid Habibullah and others, in all 229 *mujawirs* of the *maqbara* of Khwaja Muinud Din Chishti and each of the grantees had his share in his own possession in accordance with the division effected by Hasan Beg. Other details are the same as in No. 206 above. It bears the *sarnama* '*Allahu Akbar*', a square seal and a *tughra* of the Emperor on the top. On the reverse are the following endorsements *yad dasht* dated 30 *Azar, Ilahi* 12/12 *Zilhijja*, 1026 A.H./11 December 1617 A.D. prepared in the *chauki* of *Hakim* Masihuz Zaman[1], the *risala* of Sayyid Ahmad Qadiri and *waqia nawisi* of Hari Rai, giving details of the grant referred to above. There are notes under the signatures of different officials like Itimadud Daulah, Diyanat Khan[2], etc., and eight seals of Ram Rai, Sayyid Ahmad, Salim Ali and others. There is also an endorsement under the signatures of Itimadud Daulah to the effect that it has been mentioned in the *yad dasht* of Sayyid Ismail that those who have been given more than half already, in accordance with the Emperor's orders, half of the land may be restored to them and the other half may be taken away. Another endorsement gives details of the distribution of land as under:

Old Assignment

Number of assignees	Total land in *bighas*
229	27,310

Present Distribution

Assignee	Total land in *bighas*	Land taken away	Balance
Late Chandan	500	500	--
Nur Muhammad	100	100	--
Habibullah	200	100	100
Jalal	150	75	75
Daud	150	75	75

(*AS*, pp. 51-58).

4 Ardibihist, Ilahi 15/30 Jumada I, 1029 A.H./23 April 1620 A.D.

236. Copy of a *farman* of Jahangir addressed to the *karoris* states that 406 *bighas* of land was held as *madad-i maash* by Sayyid Shah Muhammad, son of Sayyid Mansur, *mujawir* of Ajmer who waited on the Emperor and explained to him his rights with the result that the Emperor has made an addition of 100 *bighas* of land to what he already possessed, i.e., in all 506 *bighas* of land. Orders the officials to hand over the possession of the land to the grantee and his sons from the beginning of *rabi Ilan-il* as *madad-i maash* after measuring and consolidating it. Directs them not to exact anything from him by way of *peshkash, jaribana, zabitana, muhrana, muhassilana, daroghana, begar, shikar, deh-nimi, muqaddami, sad-doi qanungoi*, etc. Nor should they ask him for a fresh *farman* and *parwancha* every year. It bears a square seal and a *tughra* of the Emperor on the top. On the reverse is the *yad dasht* dated 16 *Mihr, Ilahi* 11/25 *Ramazan*, 1025 A.H./6 October 1616 A.D. prepared in the *risala* of Sayyid Ahmad Qadiri, *chauki* of Khwaja Ibrahim Husain and *waqia nawisi* of Abdul Wasay, giving details of grant mentioned above. There are two seals of attestation of Mufti Abdul Halim and *Qazi* Bayazid. (*AS*, pp. 88-89, *DLFMN*, p. 70).

4 Ardibihisht, Ilahi 15/30 Jumada I 1029 A.H./23 April 1620 A.D.

237. *Farman* of Jahangir addressed to the *hukkam, ummal, jagirdars* and *karoris* states that the three villages comprising 27,310 *bighas* of land had been granted as *madad-i maash* to Sayyid Abdul Jalil and others, in all 229 *mujawirs*, of the *maqbara* of Khwaja Muinud Din Chishti and each of the grantees held his share in accordance with the division made by Hasan Beg. Other details are the same as in No. 206 above. It bears the invocation *'Allahu Akbar'*, a square seal and a *tughra* of the Emperor on the top. It has the following endorsements on the reverse: *yad dasht* dated 28 *Dai*, 13/20 *Muharram*, 1027 A.H./18 January 1618 A.D., prepared in the *chauki* of Masihuz Zaman, *risala* of Sayyid Ahmad Qadiri and *waqia nawisi* of Har Rai, giving details of the grant referred to above. The *waqia nawisi* testifies the facts given therein. Itimadud Daulah underlines the need of informing the Emperor again on the subject. Diyanat Khan in his endorsement dated 25 *Shahriwar, Ilahi* 13/26 *Ramazan* 1027 A.H. /17 September 1618 A.D. in the *waqia* of Abdul Karim testifies to the fact that the Emperor has been informed again. Another endorsement of Itimadud Daulah of *rabi Bichi-il* states that the *farman* may be written. Yet another endorsement by Itimadud Daulah states that the *farman* may be entered into the *waqia*. An endorsement by Miran Sayyid Ahmad Qadiri is to the effect that the *farman* may be entered into the *waqia* under his *risala*. Another endorsement by Miran Sayyid Ahmad Qadiri states that it is mentioned in the *yad dasht* of Sayyid Ismail that those who have got more than half already, in accordance with the *farman* of Emperor, may be allowed to retain the land as usual, while others may be made to part with the rest of their land. There is a list of the grantees as also of those whose land was resumed on their deaths. (*AS*, pp. 59-65; *DLFMN*, p. 70).

12 Khurdad, Ilahi 15/29 Jumada II 1029 A.H./22 May 1620 A.D.

238. *Farman* of Jahangir to the *hukkam, ummal, jagirdars* and *karoris* states that Sayyid Hashim has informed the Emperor that the *nuzurat* of the *rauza* of Khwaja Muinud Din Chishti were divided into five and a half shares and out of it Sayyid Hashim used to get half the share. Now it is ordered that out of the six shares, he and his sons may be given half the share as usual. Directs them not to cause any harassment to him in this regard. Nor should they demand from him a fresh *farman* or *parwancha* every year. It bears the invocation *'Allahu Akbar'* and a seal and a *tughra* of Jahangir on the top. (*AS*, p. 68; *DLFMN*, p. 70).

19 Amardad, Ilahi 15/11 Ramazan, 1029 A.H./31 July 1620 A.D.

239. *Farman* of Jahangir addressed to the *hukkam, ummal, jagirdars* and *karoris* says that the three villages comprising 27,310 *bighas* of land had been granted to Abdus Shakkur and others, in all 229 *mujawirs* of the tomb of Khwaja Muinud Din Chishti by way of *madad-i maash* and each of the grantees had his share in his possession according to the division made by Hasan Beg. Other details are same as given in No. 206 above. It bears a square seal and a *tughra* of Jahangir on the top. On the reverse is given the *yad dasht* dated 17 *Bahman, Ilahi* 12/8 *Safar* 1027 A.H./26 January 1618 A.D. prepared and endorsed in the *risala* of Miran Sayyid Ahmad Qadiri, in the *chauki* of Mutamid Khan and *waqia nawisi* of Abdul Karim, giving details of the grant mentioned above as also a statement of the land granted to and taken over from the grantees. (*AS*, pp. 101-04; *DLFMN*, p. 70).

19 Amardad, Julus 15/31 July 1620 A.D.

240. *Hukm* of Nur Jahan addressed to Mirza Raja Jai Singh asks him to send the entire amount of the *ijara*[1] money of *pargana* Amber[2] through Muhammad Hashim who has been specially deputed to collect the said amount by virtue of the *zimn*[3] and *tamassuk*[4] which are in his possession. Advises the Mirza to avoid all necessary delay in sending the money. It bears the seal and *tughra* of Nur Jahan. On the reverse are recorded details of the *ijara* money. (*JIH*, XXX Pt. I p. 266; *DLFMN*, p. 28).

1620 A.D.

241. *Farman* of Jahangir addressed to Maulana Bikaji, *Khatib* of Baroda, grants him 40 *bighas* of land situated in village Savad as a gift (*PC*, pp. 4-5).

15 Julus 1029-30 A.H. 1620-21 A.D.

242. *Farman* of Jahangir addressed to the officials states that 200 *bighas* of land, situated in *pargana* Fakharpur, *sarkar* Bahraich, have been granted as *madad-i maash* to *Musammat* Raj Gosain and others. The officials concerned are ordered to hand over possession of the land to the grantees, after measuring, demarcating and consolidating it. Further, they are directed not to realise any tax from them nor to demand a fresh *farman* or *parwancha from* them every year. It bears the invocation *'Allahu Akbar'*, a *tughra* and a seal of Jahangir on the top. On the reverse is the *yad dasht* prepared in the *risala* of Hajji Koka, *chauki* of Tatar Khan and *waqia nawisi* of Muhammad Momin. There are seven seals of Sayyid Ahmad, Abul Hasan, Itimadud Daulah and others. The endorsement refers to the mediation of Nur Jahan for this grant. (*MF, I*, pp. 30-31; *IHRC*, XXXII, Pt. I, p. 99).

24 Dai, Ilahi 15/20 Safar, 1030 A.H./4 January 1621 A.D.

243. *Farman* of Jahangir addressed to Rai Suraj Singh informs him that the Emperor and Prince Khurram along with the army, the retinue, treasury and other state paraphernalia have left Lahore and are proceeding towards his territory and that on Monday, the 24th *Dai*/20th *Safar* the royal troops have encamped at Nakodar. Hopes to crush the rebels with a stern hand. Orders him to guard his territories to the best of his ability and resources till the imperial army reaches there to punish the rebels. Assures him of all royal favours and rewards for his services. It bears the invocation *'Allahu Akbar'*, and the seal of Jahangir on the top. (*DLFMN*, pp. 40-41).

10 Isfandarmaz, Ilahi 15/6 Rabi II 1030 A.H./18 February 1621 A.D.

244. *Farman* of Jahangir addressed to Rai Suraj Singh informs him that the imperial army was encamped on the bank of the Chambal[1] on Sunday, the 10th of *Isfandarmaz* and that the Emperor, leaving behind the princes, arsenals and all luggage and equipage at Ujjain[2], has a mind of proceeding alone as far as Burhanpur[3] where he will halt for a day or so and then proceed to chastise the rebels with his forces. Orders him to join the Emperor with his troops and make every effort to uproot and annihilate the rebels completely. Assures him of all royal favours in return for the services which he would render after the arrival of the imperial forces there. It bears the invocation *'Allahu Akbar'* and the seal of Jahangir on the top. (*DLFMN*, p. 42).

14 Isfandarmaz, Ilahi 15/10 Rabi II 1030 A.H./23 February 1621 A.D.

245. *Farman* of Jahangir addressed to Rai Suraj Singh Bankri (Bikaneri), state that he is fully convinced of his (addressee's) exertions, devotion and attachment to the Emperor as is evident from the letters sent by *Khan-i Khanan*, the Commander-in-Chief. Informs him that he (addressee) will be duly rewarded for his meritorious services, sincerity and devotion very shortly. It bears the seal of Jahangir on the top. (*DLFMN*, p. 4).

28 Ardibihisht Ilahi 16/25 Jumada II 1030 A.H./7 May 1621 A.D.

246. *Farman* of Jahangir addressed to Rai Suraj Singh states that from the letters of Darab Khan[1] and the intelligence of the forces, he feels overjoyed to learn of the conquest of Khirki[2] by the imperial troops. Appreciating addressee's heroism, devotion, fidelity and exertions, assures him that he will be duly rewarded by raising his *mansab*. Hopes that he will make every effort to please Darab Khan by his services and pleasant behaviour. It bears the invocation *'Allahu Akbar'* and a seal of Jahangir on the top. (*DLMN*, p. 44).

7 Ramazan, 1030 A.H./16 July 1621 A.D.

247. *Parwana* of Bilaura Khan addressed to the official of *pargana* Haveli[1], *sarkar* Bahraich, orders them to restore the villages Shaida[2] and Panyanhiri[3] to Miran Sayyid Ziaud Din, originally awarded to him under the *farmans* of Akbar and Jahangir. (*COR*, I, p. 69).

9 Amardad, 16 julus/12 Ramazan, 1030 A.H./21 July 1621 A.D.

248. *Farman* of Jahangir addressed to the *hukkam* etc., informs them, that *Musammat* Daulat Bakht, widow of Shaikh Hajji, Nimat, widow of Hasan, Jao, widow of Allahadad and Alam Khatun, widow of Ibrahim have been collectively given 150 *bighas* of land. Alam Khatun would get 30 *bighas*, while each of the remaining three grantees would get 40 *bighas* of land. Orders them not to disturb the grant in any way. (*AS*, p. 126).

19 Amardad, Ilahi 16/22 Ramazan, 1030 A.H./31 July 1621 A.D.

249. *Nishan* of Prince Parwez to the officials confirms the *madad-i maash* grant of 200 *bighas* of land situated in village Asmahwan etc. *pargana* Manikpur, in favour of Sayyid Muzaffar who was already in possession of the land. The officials concerned are, therefore, ordered to deliver possession of the land in question to the grantee and his sons, after measuring, demarcating and consolidating it. They are directed not to realise any tax from them, nor to demand a fresh order for the grant from them. It bears the invocation *'Allahu Akbar'*, a *tughra* and a seal of Prince Parwez. On the reverse is the endoresement recording details of the grant. There are five seals of the officials. (*NF*, I, pp. 34-35).

9 Shahriwar, Ilahi 16/13 Shawwal, 1030 A.H./21 August 1621 A.D.

250. *Farman* of Jahangir addressed to the officials states that Bahaud Din and his sons have been granted 150 *bighas* of land situated in *pargana* Sadarpur, *sarkar* Khairabad, as *madad-i maash*. The officials concerned are ordered to deliver possession of the land in question to the grantees after measuring, demarcating and consolidating it. The grant is free from all taxes. They are directed not to demand fresh *farman* or *parwancha* from them every year. It bears the *tughra* and the square seal of Jahangir. All the four corners of the seal bear God's different names, i.e., '*Ya Nasir*', '*Ya Muin*', '*Ya Fattah*', '*Ya Hafiz*'. On the reverse is recorded the *yad dasht* prepared in the *risala* of Sayyid Ahmad Qadiri *chauki* of Tatar Khan and *waqia nawisi* of Fazlullah Najm-i Sani. There are seven seals of Sayyid Ahmad, Muhammad Sadiq Khan, Sabir Ali, Ram Rai and others. (*MF*, I. pp. 32-33).

9 Zilhijja, 1030 A.H./15 October 1621 A.D.

251. *Bainama* executed by Shaikh Tajud Din, Shaikh Abdur Rahim and Shaikh Alimud Din in respect of two *bighas* of land situated to the south of *qasba* Sandila sold to Shaikh Miyan Muhammad Nasir for Rs. 3 only. Boundaries of the land are also given. The vendors state that they have executed the sale-deed wilfully in their senses, voluntarily and without coercion. It bears the the seal of *Qazi* Muhammad Nasir, son of Muhammad Zakariya, as well as the seal of *Qazi* Abdul Hakim. It is witnessed by the notables of the town. (*COR*, II. p. 61).

14 Shahriwar, Ilahi 17/27 August 1622 A.D.

252. *Farman* of Jahangir addressed to Rai Suraj Singh, son of Rai Rai Singh states that he should immediately attend the Royal Court and a letter in this connection has already been sent. Has left Kashmir for Lahore and has sent Raja Sarang Dev[1] as a *sazawal*[2] there. It bears the invocation '*Allahu Akbar*' and seal of Jahangir on the top. The postscript states that Maluk Shah, son of Raja Sarang Dev, was afterwards appointed *sazawal*. (*DLFMN*, p. 46).

6 Zilqada 1031 A.H./2 September 1622 A.D.

253. *Farman* of Jahangir addressed to Rai Suraj Singh asks him not to proceed to the court since he is appointed to serve in the *thana* of Jalnapur near Amber, where his absence is not advisable. If he attends the court, he would be subjected to displeasure and his *jagir* would be taken away. It bears the *sarnama* '*Allahu Akbar*' and the seal of Emperor on the top. (*DLFMN*, p. 47).

11 Mihr, Ilahi 17/27 Zilqada 1031 A.H./23 September 1622 A.D.

254. *Nishan* of Sultan Parwez, son of Jahangir, addressed to the officials, agents, *mutasaddis, jagirdars, karoris of pargana* Saraisa states that by virtue of the *sanad* of Jahangir Quli Khan, Mir Sayyid Muhyud Din and his sons, had been granted 1,000 *bighas* of land situated in villages Jalalpur and Mirakpur in *pargana* Saraisa as *madad-i maash*. Confirms the grantees in the said grant as usual. Orders the officials to leave the land, as per schedule, in possession of the grantees and not to demand anything from them like *qunlugha, peshkash, begar, shikar, jaribana, zabitana, muhrana, muhassilana, daroghana deh-nimi, muqaddami, sad-doi qanungoi,* etc. Nor should they insist on a renewed *nishan* and *parwana* every year. It bears the *sarnama 'Allahu Akbar'* and a circular seal of Prince Parwez on the top. On the reverse is recorded the *yad dasht* dated 17 Amardad Ilahi 17/30 July, 1622 A.D., prepared and endorsed in the *risala* of the *wazir* .... and the *waqia nawisi* of . . . . . It bears the signatures of *Diwan* Mir Muhammad Husain. (*IHRC*, XXVI, Pt. II, pp. 2-5, *JBRS*, XLIII, p. 221).

21 Aban, Ilahi 17/9 Muharram, 1032 A.H./3 November 1622 A.D.

255. *Nishan* of Prince Khurram addressed to Rai Suraj Singh, Girdhar, Ishar Dayal, Hirdey Ram and Mukand states that Maluk Shah has brought imperial *farmans* urging them (addressees) to attend the court immediately. As they have been assigned important posts in the *thanas* of the Deccan, he is sending them the *farmans* through Shah Muhammad, a servant of the court. Asks them to deliver their representation in reply to these *farmans* to Shah Muhammad so that the same may be handed over to Maluk Shah who has to return to the court. Further, they are advised to send their *sazawals* separately to the court with their despatches on the same subject. The subject matter of their representation should be on the following lines: "Whereas the servants of the court of the glorious, victorious and triumphant Emperor have appointed us on important posts in the *thanas* of this *suba* and believing that the welfare of the State and the good of the government lie in our remaining here, we have sent the best of the faithfuls, to the heaven resembling court. We are, therefore staying here, till we receive reply to our representations." It bears the seal of Prince Khurram on the top. (*DLFMN*, pp. 48-49).

5 Dai, Ilahi 17/ 22 Safar, 1032 A.H./16 December 1622 A.D.

256. ***Nishan*** of Prince Parwez addressed to the *mutasaddis* and other officers of *pargana* Maner[1], *sarkar* Bihar, directs them to allow Shaikh Muhammad Mubark and Shaikh Sultan Muhammad to remain in possession of the two villages, namely Sharfuddinpur and Mustafapur. The order was passed by Prince Parwez on the representation of Shaikh Muhammad Mubarak and Shaikh Sultan Muhammad who had complained to the Prince to the effect that two aforesaid villages belonging to them had been included by Dilawar Khan in his *jagir*. (*JBRS*, XLIII, pp. 220-221).

1 Rabi I 1032 A.H./24 December 1622 A.D.

257. ***Parwana*** of Bilaura Khan addressed to the officials of *pargana* Bahraich directs them to restore village Panyanhari in Mubarakpur *pargana* Bahraich to Miran Sayyid Ziaud Din Muhammad to whom it was awarded by Akbar, but part of it was seized by the previous officials. On the reverse, there are three small seals, one of them being of Fath Chand. Other seals are not legible. There are endorsements relating to the grant in question and a note in Devanagari script as well. (*COR*, I. p. 67).

c 1622 A.D.[1]

258. *Farman* of Jahangir addressed to Prince Khurram disapproves the step the Prince has taken by raising the standard of revolt against him for the sake of the throne. Such an action is unworthy of a son like him. If he is ambitious to wield the sword and conquer countries, it will be far better for him to lead an expedition against Shah Abbas because the inhabitants of Qandhar have violated their obligations towards him (Jahangir). Advises him to be faithful and loyal to him as a son ought to be. (*JPHS*, II Pt. I, 303-4).

13 Bahman, Ilahi 17/22 January 1623 A.D.

259. *Nishan* of Prince Khurram addressed to the *hukkam, ummal, jagirdars and karoris* of *Haveli* Ahmadabad informs them that *mauza* Midra, *pargana* Haveli Ahmadabad, yielding an annual income of Rs. 2,000 has been bestowed upon Jan Beg and his sons from the beginning of *rabi Tanguz-il* as *inam*. Orders them to hand over possession of the village to the grantees and not to molest or harass him for *malujihat, ikhrajat, sairjihat, qanungoi, muqaddami, desai* and all *takalif-i diwani*. Further, they are forbidden not to demand a renewed *nishan* and a *parwancha* from him every year. It bears the *sarnama* '*Allahu Akbar*' a *tughra* and a seal of the Prince on the top. On the reverse is *yad dasht* which was recorded in the *risala* of Muhammad Taqi and *waqia nawisi* of Muhammad Muhsin Nizamul Mulki on *Marispand* 29 *Azar Ilahi* 17 Wednesday 7 Safar 1032 A.H. 12/December, 1622 A.D. It mentions some details of the grant and bears endorsements of Jumadatul Mulki, Madarul Mahami, and Khwaja Jan. It also bears several seals one of them being of Abdullah. (*MA*, pp. 14-15).

6 Bahman, Julus 17/15 January 1623 A.D.

260. *Nishan* of Prince Shahryar addressed to Mirza Jai Singh informs the Mirza that Lokman Dass is appointed *karori* at Dausa and orders him to render all possible help to him and communicate his progress. It bears the seal of Prince Shahryar. On the reverse is recorded the *waqia* of Amir Beg. (*DLFMN*, p. 28 *JIH*, XXXVI. Pts 1-3, pp. 266-67).

15 Bahman, Ilahi 17/24 January 1623 A.D.

261. *Nishan* of Prince Shahryar addressed to Rai Suraj Singh informs him that the Emperor has been duly apprised of his representation. Orders him to set out immediately with forces and equipment. It bears the invocation, *'Allahu Akbar'* and the seal of Prince Shahryar. (*DLFMN*, p. 45).

17 Bahman, Julus 17/ 26 January 1623 A.D.

262. *Farman* of Jahangir addressed to Mirza Raja Jai Singh states that he looks upon the Mirza as a very useful personage of the court. Is pleased to know that a battalion of Rajputs is stationed with him to give necessary help to the Emperor. Assures all favours and bounties to the participating Rajputs. Commands him to come with all his forces. It bears the name of Abul Hasan, *waqia nawis*. (*JIH*, Vol. XXXVI, Pts. 1-3, p. 267; *DLFMN*, p. 1).

17 Julus/1031-32 A.H./1622-23 A.D.

263. *Farman* of Jahangir addressed to the officials of *pargana* Panipat[1], *sarkar* Delhi, informs them that a grant of land measuring 130 *bighas* situated in *pargana* Panipat, *sarkar* Delhi, is conferred upon Amina, daughter of Shaikh Abdur Rahim, as *madad-i maash*. Orders them to hand over possession of the land to the grantee and forbids them to levy any tax on her. *(CDMA*, p. 25).

5 Shaban, Julus 18/25 May 1623 A.D.

264. *Parwana* of an official of Jahangir confirms grant of 55 *bighas* of land, situated in village Chak Saleha, *pargana* Bishara, in the name of *Musammat* Kabak Sultan, and her sons with directions to hand over possession of the same. It bears an illegible seal. (*SFSP*, p. 106).

17 Tir, Ilahi 18/9 Ramazan, 1032 A.H./28 June 1623 A.D.

265. *Farman* of Jahangir addressed to Raja Sur (Singh) states that Behzad and Alaud Din, while coming from Sirsa, lodged a complaint in the court to the effect that Askaran, Kesho Das and others of the Kandlot and Joya clans of *pargana* Bhatner, had raided and looted their villages and murdered Rai Jallu and others. Orders him (addressee) to punish the miscreants and recover the looted property from them and return it to the owners. It bears the invocation *'Allahu Akbar'* and the seal of Jahangir on the top. (*DLFMN*, p. 51).

8 Amardad, Julus 18/21 July 1623 A.D.

266. *Farman* of Jahangir addressed to Mirza Raja Jai Singh and Girdhar Nagar Bahadur[1] jointly, appreciates their devotion and affection referred to in the letter received from Prince Parwez and Mahabat Khan. Expresses his pleasure at the excellent work done by them. (*JIH*, XXXVI, Pts. 1-3, p. 267).

18 Amardad, Julus 18/31 August 1623 A.D.

267. *Farman* of Jahangir addressed to Raja Jai Singh appreciates his services and advises him not to act against the wishes of Prince Parwez and Mahabat Khan. (*DLFMN*, p. 1).

Shahriwar, Ilahi 18/August-September 1623 A.D.

268. *Farman* of Jahangir addressed to the *hukkam, ummal, jagirdars, karoris* of the empire states that by virtue of a grant of 30 *bighas* of land situated in *pargana* Panipat, *sarkar* Delhi, has been bestowed upon *Musammat* Aur Bano, daughter of Mubarak as *madad-i maash* from the beginning of *kharif* of *Qui-il*. Orders the officials to measure and consolidate the land and deliver its possession to the grantees. The grant being free from all taxes, the officials are instructed not to impose on her any tax like *qunlugha, peshkash, jaribana, muhassilana, zabitana, muhrana, daroghana, begar, shikar, deh-nimi, muqaddami, sad-doi qanungoi*, etc. Nor should they ask her to produce renewed *farman* and *parwancha* every year. It bears the *sarnama 'Allahu Akbar'* a *tughra* and a square seal of Jahangir on the top. On the reverse is a *zimn* giving details of the grant. There are several illegible seals. (*FS*, pp. 48-50).

Pre-1623 A.D.

269. *Hukm* of Maryam Zamani Wali Nimat Begum[1] addressed to Sayyid . . . . informs the addressee that Mudabbir Beg, one of the courtiers, has represented that he held a *jagir* in the *pargana* Chaupala[2], *sarkar* Sambhal, in lieu of his pay but Suraj Mal, *zamindar*, has embezzled and usurped the revenue thereof. Asks the addressee to inquire into the matter and get all the dues and arrears paid to Mudabbir Beg, and see that Suraj Mal is not allowed to misappropriate a single *fulus*[3] or *jital*[4]. It bears the invocation '*Allahu Akbar*' as also the *unwan* and seal of Maryam Zamani. (*IHRC*, VIII pp. 167-69).

10 Rabi II 1033 A.H./21 January 1624 A.D.

270. *Parwana of* Muhammad Murad to the *mutasaddis* of the villages assigned to the *rauza* of Khwaja Muinud Din Chishti states that *Musammat* Fatima, widow of Shaikh Qutb, was granted two *asar* of grain per diem from the *langar khana* of the *rauza* by way of *madad-i maash* in accordance with the *parwana* issued by the late Itimadud Daulah. On her death, her sons have been granted one *asar* of grain per diem from the *langar khana* for their maintenance. Orders them to supply the rations to the grantees regularly and not to disobey the orders. It bears the invocation '*Allahu Akbar*' on top and a round seal of Muhammad Murad. (*AS*, p. 154).

26 Isfandarmaz, Julus 18/6 March 1624 A.D.

271. *Farman* of Jahangir addressed to Mirza Raja Jai Singh intimates that the Emperor has sent a special *khilat* for him through Ahmed Beg[1]. Advises him to carry on the duties vigorously along with Prince Parwez and Mahabat Khan. On the reverse is given the *risala* of Abul Hasan. (*JIH*, XXXVI, Pts. 1-3, p. 268; *DLFMN*, p. 1).

26 Isfandarmaz, Ilahi 18/6 March 1624 A.D.

272. *Farman* of Jahangir addressed to Rai Suraj Singh sends a winter *khilat* through Muttalib in token of his services. Asks him to carry out his duties in collaboration with Prince Parwez and Mahabat Khan. It bears the invocation '*Allahu Akbar*' and the seal of Jahangir on the top. (*DLFMN*, p. 50).

8 Jumada II 1033 A.H./18 March 1624 A.D.

273. *Chaknama* says that in compliance with the *farman* of Jahangir and *parwancha* of Itimadud Daulah and Saif Khan[1] and *taliqa* bearing the seal of Mirza Muhammad Qasim, 100 *bighas* of land situated in the vicinity of *qasba* Navsari, *sarkar* Surat, duly measured by *gaz-i Ilahi* consolidated and demarcated by Mirza Muzaffar Husain and Khwaja Lal Chand, *Diwan*, the *desais*, the *muqddams*, ryots and residents of the area, have been bestowed upon Mulla Jamasp and Mulla Hoshang, the Parsis, with children, on the 8th *Jumada* II 1033 A.H./18 March 1624 A.D., as *madad-i maash*. It bears the *sarnama 'Allahu Akbar'* on top. Details of the boundaries are given and list of wittnesses is also attached. A portion of it is found in Gujarati. (*JBRAS*, No. LXXI, Vol. XXV, 1917-18, pp. 464-72).

3 Shaban, 1033 A.H./11 May 1624 A.D.

274. *Nishan* of Prince Khurram addressed to the officials renews the grant of village Chak Nasser situated in *pargana* Saraisa, *sarkar* Hajipur, *suba* Bihar, in the name of Maulana Zia and his sons as *madad-i maash*. Orders the officials concerned to deliver possession of the land to the grantees and not to demand land revenue or any other tax from them. It bears the seal of Prince Khurram as also other illegible seals. (*SFSP*, p. 19).

24 Amardad, Ilahi 19/ 5 August 1624 A.D.

275. *Farman* of Jahangir addressed to Rai Suraj Singh, states that he has learnt from the despatches of Prince Parwez as well as those of Mahabat Khan of the Rai's faithfulness to the Government; his meritorious services and exertions which he had to undergo in the rainy season to appear before the Prince at Allahabas (Allahabad). Orders him to extend wholehearted cooperation and help in uprooting that ungrateful and unfortunate person. It bears the invocation '*Allahu Akbar*' and the seal of the Emperor on the top. (*DLFMN*, pp. 52-53).

17 Ramazan, 1033 A.H./23 June 1624 A.D.

276. *Nishan* of Prince Khurram addressed to the officials states that Shaikh Abdus Samad and Shaikh Muhammad were granted 400 *bighas* of land situated in villages Rampur etc. *pargana* Haveli Hajjipur, *sarkar* Hajipur, *suba* Bihar by virtue of the *farman* of Jahangir as *madad-i maash*. On the death of Shaikh Abdus Samad the matter was brought to the notice of the Emperor. The imperial orders were issued to the effect that the said grant should be renewed and the share of the deceased be released to *Musammat* Bibi Sharifa and Bibi Fatima, heirs of the deceased Abdus Samad. The officials concerned are directed to hand over possession of the land to the grantees. The grant being rent-free the grantees should not be asked to pay the land revenue or any other tax. (*SFSP*, p. 10).

14 Aban, Julus 19/26 October 1624 A.D.

277. *Farman* of Jahangir addressed to Mirza Raja Jai Singh states that *Khan-i Khanan* has informed the Emperor of the Mirza's victory over *Bidaulat*[1]. Sends a *khilat* and a horse on the occasion. It bears the seal of the Emperor on the top. On the reverse is recorded the *risala* of Abul Hasan and the *waqia-nawisi* of Jafar. (*JIH*. XXXVI Pts. 1-3, pp. 267-68; *DIFMN*, p. 1).

23 Khurdad, Ilahi 20/2 June, 1625 A.D.

278. *Nishan* of Prince Parwez addressed to the officials of *parganas* Shah Hijur and Maner, *sarkar* Bihar, confirms Shaikh Muhammad Ashraf, son of Shaikh Muhammad Hafiz, and others, the descendants of Makhdum Shaikh Yahya Maneri, in the previous grant of *madad-i maash* land including the groves situated in the said *pargana*. Instructs the officials not to interfere with the said grant. (*JBRS*, XLIII, p. 221).

7 Tir, Julus 20/18 June 1625 A.D.

279. *Farman* of Jahangir addressed to Mirza Raja Jai Singh directs the Mirza to act according to the instructions of *Khan-i Jahan*[1] who is appointed guardian of the Prince and Commander-in-Chief of the Deccan. On the reverse is given the *risala* of Abul Hasan.
P.S. Sends a *khilat* for the rainy season. It bears the seal of Jahangir. (*JIH*, XXXVI Pts. 1-3; pp. 268-69; *DLFMN*. p. 1).

6 Shahriwar, Ilahi 20/18 August 1625 A.D.

280. *Farman* of Jahangir addressed to Raja Jai Singh asks the Raja to follow the instructions of *Khan-i Jahan* who has been appointed Commander-in-Chief and tutor to the Prince (Parwez). Warns him that anyone having any concern with the *Khan-i Khanan* will lose his *jagir* and incur suitable punishment. (*JIH*, XXXVI Pts. 1-3, p. 269; *DLFMN*, p. 2).

6 Shahriwar, Ilahi 20/18 August 1625 A.D.

281. *Farman* of Jahangir addressed to Rai Suraj Singh informs that the *Khan-i Khanan* has been ordered to proceed to Bengal immediately and the exalted *mansab* of the tutor to the Prince and the command of the victorious army have been bestowed upon the *Khan-i Jahan*. If anyone, hereafter, visits the house of the *Khan-i Khanan* and acts upon his advice, he would not only be dismissed from the *jagir* and *mansab* but would also be awarded exemplary punishment. It bears the seal of the Emperor. (*DLFMN*, p. 58).

24 Shahriwar, Ilahi 20/5 September 1625 A.D.

282. *Farman* of Jahangir addressed to Mirza Raja Jai Singh informs him that his indifference towards the *Khan-i Jahan* has caused to the Emperor displeasure. Orders him to rejoin *Khan-i Jahan* immediately and warns him that if anyone behaves in the like manner in future, he will be deprived of his *jagir* and *mansab*. (*JIH*, XXXVI, Pts. 1-3, p. 269; *DLFMN*, p. 2).

3 Aban, Ilahi 20/15 October 1625 A.D.

283. *Farman* of Jahangir addressed to Rai Suraj Singh states that he has learnt of his devotion and sincerity for the Emperor from the letter of Fidai Khan. Directs him to obey *Khan-i Jahan* and discharge his duties faithfully. It bears the seal of Jahangir on the top. (*DLFMN*, p. 59).

3 Aban, Julus 20/15 October 1625 A.D.

284. *Farman* of Jahangir addressed to Mirza Raja Jai Singh acknowledges receipt of the Mirza's petition through Fidai Khan reflecting his attitude of love, affection and obedience. Directs him to consider the *Khan-i Jahan* as the virtual commander of the royal army and obey his orders faithfully. On the reverse is given the *risala* of Abul Hasan. (*JIH*, XXXVI, Pts. 1-3. pp. 269-70).

9 Aban, Julus 20/21 October 1625 A.D.

285. *Farman* of Jahangir addressed to Mirza Raja Jai Singh states that he has learnt from Fidai Khan about the meritorious services rendered by the Mirza. Directs him to join the expedition and not to allow himself to be misguided by certain persons. (*JIH*, XXXVI Pts. 1-3; 268; *DLFMN*, p. 1).

11 Aban, Julus 20/23 October 1625 A.D.

286. *Hukm* of Nur Jahan addressed to Mirza Raja Jai Singh states that the Empress is highly pleased to learn through Fidai Khan that the Mirza has detached himself from Mahabat Khan. Sends her blessing and wishes that the Mirza should always behave in like manner in future. Advises him to follow *Khan-i Jahan* and assures him of her daily increasing favours. (*JIH*, XXXVI, Pts. 1-3, pp. 269; *DLFMN*, p. 28).

30 Aban, Ilahi 20/11 November 1625 A.D.

287. *Farman* of Jahangir addressed to Raja Jai Singh informs the Raja that *Khan-i Jahan* has been appointed tutor and guardian to the Prince (Parwez) and advises him to work according to the said Khan's instructions. (*DLFMN*, p. 2).

30 Aban, Julus 20/11 November 1625 A.D.

288. *Farman* of Jahangir addressed to Mirza Raja Jai Singh informs that Fidai Khan has been sent to pacify the people. He should be obeyed in all respects. (*JIH*, XXXVI, Pts. 1-3, p. 270; *DLFMN*, p. 2).

30 Aban, Julus 20/11 November 1625 A.D.

289. *Hukm* of Nur Jahan addressed to Mirza Raja Singh to the same effect as 287 above. (*DLFMN*, p. 28).

7 Rabi I 1035 A.H./27 November 1625 A.D.

290. *Sanad* issued by Fazil Khan[1] to the *mutasaddis* and *gumashtas* of *jagirdars* and *karoris* of *pargana* Ajmer states that the grant of 1,796 *bighas* of land situated in *mauza* Nandla has been made to Sayyid Hashim, etc., by virtue of the imperial *farman*. The *mutasaddis* after measuring, consolidating and demarcating the land, have delivered its possession to the grantee. Orders them not to interfere with the grant on account of the death of any grantee and not to harass the *muzari* for any *hububat*[2] like *kah charai* etc. It bears the invocation '*Allahu Akbar*' on the top and a round seal of Fazil Khan on the right-hand margin. (*AS*, p. 154; *NRPRI*, Pt. I, p. 52).

20 Dai, Ilahi 20/31 December 1625 A.D.

291. *Nishan* of Prince Khurram addressed to Mirza Raja Jai Singh states that Ram Kishan waited on the Emperor and reported of the Mirza's love, regard and affection for the Prince. The Rajputs have been always faithful to the Mughals. Assures the Mirza that he will be treated in the same way as Man Singh. Directs the Mirza to look upon Gopal Das as a trustee of the Emperor and show him due honour and respect. (*JIH*, XXXIV, Pts. 1-3; pp. 270-71; *DLFMN*, p. 28).

20 Dai, Ilahi 20/3 January 1626 A.D.

292. *Hukm* of Nur Jahan addressed to Raja Jai Singh sends a *khilat* with Khwaja Raz Bhan and assures him of Her Majesty's gradually increasing favours. (*DLFMN*, p. 28).

1625 A.D.

293. *Sanad* addressed to Bibi Amatul Azis, wife of Sayyid Shukrullah, grants 140 *bighas* of land in village Savad, Baroda. It bears the seal of Adul Hasan, *Qazi* of Baroda. (*PC*, pp. 6-7).

23 Dai, Ilahi 20/3 January 1625 A.D.

294. *Parwana* of an official of Jahangir addressed to the subordinate officials states that *500 bighas* of land situated in *pargana* Hajipur are granted to *Musammat* Khadija Begi, *Kooch* Mihr Ali *Saldoz* and *Musammat* Makh Bega, daughter of Taiyab Khan, *Kooch* Muhammad Ali, with (her) son Muhammad Yar as *madad-i maash* in accordance with the *farman* dated the 3 *Mihr, Ilahi* 11/25 September 1616 A.D. It bears an illegible seal. (*SFSP*, p. 115).

17 Bahman, Julus 20/8 Jumada I 1035 A.H./26 January 1626 A.D.

295. *Farman* of Jahangir addressed to Mirza Raja Jai Singh appreciates the services rendered by the Mirza to Fidai Khan. Directs him to work in consultation with the Prince and *Khan-i Jahan*. On the reverse is given the *risala* of Abul Hasan. (*JIH*, XXXVI Pts. 1-3 p. 270; *DLFMN*, p. 2).

17 Bahman, Ilahi 20/8 Jumada I 1035 A.H./26 January 1626 A.D.

296. *Farman* of Jahangir addressed to Rai Suraj Singh states that Fidai Khan has apprised the Emperor about the devotion and sincerity of the addressee. Advises him to look upon the Prince as his best well-wisher and to act upon the advice and suggestions of the Prince and *Khan-i Jahan*. It bears the invocation '*Allahu Akbar*' on the top. (*DLFMN*, p. 56).

15 Farwardin, Julus 21/25 March 1626 A.D.

297. *Farman* of Jahangir addressed to Mirza Raja Jai Singh states that the Emperor is highly pleased to note the Mirza's faithful and good conduct. Wishes the Mirza to act in the like manner in future so as to win the royal favours. (*JIH*, XXXVI Pts. 1-3, p. 270; *DLFMN*, p. 2).

17 Farwardin, Ilahi 21/27 March 1626 A.D.

298. *Farman* of Jahangir addressed to Raja Kalyan[1] informs him that *Khan-i Khanan* and Fidai Khan have raised the standard of revolt against the Emperor and have fled. Orders him to round them up and send them to the imperial court. If he shows any slackness in capturing them, he will have to bear the consequences. It bears the seal and *tughra* of the Emperor on the top. On the reverse are recorded the *risala* of Abul Hasan, and *waqia nawisi* of Sadiq. (*NFEJ*).

17 Farwardin, Ilahi 21/27 March 1626 A.D.

299. *Farman* of Jahangir addressed to Rai Suraj Singh states that Mahabat Khan who waited on the Emperor and paid his respects, is entrusted with the management of important affairs of the Empire. Has learnt from Mahabat Khan all the particulars of devotion and fidelity of the addressee and advises him (addressee) to discharge his duties faithfully. It bears the invocation '*Allahu Akbar*' and the seal of Jahangir on the top. (*DLFMN*, p. 60).

20 Farwardin, Ilahi 21/30 March 1626 A.D.

300. *Farman* of Jahangir addressed to Shaikh Farid states that it transpires from his *arzdasht* that he wants to leave Budaun and settle elsewhere. Informs him that he may settle anywhere he likes and that a grant of 4,000 *bighas* of land will be conferred upon him and his son in that *mahal* from the beginning of *kharif* of the current year. The officials, viz., *hukkam*, *ummal*, *jagirdars* and *karoris*, are therefore, ordered to measure and consolidate the land and hand over its possession to the grantee and not to demand any tax like *qunlugha*, *peshkash*, *jaribana*, *muhassilana*, *zabitana*, *muhrana*, *daroghana*, *begar*, *shikar*, *deh-nimi*, *muqaddami sad-doi qanungoi*, etc., from him. Nor is he to be asked to produce a renewed *farman* and *parwancha* every year. (*FS*, pp. 50-51).

29 Farwardin, Ilahi 21/8 April 1626 A.D.

301. *Farman* of Jahangir addressed to the *hukkam*, *ummal*, *jagirdars* and *karoris* of the empire states that Father Joseph and other European Fathers have bought 12 *bighas* of land with a brick-built well and some trees in *mauza* Jumah Muhzang Hari Phalwari. Orders the officials to measure the land and deliver possession to them by way of *inam* for use as a cemetery and a garden with a well and not to harass them for any tax like *qunlugha*, *peshkash*, *jaribana*, *zabitana*, *muhassilana*, *muhrana*, *daroghana*, *begar*, *shikar*, *deh-nimi muqaddami*, *sad-doi qanungoi*, etc. Further, they need not ask them for a renewed *hukm* and *farman* every year. On the reverse is the *yad dasht* dated 26 *Isfandarmaz Ilahi 20/17 Jumada* II, 1035 A.H./17 March 1626 A.D. entered in the *risala* of *Madarul Mahham* Khwaja Abul Hasan and *waqia nawisi* of Sri Ram, touching on the details of the said grant. It bears the seal of Jauhar Mal bin Chhabildas Devisahai. (*JPHS*, V. No. 1, pp. 22-23).

23 Ardibihisht Ilahi 21/3 May 1626 A.D.

302. *Nishan* of Prince Parwez addressed to the officials of *pargana* Haveli Bihar[1], *sarkar* Bihar, conveys the confirmation of the previous grant of *madad-i maash* land situated in *pargana* Haveli Bihar, *sarkar* Bihar in favour of Shaikh Abdul Latif and Shaikh Sadrud Din, descendants of Shaikh Budh *Tabib* and others. Orders them to take necessary action in the matter. (*JBRS*, XLIII, p. 221).

15 Ramazan, 1035 A.H./31 May 1626 A.D.

303. *Tamliknama* executed by *Musammat* Bibi Sappo, daughter of Miyan Shaikh Daulat, and wife of Miyan Shah Muhammad, transfers voluntarily all her rights in a plot of land in village Samauddinpura, jointly owned by Shah Muhammad and Miyan Usman, son of Miyan Shamaud Din Ahwazi, and inherited by her husband as part of her dower, to Miyan Shaikh Abdul Halim son of Miyan Shaikh Barkhurdar. Accordingly Shaikh Abdul Halim has taken over possession of the said property. The document bears 6 seals and signatures of 20 witnessess. (*COR*, II, p. 11).

27 Khurdad, Ilahi 21/7 June 1626 A.D.

304. *Farman* of Jahangir addressed to Rai Suraj Singh informs him of the death of Ambar[1] and orders him to do his utmost to extirpate the rebel[2]. Is sending Raja Sarang Deo to impress upon him how the Emperor is absorbed in the conduct of that expedition. Informs him that he will reach Ajmer very shortly. (*DLFMN*, p. 61).

28 Khurdad Julus 21/8 June 1626 A.D.

305. *Farman* of Jahangir addressed to Mirza Raja Jai Singh informs him of Ambar's death. Asks him to take all possible steps to put down the conspiracy. States that Raja Sarang Deo, who should be considered as the Emperor's true representative, is reaching Ajmer shortly. It is expected that the Mirza Raja would act upon his advice. (*JIH*, XXXVI Pts. 1-3; p. 271; *DLFMN*, p. 3).

11 Amardad, Ilahi 21/23 July 1626 A.D.

306. *Farman* of Jahangir addressed to Rai Suraj Singh orders him to proceed immediately to the court from where he will be deputed to Multan.

P.S. Is deputing Sultan Dawar Bakhsh[1] to take revenge of his father's[2] murder by putting the rebel to sword. He (addressee), accompanied by

Prince Shahryar and an army of about 20,000 horsemen, should attack and annihilate the rebel. (*DLFMN*, p. 62).

19 Shahriwar, Ilahi 21/3 September 1626 A.D.

307. *Farman* of Jahangir addressed to Raja Jai Singh desires the Raja not to proceed to his native land as Rai Suraj Singh has been deputed to Multan. (*DLFMN*, p. 3).

24 Mihr, Ilahi 21/6 October 1626 A.D.

308. *Hukm* of Nur Jahan addressed to Raja Jai Singh advises him to be rest assured on all ground and desires him to communicate everything to the royal court, but not to act against the royal orders. (*JIH*, XXXVI Pts. 1-3, p. 271; *DLFMN*, p. 29).

27 Mihr, Ilahi 21/9 October 1626 A.D.

309. *Farman* of Jahangir addressed to Rai Suraj Singh states that he has deputed Mahabat Khan to Thatta to fight against the rebel and orders him also to reach Burhanpur immediately as his presence there is very essential. It bears the invocation '*Allahu Akbar*' and the seal of the Emperor on the top. (*DLFMN*, p. 63).

11 Aban. . . . 21/24 October 1626 A.D.

310. *Farman* of Jahangir addressed to Rai Suraj Singh states that he has ordered the royal servants and the *zamindars* to annihilate Mahabat Khan Kodhi and if he or his men enter the territory of the addressee, they ought to be killed and the property seized from the rebels will be bestowed upon the addressee. If anyone of the followers of the rebel leader comes to the court or retires to his place, his sons should be regarded as pardoned. It bears a seal of the Emperor on the top. (*DLFMN*, p. 64).

11 Aban. . . . 21/24 October 1626 A.D.

311. *Hukm* of Nur Jahan addressed to Rai Suraj Singh asks him to obey the *farman* issued by the royal court faithfully and should expect favours in his service, devotion and sincerity. It bears the seal of Nur Jahan. (*DLFMN*, p. 65).

10 Rabi I 1036 A.H./19 November 1626 A.D.

312. Sale-Deed executed by *Musammat* Bibi Haibat, daughter of Miyan Madan, in respect of half of the house, sold to Miyan Abdul Halim, son of Miyan Shaikh Abdul Hamid for Rs. 2 only. It bears three illegible seals and signatures of witnesses and contains description of the boundaries of the said house. (*COR*, II p. 61).

14 Azar. . . . 21/25 November 1626 A.D.

313. *Farman* of Jahangir addressed to Rai Suraj Singh reminds him of his promise that he would return to Burhanpur immediately on receipt of the *farman* which has already been issued. Orders him to reach Burhanpur at once in order to join *Khan-i Jahan*. It bears the invocation '*Allahu Akbar*' and the seal of Jahangir on the top. (*DLFMN*, pp. 67, 74).

17 Dai, Ilahi[1] 21/28 December 1626 A.D.

314. *Hukm* of Nur Jahan addressed to Raja Jai Singh informs him that his request to attend the court could not be acceded to owing to the grave circumstances of war. Directs him to stay where he is. (*JIH*, XXXVII Pts. 1-3, pp. 271-72; *DLFMN*, p. 29).

19 Dai. . . . 21/30 December 1626 A.D.

315. *Farman* of Jahangir addressed to Rai Suraj Singh states that already a *farman* has been issued that he should reach Burhanpur as soon as possible. Informs him that Jamal Muhammad has been deputed to wait on him and that he should leave for Burhanpur immediately along with Jamal Muhammad. Has sanctioned the proposal of an increase in the grant and confers the former *jagir* upon the addressee. It bears the seal of the Emperor on the top. (*DLFMN*, p. 66).

1626 A.D.[1]

316. *Farman* of Jahangir addressed to the officers of the province of Gujarat informs them that Shantidas *Jawahari*[2], a resident of Gujarat, has been placed under the protection of Nizamud Din Asaf Khan[3], enabling him to offer gifts and presents and every kind of jewellery which he might procure for Asaf Khan. Orders them not to obstruct him (Shantidas) in any way. It bears the seal and *tughra* of Jahangir. (*IMFG*, p. 30; *JUB*, IX, Pt. I, July 1940, p. 20.)

7 Isfandarmaz, Julus 21/15 February 1627 A.D.

317. *Parwancha* of Fazil Mir-i Adl[1] addressed to the *gumashtas* of the *mutasaddis* of *qasba* Navsari, *sarkar* Surat states that since long Mehr *Tabib* held 50 *bighas* of land having trees of *khajuri* thereon and now whereas Qiam Parsi[2] attended on the Emperor and stated the real circumstances, the imperial orders are issued to the effect that the land in question with trees thereon be confirmed and settled on Qiam and his sons as *madad-i maash* from the beginning of *rabi* of *Tawishqan-il*. Orders the said officials to measure, demarcate and consolidate the land and leave the same in possession of the grantees and not to demand a renewed *parwancha* from them every year so that they may utilise the proceeds thereof in providing the means of subsistence and occupy themselves in praying for the perpetuation of His Majesty's everlasting empire. It bears the invocation '*Allahu Akbar*' on the top and three seals, one of which being that of Fazil. (*SPH*, pp. 176-77).

Roz (Isfandarmaz) Julus 21/17 February 1627 A.D.

318. *Farman* of Jahangir addressed to Mirza Raja Jai Singh states that Kutch Singh and others sought the permission of the Prince to leave for home and that Rai Suraj Singh has been deputed to Multan. Urges the Mirza to perform his duties sincerely and vigorously. On the reverse is recorded the *risala* of Mahabat Khan. (*JIH*, XXXVI, Pts. 1-3, p. 268).

22 Ardibihisht, 22 Julus/26 Shaban, 1036 A.H./2 May 1627 A.D.

319. *Hukm* of Nur Jahan addressed to Sher Khan[1] states that *Hakim* Ruhullah has submitted petition to the Empress to the effect that he has not yet been given possession of the two out of the total number of villages granted to him (*Hakim* Rahullah) by way of *madad-i maash* by the royal *farman* and that the addressee has also imprisoned his writers. Condemning this action of Sher Khan, orders him to deliver possession of the two villages to the grantee in entirety immediately on receipt of the orders with effect from *rabi, Pars-il*. And if his men have misappropriated a portion of the harvest in question, it should be returned to the grantee and he should see that in future no complaint is heard in this regard. It bears the invocation '*Allahu Akbar*' and a seal and a *tughra* of Nur Jahan on the top. (*IHRC*, XXXV, Pt. II, p. 199).

4 Khurdad, Ilahi 22/10 Ramazan 1036 A.H./15 May 1627 A.D.

320. *Farman* of Jahangir addressed to the officials states that Shaikh Ahmad has been granted 200 *bighas* of land in village Haibatpur[1], *pargana* Ander, *sarkar* Saran, *suba* Bihar as *madad-i maash*. The grant being rent-free the officials should not ask the grantee to pay any tax whatsoever. It bears a number of illegible seals. (*SFSP*, pp. 1, 5).

26 Khurdad, Ilahi 22/6 June 1627 A.D.

321. *Farman* of Jahangir addressed to the officials states that a grant of 275 *bighas* of land situated in village Koela Mahal, *pargana* Bisara, *suba* Bihar, has been conferred upon Shihabud Din, son of Sayyid Jalal as *madad-i maash*. Orders the officials concerned to deliver possession of the land to the grantee and demand no dues from him. It bears illegible seals. (*SFSP*, p. 14).

15 Shahriwar, Julus 22/28 August 1627 A.D.

322. *Farman* of Jahangir addressed to the *hukkam, ummal, jagirdars, karoris*, etc. of Ajmer states that *mauza* Gilota, *pargana* Nirania, *sarkar* and *suba* Ajmer, yielding *jama* of Rs. 750 *per annum* has been granted to Shaikh Alimud Din, nephew of Khwaja Husain as *madad-i maash*. Orders the officials to deliver possession of the village to the grantee, realise no tax from him and not to press him to produce a renewed *farman* every year. It bears a *tughra* and a seal of Jahangir on the top. On the reverse is recorded a *yad dasht* dated Mihr julus 13/15 *Shawwal* prepared in the *risala* of Musavi Khan, *waqia nawisi* of Ali Naqi, giving details of the grant. There are seals of the departments concerned. (*FS*, pp. 8-9).

8 Mihr, (22)/21 September 1627 A.D.

323. *Farman* of Jahangir addressed to Rai Suraj Singh acknowledges receipt of his letter and informs him that the whole of his *jagir* has been allotted to him in his native place in lieu of his salary and the necessary *sanads* in respect of the said *jagir* will be sent to him through his *wakil*. It bears the *sarnama* '*Allahu Akbar*' on the top. (*DLFMN*, p. 73).

16 Mihr. . . . 22/29 September 1627 A.D.

324. *Farman* of Jahangir addressed to *chaudharis, qanungos, headmen*, etc. of *pargana* Nagore, states that the said *pargana* and other places have been conferred upon Rai Suraj Singh as *jagir* from the beginning of *kharif* of *Tawishaqan-il* on the dismissal of Amar Singh. Orders them to deliver possession of the said *jagir* to him and render him all accounts of the revenues from harvest to harvest and year to year. It bears the seal of the Emperor on the top. (*DLFMN*, p. 68).

20 Aban. . . . 22/2 November 1627 A.D.

325. *Nishan* of Prince Dawar Bakhsh addressed to Rai Suraj Singh informs him of the death of Jahangir and of his own succession to the throne on the 17 *Aban*. Has issued *farman* to all the servants of the empire urging them to discharge their duties honestly and zealously and to send news about their respective places to the royal court regularly. Has given some verbal orders about certain matters to his (addressee's) agents which he (addressee) should obey without hesitation. It bears a seal of Dawar Bakhsh on the top. (*DLFMN*, p. 69).

24 Aban, Julus 22/6 November 1627 A.D.

326. *Nishan* of Prince Dawar Bakhsh addressed to Mirza Raja Jai Singh informs the Mirza of the sad demise of Jahangir and adds that with support of Nur Jahan Begam and the nobles of the court he ascended the throne on the 17th *Aban*. Advises him (Mirza) to shoulder his responsibilities in right earnest and to hope for the fulfilment of his ambitions. All *wakils* have been informed accordingly. (*JIH*, XXXVI Pts. 1-3, p; 272. *DLFMN*, p. 29).

21 Rabi I 1037 A.H./20 November 1627 A.D.

327. *Nishan* of Prince Khurram addressed to Raja Jai Singh, informs the Raja of the death of Emperor Jahangir and his departure from the Deccan towards Agra to ascend the throne. (*DLFMN*, p. 29).

Rabi I, Julus 22/December 1627 A.D.

328. *Nishan* of Prince Khurram addressed to Mirza Raja Jai Singh informs the Mirza of his accession to the throne on the 10 Azar/22 November 1627 A.D. Directs the Mirza to be all the more earnest and zealous about the performance of his duties and to be loyal and faithful to the Prince. (*JIH*, XXXVI Pts. 1-3; p. 272).

2 Rabi II 1037 A.H./1 December 1627 A.D.

329. *Hukmnamah* of *Khan-i Jahan* addressed to the *chaudharis*, *qanungos*, etc of Narot informs them that the fort of Narot has been conferred upon Raja Sur from the beginning of the autumn crop of *Tawishqan-il*. Orders them (addressees) to submit all accounts of the revenues to him regularly without hesitation. It bears the invocation '*Allahu Akbar*' and the seal of *Khan-i Jahan* on the top. (*DLFMN*, p. 70).

1627. A.D.

330. *Ṣanad* of the *suba* of Ahmadabad addressed to Bhikaji, *Khatib* of Baroda, states that 40 *bighas* of land situated near village Savad are granted to him. (*PC*, pp. 6-7).

3 Bahman, Ilahi 22/16 Jumada 1 1037 A.H./13 January 1628 A.D.

331. *Hasbul-Hukm* addressed to the officers of *pargana* Bisara orders them to measure the specified land situated in village Koela Mahal and deliver possession thereof to Shihabud Din, son of Sayyid Jalal, as *madad-i maash* as per *farman* of the Emperor (321). It bears an illegible seal. (*SFSP*, p. 208).

APPENDIX I

SUR DOCUMENTS

18 Shaban 947 A.H./18 December 1540 A.D.

332. *Sanad* of Sher Shah grants 60 *bighas* of land situated in village Hamidpur, *pargana* Sandila, as *madad-i maash* to Shaikh Mahmud on condition that the grantee leads a pious life, undertakes regular practice in archery to counteract malfactors creating disturbance and punish them in co-operation with the government officials. Advises him to offer prayers five times daily, to discharge ten arrows along with the men of his establishment, after the afternoon prayer and to assist the *shiqdar* in revenue collection. It bears the round seal of Sher Shah on the top. It is biscriptual. The upper portion is in *taliq* while the lower one is in Kaithi. (*MF*, I, p. 1).

24 Rajab 948 A.H./13 November 1541 A.D.

333. *Farman* of Sher Shah addressed to the *shiqdars* and *amils* of *pargana* Dhakdhar[1] intimates them that grant of land measuring 600 *bighas* situated in *mauza* Sotiana, *pargana* Dhakdhar has been in possession of *Qazi* Abdul Halim, son of *Qazi* Abdus Samad, and *Qazi* Majdud Din *Khatib* and *Qazi* Imad, *Hafiz*, from the times of Sultan Sikandar. Confirms the grantees in the said piece of land as usual from the year 949 A.H. and orders the officials to leave possession of the land to them without any alteration and not to demand any tax from them. It bears seal of Khalil, an official of Sher Shah. It is biscriptual both in *taliq* and *Kaithi*. On the reverse is recorded an endorsement giving briefly the details of the grant. (*OCM*, May 1933, Pt. I, pp. 125-28).

Ramazan 949 A.H./December 1542-January 1543 A.D.

334. *Sale-deed* executed by Yusuf, adopted son of Amir Adho Husain (?), Bushahri, in favour of Bhoraj, son of Dhamun, *muqaddam* of village Asauli, for selling 20 *bighas* "known and reputed as *milk* and *khoti*" of village Dhauli of *qasba* Bilgram, for 100 *tanka-i Adli* including transfer of title of trees, water canals, fruit trees, tanks, *takab*, etc., but excluding mosque and graves. (*IESHR*, Vol. IV, March 1967, p. 222).

25 Jumada II 950 A.H./25 September 1543 A.D.

335. *Farman* of Sher Shah addressed to the *shiqdar* and *amils* of *pargana* Dhakdhar intimates them that by virtue of the previous grant, land measuring 400 *bighas* situated in *mauza* Magiana, *pargana* Dhakdhar, had been in possession of *Qazi* Qutb and his brothers, etc., from the time of Sultan Sikandar. Confirms the said grant to the above mentioned persons from the year 950 A.H./1543 A.D. Advises the officials to leave possession of the land to the grantees and not to demand any tax whatsoever. It bears the seal of Khalil, an official of Sher Shah. It is biscriptual both in Persian and Kaithi and departmental endorsements are recorded in the margin in Persian and Kaithi. (*OCM*, May 1933, Pt. 1, pp. 121-22).

7 Rabi I 952 A.H./9 May 1545 A.D.

336. *Farman* of Islam Shah[1] addressed to Hafiz Luffullah and Abdul Karim, grants them 48 *bighas* of land situated in *pargana* Soraon[2], Allahabad, by way of *madad-i maash*. (*NRPR*, VI, p. 116).

21 Rabi II, 952 A.H./2 July 1545 A.D.

337. *Judgment* on a complaint brought before the *Diwan-i Shara*, Ramhuapur (?) i.e., Shamsabad, by Har Singh, son of Mankiya, and Nunu, *ganwars (villagers) muqaddams* of village Papri Buzurg, *tappa* Haveli, *qasba* Shamsabad, claiming possession *(haqq-i milk) of muqaddami* of village Papri Khurd as it has been in wrongful possession of Miran Sayyid Nizam Ishaq Husain who, on his part, denies the charge and states that he is the legal owner of the *muqaddami* of the village which he purchased from Maulana Fathullah, Abdullah and Piyare, presenting in evidence the sale-deed. The *Diwan-i Shara* dismissed the complaint. It bears the seal of *Qazi* Sadrud Din and signatures of witnesses. (*IESHR*, Vol. IV, March 1967, p. 222).

21 Rabi I 957 A.H./9 April 1550 A.D.

338. *Sale-deed* executed by *Musammat* Chaunda, daughter of Buddan, wife of Phul, and *Musammat* Mubarika, daughter of Buddh, and wife of Sikandar, in favour of Mubarak son of Yusuf, son of Amir Adho Husain Bushahri for selling a plot of residential land outside the fort of *qasba* Bilgram, divided into three sub-plots for a sum of 219 *tanka-i siyah*, 19 *jital*-i and ½ *dang*[1], the price per *gaz* being 35 *jital siyah* Islamshahi. (*IESHR*, Vol. IV, March 1967, p. 223).

15 Zilqada, 963 A.H./10 September 1556 A.D.

339. *Sale-deed* executed by *Musammat* Baini Jahan wife of Hasan, in favour of Sayyid Tajud Din and Sayyid Usman, sons of Sayyid Husain Dulara, for selling 4 *biswas* out of 20 *biswas* ("known and reputed as *milk* and *khoti*") of village Pochanpur, *qasba* Bilgram for 12 silver *tankas*. The vendor has obtained the right in satisfaction of her *mihr* claim upon her deceased husband. (*IESHR*, Vol. IV, March 1967, p. 223).

APPENDIX 2

DOUBTFUL DOCUMENTS

7 Jumada II 946 A.H./20 October 1539 A.D.[1]

340. *Hukm*[2] of Prince Muhammad Askari addressed to the officials of *sarkar* Sambhal grants a village in the said *sarkar* to Shaikh Sadullah as *madad-i maash*. It bears the *sarnama* '*Huwal Ghani*' and two headings (a) '*Bafarman i* Muhammad Humayun Badshah Ghazi, and (b) '*Hukm*[3] *i zi shan* Muhammad Askari Bahadur Ghazi as also a seal of Askari on the top. There is no endorsement or seal impression of any official on the reverse. (*AIOC*, X, pp. 465-66).

21 Rabi I 948 A.H./15 July 1541 A.D.[1]

341. *Farman* of Humayun addressed to the Bohras[2] of the Ismailia community grants them permission to trade in India without any obstruction and molestation in consideration of the meritorious services rendered by them to the Emperor when he was under unfavourable circumstances. States that the Bohras attended to the Emperor, extended their wholehearted hospitality to him and furnished guides to help him when he was crossing the frontiers of India at Marwar[3]. It was drafted by Bairam Khan[4] during the course of journey and bears the *tughra* and the round seal[5] of Humayun and the *sarnama* '*Huwa*' (He) on the top. (*FS*, p. 245).

27 Zilqada 960 A.H./24 October 1553 A.D.[1]

342. *Farman* of Humayun addressed to *umra*, *wuzara*, *sudur*, *mutasaddis*, etc. of *qasba* Machhiwara[2] and Darok, *sarkar* Tatar Khan informs them that Qazi Bahaud Din, son of Qazi Allahdad, is appointed *Qazi* of *qasba* Machhiwara and *Qazi* Abdul Halim, son of *Qazi* Abdus Samad, is appointed *Khatib* of the *qasba*. Orders the said officials to co-operate with them and not to allow any one to disturb them in the discharge of their duties, viz., drafting of *sukuk* or judgements, *sijillat*[3], administration of the property of orphans, enactment of marriages, etc. Further they are enjoined to trust this *tauqi* and not to bother them for a renewed *farman* and *parwancha* every year. The incumbents of the posts are allowed to receive all dues and fees attached to the posts. It is issued from Chahar Bagh, Agra, the capital. On the reverse is the *taliqa* under the seal of Bairam Khan, dated 9 *Shawwal* 409 (960) A.H. stating that all the matters pertaining to the *shara* may be referred to the said *Qazi* and *Khatib*. It bears the *sarnama 'Allahu Akbar'*[4] on the top. (*OCM*, May, 1933, pp. 119-21).

27 Jumuda I 968 A.H./3 February 1561 A.D.

343. *Farman* of Akbar addressed to the *hukkam, ummal, mutasaddis, jagirdars, karoris,*[1] *chaudharis, qanungos*, etc. of Gurgaon[2] grants 1,431 *bighas* and 8 *biswas* of land in *qasba* Senna[3], *suba* Delhi along with an allowance of Rs. 100 in cash per annum for the *dargah* and Rs.100 per diem for *shab chiragh*[4] and *langar khana* of the shrine of Hazrat Shah Najmul Haq[5]. Instructs the officials concerned to measure and consolidate the land and hand over its possession to the custodians of the shrines along with the *saliana*[6] and *yaumiya*[7] regularly. It bears a round seal of Akbar on the top. (*FS*, pp. 41-42, *CDMA*, p. 30).

16 Rabi I 9 Ilahi 1/2 October 1564 A.D.

344. *Farman* of Akbar addressed to the *mutasaddis, karoris*[2], *chaudharis, qanungos*, etc, states that 20 *halwar* of *khartal* land in *qasba* Didwana (*sarkar* Nagore) is confirmed as *madad-i maash* in the name of Balanath Jogi and his associates. Instructs the local officials not to interfere with them nor should they demand a *parwana* in this regard every year. (*IHC*, XXXII, 1970, V. I, p. 406).

21 Zilhijja 999 A.H./30 September 1591 A.D.

345. *Farman*[1] of Raja Man Singh of Amber addressed to the *ummal*, and *mutasaddis* of *pargana* Hajipur, informs them that in view of the attestations and verifications of the late *Qazi* Yaqub and *sanads* issued by the former *hukkam*, a piece of arable land measuring 14 *bighas* situated in *mauza* Jaruha in the said *pargana* is confirmed in the names of Shaikh Bakhsh and other *mujawirs* of the *mazar* of Sayyid Muhammad and Sayyid Ahmad *alias Mamu* Bhanja[2] by way of *madad-i maash*. Orders them to hand over possession of the land to the grantees and adds that the grant is revenue-free and that there should be no demand for a renewed *parwana* every year. The document is in Persian and has its Hindi version also with some disparity[3]. There is no seal or signature of the Raja or his official. Both Persian and Hindi versions are incomplete. (*RMSA*, pp. 171-74).

9 Khurdad, Ilahi 38/20 May 1593 A.D.

346. *Farman* of Akbar addressed to the *ummal, mutasaddis, karoris, jagirdars,* and *zamindars* present and future of the empire states that Gosain Vithal Rai, resident of Gokul, has purchased land in *mauza* Jatlipura[1], situated in the *pargana* adjoining Gordhan after paying full price therefore. On this land he has constructed buildings, gardens, *kharak*[2] of cows and *karkchanas*[3] for the temple of Gordhan Nath and is residing there. The said *mauza* has been given over tax-free to the said Gosain from generation to generation. All the officials are hereby directed to leave the said village in possession of the Gosain including the land purchased. Further, they are ordered not to molest or harass him for the forbidden *abwab.* viz *malujihat, takalif-i diwani* and *matalibat-i Sultani, sair awarizat, sardarakhhti,* etc. They should not demand a renewed *farman* or *parawana* from him, so that the *Marifat Agah* Gosain may engage himself in praying for the prosperity of the eternal empire. It bears the invocations *'Allahu Akbar'* and *Huwal Ghani*[4] as also a seal of Akbar on the top. On the back are recorded a number of endoresements including that of Munim Khan.[5] (*IF*, No. IV, *NRPR*, I, Pt. II, p.76).

1 Dai, 1004 A.H.[1] 12 December 1595 A.D.

347. *Farman* of Akbar addressed to Daud bin Qutb Shah of the *jamaat*[2] of the Bohras from the capital of Lahore states that the addressee was summoned to the court in pursuance of his own wishes and stature and consideration. The *hukkam* of the cities of Gujarat, particularly of Ahmedabad and Sayyidpur, are hereby ordered not to molest him in any way on account of his *mazhab* and *millat*[3]. Nor should they harass him for *zakat* and other imposts. The houses belonging to him which were seized and sealed may be restored to him after breaking the seals and those who are empolyed by him may not be obstructed or harassed in any way. If his property has been seized, it may be restored forthwith. All the *karroris, jagirdars,* and *mutasaddis* of Gujarat are instructed to render all possible help and assistance to him and if he needs an escort the same may be furnished so that he may travel safely through the dangerous spots. The text of the *farman* ends with the formula *'Allahu Akbar'*. (*FS*. p. 246).

22 Zilada, 1011 A.H./23 April 1603 A.D.

348. *Farman* of Raja Madhav Singh of Amber addressed to the *ummal. jagirdars, chaudharis, qanungos* and *ryots* of *pargana* Baikunthpur, *sarkar* Bihar informs them that in pursuance of the *parwana* of Maharajadhiraja Shri Man Singh dated 29 *Ashri* (sic) 1009/26 *Pus* V.S. 1657/1600 A.D. provision had been made for making offerings to Sri Thakurdawara[2] in the temple of Baikunthpur and the following articles, etc. were given over to Ram Das, Lachman and Tulsi *Zunardars* as *madad-i maash* to enable them to attend to the *bhog*[3] ceremoony. 13½ seers of ...., seer of *urad*[4], 2½ seers of *dal*[5], 1 seer of cow ghee[6], Rs.36¼ in cash per year for the dresses of the Brahmins, 227 *bighas* of land, both cultivated and fallow and 6 *arat* of *anwari* (sic) and ¼ of *baratangi* (sic) per house. The same arrangement will remain in force so that the grantees may perform the *bhog* as usual. They should not be harassed for a renewed *sanad* every year. The document is a copy and is bilingual in Persian and Hindi. There are no seals[7] and no signatures. (*RMSA*, pp. 175-8).

349. *Farman* of Akbar addressed to the officials of *sarkar* of Avadh, informs them that Sayyid Mubariz and his brothers have been granted 4,000 *bighas*[1] of land situated in *pargana* Husampur, *sarkar* Avadh as *muafi* in consideration of the services rendered by Sayyid Mubariz who served in different compaigns and rendered valuable assistance in annihilating refractory elements. Orders the officials to measure and consolidate the land and hand it over to the grantees and not to demand cesses like *malujihat, ikhrajat, zabitana, jaribana, takrar-i-zaraat, saddoi qanungoi, jizya*[2], *muhtarifa, peshkash, qunlugha, daroghana, dehnimi, begar, shikar*, etc. Nor should they demand a fresh *farman* and *parwancha* every year. It ends with the formula '*Allahu Akbar*' and bears a seal dated 1196 A.H. of *Qazi* Abdul Hakim who obviously had attested the copy. (*MF*. p.12).

19 Jumada I 1019 A.H.[1]/30 July 1610 A.D.

350. *Farman* of Jahangir addressed to the *karoris, jagirdars*, and *mutasaddis* of *suba* Gujarat orders them not to cause any obstruction to Shaikh Daud Gujarati and his party which consists of educated and holy persons. They must show all respect and regard to them and those who defy the orders will be suitably punished. It bears *tughra* on the top but no seal[2]. It was prepared in the *risala* of Maulana Ali Ahmad, *chauki* of Mahtab Khan and *waqia nawisi* of Khwaja Naqi Muhammad. (*FS*, p. 247).

COMMENTARY

1

1. *Farman* (P) edict, mandate, decree, royal order, royal patent, charter, command, grant. (J.T. Platts, *Dictionary of Urdu, Classical Hindi and English,* London 1884). It is the most loosely applied term to every imperial order and missive issued by the sovereign or chancellery bearing the royal seal and the *tughra.* Its first two lines are generally abbreviated in order to distinguish it from other documents. (J.N. Sarkar *Mughal Administration,* New Delhi, 1972 pp. 152-60).

2. Zahirud Din Muhammad Babur, founder of Mughal rule in India (1526-30 A.D.)

3. *Mauza* (A). A village; hamlet; a parcel or parcels of lands having a separate name in the revenue records, and of known limits. In the 13th century it was generally used in a wide sense as a place or locality but later on it became a synonym of *deh*, or village. (W.H. Moreland, *The Agrarian System of Muslim India*, Delhi, 1958, p. 275).

4. Sahrgul Pindori. It seems to be identical with Pindori which is a village in *tahsil* Batala, district Gurdaspur, Punjab, with an area of 1,022 acres and population of 1,381. (*Census, 1971, Series 17, Gurdaspur District, Punjab*, p.228, No. 384).

5. *Pargana* (P). The Indian name for an aggregate of villages. It came into official use in the 14th century partially superseding *qasba*. (Moreland *op. cit.*, p.276). Subsequently it connoted sub-division of *zila* or district. As an administrative unit, it existed under the Sultanate. Under Akbar it was equal to a *mahal* which constituted a sub-division of a *sarkar*. (Irfan Habib, *The Agrarian System of Mughal India*, Bombay 1963, p.2).

6. Vatala or Batala, a town founded by Rai Ram Das in 1427 A.D., but now a *tahsil* in Gurdaspur District of Punjab. (*Punjab District Census Handbook, No. 14 Gurdaspur District*, p.10).

7. *Tanka-i siyah* or copper *tanka*, also called *tanka-i Dihli or tanka-i Muradi*. It was gradually replaced by *dam* in Akbar's reign when its value was supposed to be equal to two *dams*. (Irfan Habib, *op. cit.*, p. 381).

8. Qazi Jalal appears to have held the post of *Qazi* of *pargana* Batala, since the time of the Lodis, but after the defeat of Ibrahim Lodi in 1526 A.D.. and subsequent change of government, he was required to get renewed and confirmed his legal possession of the old grant and the income there from as his assignment. (*Indian Historical Research Commission*, (*IHRC*), 1961, pp.51-52).

9. *Qazi (A)*. An official in the Islamic system with duties mainly judicial, but also executive. There is no precise English equivalent, but in the Mughal period he might be described as the judicial assistant of the Governor, (Moreland, *op. cit.*, p. 276). *Qazis* were appointed in large and some small towns, but n villages. Separate *Qazis* were appointed for the army under the direct control of the *Qazi-i Lashkar*. Besides settling disputes between the Muslims according to the Shariat, they also maintained peace and settled petty quarrels. (P. Saran. *The Provincial Government of the Mughals*, 1526-1658, Bombay, 1973, p.34).

10. The general term used for the various allowances granted in cash or land during the early Mughal period was the Mongol word *soyurghal* from *soyurkhal* meaning hereditary grant. This Mongol word appears to have come to India in the wake of Babur and it perhaps found its first documentary evidence in the present *farman*. (Momin Mohiuddin, *The Chancellery and Persian Epistolography under the Mughals*, Calcutta, 1971, p.60).

11. *Mutawajihat*. This term is frequently met with in the Timurid documents and appears in India for the first time in the present *farman*. Subsequently, it seems have been replaced by the more frequent terms like *sairijihat*, *awarizat* and *ikhrajat*. (Momin, *op.cit.*, p. 81).

12. *Mal u jihat* (A). There is a general agreement on the meaning of the term '*mal*' as land-revenue, but not on the connotation of *jihat*. The Mughals obviously borrowed these terms from the Turcomans, Timurids and Safavids in whose documents they frequently occur. We are told by Abul Fazl that the tax imposed on cultivated land by way of quit-rent was termed *mal* as was the practice in Iran and Turan. Imposts on manufactures of respectable kinds were called *jihat*. (Abul Fazl, *op. cit.*, *Ain* I p. 294). It is also taken to mean cesses in addition to *mal* as well as taxes on certain trades. (Irfan Habib, *op. cit.*, pp. 201, 243). By Aurangazeb's time, the term *jihat* got intergrated with *mal* and the combined term came to mean the revenue and the charges for its collection. (Noman Ahmad Siddiqui *Land Revenue Administration under the Mughals*; *1700-1750*, Bombay, 1960, pp. 155-61).

13. *Parwancha* or *Parwana* (P). It was a Mughal substitute for the *amsila* of the Sultanate period, and was the official term for the rescripts of the ministers, grandees, etc. of the Mughal empire. In fact it was a *farmancha* or little *farman.* We are told by Abul Fazl that a *parwancha* differed from a *farman* in as much as it did not require the royal seal and its first two lines were not abbreviated. In the early Mughal period, the *parwancha* tended to support and supplement royal orders, but later on it came to be issued for all such orders as did not require a *farman*. (*Ibid.*, p. 85).

14. *Sarnama* (P). The sacramental superscription which figures at the top of documents. It was customary to begin every document with one of the attributes of God as a token of benediction.

15. *Huwal Ghani.* Literally it means 'He' (God) is Independent. This superscription is found on the documents of Babur and Humayun. In the reign of Akbar, it was, however, replaced by '*Huwal Akbar*' (He is Great) in 986 A.D. (Document, 46 *supra*).

16. *Unwan* (A). Title-page, front-piece; superscription. (Steingass F. *A Comprehensive Persian-English Dictionary*, Delhi, 1973).

17. *Badashah* or *Padshah* was the title formally assumed by Babur in 1507 A.D. when he had established himself securely in Kabul. The Ottoman Sultans held the title of '*Qaisar*', the Safavids of '*Shah*' and Shaibanides of '*Sultan*'. The high and dustinctive title of '*Badshah*' was subsequently held by the successors of Babur. (R.P. Tripathi, *Some Aspects of Muslim Administration,* Allahabad, 1956, pp.110-111).

18. *Ghazi* (A). A champion, a hero; especially one who fights against an infidel. (H.H. Wilson, *A Glossary of Judicial and Revenue Terms,* London, 1855). The championship of Islam is generally associated with this term, but with Akbar its use perhaps would signify nothing more than a convention or a legacy from his forebears.

19. The dynastic seal of Babur consists of two circles. The inner circle contains the name and title of the Emperor while the outer circle traces his pedigree to Timur.

20. Zainud Din Khwafi, with *nom de plume* of *Wafai*, (d. 940 A.H./ 1533-34 A.D.) held the combined charge of the offices of *Sadrus Sudur* and *Mir Munshi* in the reign of Babur. It was in the latter capacity that he used to draft *fathnamas* or letters of victory of political interest and *farmans* of ecclesiastical significance. (Zahirud Din Muhammad Babur, *Baburnamah* translated by A.S. Berveridge, New Delhi, 1979, pp. 553-79).

21. *Dastur* (P). A high priest of Zoroastrians; a *wazir* or Prime Minister; a confidential person, a councillor of state; a model, exemplar; a book or record or anything to which people have recourse; a customary fee, tax or percentage. (Steingass, *op. cit.*, s.v).

22. *Sadr* (A). Head of Ecclesiastical department which dealt with gifts, endowments, etc. granted to religious men, poets, scholars, astronomers, widows, poor men, orphans, judicial officers and the like. The *sadr* was selected not on the ground of his administrative abilities, but particularly, for his scholarship and theological attainments. (Tripathi, *op. cit.*, p. 233).

2

1. *Diwan* (P). A royal court, a council of state, a tribunal of revenue or justice; a minister, a chief officer of state. Under the Muslim government, it was especially applied to the head financial minister. In keeping with the policy of the Turkish Sultans of Delhi, Babur himself appears to have appointed *diwans*. Muhammad Zaman was posted as commander or rather viceroy of Bihar and Murshid Iraqi as *Diwan*. (Tripathi, *op. cit.*, p. 297).

2. He seems to be identical with Muhammad Sultan Mirza, grandson of Sultan Husain Mirza of Khurasan and one of the favourite officers of Babur. In 1527 A.D. the country beyond the Ganges was still disturbed by the Afghan chief, Baban, who forced Muhammad Sultan to abandon Kanauj. Subsequently, when Muhammad Sultan crossed the Ganges, Baban retired once more into the upper country. In 1528 Muhammad Sultan was again defeated by the Afghans and was forced to abandon Lucknow. Babur then pursued and routed the Afghans near Ajodhya. (W. Erskine, *A History of India under the Two First Sovereigns of the Houses of Babar and Humayun*, London, 1854, pp. 477-84).

3. Auhadpur is a village in Bilgram *tahsil* of Hardoi District in U.P. (*District Hardoi, Census 1971*, Lucknow, 1972, p. 117).

4. *Tappa* (H). A small tract or division of country, smaller than a *pargana*, but comprising one or more villages; a division of country for the revenue of which only engagement is entered into with government. (Wilson, *op. cit.*, s.v.).

5. *Haveli*. It is now a low-lying tract between the Sasur Khanderi and Chhoti Nadi in Katoghan, a *pargana* in *tahsil* Khage of Fatehpur district, U.P. (H.R. Nevill, *Fatehpur, A Gazetteer*, Allahabad, 1906, p. 239).

6. *Qasba* (A). The earliest writers used it to denote a *pargana*. From Afif onwards it seems to have been replaced by *pargana*, but *qasba* survived as an occasional synonym. (Moreland, *op. cit.*, p. 276). Subsequently, it came to mean a small town or large village, the chief or market town of a district. (Wilson, *op. cit.*, s.v.).

7. Sandi. It seems to be identical with Fatehpur which is now a village in Bilgram *tahsil* of Hardoi district in U.P. (*Hardoi District Census, op. cit.*, p. 118).

8. *Jama* (A) Amount, aggregate, total in general, but applied especially to the rental of an estate; it is also applied to the revenue assessed upon the land alone (Wilson, s.v.). It signified the amount assessed as opposed to *hasil* or the amount collected. In accordance with the great seasonal division of the agricultural year in India, the assessment was separately made for the *kharif* or autumn and *rabi* or spring harvests. (Irfan Habib, *op. cit.*, pp. 96-97).

9. *Bigha* (H). The ordinary unit of area; a measure of land, varying in extent in different parts of India, and in different times. (Wilson *op.cit.*,s.v.). Prior to the introduction of *jarib* or bamboo measuring rod in the 19 *Julus* the *bigha* used to be 13 per cent smaller than its true size because the wet rope would shrink from the length of 60 *gaz* to 56 *gaz*. The *gaz-i Sikandari* consisted of 32 *angushts* or digits, while the *gaz-il Ilahi* had a length of 41 digits. (Irfan Habib, *op. cit.*, p. 354).

10. Abdud Daim *alias* Dademiyan, son of Qazi Mahmud Ilhadad, was the *Qazi* of Bilgram till his death, some time after 948 A.H./1541 A.D. (*TKTB*, 137-49).

11. *Hasil* (A). Sometimes used as synonym for *mahsul* denoting either produce or demand according to the context. (Moreland, *op. cit.*, p. 272).

12. *Madad-i maash.* (A) Literally, it means aid for subsistence. The grants by which the king alienated his right to collect the land-revenue and other taxes for the lifetime of the grantee or in perpetuity. In the Mughal period such grants were known as *milk, amalk, suyurghal, madad-i maash, aimma*, etc. There was a separate department charged with looking after these grants. It was presided over by the *Sadr* or *Sadrus Sudur* at the Imperial Court under whom were provincial *Sadrs*. (Irfan Habib, *op. cit.*, pp. 298-99).

13. *Ikhrajat* (A). It means occasional expenses and denotes various levies as in the Timurid and Safavid documents. (Momin, *op. cit.*,51). It covered petty burdens imposed by officials. (Irfan Habib, *op. cit.*, pp. 243, 299.)

14. *Sali* (H). Annual, relating to the year; land taken up for the year; a rate in the cultivator's lease when two or more crops are raised from the soil in the same year, that is to say, when the ground is worked throughout the year, not in one season only. (Wilson, *op. cit.*, s.v.).

3

1. *Milk-khoti*. It seems to be identical with the term '*khoti*' frequently used by Barani in his account of the revenue measures adopted by Alaud Din Khalji and Ghiyasud Din Tughluq. Subsequently, it seems to have disappeared in the very region with which Barani's account was concerned but the term appears to have survived in Shamsabad and Bilgram as also in Gujarat. (S.H. Hodiwala, *Studies in Parsi History*, pp. 205-08). The term was afterwards replaced by the word '*muqddami*'.

2. *Biswa* (H). Literally, it means twentieth but is applied especially to the twentieth part of a *bigha* (Wilson, *op. cit.*, s.v.). It sometimes represented a twentieth part of a village and subsequently came to mean simply a share in the *zamindari* of a village. Thus we have reference to the *biswas* of the *Zamindari* of half of the village. (Irfan Habib, *op. cit.*, p. 140 n.).

3. Papri Khurd is a village in Kaimganj *tashil* of Farrukhabad district, U.P. (*District Census Handbook, Farrukhabad District*, 1961, Allahabad, 1966 p. viii).

4. *Khitta* (A). A piece of ground, a plot of land; region, territory, country, district. (Platts, *op. cit.*, s.v.).

5. *Shamsabad*. One of the *mahals* of *sarkar* Kanauj, *suba* Agra yielding a revenue of 71,38,453 *dams*. The modern town is said to have been found in 1585 by Mirza Tahir. Now it is a *pargana* of district Farrukhabad, U.P. (Abul Fazl, *op. cit., Ain* p. 49). (*Farrukhabad. A Gazetteer*, Allahabad, 1911, pp. 255-58, Alakh Chari, *Raja Rai Singh*, Bikaner, 1935, pp. 100-102).

6. *Tanka-i Adli Sikandari* appears to be a well-known bullion *tanka*, with only a trace of silver issued by Sikandar Lodi. (Wright, *Coinage and Metrology of the Sultans of Delhi*, Delhi, 1935, pp. 260-61).

7. *Tughra* (A). Ornamental Arabic character, the imperial signature, the sign-manual on a royal grant. (Wilson, *op. cit.*, s.v.).

4

1. *Amir* (A). In the 13th and 14th centuries a rank of nobility inferior to *Khan* and superior to *Malik*. In the 15th century it also meant provincial governor. (Moreland, *op. cit.*, p. 270).

2. *Wazir* (A). In the 13th and 14th centuries it denoted Prime Minister who in practice held charge of the revenue and financial administration.

In the Mughal period, when there was a *wakil*, the *wazir* was Revenue and Finance Minister and was sometimes described as *diwan*. When there was no *wakil*, the *wazir* was in charge of general, as well as revenue, administration. (Moreland, *op. cit.*, p. 278).

3. *Shiqdar* (P). At first a military rank, later an officer appointed to collect the revenue from a *shiq* or a division (Platts, *op. cit.*, s.v.). Under Sher Shah each *paragana* used to have a *shiqdar* who had the charge of revenue collection as well as of maintaining law and order. *Shiqdar* and *amil* probably continued to be used synonymously, but subsequently the former seems to have been used rather for a subordinate collector under *karori*. (*Ibid.*, p. 277, 74 & n).

4. *Mutasaddi* (A). A writer, a clerk; under the Mughals the term was usually applied to the officials. (Tirmizi, S.A.I., *Edicts from the Mughal Harem, Delhi*, 1979, p. 72).

5. *Sarkar* (P). The word literally means a chief, a superior, a government. Under Sher Shah it denoted an administrative district, i.e., an aggregate of *parganas*. Under Akbar it was a territorial division of a *suba* or province. A *sarkar* was sub-divided into *parganas* or *mahals* which were aggregated into *dasturs* or districts. Between *sarkar* and *dastur* there appears a connection, the former meaning chief and the latter standing for minister.

6. Sarkar Tatar Khan seems to have been so named after Tatar Khan who appears to have held the whole of Jullundur Doab in the days of Babur. He was in possession of the whole of Punjab under Humayun, but joined Sher Shah who made him Governor of the province. When Humayun returned from exile, he defeated Tatar Khan, but afterwards took him into service. The Pathans of Dhogri, about six miles north-east of Jullunder, claim to be the descendants of Tatar Khan (*Jullundur District Gazetteer, Lahore, 1908*, p. 102).

7. *Wazifa* (A). Pension, stipend, grant of land rent-free or at a quit rent, to pious persons or for past services. (Wilson, *op. cit.*, s.v.).

8. *Sanad* (A). Order, written authority, royal ordinance, mandate or decree, any deed or grant from one in authority, document warrant, character diploma. (Platts, *op. cit.*, s.v.).

9. Sultan Ibrahim. The son and successor of Sultan Sikandar Lodi. He was defeated and killed in the battle with Babur in 1526 A.D.

10. *Tauqi* (A). Denoted *hukm* or royal order as also *misal* or ministerial edict. Under the Mughals the former disappeared in favour of *farman* while the latter was replaced by *parwancha*. (Momin, *op. cit.*, 45).

11. Sultan Sikandar (1488-1517 A.D.), the son and successor of Bahlol Lodi, Sultan of Delhi.

12. *Taufir* (A). Literally, it means an increase, but in revenue language it connotes augmentation of the revenue either from extended cultivation or the lapse or resumption of alienated assignments, excess above an intended amount of assignment, which, when realised in a *jagir*, was considered to be the right of the state, although rarely acknowledged or paid. (Wilson, *op. cit.*, s.v.).

13. *Ushr* (A). A tenth part, tithe. It is applied to the tithe assessed on lands occupied by the Muslims (Wilson, *op. cit.*, s.v.). The tithe was levied under Islamic law. A *ushri* denotes country liable to tithe as opposed to *kharaji*. (Moreland, *op., cit.* p. 278).

14. *Daroghana* (P). It denotes the charges of the *darogha* or superintendent of the locality and is included as in the charts of the Turcomans and the Safavids, in the list of forbidden cesses and imposts (Momin *op. cit.*, 83) the pay or fees of a *darogha*, taxes levied for the payment of *darogha*. (Wilson, *op. cit.*, s.v.).

15. *Shiqdarana* (P). It probably danotes share of the *shiqqdar*. There is no evidence available in contemporary accounts to show the share of the *shiqqdar* in the revenue of his *pargana* under the Lodis, but the earlier evidence reveals that he did get a specific portion of the revenue collected. (Moreland, *op. cit.*, p. 270).

16. *Takalif-i diwani* and *Lawasimi sultani*. Ministerial and royal perquisites respectively.

5

1. Sharfuddinpur is a village in Bilgram *tahsil* of Hardoi district of Uttar Pradesh. *(Census 1971, District Census Handbook-District Hardoi, p. 120).*

2. Shaikhanpur. It is probably Shaikhpur, a village in Bilgram *tahsil* of Hardoi district in Uttar Pradesh. *(Ibid. p. 120).*

3. Bilgram is now a *pargana* and *tahsil* in *Hardoi* district, U.P. (H.R. Nevill, *Hardoi, A Gazetteer* Naini Tal, *1905, pp. 176-84).*

4. Tanka-i Adli. This coin seems to have been named after Muhammad Shah Adil who succeeded Salim Shah Suri. *(Report of the Regular Settlement of the Hardoi District* Allahabad, 1880. p. 113).

5. *Takab.* Land cut into by stream. (Steingass, *q.v.*).

6. Malanwa or Mallanwan. According to the *chaknama* (No. 140) it was a *pargana* in *sarkar* Lucknow, *suba* Avadh yielding 35,98,713 *dams*. In the Mughal rule, it was named Malawan. Now it is a town in *Tahsil*

Bilgram, District Hardoi, U.P. (*Hardoi, A Gazetteer.* Nevill, H.R., VA, XLI, *Naini Tal*, 1904, pp. 135, 211).

7. Bochanpur is a village is Bilgram *Tahsil* of Hardoi district, U.P. *(C.D.H., 1971, p. 117).*

8. Ka(n)dhariya. Khandarya or Khandariq. It seems to be identical with Khandiyara Khanjhanpur, which is a village in Bilgram *tahsil* of Hardoi District, U.P. (*Ibid.*, p. 119).

6

1. Farid, name of Sher Khan, who after finally defeating Humayun assumed the title of Sher Shah in 947 A.H./1540 A.D. After ruling for a short spell of five years he passed away in 952 A.H./1545 A.D. (Beale, *op. cit.*, pp. 380-81).

7

1. *Diwan-i shara* (A). A tribunal, a hall or court of justice where justice is done according to the Shariat or Islamic law.

2. Dhauli. It seems to be identical with Dauli now a village in Hardoi *tahsil* in Hardoi district of U.P. *(Hardoi District Census 1971,* pt. XA p. 70).

3. *Biswansa* or *biswani* (H). The fraction of a *biswa* usually the twentieth. (Wilson, *op. cit.*, s.v.).

4. *Hakam* (A). An arbitrator, a judge. (Wilson, *op. cit.* s.v.).

8

1. *Hukm.* Strictly speaking it was an edict of either the Queen Mother or Royal Consort, but it was a privileged order, also of *Khan-i Khanan* during the reign of Akbar as is borne out by the orders of Bairam Khan and Munim Khan who had the honour of issuing *hukms*, though they could, as a rule, issue *parwanchas* only. (Tirmizi, *op. cit.*, pp. 27-28).

2. Bairam Khan. The distinguished general of Humayun who accompanied his master on his exile. He joined Humayun at Jun on the banks of the Indus in 950 A.H./ 1543 A.D. on his way to Persia. He was with Humayun when he returned from Persia to India and victoriously fought the battle of Machiwara. At the time of the death of Humayun in 963 A.H./ 1556 A.D., he was regent of Akbar who on his accession made him *wakilus saltana* or vice-regent. Subsequently, he was removed from this office and killed in 1561 A.D. (Shah Nawaz Khan, *Maasirulumara*, I pp. 371-75).

3. Prayag or Payag, sometimes called Ilahabad, now known as Allahabad is a city, *tahsil* and district in U.P. It is situated on the left bank of the Yamuna, on the edge of land formed by its confluence with the Ganges. Prince Salim was the Governor of Allahabad for some time in the life time of his father. *(Uttar Pradesh District Gazettee*, Allahabad, 1968, pp. 1, 41).

10

1. Bawanipur, now called Bhawanipur, is a village in *tahsil* Sambhal, District Moradabad, U.P. *(Jan Ganna 1971, Zila Moradabad, Granth Mala, 21*, p. 75, S. No 319).

11

1. Sayyid Alam was the son of Mahmud Husaini, who seems to be identical with Sayyid Mahmud Barha. (Shah Nawaz Khan, *op. cit.*, II. p. 409).

2. *Chaudhari* (H). A headman of a *pargana*, he was an important functionary for revenue administration in Northern India. Designated as *Desai* in Gujarat and *Deshmukh* in the Deccan, he was invariably a *zamindar*. His position was usually hereditary, but an imperial *sanad* had to be secured by each incumbent. He collected the revenue from the *muqaddams* and *zamindars* and passed it on to the *amil*. (Irfan Habib *op.cit.*, pp. 291-93).

3. *Muqaddam* (A). It literally means one who is placed first. It came to be used in the specific sense of a village headman very early in Mediaeval India. In the Deccan he was designated as *Patel*. His office was generally hereditary but it could also be bought or sold a testimony to the growth of money economy. He was never, strictly speaking, a government servant, but the revenue authorities could at times depose him for his failure in his obligations. Morever, they exercised the power of nominating *muqaddams* for villages that were newly settled. (Irfan Habib, *op. cit.*, pp. 129-30).

4. *Qanungo* (P). He was the *pargana* accountant and registrar. The position must have existed in ancient India but the Hindi designation does not appear anywhere in the contemporary works. The word *Qanun* in the 13th-14th century had not acquired the modern sense of 'law' but denoted 'custom' or 'practice' and as such *qanungo* interpretted. He was not 'expounder of law' but an 'interpreter of custom', i.e., he denoted the man to whom the Muslim administrators looked for information regarding the customs of their Hindu subjects. (Moreland, *op. cit.*, 276). He

generally belonged to one of the 'accountant-castes', (Kayastha, Khatri, etc.) and his office generally ran in the family, but an imperial order was necessary for the recognition of the rights of any incumbent. He was formerly paid an allowance out of the revenue amounting to 1 per cent, but Akbar replaced this by fixed salaries in lieu of which he was granted revenue-free land. Later on, in some cases at least, he drew cash allowance called *nankar*, in addition to the land held by him. (Irfan Habib, *op. cit*., pp. 288-99).

5. Ajmer was annexed to the Mughal empire by Akbar who restored it to its past glory by making it one of the *subas* of his empire. (Abul Fazl, *Akbarnama*, II, Eng. Tr. Beveridge, Calcutta, 1912, pp. 71-72). It was the capital of the *suba* where the Governor, *diwan* and other top-ranking Mughal officers had their headquarters. It was made the nerve centre of Mughal power in Rajputana and the *dargah* or shrine of Khwaja Muinud Din Chishti enhanced its popularity. *(Rajasthan District Gazetteers, Ajmer*. ed., Dhoundiyal, B.N., Alwar, 1966, pp. 60-61).

6. *Inam* (A). Literally, it means favour, benefaction, gift or present given by a superior to an inferior (Wilson, *op. cit*., s.v.) but in revenue parlance it denotes land held on this basis as *jagir*, but not against any rank or with any obligation. (Irfan Habib, *op. cit*., p. 25).

7. Shaikh Qutban, son of Ali, was one of the *khadims* or attendants of the shrine of Khwaja Muinud Din Chishti. (Abdul Bari. *Asanidus Sanadid* Ajmer 1952, pp. 11-13).

8. Khwaja Muinud Din Sijzi brought the Chishtia *silsilah* or order to India in the 12th century A.D. and firmly established a mystic centre at Ajmer before he passed away in 633 A.H./1235 A.D.. (K.A. Nizami, *Some Aspects of Religion and Politics in India during the Thirteenth Century*, Aligarh 1961. p. 58).

9. *Wujuh* (A). Its plural is *wujuhat* which mean taxes other than land revenue. Such taxes were divided in to *jihat* or taxes on certain trades and *sair jihat* or market and transit dues. (Abul Fazl, *op. cit., Ain* I pp. 294, 301). Some are of the view that *wujuhat-u sairjihat* are synonymous with *ikhrajat-u awarizat*. (Goswamy and Grewal, *op.cit*., p. 69).

12

1. *Hukkam* (A). Plural of *hakim*. Not a precise designation, but used to denote any high executive officer whether Viceroy of a province or Governor of a smaller area (Moreland, *op. cit*., p. 272). Subsequently, it came to mean the supreme administrative authority in a district, also a judge. (Wilson *op. cit*., s.v.).

2. *Ummal* (A). Plural of *amil* which in 13th-15th centuries stood for an executive official in general. From Akbar's time onward, it has acquired the specialised meaning of collector of *khalisa* or reserved revenue, as a variant of the official designation *'amalguzar'*. In this sense, it is synonymous with *karori*. In the 18th century it was used also to denote a Governor, i.e., an officer in charge of the general administration. (Moreland, *op. cit.*, p. 270).

3. Shaikh Husain seems to be identical with Khwaja Hussain who was *Mutawalli* or Superintendent of the mausoleum of Khwaja Muinud Din Chishti when Akbar visited Ajmer in 977 A.H./1569 A.D. consequent on the birth of Prince Salim. He considered himself to be a descendent of the Khwaja from his daughter's side. He was banished to Mecca and had to suffer, with other scholars, various persecutions. He lies buried at Ajmer behind the Shah Jahani mosque. (S.A.I. Tirmizi, *Ajmer Through Inscriptions*, Delhi, 1969, pp. 31, 43).

4. *Tauliyat* (A). Trusteeship or superintendence of a religious foundation; management of the funds appropriated to its support; appointing a person to such an office, transferring property to him for such a trust. (Wilson, *op. cit.*, s.v.).

5. *Sajjadanashin* (P). Literally it means occupant of the prayer-carpet. It stands for a Muslim priest when saying prayers, the spritual superior of religous endowment as distinguished from the *mutawalli* or secular superintendent. (Platts *op. cit.*, s.v.).

6. *Mutawalli* (A). It is derived from *wali* or Governor or guardian. It denotes a superintendent or treasurer of a mosque; administrator or trustee of a religious or charitable foundation. (Platts *op. cit.*, s.v.).

7. *Langar* (P). Victuals distributed amongst mendicants; an alms-house, a public-kitchen. (Platts *op. cit.*, s.v.).

8. *Tanka-i Muradi* (P). The copper *tanka* was sometimes also called *tanka-i siyah* and *tanka-i Dilhi*. In Akbar's time, one *tanka* was equal to two *dams*. (Irfan Habib, *op. cit.*, p. 381).

9. Mujawir (A). An attendant at a mosque or shrine. (Platts, *op. cit.*, s.v.).

13

1. *Lakhnau*, or Lucknow, derived from Lakhana. In Akbar's reign, it was one of the *sarkars* of the *suba* of Avadh, now capital of Uttar Pradesh. (Abul Fazl, *Ayeen Akbary*, tr., Gladwin, p. 469).

14

1. *Haveli* (P). A house of brick or stone; house, mansion; the district or lands attached to and in the vicinity of town. (Platts, *op. cit.*, s.v.).

15

1. *Jagirdar* (P). It literally means the holder of any assignment of revenue. The use of this word in this technical sense is confined to India and came into vogue only in the 15th century. In the reign of Akbar the whole country with the exception of the *khalisa* was held by the nobility as *jagir*. The *jagirdars* were usually *mansabdars* holding *mansabs* or ranks which were generally dual, viz. *zat* and *sawar*. The former chiefly meant to indicate personal pay, while the latter determined the contingents which the *mansabdar* was obliged to maintain. (Irfan Habib, *op. cit.*, pp. 257-58).

2. *Munsif* (A). Under Sher Shah each *pargana* used to have a *shiqqdar* who was assisted by *Munsif*. The latter appears to be identical with *Amin*. (Irfan Habib, *op. cit.*, 274-75).

3. *Sandila* or *Sandylh* in the reign of Akbar, was one of the *mahals* in the *sarkar* of Lucknow, *suba* Avadh yielding a revenue of 1,06,23,901 *dams*. Now being headquarters of the *tahsil*, it lies nearly midway between Lucknow and Hardoi at a distance of 32 miles north of Lucknow, U.P. (Abul Fazl, *Ayeen op. cit.*, p. 490, Hardoi, A *Gazetteer*, ed. Nevill, H.R., Vol. XII Naini Tal, 1904, pp. 134, 135, and 249).

4. Mahirpur located in the Hardoi *tahsil* of Hardoi district in U.P. (*Hardoi District Census Handbook, 1971, Pt. X-A.* p.71).

16

1. *Wukala* (A). Plural of *wakil* which denotes an agent, deputy, delegate, an attorney, a pleader, an ambassador. (Platts *op. cit.*, s.v.).

2. Mirza Sharfud Din Husain was appointed *Hakim* or Governor of Ajmer and Nagore in the 5th year of Akbar's reign. Earlier, he was *panjhazari* (5,000). In 969 A.H. (1561-62 A.D.) he joined Akbar in the siege of Mairtha. Thereafter he led a chequered career and was ultimately poisoned. (Abul Fazl, *op. cit.*, *Ain* I, p. 339-40).

3. *Maqbara* (A). A tomb, a mausoleum. (Platts, *op. cit.*, s.v.).

17

1. This undated *hukm* seems to have been issued some time in August 1564 A.D. when Akbar along with Munim Khan went to Mandu to suppress the rebellion of Abdullah Khan and stayed there for nearly a month to set the administration of Malwa in order. (Abul Fazl, *op. cit.*,

Ain, II, 229).

2. Munim Khan, *Khan-i Khanan*, was a grandee of Humayun's court. He did not, however, accompany Humayun to Persia but rejoined him immediately on his return. In 961 A.H./1553-54 A.D. he was appointed *ataliq* of Prince Akbar; he was Governor of Kabul where he remained till Bairam Khan fell into disgrace; he joined Akbar in 967 A.H. (1559-60 A.D.) at Ludhiana where he was appointed *Khan-i Khanan* and *wakil*. In the eighth year of Akbar's reign, he was again sent to Kabul to quell disturbances but he fled to the Ghakkars and being humiliated he hesitatingly rejoined Akbar, who appointed him commander of the fort of Agra. In the 12th year he was appointed to his *jagir* in Jaunpur; in 982 A.H./1574-75 A.D. he was made Governor of Bihar. He died at Gaur of fever. (Abul Fazl. *op. cit*., *Ain* I, pp. 333-34.).

3. *Pargana* Khargon is mentioned without any reference to *sarkar* Bijagarh. This suggests a hint that perhaps by the time of the issue of the *hukm*, the administrative division of Malwa into 12 *sarkars* was not finalised.

4. Khargon, *pargana*, headquarters of the Nimar district Indore State, Central India, situated in 21° 50'N. and 75° 37'E on the left bank of the Kindi river. Khargon appears to have been founded under the Mughal. It was the chief town of a *mahal* in the Bijagarh *sarkar* of the *suba* of Malwa. (*Imperial Gazetteer of India*, Vol. XV. p. 253).

5. In the absence of Abdullah Khan, who had fled to Gujarat, Munim Khan addressed the *hukm* to the 'officers and servants of *pargana* Khargon.

6. It would not be wrong to conclude that even after the conquest of Malwa, Akbar allowed his officers to continue the prevalent system of revenue collection with the help of officers appointed by the former rulers of Malwa.

7. The legend Akbar Shah *Banda-i Khan-i Khanan* as deciphered by Mr. Bhatt (*IHC*, XXX, 1968, p.183) is obviously wrong.

18

1. *Malik* (A). Proprietor, owner, master, employer, lord, possessor. (Platts, s.v.). In Islamic law, it is applied to an occupant of land, and is used in one of Aurangzab's *farmans* to denote a peasant. (Moreland, *op. cit*., p. 274).

2. *Malikana* (P). It was a fiscal claim of the *zamindar* upon the land lying within his *zamindari*. This claim was met either through the holding of a portion of the land revenue-free or a cash allowance from the revenue collected from the entire land by the authorities. In Northern India and Bengal it was called *malikana* and *do-biswi*, while in Gujarat it was designated as *banth* and in the Deccan as *chauth*. (Irfan Habib, *op. cit.*, pp. 149-50).

3. *Fatwa* (A). A judicial sentence, a judgement; but more usually applied to the written opinion of the jurist of the Islamic law. (Wilson q.v.).

4. *Shariat* (A). The divine way of religion, the Islamic law. (Platts, *op.cit.*, s.v.).

19

1. Dr. Ansari has omitted the date (*Ansari, op. cit.*, p. 206) which has been furnished by Mr. Jalalud Din ("Some Important Farmans and Sanads, of Mediaeval Period in the Institutions of U.P." published in *Studies in Islam*, XV, No. 1 January, 1978, p. 46).

2. *Amil* (A). It literally means a functionary and denotes an official in charge of both the assessment and collection of revenue. He was not expected to have any local ties or links in the area to which he was appointed. Uncertain about his tenure, he tended to be rapacious and levied extortions from the *muqaddams* and other revenue officers. His accounts were subjected to audit. (Irfan Habib, *op.cit.*, pp. 230,280,287).

3. Haveli Benares was one of the 8 *mahals* in *sarkar* Benares, *suba* Allahabad and yielded a revenue of 17,34,721 *dams* in the reign of Akbar. Today it is a city and district of the same name in U.P. (Abul Fazl, *op. cit.*, *Ayeen*, p. 482).

4. Malik Arjunmal Jangam was the title of the Head priest of the Jangam Bari Math at Benaras. This Math is associated with the followers of the Shaivite sect which come from South India. Since its inception in the 6th century A.D., this Math had been enjoying Imperial grants and favours. Its followers had a number of Shiva temples built at Benares, Arain, Prayag, and Gaya. (Jalalud Din, *op. cit.*, p. 46).

5. *Mahal* (A). Under Akbar *mahal* was a revenue subdivision corresponding usually, but not invariably with *pargana*. The term was occasionally applied also to a head of miscellaneous revenue. The modern form of *mahal* does not appear before the 18th century. (Moreland, *op.cit.*, p.274). The markets of larger towns and the ports were constituted into separate *mahals* as distinct from *pargana* or territorial *mahals*. (Irfan Habib *op. cit.*, p. 259).

6. *Awarizat* (A). It has been defined by Jhaveri (IV) as taxes like the

peshkash and *jaribana*. Goswamy and Grewal (p. 56) consider it synonymous with *sairjihat* and *ikhrajat*.

7. *Qunlugha* (T). Like many Chaghtai Turki words, this term also came to India in the wake of Babur who refers to it twice in his Memoirs under the year 935. A.H. coupled with *ulufa*. It has been translated as (i) "daily allowance and lodging of envoys going backward and forward" and (ii) "allowance and lodging". (Babur, *op. cit.*, II, pp. 646, 658). This was one of the exactions forbidden by Akbar. (Abul Fazl, *op. cit.*, *Ain* I, p. 301). The Indian sense of the word as in Mughal documents is "a diet obtained by officers from the ryots" (*Islamic Culture*, XI, 14 October 1947 Art. Maulavi Muhammed Shafi, Qonalgha, pp 90-93). It has also been defined as a gift made to the *hakim*, more particularly, the pot of yogurt which a *zamindar* was expected to take with him to the *hakim* when paying a visit. (Irfan Habib, *op.cit.*, p. 247).

8. *Peshkash* (p). Literally it means what is first drawn; first fruits; fixed amount; tribute. (Wilson *op. cit.*, s.v.). It was usual under the Mughals to demand from the chieftains *peshkash* which was regarded as both the hall-mark and substance of submission. It was possibly to require a chieftain to pay both, an amount as *jama* and an additional sum as *peshkash*. It was paid in the imperial treasury also and was probably never assigned in *jagir* to any one. (Irfan Habib, *op.cit.*, pp. 184-85).

20

1. Sarwarpur. No village of this name is traceable. It may be Sarwarpur Zaptmapi, which is lying unpopulated today. Another possibility is that the name of the village was changed to Sakharpur Alampur occupying an area of 251 acres. It does not seem to be Shaikhupura as there is no such village of this name, as opined by Iqtidar Alam Khan. Sakharpur Alampur appears to be the village where a family claiming to be the descendents of *Qazi* Alam, the recipient of the above grant, still reside. (Jangarna, 1971, Granthmala 21, Uttar Pradesh Bhag X-B, Farrukhabad, p. 68 (S. No. 179), p. 78, S.No. 324; Iqtidar Alam Khan, *The Political Biography of the Mughal Noble Munim Khan Khan-i Khanan*, p. 96 n. 4).

2. Maipur *tappa* is four miles to the west of Bhojpur. (Iqtidar Alam Khan, *op. cit.*, p. 96, n. 5).

3. *Kharif* (A). Autumn; autumnal harvest, the crops which are sown before the commencement of the rains and reaped after their close. (Wilson, *op.cit.*, s.v.).

4. *Pars-il* (T). The leopard year of the Turkish Duodenary cycle which consists of 12 solar years and every new year begins on the sun's entry into the Aries and thus every new year day falls on the 21st March. Every year of this cycle is named after an animal and is followed by the Turkish word *il* meaning a year.

5. *Bhojpur*. From the time of Akbar until the establishment of the Bangash dynasty in 1713, *pargana* Bhojpur was the special charge of an *amil*. In Akbar's reorganisation of empire, it was one of the *mahals* in the district of Farrukhabad, *suba* Agra. Now it is a village situated in 270° 17' N and 79° 41'E, six miles from Fatehgarh on the bank of the Ganges. (Neave, E.R., *Farrukhabad*, A *Gazetteer*, Vol, IX, Allahabad, 1911, pp. 134, 184-185).

6. *Darul khilafa* (A). Residence of Caliph; seat of Government, capital. (Wilson, *op. cit.*, s.v.).

7. Agra, it was the headquarters of the kingdom of Sikandar Lodi. In 1505 A.D. Akbar made it the capital of his empire and this status it continued to enjoy for over a century. It was also one of the *subas* of the Mughal empire. (Abul Fazl, *op. cit. Ayeen*; pp. 326-27; *Agra District Gazetteer*. E.B. Joshi ed., Lucknow, 1965 p. 346).

8. *Muzarian* (A). Cultivators who were identical with *muqaddams* or headmen. (Irfan Habib, *op. cit.*, pp. 130, 143).

9. *Sair ikhrajat* (A). Extra or miscellaneous expenses. (Wilson, *op cit.*, s.v.).

10. *Savi*. This term could not be identified but from the context it seems to be a cess; Iqtidaar Alam Khan has read it as *Sairi* (Iqtidar Alam Khan, *op. cit.*, p. 95) which does not appear to be correct.

11. *Jaribana* (P). An assessment on the cultivators for the expense of measurement by *jarib* (Wilson *op. cit.*, s.v.). *Jarib* was the form or measuring instrument and the suffix '*ana*' of Persian is added to the Arabic word '*jarib*' to denote the rate for defraying the charges of measurement of land by *jarib*.

12. *Zabitana* (P). A cess levied on land to meet the cost of maintenance of the measuring parties. In the days of Akbar the measuring parties used to get 58 *dams* daily as *zabitana* from the treasury. This was converted into a cess of one *dam* per *bigha*. Todar Mal's regulations provided for a minimum area to be measured every day by the staff. The daily allowances in cash and kind for the survey staff were provided out of *zabitana*. (Irfan Habib, *op. cit.*, p. 214).

13. *Muhrana* (P). In the context of land grants it means the fee paid to the *Qazi* or the *sadr* in charge of *suyurghal*. The *Qazi* used to charge fee for imprinting seals on all civil contracts. (Wilson *op. cit.*, s.v.).

14. *Sad doi-i qaunugoi* (P). It was a commission paid at the rate of two per cent to a *qanungo*. (Irfan Habib, *op. cit.*, p. 135).

15. *Takrar-i Zarat* (P). Literally, it means repetition of the crop. It denoted a cess levied on the ryots at the time of repetition of the crop. (Aziz Jang Wila, *Jamiul Atiyat, ed.,* Ziaud Din Ahmad Shaheb and Hasnud Din Ahmad, Hyderabad, 1974, p. 137).

16. *Hari kharch*. Miscellaneous charges. (Iqtidar Alam Khan, *op. cit.*, p. 96).

17. *Jizya* (A). A poll-tax which the Muslim rulers imposed on non-Muslim subjects. (Wilson, *op. cit.*, s.v.).

18. *Muhtarifa* (A). It was a tax levied on artisans. (Irfan Habib, *op. cit.*, p. 259).

19. *Taughana* (P). From *taugha* which means a dish prepared from lamb's meat, flour and pickles. (Steingass, *op. cit.*, s.v.). Probably here it means charges or cess for entertainment.

21

1. Amroha, town and *tahsil* in Moradabad District, Uttar Pradesh. In Akbar's reign it was a *pargana* and belonged to the *sarkar* of Sambhal. (Abul Fazl, *op. cit.*, *Ain* I, p. 485).

2. Sambhal. Town and *tahsil* in Moradabad District, U.P. It was awarded to Humayun in 1526 A.D. Under Akbar Sambhal was the headquarters of *sarkar* of the same name and copper coins were minted here. (Abul Fazl, *op. cit.*, *Ain* I, pp. 32-33, 328, 537, H.R. Nevill, *Moradabad District Gazetteer*, Allahabad, 1911, pp. 253-270).

3. Khanpur, also called Khanpur Sarai *urf* Alampur, is situated in Moradabad District, U.P. (*Moradabad District Census Handbook, 1961, Allahabad, 1966*, p. liii).

22

1. This *farman* was most probably issued soon after the Mughal conquest of Chittor in 1568 A.D. when Akbar paid a visit to the mausoleum of Khwaja Muinud Din Chishti.

2. Nabera. This name is not forthcoming in the Gazetteers and in the list of villages under Ajmer in the Census Report. It is doubtful if it is Nimbahera, which is a village in *tahsil* Gangrar, Chitor, Rajasthan. (*Census of India. 1961, Rajasthan Chitorgarh District*, p. 316.)

3. Chitoor (also Chittor, Chitor, or Chitore) district of Rajasthan, formerly a great princely state of Mewar. During the second half of Akbar's reign, when it was conquered in 1568 A.D., a large portion of Maharana Pratap Singh's territories constituted the *sarkar* of Chitor and included in the province of Ajmer. (P. Saran, *The Provincial Govt. of the Mughals,* Bombay 1973, p. 124).

4. *Gumashta* (P). An agent, a steward, a confidential factor; an officer employed by *zamindars* to collect their rents, by bankers to receive money, by merchants to carry on their business in places where they themselves did not reside. (Wilson *op. cit.*, s.v.).

23

1. This undated *farman* was most probably issued sometime after Akbar's visit to the mausoleum of Khwaja Muinud Din Chishti in 977 A.H./1570 A.D. after the birth of Prince Salim.

2. Savai, village not traceable in the Postal Directory and Census Report of Rajputana Agency, 1931. However, there are four villages of the names of (i) Sawai Madhosinghpure, (2) Sawai Mansinghpura, (3) Sawai Jaisinghpura, and (4) Sawaipura. (*Census of India 1961, Rajasthan, Jaipur District,* pp. 396, 425).

3. Naraina, district, headquarters of *talluqa* or Subdivision of the same name. It is at a distance of 41 miles west of Jaipur and 43 miles north-east of Ajmer. (*Imperial Gazetteer of India,* Vol. XVIII. 370).

4. Sanghar, town and lake, one of the 28 *parganas* in *sarkar* Ajmer. (*Rajasthan District Gazetteers, Ajmer.* Dhoundiyal B.N., ed. Alwar, 1966, pp. 58, 59). It was worked by the Imperial administration of Akbar and his successors upto the time of Ahmad Shah (1748-54). The town was within the joint jurisdiction of Jaipur and Jodhpur in Rajputana. (*Imperial Gazetteer of India* Vol. XXII, pp. 20-21). Akbar married the daughter of Raja Bihari Mal at Sambhar in 968 A.H./1555-56 A.D. (Abul Fazl, *op. cit., Ani I,* p. 322).

24

1. Umdatul Mulk (A). Pillar of the state. It was the title of Nizamud Din Muhammad Qasim Khan.

2. Nizamud Din Muhammad Qasim Khan Umdatul Mulk of Nishapur served under Bairam Khan. He was sent against Hajji Khan, as old servant of Sher Khan. He defeated Hajji Khan and took possession of Nagore and Ajmer which for a long time remained the south-western frontier of Akbar's empire. In the 9th *Julus* he was sent to Sarangpur in

Malwa. Subsequent part of his career is not known. (Abul Fazl, *op. cit.*, *Ain I*. 379, Shahnawaz Khan, *op. cit.* III.50-52).

3. *Mutamidul Mulk* Tardi Beg Sultan. It refers to Tardi Sultan, a noble of high rank. After the recapture of India by Humayun, Tardi Beg got Mewat as *jagir* and on Humayun's death, he read the *khutbba* at Delhi on behalf of Akbar. He was made commander and Governor of Delhi by Akbar. (Abul Fazl, *op. cit.*, *Ain* I, 334-36).

4. *Muqaddami. (H).* It was a customary perquisite exacted by a *muqaddam* from the villagers individually. In Akbar's *farman* of 1575 A.D. *muqaddami* and *deh-nimi* (5%) are put at a distance, but from Jahangir's reign, they invariably appear paired together. (Irfan Habib, *op. cit.*, pp. 131-32).

25

1. He seems to be identical with *Qazi* Nizam called Ghazi Khan. He was a native of Badakhshan. He studied law and *Hadis* under Mulla Isamud Din Ibrahim and was looked upon as one of the most learned of the age. He had access to the court of Sulaiman, King of Badakshan, who conferred upon him the title of Ghazi Khan. He came to India and was appointed *parwanchi* or writer by Akbar. Soon he was made a Commander of one thousand and the title of *Ghazi Khan* was bestowed upon him by Akbar. He fought bravely against the Rana and distinguished himself against the rebellious grandees in Bihar. He received Avadh as *tuyul* and died there at the age of 70 in the year 992 A.H. He wrote several books. (Abul Fazl, *op. cit.*, *Ain* I, pp. 487-88).

2. Bijnor, *pargana*, *tahsil* and district in Uttar Pradesh was included in the *sarkar* of Sambhal in the *subah* of Delhi. It was a thickly inhabited place in Akbar's reign. (*Bijnor A Gazetteer*, Vol. XIV, H.R. Nevill, Allahabad, 1908. pp. 169. 171).

26

1. *Makhadim* (A) Religious leaders. When Akbar passed by Sirhind in 1585 A.D. the *makhadim* of the *pargana* around did not come to pay him their respects. In his indignation Akbar ordered resumption of their *madad-i maash* grants. It was then that a few appeared but owing to Abul Fazl's intervention most of them received back their grants. (Irfan Habib, *op. cit.*, p. 310).

2. Jama Masjid (A). The congregational mosque. (Platts, s.v).

3. Probably Baroli, a village in Bilgram *tahsil* of Hardoi District, U.P. (*Hardoi District Census Report*, 1961, p. LXXXV).

4. Khadkanian. It could not be identified, probably it is a village in *tahsil* Bilgram, Hardoi District.

5. Probably Bhadeona, a *mahal* in Hardoi District, U.P. (*Hardoi District Gazetteer, op. cit.*, p. 111).

27

1. Bijagarh, a village situated in 23° 42' North and 77° 11' East, 2 miles south of the Narsinghgarh town. (*Western States (Malwa) Gazetteer*, Vol. V. Pt. A. Text. compiled by Capt. C.E. Luard, Bombay 1908, p. 165). In the *suba* of Malwa, in 969 A.H. (1561-62 A.D.) in the reign of Akbar, Pir Muhammad defeated Baz Bahadur, invaded his country, drove him away, and took Bijagarh from Itimad Khan, Baz Bahadur's general. (Abul Fazl, *op. cit.*, *Ain* I, pp. 129, 343).

28

1. *Hasbul hukm* (A) Imperial order issued through court officials as distinct from *hasbul amr* or order issued on behalf of a prince. (Irfan Habib, *op. cit.*, p. 282).

2. Shihabud Din Ahmad Khan Hasani, a relation and friend of Maham Anga, was instrumental in bringing about Bairam's fall. From the beginning of Akbar's reign, he was commander of Delhi, served in Malwa against Abdullah Khan. In 975 A.H. (1567-68 A.D.) he was appointed Governor of Malwa. In the 13th year he was put in charge of the Imperial domain lands. In the 21st year he was promoted to a command of 5000 and was again appointed to Malwa. He distinguished himself in the conquest of Broach in 992 A.H. (1574-75 A.D.) and again was made Governor of Malwa. He died in Malwa in 999 A.H. (1581-82 A.D.). (Abul Fazl, *op. cit., Ain* I, pp. 352-53).

3. *Dasturul amal* (A). Rule, regulation; body of regulations agreed upon by any number of persons for their future guidance. A body of instructions and tables for the use of revenue officers. (Wilson, *op. cit.*, s.v.).

29

1. Habibullah Kamal. Probably a descendant of Shaikh Niamatuallah of Gopamau upon whom had been bestowed two villages in Gopamau *pargana* by Humayun. (*IHRC* XXII. p. 33).

2. *Tuyul*. It was a term used in Persia from the 14th century onwards but in India its use became perhaps more common than of *iqta* but it still

remained a secondary synonym of *jagir*. (Irfan Habib, *op.cit.* p. 258).

3. Khwaja Mahmud and Sulaiman. They appear to be local officials in the Eastern Sarkars. Khwaja Sulaiman was *Bakhshi* of the Punjab in the 47th year of Akbar's reign. (*IHRC*, XXII. p. 33).

4. Afzal Sultan, probably Khwaja Afzal Khan, Sultan Ali Turbati. He was *Mushrif-i Buyutat* (Store Accountant) in 956 A.H. (1548-49 A.D.). Next year he was imprisoned at Kabul by Mirza Kamran who forced him to pay large sums of money. Humayun appointed him *Mir Bakhshi*. He was with Tardi Beg when Humayun died. He was imprisoned for his failure to defend Delhi against Hemu. He escaped from the prison. In the 5th year of Akbar's reign, he was favourably received at court and made a commander of 3,000. (Abul Fazl, *op. cit.*, Ain I, p. 408; *IHRC*, XXII 1945, p.33).

30

1. *Gopamau*, town, *pargana* and *tahsil* in District Hardoi, situated in latitude 27° 32' north and lingitude 80° 18' east, at a distance of 15 miles north-east of Hardoi. The *Qazi* acquired distinction in the days of Akbar. (H.R. Nevill, *Hardoi, A Gazetteer*, Vol. XLI. Naini Tal, 1904. pp. 186, 188).

31

1. *Ruz* (P). Literally, it means a day.

2. *Ormuzd* or *Ormuz*. The first of the 32 days of Persian month. (Bendrey, *op. cit.* p. 17).

3. *Mah* (P). Literally, it means a month.

4. *Shahriwar, Sharewar, Shahrever* is the sixth month of the persian calendar. (Bendrey, op. cit., p. 24).

5. These persons were the acknowledged leaders of the Parsi community at Navsari at that time. (Hodivala, *op. cit.*, p. 215).

6. Navsari a *mahal* in the *sarkar* of Surat, is situated about 18 miles to the south of Surat. It is one of the principal centres of the Parsi population in Gujarat, with a considerable number of priest families. (Commissariat, M.S., *A History of Gujarat*, Vol. II, Bombay, 1957, p. 223). The Parsis named the city Navsari, or New Sari, and since it has been known as Navsari Nagmandal instead of its former name Nagamandla. (Karake, Dosabhai Framji, *History of the Paris*, Vol. I, London, 1884, p. 37).

7. Dastur Mehrji Rana, or Dastur Mahyar Rana, or Adhyaru Mehrji Vachcha popularly known as Mahrvaid, was Akbar's physician and principal teacher in Zoroastrian lore, a leading *mobed* or theologian from

Navsari in Gujarat, whose acquaitance Akbar had made at the time of the siege of Surat in 1573. Meherji, in response to Akbar's invitation, accompanied him to his capital in 1573. His eminent services rendered at the court to the religion of his forefathers justly won the gratitude of his colleagues who formally recognised him as their head, an honourable position he held until his death in 1591. Akbar rewarded him with a grant of 200 *bighas* of land as *madad-i maash.* The Dastur acquainted Akbar with the peculiar terms, ordinances, rites and ceremonies of his creed, laying stress on the reference of the Sun. (Hodivala, *op. cit.*, pp. 149-50).

8. When Surat was conquered by Akbar in 1573 A.D., Qilij Muhammad Khan was entrusted with the charge of the fort and the adjoining district which obviously included Navsari. He is spoken of as *jagirdar* of Surat in 992 A.H./ 1584 A.D. His connection with Gujarat does not appear to have terminated before 996-97 A.H./1588-89 A.D., when he was appointed assistant to Todarmal. After the execution of Shah Mansur, the management of the *wizarat* was entrusted to him. (Shah Nawaz Khan, *op. cit.*, III, pp. 69-74; Hodivala, *op. cit.*, p. 217).

9. Pipalis seems to be identical with Pipaliewady. (Hodivala, *op. cit.*, p. 215).

32

1. Gobri. Probably Gajobari in *pargana* Charde under Mallahpur thana, Bahraich District, U.P. *(District Census Handbook, Census of India 1951, Uttar Pardesh, Bahraich District,* Allababad, 1955 p. 136).

33

1. Ahmedabad, town and district in Gujarat, was one of the nine *sarkars* of the *suba* of Gujarat, containing 28 *mahals* in the reign of Akbar; presently it is a flourishing industrial town of Gujarat. (Abul Fazl *op. cit., Ayeen*, II, p. 516).

2. *Takas* (S & Mar). A coin the value of which appears to vary in different parts of India. In northern India it was said to be a copper coin equal to two *paisa* while in Deccan it was called an aggregate of four *paisa*, and in Gujarat an aggregate of three *paisa* in Bengal it was synonymous with a rupee. (Wilson *op cit.*, s.v.).

3. Aziz Koka, commonly called Shamsud Din and Mirza Koka was the foster brother of Akbar. In the 17 year of Akbar's reign, he was appointed Governor of Gujarat. He was promoted to a command of 5000, got the title of *Khan-i Azam* and was sent to Bihar to crush the rebellion. He crushed the revolt successfully. In 994 A.H. he was sent to the Deccan, but soon returned to Gujarat. In the 22 year of Akbar's reign, he gave his daughter in marriage to Prince Murad. He went on pilgrimage to Mecca where he was much "fleeced". On his return from Mecca he became a member of Din-i Ilahi, was appointed Governor of Bihar and got Multan as *jagir*. He served Jahangir who appointed him Governor of Gujarat. He died at Ahmedabad in 1033 A.H. (Abul Fazl, *op. cit., Ain* I, pp. 343-46; Jahangir, *op. cit.*, Vol. I, pp. 153, 183, *passim;* Vol II, pp. 256).

4. *Amatya* (Mar). A minister, one of the eight principal officers of Maratha state. (Wilson, *op. cit.*, s.v.,).

34

1. Khurshed or Khur (p). The eleventh of the 32 days of a Persian month. (Bendrey, *op. cit.*, p. 17).

2. Tir (P). The fourth month of the Persian calendar. (Bendrey, *op. cit.*, p. 15.)

3. The original is Gujarati.

4. Gardis were Vohras, small traders by profession and were Behdins or laymen. (Hodivala, *op. cit.*, p. 248).

5. Ervad Padam Mahyar. Probablly Padam Mahyar Jainsang Dhayyan, son of Mahyar Jaisang. (Hodivala, *op. cit.*, p. 249).

6. *Tanka Pratabahra.* The word is a corruption of Pratap Varaha the name of a mediaevel Hindu coin which was further corrupted by the Portuguese into '*Par dao ouri*'. It seems to be identical with the silver coin *Muzaffari* which was known among common people by the old Hindu name and was equal to 3/5 of rupee. (Hodivala, *op. cit.*, pp. 195-97).

7. *Dokda* (Mar). A small copper coin, a half pice. (Wilson, *op. cit.*, s.v.).

8. *Amal* (A). Business, affairs, an office for collection of revenue, administration of justice, management of any land or business on behalf of another authority, government. (Wilson, *op. cit.*, s.v.).

9. Nagmandal is the old name of Navsari. (Hodivala, *op. cit.*, p. 249).

35

1. Arail, also called Jalalabad, ancient village and headquarters of the *pargana* of the same name, lies opposite to the fort on the right bank of the Yamuna in Allahabad. (*Uttar Pradesh District Gazetteers, Allahabad,* Esha Basanti Joshi, *ed,* Allahabad, 1968 pp. 44, 371).

2. *Gumbad* (P). An arch or vault, a dome, cupola, a tower, a bastion. (Platts *op. cit.*, s.v.).

36

1. *Karori, kirori* (H). Written also as *Carori.* The word means possessor or collector of a *karor* or ten million of any given kind or money. When Akbar introduced his revenue reforms in the 19th *Julus*/ 1574-75 A.D. he put zealous and upright men in charge of revenue, each over one *karor* of *dams.* A *karori* reveived 8 per cent upon the amount of his collection, beside perquisites. This system lasted till 1639 A.D. In the reign of Shah Jahan, his minister Islam Khan deputed a separate *Amin* to every *pargana* for purpose of fixing the *jama,* and the *karori* was left in charge of the collection to which the duties of *faujdar* were added with an allowance of 10 per cent on the collections. Saduallah Khan, who succeeded Islam Khan, combined the duties of *amin* and *faujdar* in one person and appointed him superintendent of a *chakla* of several villages and placing the *karori* entirely under his orders, established 5 per cent on collections as the amount of the *karori's* allowance and of this 1 per cent was subsequently deduced. This system continued in the reign of Aurangzeb. (Abul Fazl, *op. cit., Ain* I, p. 13; H.N. Elliot, *Memoirs of the History, Folklore and Distribution of Races of the North Western Provinces of India, II.* London, 1859 pp. 197-99).

2. *Karkun* (P). Literally, it means an agent, or deputy. From 16th century it usually means a clerk or writer. The same meaning is applicable in some 13th-14th centuries passages, but they do not show with certainty whether the word had become specialised by that period. (Moreland, *op. cit.,* p. 273). In the *Ain* it is used as synonymous with *bitickchi* denoting accountant who was one of the officials posted to each *pargana. (*Abul Fazl, *op. cit., Ain,* I, p. 288).

3. *Roshanai-i Chiragh* (P). Lighting lamp at a shrine.

4. Maund. Anglicised form of *man,* a unit of weight which varied with both time and locality (Moreland, *op. cit.,* p. 274). In Akbar's time the *man* based on the *ser* of 28 *dams* was equal to about 51.63 Ibs. and that of 30 *dams* to the *ser* called *Akbar Shahi* or *Akbari* to about 55.32 Ibs. *The man-i Jahangiri* was based upon the *ser of* 36 *dams* and in terms of avoirdupois weights the new unit must have been equal to about 66.38 Ibs. (Irfan Habib, *op. cit.,* p. 368).

5. *Uzuk* (T). It was the most important of the royal seals entrusted to the most trusted person and was not as a rule placed in the charge of the *Wakil* or the *Diwan.* It remained in the female apartment. (Ibn Hasan, *The Central Structure of the Mughal Empire,* New Delhi, 1970, pp. 100-102).

6. Shaikh Abdun Nabi, *grandson of* Shaikh Abdul Quddus of Gangoh, was the first of his time in literary sciences, *naqlia* the science of *Hadis* (traditions). In the 10th year of Akbar's reign, he attained the office of *Sadrus Sudur (Principal Sadr)* of India, his intimacy with the Emperor became so great that Akbar used to go to his house to hear the traditions; but his bigotry and censures displeased Akbar and he fell in his estimation. As a result he was sent off to Mecca. In the 27 year he returned and arrived at Ahmedabad but was imprisoned and Abul Fazl strangled him there in 992 A.H./1584 A.D. (Shah Nawaz Khan, *op. cit.*, pp. 41-44; Abul Fazl, *op. cit., Ain* I. pp. 615).

7. Khwaja Ghiyasud Din (Ali Qazwini), Asaf Khan, son of Aga Mulla *Dawat-dar* (inkstand-holder), was distinguished for his eloquence, courage and industry. Akbar appointed him *Bakhshi*. In 981 A.H./1573 A.D. he took part in the battle at Ahmedabad and received the title of Asaf Khan. In 989 A.H./1581 A.D. he died in Gujarat. (Shah Nawaz Khan, *op. cit.*, pp. 281-82; Abul Fazl, *op. cit., Ain* I, p. 479).

38

1. Haveli was one of the four *mahals* of *sarkar* Kara in *suba* Allahabad; had a cultivated area of 9,638 *bigha,* paid a revenue of 51,92,170 *dams* and contributed a contingent of 100 horses and 1000 foot during the reign of Akbar. It is now insignificant village in *tahsil* Sirathu on the banks of the Ganges 65.5 km. from Allahabad. (*Uttar Pradesh District Gazetteers*, Allahabad, ed., Esha Basanti Joshi, Allahabad, 1968, pp.44-45).

2. Kara. The *sarkar* of Kara comprised six *mahals,* viz., Haveli, Kara, Baldhkara, Karari and Atherban. Kara is now an insignificant village 65.6 km. from Allahabad. (*Ibid.*, p. 44).

3. *Khalsa sharifa* (P). Literally the word means pure. If and when applied to land, it stands for those lands the revenue of which becomes the property of the government exclusively and is not shared in *jagir* or *inam* by any other party. It also refers to land or villages of which the state is the manager, or holder. In other words it connotes domain lands reserved for imperial treasury. Subsequently, it came to mean the exchequer and as the collective denomination of the Sikh government and people. (Wilson, *op. cit.*, s.v.).

4. Dilwarpur. There is no village of this name in the *tahsil* of Sirathu; probably it is Dilawalpur which is a small village in *pargana* Kara, *tahsil* Sirathu. (*District Census Handbook,* 1951, *Uttar Pradesh* 22-*Allahabad District*, Allahabad, 1955, p. 218 S. No. 104.).

5. *Khudkashta* (P). Literally it means personally cultivated land. The *Ain* cautions the revenue officials against entering *raiyat kashta* or peasant holding as *khudkashtai* of *madad-i maash* holders in their records. (Abul Fazl, *op. cit., Ain* I, p. 289).

6. *Raiyat kashta* (P). It literally means the land cultivated by the peasant and denotes peasant holding. The *madad-i maash* holders could not interfere with the occupancy rights of the peasants. The *Ain* lays down that the revenue collectors should prevent *raiyati* land from being converted into *khudkhashta* by the grantees. (Abul Fazl, *op. cit., Ain*, I, p. 287).

7. *Qazi* Abdus Sami. He was of Miyal Kali, a hilly tract between Samarqand and Bukhara and played chess for money and drinking wine. In 990 A.H. Akbar made him *Qaziul Quzzat* in place of *Qazi* Jalaud Din Multani. (Abul Fazl., *op. cit., Ain* I, p. 615).

39

1. *Hukmnama* (P). Written order, decree, writ, warrant, written award or judgement, injunction, a deed conveying certain authority (Platts, *op. cit.*, s.v.). *Hukmnamas*, like *parwanas*, purport to confirm, support and execute a preceeding *farman* or *sanad* pertaining to *suyarghal* or royal privilege. (Momin, *op. cit.*, p. 89).

2. *Khan-i Jahan* Hussain Quli Khan , son of Wali Beg Zulqadr, rendered continuous meritorious service in the reign of Akbar. In the 18th year he pounced upon the rebellious Mirzas in the Punjab, defeated them and seized Masud Hasani whom he presented before Akbar. He was raised to high office and got the title of *Khan-i Jahan* ; after the death of Munim Khan Akbar sent him along with Raja Todar Mal, as *subadar* of Bengal. He was a *panj-hazari* (5,000) among Akbar's nobles. In 986 A.H./ December 1587 A.D., he died. (Shah Nawaz Khan, *op. cit.*, I, pp. 645-49).

3. Banahra. According to Sayyid Hasan Askari's contention it is the old name of Bhagalpur in the *sarkar* of Monghyr. (*IHRC*, Vol. XXIV, Pt. II, Delhi, 1951, p. 6, 19 n). It is not correct. As a matter of fact, Banahra exists today as a large and an important village in Bhagalpur District, situated just west of Amarpur. In the reign of Shah Jahan, Shah Shuja had his headquarters in this village. (*Census* 1961, *Bihar District Census Handbook*, 9, *Bhagalpur*, Patna, 1967, p. XLIV).

4. Monghyr, district situated between 24°22' and 25°49'N and 85°36' and 86°51'E in Bihar, in Bhagalpur Division, was one of the *sarkars*

under Akbar, who sent Raja Todar Mal to quell the disturbances in Bihar. Todar Mal for fear of teachery, shut himself up in the fort of Monghyr. (*Imperial Gazetteer of India,* Vol. XVII, pp. 389, 393).

5. Miran Sayyid Ali Muhammad was the son of Sayyid Husain, a brother of Sayyid Ahmad called Pir Damariai. His son, Sayyid Mir and his descendants, were recipients of grants from time to time. (*IHRC*, Progs. Vol. XXVI, Pt. II, p. 6, n. 22).

6. Sultanpur, a village in *pargana* Banihra, in Anchal Amarpur, Bankapur subdivision, Bhagalpur District. (*Ibid.*, pp. 169).

7. *Qazi* Yaqub was the chief *Qazi* and one of the veteran lawyers of his time. He took part in the discussion with Akbar about the number of free born women a Muslim could marry by *nikah* as the Emperor had more than four in his harem. The said *Qazi* made very long face at the proceedings of the issue. He was afterwards sent to Gaur as District *qazi* and in his place was appointed Maulana Jalalud Din of Multan as Chief *Qazi* of the empire. (Abul Fazl, *op. cit.*, *Ain*, pp. 183-84; A. L. Srivastava, *Akbar-the Great*, Vol. I, Delhi, 1962, p. 175).

8. *Sichqan-il, Sachqan-il* (T). The mouse year of the Turkish Duodenary Cycle. It is the first year of the said cycle. The use of any lunar calendar was inconvenient both to the tax-payer and tax-collector because of its non-concurrance with the harvests. This was perhaps the reason why almost all the Mughal emperors used the Turkish Duodenary Solar Cycle particularly in their documents concerning land grants, remission or exemption of taxes, payments of wages or pensions and other agrarian matters. (For details *see* G.H. Khare, *Select Articles*, Poona, 1966, pp. 174-202).

40

1. Shoram, there is no *pargana* or place of this name in district Muzaffarnagar; however there is a village of the name of Shoron in *pargana* Shikarpur,. *tahsil* Budhana, District Muzaffarnagar; but from the context of the document it is evident that the *pargana* had quite a number of temples. As such the place appears to be Soron, a town in the Kasganj *tahsil* of Etah District, U.P., on the Burhiganga. It is important for its religious associations; a temple dedicated to Sita and Rama stands on the mound, besides having other temples. (*Muzaffarnagar, A*

Gazetteer, Vol. III H.R. Nevill, ed., Allahabad 1903 p. 322; *Imperial Gazetteer ofIndia, Provincial Series, United Provinces of Agra and Oudh*, Vol. I, Calcutta 1908, pp. 480-81).

2. Akbar abolished *jizya* in 1564 A.D.

41

1. This undated *farman* must have been issued some time after 983 A.H./1575-76 A.D. in as much as it bears a seal bearing the invocation *'Allahu Akbar'*. This formula was engraved on the Imperial seal about the year 983 A.H./1575-76 A.D.(Badauni, *op. cit.*, II, pp. 213-14).

2. Sayyid, Fathullah, according to *Kitab-i Auhda-i Taulit*, which Abdul Bari Maani quotes, was a *mutawwali* of the shrine of Khwaja Muinud Din Chishti at Ajmer during the reign of Akbar. (Abdul Bari Maani, *op. cit.*, p. 10).

42

1. Nadila, probably Nandla, a village in *tahsil* Ajmer with an area of 4,075 acres and population of 1,414. *(Census 1971, Rajasthan*, Series 18, Pts. XA and XB., *10 Ajmer District*, Jaipur, 1972, p. 12).

2. Haveli *pargana*, one of the 28 *mahals* in the *sarkar* and *suba* of Ajmer under Akbar containing a fort on the mountain. (Abul Fazl, *op. cit., Ayeen Akbery*, Vol. II, p. 522).

3. *Hazrat* (A) Presence, dignity; applied to any great man, the object of resort, Your or His Majesty. (Platts, *op. cit.*, s.v.).

4. *Urs* (A). Literally, it means marriage nuptials; a marriage feast, a religious ceremony celebrating the union of the soul of a deceased saint with the Supreme Spirit. The disciples of the saint gather round his grave on the day of his death and recite the *fatiha* and offer food, incense, lights, etc. (Platts, *op. cit.*, s.v.).

5. *Riaya* (A). Plural of *raiyat* which literally means 'a herd at pasture' and connotes a peasant. The preamble to Aurangzeb's *farman* to Rasikdas refers to the two categories of cultivators, viz., *mustajirs* or revenue farmers and *riaya* or peasants. (Wilson, *op. cit.* s.v.; Henry Yule and A.C. Burnell, Hobson-Jobson, London, 1903, p. 777; Irfan Habib, *op.cit.*, p. 235).

6. It is interesting to note that the endorsement on the reverse of the *farman* of Akbar bears the date 4th *Shahriwar, Ilahi*, 5th regnal year of Jahangir and is followed by seals, one of them being of Asaf Khan of 989 A.H./1581 A.D. Thus it is obvious that the endorsement is not a part of the

document. Copy of the *farman* of Jahangir in the same context is given by Maani on pp. 30-32.

43

1. *Mihr* (P) The sixteenth of 32 days of a Persian month. (Bendrey, *op. cit.*, p. 17).

2. *Amardad* (P). The fifth month of the Persian Calendar. (*Ibid.*, p. 24).

3. The original is in Gujarati.

4. Adhyaru Mehrji Vachcha. Mehrji Rana was also called Mehrji Vachcha on account of his having been adopted by his uncle, Vachcha Jaisang. (Hodivala, *op. cit.*, p. 216).

44

1. Jalalpur Nulkhan. There is no place of this name traceable in the *Gazetteer of India, Uttar Pradesh*, Allahabad, 1968. Jalalpur, a village, situated in Lat. 25° 28'N and Long. 82° 6' E. is 16 km. north-west of *tahsil* Handia. It possesses a ruined fort and a tomb, and it was named Jalalpur after the name of Emperor Akbar. (*Uttar Pradesh District Gazetteer, Allahabad, op. cit.*, p. 379).

2. Manikpur, in the reign of Akbar, was one of the *mahals* in *suba* Allahabad; (Abul Fazl *op. cit., Ayeen*, p. 481). Situated on the opposite bank of the Ganges, it remained an important seat of Government in the early medieval period. A number of ruined mosques and palaces dating from the reign of Akbar bear testimony to its being an important place which is now a mere village. (*Imperial Gazetteer of India, Provincial Series, United Provinces of Agra and Oudh*, Vol. II, Calcutta, 1908, pp. 431-32).

45

1. Vithaldas or Vithaleshwar or Bithaleshar was the second son of Vallabhacharya (d. 1587 A.D.) who is reported to have impressed Akbar with his learning and piety to such an extent that the Emperor called him *Marifatagah* or Possessor of Divine Knowledge. (K.N. Jhaveri, *Imperial Mughal Farmans*, Bombay, Preface).

2. Gokul, *qasba*, lies in the west of *tahsil* Sadabad on the left bank of the Yamuna in Lat. 27°27' N and Long. 77°44' E, and is situated 1.61 km. north-west of Mahaban and 6.44 km. south-east of Mathura. (*Uttar Pradesh District, Gazetteer, Mathura*, Lucknow, 1968, p. 326).

46

1. *Chaupal* (H). A shed in which the village community assemble for public business, generally erected by the headman of village and used by him as an office. (Wilson, *op. cit.*, s.v.).

2. *Tumar* (A). A roll, a record, a register, an account. (Wilson, *op. cit.*, s.v.).

3. *Huwal Akbar* (A). It literally means He (God) is great. This symbolical formula replaces '*Huwal Ghani*' as invocation for the first time in this document and continues to be employed as such till 992 A.H./ 1584 A.D. when it was substituted by '*Allahu Akbar*'. (70).

47

1. Mamraspur, probably Maharajpur, a village in *tahsil* Khair, with an area of 551 acres, situated at 27 km. from Aligarh. (*Census 1971, Uttar Pradesh, Aligarh District,* Series 21, Pt. X-A, pp. 30-31; Code No. 152.).

2. Bisara, now a village in *tahsil* Khair having an area of 1,851 acres, situated at 30 km. from Aligarh. (*Ibid., Code No. 172.).*

3. Risaldar (P). The commander of a *risala* or body of horse. (Steingass, *op. cit.*, s.v.).

48

1. *Guad.* It seems to be identical with *Bad* the 22nd day of a Persian month. (Bendrey, *op. cit.*, p. 17).

2. Anjuman (P). Assembly, meeting, company, society institution, party, banquet. (Platts *op. cit.*, s.v.).

3. Sarosh or Sraosh, the guardian deity presiding over the soul of the dead, especially during the first three days after death. (Karaka, Desabhai Frangi, *History of the Parsis,* Vol. I, London, 1884, p. 202). The ceremonies are performed by the Parsis in honour of the dead during the first three days, most of which are performed in their Fire Temples. (*Gujarat State Gazetteers, Surat District*, Ahmedabad, 1963, p. 296).

49

1. Kahjari, probably Khajuri, a village situated in *pargana* Sharda under *thana* Sujauli, District Bahraich, U.P. *(Bahraich District Census Report, 1951*, Allahabad, 1955, p. 138).

51

1. *Dai (P).* Name of the tenth month of the Persian Calendar. (Bendrey, *op. cit.*, p. 24).

2. Kaikobad Mahiyar, probably Dastur Kaikobadji Meherji Rana, who succeeded to the *Desaigiri* of Navsari and also of *pargana* Parohol. He was the son of Dastur Meherji Rana, both of whom had been to the Mughal court at Delhi and obtained grants of extensive *wazifa* lands. (300 *bighas*) (*Gujarat State Gazetteers, Surat District*, Ahmedabad, 1962, p. 94).

3. *Agiary* (H). The fire temple where the religious ceremonies of the Zoroastrians are performed. (B.P. Ambasthy, *Contributions on Akbar and Parsees*, Delhi, 1976, p. 150).

4. *Siav, Siev*. The consecrated cloths which are presented by the Parsis to the priests as a part of their fees. (Ambasthya, *op. cit.* p. 150).

5. *Sanjana.* The fees of the ceremonies falling to the lot of the Zorastrian priests who had gone to Navsari from Sanjan with the sacred fire of the first great fire temple founded in India. (*Ibid.*, p. 150).

6. *Nav-so* or *nou shav* meaning a new bath. The sacred bath given every third day during the Zorastrian Barashnum ceremony of nine days. (*Ibid.*, p. 147).

7. *Bhagar* or *Bhangar* (H). The *bhag* or share of fees falling to the lot of the original priests of Navsari out of the sacred breads presented at the fire temple by different parties for the recital of the *baj*, the officiating priest removes one from each *baj* and all from the *saraosh baj.* The collection so made is afterwards divided by the priests as a part payment of their fees (*Ibid.*, p. 150).

53

1. Jhajjar, one of the 48 *mahals* of the *suba* of Delhi. (Abul Fazl *op.cit.*, *Ayeen*, p. 528). Town and *tahsil* in Rohtak District, Punjab, now in Haryana. (*Imperial Gazetteer of India*, XIV, pp. 107-108).

2. *Makhdum* Majdud Din *Hajji*. A great Shaikh, he was a mystic of note and a disciple of Shaikh Shihabud Din Suhrawardi. He made pilgrimage to Mecca twelve times and came to Delhi in the reign of Sultan Shamsud Din Iltutmish who appointed him *Sadr*. He was in this office for two years and discharged his duties to the entire satisfaction of the Sultan. He died at Delhi on the 12th *Zilhijja* 640 A.H./1242 A.D. and was buried within the precincts of the shrine of Khwaja Qutbud Din Bakhtiyar Kaki. During the days of the celebration of *Iduz Zuha* which are called the *Ayyamul tashriq*, (the days of distribution of meat in the name of God) the public of Delhi assembled at his shrine and this assembly was called *Khatm-i Majd* Hajji the ceremonial feast of Majd Hajji. (Shaikh Abdul Huq of Delhi, *Akhbarul-Akhyar*, Delhi, p. 49;

Maulana Ghausi, *Azkar-i Abrar*, Agra, 1326 A., p. 44; *IHRC*, Vol, XXXV, Pt. II, pp. 59-60).

54

1. *Rauza* (A). A mausoleum, a shrine, a tomb of some reputed saint at which prayers are recited and offerings made. (Wilson, *op. cit.*, s.v.).

2. *Nuzurat* (A). Double plural of *nazr* which means a vow, a promise made to God ; offerings to God. (Platts, *op. cit.*, s.v.).

55

1. This Shaikh Gadai is a different person and should not be confused with Shaikh Gadai Kambuh, the *Sadr* of Akbar, who passed away in 976 A.H./1568-69 A.D. (Shah Nawaz Khan, *op. cit.*, II, pp. 539-41).

56

1. *Khadim* (A). A servant; a servant in charge of a mosque or shrine; one who has charge of religious bequest or endowment. (Platts, *op. cit.*, s.v.).

57

1. *Desai* (Mar). *Desai* was an important functionary for the administration of a *pargana* in Gujarat. He was identical with the *chaudhari* in Northern India and *Deshmukh* in the Deccan. (Irfan Habib, *op. cit.*, p. 291).

2. Mehr Tabib Parsi. He is identical with Meherji Rana who was commonly known as Mahrvaid. (Hodivala, *op. cit.*, pp. 99, 149-88).

3. *Aul, Ol, Aual.* It is evidently the local name of some old unit of land-measurement. A land measure frequently met with in old Chalukya grants from Gujarat is the *hala*, which signified as much land as could be tilled by a single *hala* or plough in a day. An inscription of 858 A.H./1452 A.D. from Ahmadabad records the grant of six ploughs of land to Malik Shabban. A similar measure prevalent in Saurashtra was called *santhi* meaning plough. (Hodivala, *op. cit.*, p. 172-73). According to Wilson, *santhi* was equal to either 60 or 90 *bighas* of land each *bigha* being equal to 160 yards by 10 (1600 yards). (Wilson, *op. cit.*, s.v.).

4. *Wazifa* is here used not in the sense of pension or stipend in money, but in that of a grant of land rent-free or at a quit-rent, to pious persons or for past services. (Wilson, *op. cit.*, s.v.).

5. *Khajur* (H). Date tree. (Platts, *op. cit.*, s.v.).

6. The prince or noble who was given the power of *risala* used to write his *risalatun* on the back of the *farman* and affix his own seal. Below the *risala*, the *Diwan* wrote his *marifat* or the note to the effect that the *farman* was transmitted through his hands. (Jadunath Sarkar, *Mughal Administration*, Calcutta, 1952, p. 224).

7. *Mustaufi* (A). An examiner or auditor of accounts, the principal officer of the department in which the accounts of ex-collectors or farmers of the revenue were examined. (Wilson, *op. cit.*, s.v.).

60

1. Hamida Banu was the wife of Humayun. She was a descendant of Ahmad Jam Zindafil. Her father was tutor to Mirza Hindal and for this reason Hamida Banu was with the Mirza's household. She was married to Humayun at Pat early in 948 A.H./1541 A.D. and remained in Sind until she made the arduous journey to Umarkot with her husband where Akbar was born. She accompanied her husband to Iran. In November 1554 A.D. when Humayun set out for Hindustan, she remained at Kabul. She rejoined her son in 2 *Julus* 964 A.H./1557 A.D. together with Gulbadan and other royal ladies. She was closely associated with Gulbadan in Akbar's court. Together they interceded for Prince Salim when the latter rose in rebellion. She died on 19 *Shahriwar* 1013 A.H./1604 A.D. at the age of about 70. (Gulbadan Begam, *Humayun Nama*, A.S. Beveridge, ed., London, 1902, pp. 237-41).

2. Mahaban. (or Mehawen), was one of the 33 *mahals* in the *suba* of Agra, presently *tahsil* in Mathura District, situated in 27°27' N, and 77°45' E near the left bank of the Yamuna. It is a place of pilgrimage for the Hindus as there are a number of temples in it. (*Uttar Pradesh District Gazetteers, Mathura*, Lucknow, 1968, pp. 1, 2, 331).

3. *Zunnardar* (P). Wearer of the sacred thread, Brahmin.

61

1. Pathan, *tahsil* of Gurdaspur District, Punjab, headquarters of the *tahsil* of the same name situated in 32°16' N and 75°40' E. (*Imperial Gazetteer of India*, Vol. XX, p. 27).

2. Punjab perhaps refers to Bari doab of the *suba* of Lahore. (B.N. Goswamy and J.S. Grewal, *The Mughals and Jogis of Jakhbar*, Simla, 1968, p. 54).

3-4. *Mazru* (A). Literally it means cultivated and *uftada* means cuturable waste. Under Akbar the standing rule was to give half the area of the grant in land already cultivated and the other half in cultivable waste and if the latter was not available, the area of the grant was to be reduced by one-fourth. (Irfan Habib, *op. cit.*, p. 302).

5. *Tanabi bans* or *jaribi bans* was a bamboo rod used in measuring land. It was introduced by Akbar in the 19th year of his reign as a measure of length to obviate the decrease in the *jarib-i san* or the hemp-rope when wet. The former was, supposed to consist of 56 *gaz* while the latter of 60 *gaz*. Therefore a *bigha* or a square *jarib*, by the new measures would be larger than the one by the old. The size of the *bigha* is believed to have increased by 13 or 13.02 per cent. In order to convert the old *bighas* into new, a reduction of 13 or 13.02 per cent was made. (B.B. Grover, *Raqba Bandi Documents*; *IHRC*, XXXVI, I, p. 58 n. 11; Irfan Habib, *op. cit.*, p. 355). In this document, however, the reduction is 15 per cent. There were, obviously, regional differences in the percentage.

6. Boh or Bhoa, a small village, with an area of 1,108 acres, 13 km. far from Pathankot, overlooking the old bed of the Ravi, towards the south-west of Jakhbar. It is looked upon by the *mahants* of Jakhbar as the original place of *gaddi* of the *Jogis*. (*Census 1971*, *Series* 17, *Gurdaspur District*, Punjab, pp. 28-29, Code No. 161).

7. Udwant Nath, Jogi, the founder of the Jakhbar *gaddi*, originally he is said to have lived in village Bhoa. After its destruction by flood, the *Jogis* moved out of Bhoa and settled at Jakhbar. He is referred to always in association with Akbar, who after witnessing of his occult powers, won his admiration. The time of the *guru's* death is not known but probably he remained alive up to 1597 A.D. (*Goswany and Grewal, op.cit.*, pp. 6-8, 54-55 n. 8).

62

1. The unit figure has disappeared from the original. It seems to have been sealed by Qilij Khan as Governor of Surat or as *Diwan* of the empire about 989 A.H./1581 A.D. (Hodivala, *op. cit.*, p. 170).

2. *Mutiul Islam*, obedient to Islam and can be taken as synonymous with *zimmi* or protected subject. (*Ibid.*, p. 169).

3. These phrases appear to have been parts of the official terminology of the day. Each of them was peculiar to some departmental head, was used by him for recording documents, and was a sort of password which was perfectly understood by his colleagues who were able at once to tell through which hands or opinions the paper had passed. (*Ibid*, p. 168).

63

1. 5 Rabi II, 1082 A.H. which falls in the reign of Aurangzeb, cannot be the date of this *farman* of Akbar. It may, at best, be taken as the date of attestation of the present copy. Since Tirhut was conquered by Akbar in 1574 A.D. the *farman* could not have been issued prior to that date. Moreover, Gopal Thakur's period is 1569-81 A.D. (S.N. Singh, *History of Tirhut*, Calcutta, 1922, p. 216). The *farman*, therefore, appears to have been issued about 1581 A.D.

2. Tirhut, under the Mughal empire formed a *sarkar* or division of the *suba* of Bihar. It comprised a very large tract of country, being bounded on the north by Nepal, on the south by *sarkars* of Hajipur and Monghyr and on thc cast by *sarkars* of Monghyr and Purnea. In 1875 it was divided into the districts of Muzaffarpur and Darbhanga. In Akbar's reign the *sarkar* of Tirhut included 74 *mahals* (Abul Fazl, *op. cit., Ayeen*, p. 479; *Bihar District Gazetteers, Darbhanga*, Chaudhury, P.C. Boy, ed., Patna, 1964, p. 1).

3. Ajit Thakur was one of the four sons of Mahesh Thakur, the founder of Darbhanga Raj. (*IHRC*, XXXVI, pt II, p. 93).

4. Gopal Das or Gopal Thakur succeeded his father, Mahesh Thakur in 1569 and administered Tirhut till 1581 A.D. (Singh, *op. cit.*, p.216).

64

1. Jakhneli. No village of this name could be traced in the Shamsabad *tahsil* of Hardoi District, U.P.

2. Saunek. This could not be identified with any of the existing villages of the Shamsabad *tahsil* of Hardoi District, U.P.

65

1. This undated document must have been issued some time after 1578 A.D. when investigations were made in the *aima* lands in compliance with Akbar's *farman* dated 27 *Rabi* II, 986 A.H./3 July, 1578 A.D. calendered above. (46). The *sarnama 'Allahu Akbar'* as deciphered by Dr. Ansari is obviously a misreading for *'Huwal Akbar'* in as much as the former invocation began to be employed from 992 A.H./1584 A.D. (Abul Fazl *op. cit., Ain* I, p. 212). The formula *'Huwal Akbar'* is founded on documents up to 1582 A.D. This documents can, therefore, be dated between 1578 A.D. and 1582.A.D.

66

1. *Mir-i Mal* (P). Master of the Treasury. According to Abul Fazl the *Mir-i Mal*, the *Khan-i Saman*, the *Parwanchi*, etc., seen on the second fold, but in such a manner that a smaller part of their seals goes to the first part. (Abul Fazl, *op. cit., Ain* I, 363).

2. *Mandvi, Mandavi* (Guj., Mar.). A building into which goods are received from ships in sea-ports, a store, a warehouse, a custom-house (Wilson, *op. cit.*, s.v.). It also means market tolls or market dues. (Hodivala, *op. cit.*, p. 181).

3. Gandevi, A small town about ten miles distant from Navsari. (Hodivala, *op. cit.*, p. 181).

4. *Qabzul wasul* (A). A receipt, an acknowledgement; a document acknowledging the receipt of money or other valuables. (Wilson, *op. cit.*, s.v.).

67

1. Ekda, perhaps Ikra is meant. *(Purnea District Census Report*; 1961, p. 186).

2. Bangawan, village in Thana Kishanganj, District Purnea, Bihar, having an area of 1023 acres. *(District Census Hand Book, Purnea*, Patna, 1956, p. 228, no. 447).

3. Powakhali or Pawakhali, was a *pargana* in Purnea District, Bihar, having an area of 126 square miles. *(Bengal District Gazetteer, Purnea*, Calcutta 1910, p. 165.) Today it is a big village in *thana* Thakurganj, District Purnea, with an area of 1,078 acres having Lower Primary School and a Library. (*District Census Handbook*, Purnea, Patna, 1956, p. 276, no. 453).

4. *Bishnuprit* (H). Land granted rent-free to the Brahmins in honour of Bishnu or Vishnu or to maintain his worship. (Platts, *op. cit.*, s.v.).

68

1. Akbarbad, old name of Agra, historical town and one of the *subas* in the reign of Akbar, and capital of the Mughal Empire. (Abul Fazl, *op. cit., Ayeen*, Vol II, p. 491).

2. Lahore. It was a *suba* in Akbar's reign; city, *tahsil* and district in Punjab, now in Pakistan. From 1584 to 1598 A.D Akbar apparently made it his headquarters and undertook from there conquest of Kashmir. (*Gazetteer of the Lahore District*, Walker G.C., (ed.), Lahore, 1894, p. 29).

3. Multan city, *tahsil* and district in Punjab, one of the *subas* in the reign of Akbar, now in Pakistan. (*Ibid.*, p. 540).

4. Hiravijaya Suri, supreme pontiff of the Svetambar branch of Jainism and the most outstanding personality in the religious history of Jainism in modern times. Born in Palanpur in 1526 A.D. he was made Acharya in 1554 at Sirohi. In 1566 he held the high position of *guru*. He was the religious head of the Jain community. On 7 June 1583, on invitation of Akbar, he visited his court at Fathepur Sikri, where he was honoured by Akbar with the title of *Jagat Guru*. He died in 1594. (Commissariat, M.S., *A History of Gujarat*, Vol. II, Bombay, 1957, pp. 229-231).

5. Acharya (S). Guide or instructor in religious matters, especially one who invests a student with the sacrificial thread and instructs him in the Vedas, in the law of sacrifice, and the mysteries of religion; priest, founder or leader of a sect; a title affixed to the names of learned men. (Platts, *op. cit.*, s.v.).

6. Jaina (S). The name of religion differing from Hinduism. Jains are met with in considerable numbers, especially among the merchants and bankers in central and western India. (Wilson. *op. cit.*, s.v.).

7. Svetambar (S). A religious mendicant wearing white garments, especially applicable to one of the two great divisions of Jains. (Wilson, *op. cit.*, s.v.).

8. Jagat Guru (S). The leader of the world, an epithet of Brahma, of Vishnu, and of Shiva; a senior or elder in religion. (Platts, *op. cit.*, s.v.).

9. Siddhachal, hill, appears to be one of the sacred summits of the Jains.

10. Girnar, sacred hill in Gujarat, temple of Neminath, the largest and oldest, is situated on a lodge. It was one of the sacred seats of the Jains. (*Imperial Gazetteer of India*, Vol. XII, pp. 247-48).

11. Taranga hill, situated 20 miles south of Danta. It is sacred to the Jains as it contains two temples dedicated to Ajitnathji and Shambhav Nathji. (Commissariat, *op. cit.*, p. 234, no. 12).

12. Keshrinath hill, is sacred to Jains. The temple of Keshrinath is situated in the village of Dhulena, about 36 miles from the town of Udaipur, in Rajasthan. (*Ibid.*, p. 234, n.12).

13. Abu a hill to the south of Sirohi in Rajasthan. On it are situated five Jain temples, two of them being unrivalled in India; the first is dedicated to Adinath, the first of the 24 Tirthankas and the second is dedicated to Neminath. (*Imperial Gazetteer of India*, Vol. V, pp. 3&6).

14. Rajgir hill, is situated 14 miles south-west of Bihar Sharif and is connected by *pucca* road with Patna and Gaya. It is a sacred place of pilgrimage for Hindus, Jains and Buddhists. Jains regard it sacred on account of its being the birth place of their twentieth Tirthankara Muni Surata. According to the Jain tradition, the hills that encircle Rajgir are Vipula, Ratna, Uday, Swarna and Vaibhar, and all the five of them have Jain temples on their tops. (*Bihar District Gazetteers, Patna*, ed., Kumar, N., Patna, 1970, pp. 663-64).

15. Parasnath, originally called Samet Shikhar, hill and place of Jain pilgrimage in the east of the Giridih subdivision of Hazaribag District, (now in Bihar). (*Imperial Gazetteer of India*, Vol. XIX, p. 409).

16. *Kothi* (H). A storehouse; warehouse; granary; factory, banking-house, bank; a mercantile house or firm. (Platts, *op. cit.*, s.v.).

17. *Paryushan*. The holy festival of the Jains. (Commissariat, *op. cit.*, II, p. 231).

18. *Bhadrapad* (S). Name of the third and fourth lunar asterisms. (Platts, *op. cit.*, s.v.).

69

1. *Gul* (P). A flower, a rose. (Platts, *op. cit.*, s.v.).

2. *Post* (P). Skin, outer coat, rind, crust, shell capsule, covering. (Platts, *op. cit.*, s.v.).

3. Daniyal, Shaikh, was the father of Shaikh Kamal; follower of Muinud Din Chishti, to whose tomb at Ajmer, Akbar often made pilgrimages. (Abul Fazl, *op. cit. Ain* I, p. 322).

4. *Adalat-i Alia* (P). Supreme court of justice where both civil and criminal cases were dealt with and justice administered. It was under the charge of the Emperor himself and was a sort of a court of appeal. (Yule and Burnell, *op. cit.*, s.v.).

5. Fathepur or Fathpur Sikri. Before Akbar's reign it was a village dependent on Bayana, then called Sikkery or Sikri; when Agra was made the seat of government, it also became a city. It is situated at a distance of 12 *kos* from Agra. Sikri was doubly dear to Akbar, who on his victory over Gujarat, affixed to the name of Sikri the *praenomen* "Fathepur" the City of Victory. Today it is a historic town near Agra. (Augustus, Frederick, *The Emperor Akbar I*, tr. Bevaridge, pp. 201-202).

70

1. Siddhaur or Seedhore, was one of the *mahals* in *sarkar* Lucknow, *suba* Avadh in the reign of Akbar. A *tahsil* and *pargana*, situated in

26°46' N and 81°24' E lies to the north of the Gomti, presently a *pargana* in district Barabanki, U.P. (*Uttar Pradesh District Gazetteer, Bara Banki,* Joshi, Esha Basanti, ed. Allahabad, 1964, pp. 30, 282).

2. *Allahu Akbar* (A). It literally means God is great. This formula was adopted by Akbar as a legend for his seal and invocation for his documents. It was in 983 A.H./1575 A.D. that he asked the *ulema* as to how the people would like if he ordered the formula to be engraved on his seal and coins. There was a general approbation for it, but one Hajji Ibrahim observed that the formula had a ambiguous meaning. As the public at large expressed their approval, the formula was engraved on the imperial seal. It was however, in 992 A.H./1584 A.D. that Akbar ordered it to be used as an invocation and held ground throughout the reign of Jahangir and for some time in the reign of Shah Jahan. (Badauni, *op. cit.*, I p. 212). It should be noted in this connection that the selection of symbolical punning motto for coins, seals and as invocations has been a very common practice and the devoutest Muslims have not seen any livity or irreverence in a *Jau de mot* or paronomasia on a Quranic text but have regarded it as a proof of ingenuity.

3. *Yad dasht* (P). It literally means memorandum. The diary of the *waqia nawis* or news-writer after inspection by concerned officer was approved by the Emperor and each order thus approved was a called *yad dasht*. (Ibn Hasan, *op. cit.*, p.93).

4. Abul Fath, Hakim, arrived in India from Gilan in the 20th regnal year of Akbar and in the 24 regnal year was made *Sadr* and *Amin* of Bengal. He rose higher and higher in Akbar's estimation. In the 34th regnal year he accompanied Akbar to Kashmir and Zabalistan; on the march he died, at Dhamtur and was buried at Hasan Abdal. (Farid Bhakkari, *Zakhiratul Khawanin,* Karachi, 1961, p. 195. Abul Fazl. *op. cit., Ain* I, p. 469).

5. *Chauki*, a station of police or of palanquin-bearers, horses, etc., a custom or toll-station; the act of watching or guarding; a mounting guard. (Yule and Burnell, *op. cit.*, pp. 205 b, 206 a).

6. Abul Fazl, Shaikh, second son of Shaikh Mubarak Nagori, Secretary and minister of Akbar. He advanced through his scholarly gifts, *Akbarnama* and the *Ain* are monuments to his toil. He wrote several other books but his success embittered Prince Salim who got him assassinated on 4 Rabi I, 1011 A.H. /12 August 1602 A.D. (Shah Nawaz Khan, *op. cit.*, I, pp. 117-123).

7. *Waqia nawisi* (P). It literally means news-writing. Separate staff was appointed for recording the Emperor's orders, movements and

sayings in the *darbar* and on all other public occasions. The *waqia nawis* recorded in his diary whatever the Emperor did or said and whatever the officers of the state brought to his notice. (*Ibid.*, p. 93).

71

1. Bhatner, according to Abul Fazl. The *pargana* of Bhatner was named as Tahneer, having a brick fort. (Abul Fazl, *op. cit.*, *Ayeen*, p. 33. Sir H. Ellict's *Supplemental Glossary*, pp. 132-55). It was a *mahal* of the *sarkar* of Hissar Firoza. (*Punjab District Gazetteers*, Vol. II, *Hisar District*, Pt. A., Lahore, 1907, pp. 23-25).

2. Hissar-Firoza, in the reign of Akbar it was a *sarkar* under the *suba* of Delhi and was a place of considerable importance. It was the headquarters of the revenue division or *sarkar* of Hissar Firoza. (*Ibid.*, p. 23).

3. Rai Singh, Rai, was the son of Raja Kalyan Mal, belonged to the Rathors of Bikaner. He entered Akbar's service in his 15th regnal year. From time to time he was sent on various expeditions. In the 17th *Julus*, he was given the charge of Jodhpur to keep a watch over the route to Gujarat. In the 28th year he served in Bengal; in the 30th year he led successfully an expedition against the Baluchis. In the 31st *Julus* he was appointed *Amin* of the *suba* of Lahore. The same year he married his daughter to Prince Salim. He was also given the title of Raja Khan. He was a commander of 4,000 and Jahangir made him a commander of 5,000. He died in 1021 A.H. (Abul Fazl, *op. cit.*, *Ain I*, pp. 384-86; Gauri Shankar Ojha, *Rajputanaka Itihas*, Vol II, Part I, pp. 117-18).

4. *Takhaqui-il* (T). The fowl year of the Turkish Duodenary cycle. It is the tenth year of the cycle. (Tirmizi, *op. cit.* EMH, p. 119).

5. Lakhipur. Lakhipur seems to be a village in *pargana* Dibalpur. According to Alakh Dhari, the *pargana* of Dibalpur was called Dibalpur Lakhi and it formed part of Bikaner territory. It was conquered by Rao Bikaji and was inhabited mainly by Jats and Bhattis. It has a big fort. The area of agricultural land was 2,42,344 *bighas* and the annual revenue amounted to 1,35,14,059 *dams* or Rs. 3,37,850. Alakh Dhari has referred to this *farman* of Akbar (dated 3 July 1585). Dibalpur is now situated in District Montgomery and is a place of no importance. (Alakh Dhari, *Raja Rai Singhji, 1541-1612*, Bikaner, 1935, p. 104; P.J. Fagan, *Montgomery District Gazetteer, 1898-99*, Lahore, 1900, pp. 232-34).

6. Dibalpur. Also called Deobalpur, it is now called Dipalpur which is the headquarters of the *tahsil* of the same name in Montgomery District, Punjab (Pakistan). In 1524 it was stormed by Babur and under

Akbar it became the headquarters of one of the *sarkars* of the province of Multan. (*Imperial Gazetteer of India*, Vol. XI, Oxford, 1908, pp. 358-60; P.J Fagan, *Montgomery District Gazetteer*, 1808-99, Lahore, 1900, p. 34).

72

1. Jarha, village having an area of 1,252 acres in *tahsil* Sandila, District Hardoi, U.P. It is at a distance of 11 km. from Sandila. (*Census 1971, Series 21, Uttar Pradesh, District Hardoi*, Pt. X. A., pp. 172-173, no. 26).

73

1. Kuroh (P). A measure of distance which in the days of Jahangir consisted of 5,000 *diras*, one quarter of which equalled two *dira-i shari* of 24 *digits* each. This means a *dira* used in the *kuroh* consisted of about 38 *digits*. (Irfan Habib, *op. cit.*, p. 361).

2. Bhusahi Buzurg is a village in Thana Malwa, Hajipur subdivision, Bihar, having an area of 174.40 hectares with a population of 993. (*Census 1971, Series 4, Bihar, Muzaffarpur District*, p. 182. n. 89).

3. Probably Saraisa or Serreysa. It was one of the 11 *mahals* in *sarkar* Hajipur, *suba* Bihar, famous for tobacco cultivation. Name of this *pargana* could not be located even in the *Census Report*. (Abul Fazl, *op. cit., Ayeen*, p. 478; *Bengal District Gazetteers, Muzaffarpur*, Calcutta, 1907, p. 59).

4. Hajipur, one of the *sarkars* of *suba* Bihar in the reign of Akbar, subdivision and town on the eastern bank of the Gandak in Bihar. (*Ibid.*, p. 478; *Ibid.*, p. 144).

5. Shaikh Abdul Qadir Jilani, the celebrated founder of the Qadiriya order (d. 1166 A.D). His *chillas* are believed to be at different places in India. (Beale, *op. cit.*, p. 3).

74

1. Abul Qasim, brother of Abdul Qadir Akhund, was a native of Tabriz and his brother was Akbar's teacher (Akhund). In 991 A.H. Abul Qasim was made *Diwan* of Gujarat. (Abul Fazl, *op. cit., Ain*, p. 542).

76

1. This undated *farman* must have been issued about 1587 A.D. because Akbar arrived at Lahore on 27 May 1586 A.D. (Smith, *op. cit.*, p. 457).

2. Lahore. It was a *suba* in Akbar's reign, *tahsil* and District in Punjab, now in Pakistan. From 1584 to 1598 A.D. Akbar apparently made it his headquarters and undertook from there the conquest of Kashmir. (*Gazetteer of the Lahore District,* Walker G.C., ed., Lahore 1894, p.29).

77

1-2. Azar. Name of the ninth day as also of the ninth month of the Persian Calendar. (Bendrey, *op. cit.*, pp. 15-17).

3. *Khan-i Khanan* was a title which Akbar conferred on Bairam Khan. After his death Akbar took charge of his son, Mirza Abdur Rahim. His surname was Mirza Khan. His valour and courage in the various fields of battle won him the admiration of Akbar. In 1584 A.D. he was made *Khan-i Khanan* and a commander of five thousand. In Jahangir's reign also, he held the post of *Sipah Salar*. He became supporter of Prince Khurram, but was pardoned. He was proverbial for his liberality and love of letters. He wrote Persian, Turkish, Arabic and Hindi with great fluency. As a Hindi poet he wrote under the name of Rahim. (Abul Fazl., *op. cit., Ain.* I pp. 354-60).

4. Sipah Salar (P). Commander of an army, a general. (Platts, *op.cit.*, s.v.).

5. Aao from the list of *mahals* under *sarkar* Agra, this appears to be one of the *parganas*. (Abul Fazl, *op. cit., Ayeen*, p. 491). It is said to be a *pargana* or village in District Mathura, *sarkar* Agra. (Srivastava, *op. cit.*, Vol. I, p. 239).

6. *Chiragah* (P). Grazing ground, pasture (Platts, *op. cit.*,s.v.).

7. Savi, a village in Mathura District, U.P. (Srivastava, *op. cit.*, p. 239).

8. Govardhan. Town, *pargana* and *tashil* in Mathura District, U.P., Govardhana, which literally means 'fosterer of cows' is situated west of Mathura on the provincial highway to Dig and is a famous place of Hindu pilgrimage. The place is associated with Krishna and there is a sandstone temple of Harideva, built by Raja Bhagwan Das, father of Raja Man Singh of Amber. (*Uttar Pradesh District Gazetteer, Mathura* Lucknow, 1968, pp. 327-29).

9. *Quruq*. Watching charges. (Platts *op. cit.*, s.v.).

10. *Gaushumari* (P). An enumeration or census of kine, a tax upon kine. (Wilson, *op. cit.*, s.v.).

78

1. This undated *farman* must have been issued about 1588 A.D. It was in this year that the Raja of Rajauri is reported to have personally waited upon Akbar when the Emperor was on his way back from Kashmir and received the title of *Mirza* for his family members.

2. The Raja of Rajauri first came in contact with the Mughals on the eve of the Mughal invasion of Kashmir. Mast Khan, the then Raja of Rajauri, is said to have accompanied the Mughal forces on their way to Kashmir. The Raja was rewarded with a *khilat* and a *jagir*. (A.R. Khan, *Chieftains in the Mughal Empire during the Reign of Akbar*, Simla, 1977, p. 22).

3. Rajauri or Rajapur, also called Rampur by the Dogras, with an elevation of 3,094 feet, is a walled town near Naushahra in Kashmir, situated about 150 feet above the right bank of the Tawi river. It was a stage on the old Mughal route. (Sufi, G.N.D. *Kashir-Being a History of Kashmir, Vol. II*, Lahore, 1949, .p 761).

79

1. *Tarbuzfarosh (p)*. Water-melon seller. (Platts, *op. cit.*, s.v.).

2. *Riwaq* (A). A tent or canopy supported on one pole in the middle thereof; portico, porch, a lofty building resting on one column. an apartment. (Wilson, *op. cit.*,s.v.).

3. *Kothri* (H). A chamber, an apartment. (Wilson, *op. cit.*, s.v.).

4. *Safed-baf (P)*. One who weaves white cloth.

80

1. *Parwana* as given by Zafar Hasan (*AIOC*, X, p. 467) is obviously wrong in view of specific mention of '*hukm*' in the *unwan* of the text.

2. *Hukm-i rahdari* (P). Like *farman-i rahdari*, it was a permit issued by the *Khan-i Khanan* to a foreign traveller or trader, or to any servant of the state proceeding on a journey on official business or state mission. It was issued in the names of the officials of each and every territory through which the bearer had to pass. They were required to record the name and nature of the business. The privileged and other highly placed officials of the state also issued *parwana-i rabhari* called *dastak-i rahdari* in official parlance. Under the Aq Qoyunlu the *farman-i rahdari* was more explicitly called *ijazanama-i mahmil* and was issued to *hukkam, daroghas, mubashirs* (deputies), *tamghachis, rahdars, bajdars* and *kutvals*. (Momin, *op. cit.*, pp. 62, 97).

3. Jalalabad, a large district in Afghanistan, it is bounded on the north by Badakhshan, on the east by Chitral, on the south by Afridi Tirah and on the west by the Kabul province. The district is drained by the Kabul basin. Jalalabad town was founded in 1570 by Emperor Akbar. *(Imperial Gazetteer of India* Vol. XIV. Oxford, 1908. pp. 11. 13).

4. Kabul the central and most important province of Afghanistan became a capital when Babur made himself master of it in 1504. On his death it passed to his younger son Kamran Humayun left it to his infant son, Mirza Hakim, on whose death in 1585, it passed to the latter's elder brother, Akbar. (*Ibid.*, Vol. XIV. pp. 241, 243.)

81

1. *Bahadins* or *Behdins,* laity, laymen or unprofessional people and those outside any particular learned profession. (Karaka, Dosabhai Framji, *History of the Parsis,* Vol. I, London, pp. 216. 220. 221).

2. Diu, island, once forming a portion of Portuguese possessions in Western India. Now Daman and Diu form part of the Union Territory of India. For details *see Imperial Gazetteer of India. Vol. XI.* Oxford, 1908, pp. 362, 64.

3. *Hirbeds, Mobeds,* and *Dasturs* are the three classes of Zorastrian priests, the first being the highest. (Hodivala, *op. cit.,* p. 108).

4. *Bareshnum.* It is derived from Avesta *Baresma* meaning a bundle of sacred twigs which are an indispensable part of the ceremonial apparatus. It is held in the hand of the officiating priest while reciting many parts of the liturgy and is frequently washed with water and sprinkled with milk. It consists of a number of slender rods varying with the nature of the ceremony, but usually from five to thirty-three. These rods were formerly twigs cut from some particular trees, but now thin metal wires are generally used. (Hodivala, *op. cit.,* p.107).

5. *Afrings* are the only prayers of the Khordeh-Avesta that are required to be recited by the Zoroastrian priests alone, and also with some rites and ceremonies different from those of the *Yasna.* They are recited on a carpet spread on the floor, on which are placed either in a metallic tray or on plaintain leaves the choicest fruits and the most fragrant flowers of season, while glasses are filled with fresh milk, pure water, wine and *sherbat.* These prayers are recited either with the object of expressing remembrance for the souls of the dear departed or with that of invoking the aid of guardian angles. *(Karaka, op. cit.* Vol. II, p. 171).

6. *Baj.* It is derived from Avesta *Vak* which in Pahlvi became *vij* and in Persian *baz* . The last got corrupted into *baj* . It is a kind of Zorastrian

prayer comprising a formula, the beginning of which is to be muttered in a kind of whisper strictly abstaining from all conversations until the completion of the act, when the *baj* or conclusion of the formula is to be uttered aloud. (Hodivala, *op. cit.*, p.107).

7. *Gehsarna.* When a man dies among Parsis, a number of priests attend and say the prayers for the dead, two of them chosen for the occasion recite *Avunvat Gatha,* a portion of the *Yasna* which is called *Gehsarna.* (*Gujarat State Gazetteers, Surat District,* Ahmedabad 1962. pp. 294-95).

82

1. *Ulum-i din* (P). Religious sciences. (Platts, *op. cit,* s.v.).

2. *Hafiz* (A). It literally means a keeper, guardian, protector, preserver and denotes one who has learnt the whole Quran by heart. (Platts, *op. cit,* s.v.).

83

1. This undated *farman* seems to have been issued soon after the death of Mahyar in 1591 A.D. Local tradition states that after the death of Mahyar, Dastur Kaikobad went in person to Akbar's court for securing renewal of the grant made to his deceased father and evidently impressed the Emperor so favourably that the latter made an addition of 100 *bighas* to the original amount. (Commissariat, *op. cit., A History of Gujarat* II, p. 224).

84

1. When this *farman* was issued, Rai Singh was at Bikaner. In 1591 A.D. he was sent to Sind to help *Khan-i Khanan* Abdur Rahim Khan to fight against Mirza Jani who was defeated. Thereafter Rai Singh appears to have returned to Bikaner, when in 1592 Akbar sent his *farman* to the Rai. (*Ojha, op.cit.,* Vol. II. Pt. I. pp. 181-82; Smith *op. cit.*, p. 245).

85

1. Jhalra. It is an artificial reservior of water between the shrine of Khwaja Muinud Din Chishti and the northern spur of Taragarh formed by putting two dams across the old *nala* which drained the rain water of Inderkot and diverting the course of the *nala* from behind to the front of the spring during the time of Akbar. (Har Bilas Sarda, *Ajmeri : Historical and Descriptive,* Ajmer, 1941 pp. 96).

2. *Nala* (H). A water-course, channel, a ravine, a rivulet, brook. (Platts, *op. cit.*, s.v.).

3. *Takia* (P). The stand or seat of a *faqir;* the spot where he usually abides, whether it be open or enclosed. (Wilson, *op. cit.*, s.v.).

86

1. *Gaz-i Ilahi*. It was a unit of measurement introduced by Akbar in 31 or 33 *Julus* in place of *Gaz-i Sikandari* which was in vogue. It was equal to 41 *angushts* or finger-breadths and its length lay some where between 32-00 and 32-25 inches. (Irfan Habib, *op. cit.*, pp. 353-62).

2. *Lui-il* (T). The crocodile year which is the fifth year of the Turkish Duodenary cycle. (Tirmizi, *op. cit.*, *EMH*, p. 119).

3. *Aimma, aima*. The term seems to have been used first for the grantees perhaps as a complimentary epithet. Subsequently, while *aimma* came to mean the land granted, the term *aimmadar* or holder of *aima* was coined for the grantee. (Irfan Habib, *op. cit.*, p. 298).

87

1. This undated *hibanama* was probably executed about 1000 A.H./1593 A.D. as Taj Muhammad the donee mentioned in the *hibanama* seems to be indentical with one referred to in the *sanad* dated 995 A.H./1587 A.D. (75).

2. *Hibanama* (P). It is a deed of gift in which a property held in proprietary right is conferred on a beneficiary in order that he may derive a benefit therefrom. As such it denotes a transfer of ownership made without consideration, with the object of manifesting affection of the benefactor towards the donee. (Momin, *op. cit.*, p. 117).

3. *Chahardiwari* (H). A courtyard, enclosed area; a wall around a town, rampart. (Platts, *op. cit.*, s.v.).

4. *Suffa* (A). A kind of vestibule or portico for shade and shelter, open in front; a place for reclining on before the doors of eastern houses. (Platts, *op. cit.*, s.v.).

5. *Astana* (P). Entrance, entrance to a shrine, abode of a *faqir* or holy man. (Platts, *op. cit.*, s.v.).

88

1. Aimi. There is no village or *pargana* of this name. However, there is a village called *Ain* in *tahsil* Lucknow with an area of 2,442 acres and a population of 2,386. *(Census of India, 1951, District Census Handbook,*

Uttar Pradesh, 40, Lucknow District, Allahabad, 1953. p. 92, Code No.7).

2. Jamalpur. There are two village of this name. One is called Jamalpur Dadri and the other is named Jamalpur Kurmiyan. (*Lucknow District Census Report,* 1971, p. 84).

89

1. Mathura, was a *mahal* in the *sarkar* and *suba* of Agra; presently a district of Uttar Pradesh and place of pilgrimage for the Hindus. (*Uttar Pradesh Gazetteers, Mathura,* Lucknow, 1968, pp. 1-2).

2. Sahar, was the name of both a *sarkar* and a *mahal,* 25.6 km. north-west of Mathura on the road to Delhi. (Abul Fazl, *op. cit., Ayeen,* p. 500).

3. Mangotah or Mangotla or Muhgootelah. In Akbar's reign it was a *mahal* in the *sarkar* and *suba* of Agra. It had an area of 74,974 *bighas* and revenue 11,48,035 *dams*; presently it is a *pargana* in District Mathura, U.P.(*Ibid.,* p.49).

4. *Zabh, Zibah* (A). Slaughtering, slaying, sacrifing. (Platts, *op. cit.* s.v.).

5. *Shikar* (P). Hunting; prey, game, booty, plunder, pillage. (Platts, *op. cit.,* s.v.).

6. Peacock is considered sacred by the Hindus and held in great veneration. Saraswati, goodness of learning, is supposed to ride it.

7. In 999 A.H./1590-91 A.D. Akbar is reported to have forbidden the eating of flesh of oxen, buffaloes, goats, or sheep, horses and camels. Fishing was also prohibited for some time when Akbar visited Kashmir in 1592 A.D. (Sri Ram Sharma, *Religious Policy of the Mughal Emperors,* Bombay, 1962, p. 28).

8. Abul Fazl. He was the son of Shaikh Mubarak and younger brother of Faizi. When Akbar became alienated from the bigoted *ulama,* Abul Fazl and Faizi vehemently opposed Shaikh Abdun Nabi and Makhdumul Mulk. In 37 *Ilahi* he was raised to the rank of 2,000. (Shah Nawaz Khan, *op. cit.,* II, pp. 608-22). Shaikh Mubarak, father of Abul Fazl, after retiring from active service was ailing at Lahore where he passed away on 4 September 1593 A.D. This must be the reason why Abul Fazl is found in the *risalah* of Akbar when this *farman* was issued from Lahore. (Jhaveri, *op. cit.,* No. IVA, Notes).

9. This lineal or dynastic seal was the Great Seal of Akbar. In the beginning of his reign, Maulana Maqsud, the seal engraver, engraved the Emperor's name and also of his ancestors up to Timur on a round piece of steel in the *riqa* characters. This seal was originally meant for

diplomatic correspondence, but later on, came to be used on the *farmans* also. (Abul Fazl, *op. cit.*, *Ain* I, p.52).

90

1. Hisampur, in the reign of Akbar, was a *mahal* in *sarkar* Bahraich, *suba* Avadh, consisting of 1,07,400 *bighas* of cultivation and yielded a revenue of 47,07,035 *dams*. It occupies the extreme southern corner of district Bahraich and is bounded on the south and west by the Ghagra river. (Abul Fazl, *op. cit.*, *Ayeen*, p. 488; *Bahraich, A Gazetteer*, Vol. XLV, Allahabad, 1903, pp. 125 and 185). Presently it is a prominent village in *tahsil* Kaisarganj, District Bahraich, U.P., having an area of 136 acres and is 45 km. far from the *tahsil* headquarters. (*Census 1971 Series 21, Uttar Pradesh, District Bahraich*,. p. 110 Code No. 476).

2. Kasraula. It is not traceable. Probably it is Kasmara, a village in Bahraich District. (*Bahraich District Census Report*, 1951, p. 122).

91

1. On 29 *Mihr*/22 *Muharram* 1002 A.H./8 October 1593 A.D Akbar ordered Rai Singh to go with Prince Daniyal to the Daccan to punish Burhanul Mulk. The same year the Emperor gave Rai Singh the province of Junagarh which had been conquered and annexed to the Mughal empire by Azam Khan. It was probably after this period and till 1597 that no details of the movement of Rai Singh are so far available. From the tenor of the *farman* it is evident that the Rai remained engrossed either in Bikaner or somewhere else, but remained away from the court. That is the reason why Akbar complains of his inaction and suggests him to proceed to some *tirath*. (Ohja, *op. cit.*, Pt. I. pp. 183-185; Karni Singh, *The Relations of the House of Bikaner with the Central Powers, New Delhi, 1974*. pp. 52-53).

2. *Tirath* (H). A bathing place, a shrine or sacred place of pilgrimage especially the one situated along the course of a sacred stream. (Platts, *op. cit.*, s.v.).

3. Dalpat Singh, was the eldest son of Rai Singh of Bikaner. Born on 24 January 1565, he had incurred his father's displeasure as he had created disturbances in Bikaner. In the 46th regnal year of Akbar's reign, Rai Singh brought him to his senses and Dalpat asked his father to be pardoned. After his father's death, Jahangir raised him to the *gaddi* of Bikaner on 28 March 1612, but he was treacherously seized in a battle against the Mughal Commander, Ziaud Din, and was imprisoned and killed in January 1614. (Abul Fazl, *op. cit.*, *Ain*, I. pp. 385, 385n, 386,

517, 548; Ojha, *op. cit.*, Pt. I, p. 206, 210).

4. *Ahadi (A)* Literally it means single or alone and connotes gentleman or trooper; he ranked between the *mansabdar* and the *tabinan* on the one hand and *ahsham,* on the other. (Irvine, *The Army of the Indian Mughals,* London, 1903, p.43).

93

1. The year is missing, but it appears to have been issued about 40 *Julus*/1595 A.D. when Akbar added 100 *bighas* to the *madad-i maash* grant of Kaikobad, son of Mehrji Rana.

2. Navsherwan Bahman Manek Changa, a hereditary Desai of Navsari, had been thrown into prison at Lahore for his failure to pay the imperial dues. (*Hodivala, op. cit.,* p.218).

3. Kikaji. Kikaor Kaikobad was the name of Navsherwan's son. He was called *Behdin* Kaikobad Navsherwan and also *Behdin* Sheth Kika. (*Ibid.*, p. 221).

4. Kaka Meherji. His full name was Dastur Kaka (Kaikobad) Meherji Rana. He was the son of Dastur Meherji Rana and was popularly called Kaka, i.e., uncle. (*Ibid.*, pp. 219, 221. f.n. 50).

5. *Bania* (H) Merchant, trader, shopkeeper, grainseller, vendor of provisions. (Platts, *op. cit.*, s.v.).

6. *Namaskar* (S). Uttering the exclamation *namas* respectful or reverential address or salutation. (Platts, *op. cit.*, s.v.).

94

1. *Infandarmaz.* (P). Name of the 12th month of Persian calendar adopted by Akbar as *Ilahi* era. (Bendrey, *op. cit.*, p.15).

2. Surat, in Akbar's reign, was one of the *sarkars* in *suba* Gujarat. It contained 31 *mahals;* with its famous castle, its port and various *parganas,* which last came to be commonly known at a later date as the Surat Athavisi. It was placed by Akbar under the *Qaladar* or commandant and the *Mutasaddi* or governor. (Abul Fazl, *op. cit., Ain,* I, p. 519; Commisariat, *op. cit.*, Vol. II, p. 5).

3. *Tar* (S). Palm tree. It is applied to both the *Palmyra or borassus flabe lil formis,* and *corypha talliera,* and loosely to various other kinds of palms. It is most appropriate to the *palmyra* from the stem of which juice is extracted which becomes *tari* or vulgarly, *toddy.* (Wilson, *op. cit.*, s.v.).

4. *Khurma* (P). Date or fruit of date tree. (Platts, *op. cit.*, s.v.).

5. *Qui-il Qawi-il*, (T). Literally it means the sheep year and connotes the eighth year of the Turkish Duodenary cycle (Tirmizi, *EMH*, p. 219).

6. *Muhassilana* (A). Fees of the *muhassil* or tax-gatherer or bailiff. (Wilson, *op. cit.* s.v.).

7. *Dehnimi* (P). It literally means half of ten or five per cent and denotes a tithe of 5 per cent. (Platts, *op. cit.* s.v.). This tax was imposed on manufactures. Akbar reduced it from ten to five per cent. (Ambasthya, *op. cit*, p. 101).

8. *Taliqa* (P). The gist or abridgement of the *yad dasht* signed by the *waqia nawis*, the *risaladar*, the *darogha* and finally by the Minister. (Ibn Hasan, *op. cit.*, p. 94).

9. *Aban* (P). Name of the eighth month of the Persian calendar which was adopted by Akbar as *Ilahi* era in 992 A.H./1584-85 A.D. (Bendrey, *op. cit.*, p. 15).

10. The reference obviously is to Abdur Rahim who was *Khan-i Khanan* at that time.

95

1. Jaitore, probably it is a misreading of Jaitpur which is somewhere in Bikaner. (*Post and Telegraph Guide* pt. II October 1954, p. 275).

2. Bhatiani, the reference is probably to Bhatiani Amolakh Devi, who out of love and devotion for her husband, Rai Sing, burnt herself along with the two other *ranis* on his funeral pyre and became *sati*. (Alakh Dhari, *Raja Rai Singh*, Bikaner, 1935, p. 149).

3. Tujia, this may be a misreading of Teja, who was personal servant of Rai Singh. In 1597 or a little prior to this, there was an occasion for friction between Akbar and Rai Singh over an incident which happened while Rai Singh was at Bikaner and Nasir Khan, one of Akbar's fathers-in-law, was staying with him. Teja was deputed to look after comforts of this relative of Akbar. But Teja resented Nasir Khan's conduct and reported to Rai Singh about the guest having misbehaved with a Khatri girl. Rai Singh allowed Teja to use his discretion to bring Nasir Khan to his sense. Teja got an opportunity when Nasir Khan, on account of some defect in the supplies sent to him, addressed Teja in foul language where upon Teja and his men beat Nasir Khan, who, on returning to Delhi, complained to Akbar against Teja and Akbar ordered Rai Singh to send Teja to him. But Rai Singh reported that Teja had fled. The Emperor was so put out that he deprived Rai Singh of the gift of Bhatner and granted it to Dalpat, the Rai's rebellious son. (Karni Singh, *op. cit.*, p. 53 and n. 44).

96

1. Niryad or Neryad, Nadiad, *talluqa* and town in Kaira District, Gujarat. In the reign of Akbar it was a *mahal* in *sarkar* Surat, *suba* Gujarat, yielding 1,30,900 *dams*. (Abul Fazl. *op. cit., Ayeen*, p. 520).

2. Tahara, (Tahirpur in Bengal?) no *pargana* of this name could be located. There is *thana* Tehata in the Meherpur Subdivision, District Nadia, Bengal. There is also another place Tahirpur in Nadia District. (Alakh Dhari, *op. cit.*, p. 100, *Bengal District Gazetteers, Nadia*. Garett, J.H.E., ed., Calcutta. 1910, pp. 42 and 119., *Posts and Telegraphs Guide* Pt. II, October 1954, p. 678).

3. Qasur, is the most important town in district Lahore, now in Pakistan. In the reign of Akbar it was a considerable principality, with territory of both sides of the Sutlej. It was one of the 52 *mahals* in the *sarkar* of Doaba Bari, *suba* Lahore, yielding revenue of 39,15,506 *dams*. (Abul Fazl, *op. cit., Ayeen*, p. 536; *Punjab District Gazetteers, Lahore District*, Vol. XXXA, Lahore, 1916, pp. 24,251).

4. Atgarh, or Athgarh, in the reign of Akbar, it was a *pargana* with a strong fort in Orissa inhabited mainly by the Brahmins, and it was garrisoned by a military force of 7,000 infantry and 200 cavalry. Latter on it became a tributary state in Orissa, Bengal. (Alakh Dhari, *op. cit.*, p.100 and n.1; *Imperial Gazetteer of India*. Vol. VI. pp. 121-22).

5. *Bichi-il* (T). It literally means the monkey year and denotes the 9th year of the Turkish Duodenary cycle. (Tirmizi, *EMH* p.119).

98

1. This undated *farman* was most probably issued about 22 *Aban-Ilahi*, the date of the *zimn*.

2. Miran Sadr-i Jahan was made *Mufti* through the influence of Shaikh Abdun Nabi; in the 34th regnal year he was made *Amir* and got *mansab* of 2,000. In the 41st year he was *Sadr-us Sudur*, the chief justice of the empire, whose duty was to consider *suyurghal* petitions and confer *madad-i maash* and charitable grants. (Abul Fazl, *op. cit., Ain* I, p. 522; Jahangir *op. cit.*, I, pp. 46, 140).

3. Raidas Kachhwaha, seems to be misreading for Ram Das, one of the Kachwaha nobles who returned to the Punjab in 1583 A.D. and remained with the Emperor till the latter's death. (Refaqat Ali Khan, *The Kachwahas under Akbar and Jahangir*, New Delhi, 1976. p. 173).

99

1. He seems to be identical with Niran Sadr-i Jahan referred to at 98 supra.

100

1. This document was most probably issued soon after Kaikobad presented the Imperial *farman* to the *Qazi* on 26 Rabi II 1005 A.H./ 1596 A.D. which is also the year of the death of Sadiq Muhammad Khan referred to in the text. (Ambashtya, *op. cit.*, p. 145).

2. *Mahzarnama* (P). Literally it means a document or a petition attested by a number of witnesses laid before a judge with a view of promoting a suit. (Platts, *op. cit.*, s.v.). It served the following objects: (i) as a legal document for proof, (ii) a public recognition of a *bona fide* claim, and (iii) a documentary evidence in an indictment. (Momin, *op. cit.*, p.110).

3. Sadiq Muhammad Khan, Nawwab Namdar, was the son of Muhammad Baqir of Herát. Since his youth, he had been in Akbar's service. In the 36th year, he was appointed *ataliq* to Prince Murad in Gujarat. In the beginning of the 41st year he was made a commander of five thousand; he was made governor of Shahpur and died in 1005 A.H. there. (Abul Fazl, *Ain*, I, pp. 382-84; *Journal of the Bombay Branch of the Royal Asiatic Society*, Vol. XXI, 1900-1903, Bombay, 1904, pp. 212-13).

4. *Shar-i Sharif* (P). Court of Justice presided over by the *Qazi*. (Ambashtya, *op. cit.*, p. 143).

5. *Gumashta-i shumari* (P). Officer making calculations. (*Ibid.*, p. 142).

101

1. Khambaiyet or Cambay, in Akbar's reign it was one of the *mahals* in *sarkar* Ahmadabad, *suba* Gujarat, yielding revenue of 2,01,47,986 *dams* and lying between 22°9' and 22°41' N and 72°20' and 73°5' E. It is situated in the western part of Gujarat. (Abul Fazl, *op. cit.*, *Ayeen*, p. 516; *Imperial Gazetteer of India*, Vol. IX, p. 292).

2. *Padri* (H). A Christian priest, clergyman, chaplain, missionary. (Platts, *op. cit.*, s.v.).

3. The reference is to the Jesuits. The Jesuit Mission under Padre Jerome Xavier was despatched from Goa and on 5 May 1595 reached Lahore. Gracious was their reception from Akbar, who gave them permission to build a church at Lahore and to baptise in Cambay. In a letter written to the Father-General in 1598 A.D. Father Jerome conveyed

the happy news that Akbar had given the society permission to build a church at Cambay. (Augusts, Frederick, *op. cit.*, Vol. I, p. 332; Commissariat, *op. cit.*, Vol. II, pp., 274-75).

4. The concession thus made by Akbar furnishes the most abundant testimony to the catholicity of his character and policy in an age noted for its uncompromising religious intolerance in Europe.

102

1. *Nishan* (P). It is an order or a missive of a prince, princess, princes-consort. It ranks next to *farman*, but higher than *parwancha*. It resembles a *farman* in technical and literary form, but purports to convey emperor's command as is the case with the *parwanchas* of ministers. The *tughra* of the prince or princess always figures below that of the emperor. (Momin, *op. cit.* p. 137).

2. Prince Salim, son of Akbar, and Mariyam Zamani, was born at Sikri, on Wednesday, 17th *Rabi* I, 977 A.H./31 August 1569 A.D. He was called Salim on account of his birth in the house of and by the prayers of Shaikh Salim Chishti who resided in Sikkri, now called Fatehpur Sikri. His mother was the daughter of Raja Bhar Mal Kachhwaha. Salim ascended the throne under the title of Nurud Din Muhammad Jahangir after the death of his father on 16 October 1605. He reigned 22 years, 8 months and 15 days and died on Sunday, the 28 *Safar*, 1037 A.H./28th October 1627 near Rajauri in Kashmir, and was buried at Lahore. After his death he received the title of '*Jannat Makani*'. (Abul Fazl, *op. cit.*, *Ain* I, 223n, pp. 322-3, *passim*; Srivastava, *op. cit.*, pp. 125-6 *passim*; Beale, *op. cit.*, p.128).

3. This obviously refers to Abdur Rahim who was *Khan-i Khanan* at that time.

4. Cheeta (H). Hunting dog or leopard. (Platts, *op. cit.*, s.v.).

5. *Farghul* (P). A wrapper; quilted cloak or cloak; a great coat. (Platts, *op. cit.*, s.v.).

103

1. Junagarh, formerly native state in Kathiawar Political Agency. In Akbar's reign, it became a dependency of Delhi and was under the immediate authority of the Mughal Viceroy of Gujarat; the Emperor gave Rai Rai Singh the province of Junagarh in 1593 A.D. (Karni Singh, *op. cit.*, 53-54; *Imperial Gazetteer of India*, Vol. XIV. pp. 236).

105

1. The agreement is in Gujarati.

2. Roti (H). A loaf of bread; a cake of flour or meal roasted on an earthen or iron dish or plate. (Platts, *op. cit.*, s.v.).

3. *Darun*. Consecrated bread which is eaten on the day of *Farwardin*. (Karaka, *op. cit.*, Vol. I, p.140, and Vol. II, pp. 177 and 182).

4. *Karole*. Platains. (Hodivala, *op. cit.*, p. 230).

5. *Frasast*. It is a sacred cake marked on the upper side with nine superficial cuts (in three rows of three each) made with a finger-nail while repeating thrice the words *Humat, Hukht*, and *Huvarsht* meaning well-thought, well-spoken, and well done. It is placed before the right side of the consecrating priest, while the ordinary sacred cakes are kept on his left. (Hodivala, *op. cit.*, p. 230).

6. *Chashni* (P). Taste, flavour, relish, a mixture of sweet and sour; a taste by way of a sample. (Platts, *op. cit.*, s.v.).

7. Ervad Hirji. Meherji Rana was a recognised Dastur from 1579 to 1580 A.D. He left three sons, Kaikobad, Hirji and Bahram. Kaikobad. was acknowledged as his successor on account of his being the eldest of his brothers. (Hodivala, *op. cit.*, p. 229).

8. Hoshang Asha. Dastur Hoshang Asha was the lineal descendant of Khurshed Kamdin Sanjana who occupied a prominent position in his community after the death of Mehrji Rana Din 1591 A.D. (*Ibid.*, 231).

106

1. The *sanad* calendared at 73 *supra* is more or less to the same effect.

107

1. Murad, Prince, Akbar's fourth son, born on Thursday, 3 *Muharram* 978 A.H. was nicknamed Pahari. His unsuccessful expedition against Ahmadnagar told on his health and reputation. Thereafter he was seized with violent fits of epilepsy near Dibari (or Dihbari) on the banks of the Purna, 20 *kos* from Daulatabad, and on 2 May 1599, he died in an unconscious state. (Abul Fazl, *op. cit.*, *Ain*, I, p. 322; Srivastava *op. cit.*, p.437).

108

1. Burhanpur, the southern *tahsil* of district Nimar, lying between 21°5' and 21°37'N and 76°48'. It was annexed to Akbar's dominion in 1600 A.D. and became seat of Government of the Deccan provinces of the Mughal empire till 1635 A.D.(*Central Provinces District Gazetteers,*

Nimar District. Vol, A. Russell. R.V., ed., pp. 208 and 213).

2. Asirgarh, the impregnable fortress of Asir, on a spur of the Satpura range, 2000 ft. above sea level, is situated on the main road to the Deccan and at a distance of 12 miles from Burhanpur. The fortress was besieged and its possessions was delivered to Abul Fazl's son, Abdur Rahman, on 17 January 1601. (Srivastava, *op. cit.*, pp. 445 and 450).

3. Rana, reference is to Rana Amar Singh, son of Rana Pratap Singh of Udaipur. Prince Salim was ordered to march against the Rana of Udaipur who had rebelled and recovered a part of his ancestral dominions. He was no match to his brave father and unable to withstand the hardships. He died in 1619 A.D. (Srivastava, *op. cit.*, p. 439; Augustus, Frederick, *op. cit.*, Vol. II, pp. 373, 374).

4. Prince Murad according to Khadgawat is not correct in as much as the said prince had passed away on 2 May 1599 A.D. (Srivastava, *op. cit.*, p. 437). It was Prince Daniyal who laid siege to Ahmadnagar at the time of issue of this *farman*. He was born at Ajmer in 1572 A.D. and in 1597 A.D. was made Governor of Allahabad and after the death of Prince Murad, he was deputed to the Deccan. In 1601 he was made Viceroy of the Deccan and died at Burhanpur on 11 March 1605 A.D. (Srivastava, *op. cit.* pp. 143, 408, 438, 455, 481).

5. Ahmadnagar, a renowned and historical fort in District Ahmadnagar, Maharashtra. It is said to have been built by Husain Nizam Shah (1553-1565 A.D.). Its great strength was shown in its brilliant and successful defence by Queen Chand when a great Mughal army under Prince Murad besieged it in vain from November 1595. Again in July 1600 A.D., the fort was besieged by Prince Daniyal and the *Khan-i Khanan* and Queen Chand was murdered. (*Maharashtra State Gazetteers, Ahmadnagar District*, Bombay, 1976, pp. 874-75).

6. Mahmudabad, Mahudabad or Mehamdabad, north-eastern *taalluqa* of Kaira District, Gujarat. In Akbar's reign it was a *mahal* of *sarkar* Ahmedabad. It was founded in 1479 by Mahmud Begada. (Commissariat, *op. cit.*, Vol. II, p.80).

109

1. *Begar* (P). One who works without any compensation or wages, a forced labour (Wilson, *op. cit.*, s.v). It was an exceptional form of labour imposed upon some inhabitants by the authorities, rather than a regular part of productive work. (Irfan Habib, *op. cit.*, p. 239).

2. Prince Salim, who had unwillingly undertaken expedition against Rana Amar Singh of Mewar, rose in rebellion against Akbar. He marched from Ajmer to Agra confiscating more than a *karor* worth of cash and effects of Sahbaz Khan Kambuh who had died sometime before 11 November 1599 A.D. Qilij Khan, Governor of Agra, firmly refused to betray the charge while Akbar was in the Deccan. Salim, therefore, marched to Allahabad, assumed the title of Sultan and set up an independent court. (Srivastava, *op. cit.* pp. 463-65). By September 1602 A.D. Akbar had sent Salima Sultan Begam who wielded great influence on her husband Akbar and on her step son, Salim. She wrote from Allahabad that Salim was willing to submit. The death of Gulbadan Begam on 7 February 1603 A.D., however, delayed the successful consummation of the diplomatic parleys. (Srivastava, *op. cit.*, p. 472).

110

1. Nagaur or Nagore, presently a district of Rajasthan, is on the north bounded by Bikaner and Charu districts, on the east by Sikar and Jaipur, on the South by Ajmer and Pali and on the West by Jodhpur. It was the place of residence of Shaikh Muharak, father of Abul Fazl and Faizi, the noted scholars. In the reign of Akbar there was a mint at Nagore for striking copper coins. It was here that Dalpat, son of Rai Rai Singh, had fomented rebellion. (Abul Fazl, *op. cit., Ayeen*, pp. 33, 422, 548; *Rajasthan District Gazetteer, Nagore,* Sehgal, ed., Jaipur, 1975, p. 1).

2. Madho Singh. Probably Madho Singh Kachhwaha, son of Raja Bhagwan Das. He was present in the fight at Sarnal. In the beginning of the 21st year (*Muharram*, 984) he served under Man Singh against Rana Kika, and distinguished himself in the battle of Gogunda (21st *Rabi I*, 984 A.H). In the 30th year he accompanied Mirza Shah Rukh on his expedition to Kashmir. In the 31st year, after the death of Sayyid Hamid, he took the contingent of Raja Bhagwan Das from Thana Langar where he was stationed, to Ali Masjid, where Man Singh was encamped. In the 48th year, he was made a commander of 3,000 *zat* 2,000 *swar*. In 1001 A.H. he had been a commander of 2,000. (Abul Fazl., *op. cit., Ain.* pp. 460-61; Shah Nawaz Khan, *op. cit.*, III, pp. 321-22).

111

1. Kahalgaon or Colgong, town in the headquarters sub-division of Bhagalpur District, now in Bihar, is situated in 25°16' N and 87°14' E on the south bank of the Ganges. In Akbar's reign it was a *mahal* by the name of Khelgaon of *sarkar* Monghyr, *suba* Bihar yielding a revenue of 28,00,000 *dams*. (Abul Fazl, *op. cit., Ayeen*, p. 477; *Imperial Gazetteer of India, Provincial Series, Bengal,* Vol.II, Calcutta, 1909, p. 178).

2. Bihar, historic name of a *suba* under Akbar, presently a state administered by a Governor.

3. Usthoo, this village could not be located. According to Sayyid Hasan Askari it is still in possession of Khalifa Bagh family. (*IHRC*, XXVI, Pt. II. p. 7 fn. 28).

112

1. Lal Miyan, also called Lal Kalawant, belonged to Gwalior. He was a singer. He died in the 3rd year of his reign at the age of sixty or rather seventy years. He served Akbar from his youth. One of his concubines was so affected at his death that she poisoned herself and died. (Abul Fazl, *op. cit.*, *Ain.* I, p. 681, 681n).

114

1. The date of issue must be posterior to 1011 A.H. which is the date of the seal.

2. Jamil. Probably his name was Jamil Beg and was the son of Tash Beg Khan Mughal, commonly known as Taj Khan. (Abul Fazl, *op. cit.*, *Ain,* I, p. 508).

3-4. Tan Nath and Ban Nath. Neither of them occupied the *gaddi* at Jakhbar after Udwant Nath. It is possible that they might have represented the case before the Mughal authority and so their names are recorded in the document. (Goswamy and Grewal, *op. cit.* p. 60).

5. Narot, properly called Narot Mehra, a large village lying south-east of Jakhar at a distance of one mile, in Gurdaspur District. (*Ibid.*, p. 39, n. 3; and p.105, *Gazetteer of the Gurdaspur District*, 1914, p. 64).

115

1. In the *unwan* this document has been called *hukm* while in the text it has been referred to as *farman*. This indicates that Salim had not given up the rebellious designs while Salima Sultan Begam was busy with her diplomatic parleys at Allahabad. In March 1603 A.D. she reported that "she had cleansed the stain of savagery and suspicion from his heart and that she would soon bring him to court". (Srivastava, *op. cit.*, p. 472).

2. Sadarpur, village and *pargana* in *tahsil* Sidhauli. It lies in the south-east of Sitapur District, between Muhamudābad on the west and south-west and the Chauks river on the east. It was founded in 974 *Fasli*/1567 A.D. by Sadr Jahan Pihani. In the reign of Akbar, it was a *mahal*, of *sarkar* Khairabad, *suba* Avadh, yielding 8,31,185 *dams* as revenue. (Abul Fazl, *op. cit.*, *Ayeen.* p. 489; and *Sitapur, A Gazetteer*, Vol. XI Navill, H.R., ed., Allahabad, 1905, p. 207).

3. Khairabad, in Akbar's reign, was one of the *sarkars* in the *suba* of Avadh. Today it is a *tahsil* of Sitapur District bounded on the north by Hargam, on the east by Lakharpur and Biswan, on the west by Sitapur and Ramkot, on the south-west by Machbrebta and on the south-east by Pirnagar. (*Ibid*., pp. 486; *Ibid*., p. 164).

4. *Hissa-i rasasad* (A). An equal share, a proportional share, part or contribution, a fractional share of land; a divident on a share, a rate, cess. (Platts, *op. cit*., s.v).

5. In the *madad-i maash* documents *zabt-i harsala* is used to denote annual measurement of the land. (Irfan Habib, *op. cit*., p. 216).

6. *Tashkhis-i Chak* (P). It connotes demarcation of boundaries of land. (*Ibid*., p. 216).

7. *Ya Malikul mulk* (A). Oh, Lord of the domain. This invocation was employed by Salim when he rebelled against his father.

8. The round seal of Salim contains the following legend: '*Muzaffarud duniya wad din Sultan Salim Badshah Ghazi*.' This signifies the independent status of the rebel Prince.

9. This means universally obeyed edict of Abul Muzaffar Sultan Salim, the king, the valiant.

10. Absence of Akbar's *tughra* proves denial of the authority of the Emperor.

11. Lal Beg. After the revolt at Allahabad by Prince Salim, Lal Beg was sent to Jaunpur. Soon after the accession of Jahangir to the throne, Lal Beg came to be known as Baz Bahadur and was raised to the *mansab* of 4,000 and appointed Governor of Bihar. (Beni Prasad, *History of Jahangir*, Allahabad, 1962, pp. 44. 125).

12. Nurullah, probably he is Mir Nurullah of Shustar. Introduced to Akbar by Hakim Abul Fath, he was appointed as *Qazi* of Lahore. After Jahangir's accession, he was recalled, and when he offended the Emperor by a hasty word, he was executed. (Abul Fazl, *Ain*, I, p. 615).

13. Sharif Khan, son of Shaikh Abdus Samad, was a school companion of Prince Salim. While the Prince had occupied Allahabad in rebellion against Akbar, he, instead of advising him fidelity to Akbar, widened the breach between them and gained ascendency over Salim. On Jahangir's accession, he was made *Amirul umara, wakil*, and was entrusted with the Great Seal. He was made a commander of 5,000 and was appointed Governor of the Deccan, where he died in the 7 year of Jahangir. (Abul Fazl, *op. cit*., *Ain*, I, p.583).

117

1. This obviously is the converted date inasmuch as *Ilahi* era was in vogue at that time.

2. Gobindpur, village in the Buxar sub-division, District Shahabad, Bihar, with an area of 32.37 hectares. (*Census 1971, Serial 4, Shahabad District, Bihar*, p. 300).

3. Chausa, village with an area of 267.90 hectares with a population of 3,816 in 1971, in Buxar subdivision, District Shahabad, Bihar, is situated close to the east bank of the Karamnasa river, four miles west of Buxar. In Akbar's reign it was a *mahal* in the *sarkar* of Ghazipur, *suba* Allahabad, yielding a revenue of 794,853 *dams*. (Abul Fazl, *op. cit., Ayeen*, p. 482. *Census 1971, Series 4, Shahabad District, Bihar*, p. 296; *Bengal District Gazetteers, Shahabad*, ed., O. Malley, L.S.S., Calcutta 1906, pp. 136-37).

118

1. *Mihr* (P). Name of the seventh month of the Persian calendar adopted by Akbar as *Ilahi* era. (Bendrey, *op. cit.*, p. 15).

2. *Zakatul Jihati* (A). *Zakat* came to mean an impost like *baj, tamgha*, by the time of Akbar, if not earlier. (Irfan Habib, *op. cit.*, p. 65). The compound word, therefore, would mean imposts on manufactures.

3. *Ikhrajat-i Sultani* (P). It probably means petty burdens imposed by officials as royal obligations and seems to be more or less synonymous with *Mutalibat-i Sultani*.

4. Asaf Khan, commonly called Mirza Jafar Beg, was the son of Mirza Badiuz Zaman. His uncle Mirza Ghiyasud Din introduced him to Akbar. In 1581 A.D. on the death of his uncle the office of *Bakhshigiri* was conferred on him with the title of Asaf Khan; the office of *Diwan-i Kul* was entrusted to him by Akbar in 1598 A.D. Jahangir raised him to the high post of *wizarat*. He died in 1021 A.H./1612 A.D. (Abul Fazl, *op. cit. Ain*, I, pp. 451-53).

5. Fathullah, Khwaja, son of *Hajji* Habibullah Kashi, was one of the servants of Akbar. In the 29 year he was appointed to watch the Bengal officers, in the 37 year he was made *Bakhshi*, he reordered valuable services to the Emperor and in the 48th year, he obtained the rank of 1,000 and was attached to Prince Salim. After Jahangir's accession, he was made *Bakhshi*. (Shah Nawaz Khan, *op. cit.*, Vol. I, pp. 536-37).

119

1. Tulari, probably it is Tellery, in Akbar's reign it was a *mahal* in *sarkar* Surat, *suba* Gujarat, yielding a revenue of 9,17,890 *dams*. (Abul Fazl, *op. cit., Ayeen*, p. 519).

2. *Wazifadaran* (P) Plural of *wazifadar* or holder of rent-free land; stipendiaries or scholarship holders. (Platts, *op. cit.*, s.v.).

3. Tavri. A village in Surat district of Gujarat. (M.R. Palande, *Surat District Gazetteer*, Ahmadabad, 1962, p. 115).

4. Mirza Hasan Ali Beg. He seems to be identical with Mirza Ali Beg of Badakhshan. In the Deccan compaign he was an auxiliary of Prince Murad. He helped Prince Daniyal in the siege of Ahmadnagar, and in the 46 *Ilahi* he was rewarded with a flag and a drum. He was for long time in the Deccan as an assistant of the *Khan-i Khanan*. In the time of Jahangir he got the rank of 4,000 and was made Governor of Kashmir. Thereafter, he was given the fief of Oudh. He passed away at Ajmer on 22 *Rabi* II 1025 A.H./30 March 1616. A.D. (Shah Nawaz Khan, *op. cit.*, III, pp. 355-57).

120

1. Jhunjhunu, *tahsil* and its headquarters of the same name and of the Shekhawati *Nizamat* in Jaipur, Rajasthan, situated in 28°8' N and 75°23' E. (*Imperial Gazetteer of India*, Vol. XIV, p. 164).

121

1. Nurpur. It was situated on the east bank of the Ganges and Shamsabad on the opposite bank. Both Shamsabad and Nurpur had been in possession of the Rathors in the past and were conferred upon Rai Rai Singh in recognition of his eminent services to the Mughal Empire. (Alakh Dhari, *op. cit.* pp. 100-101).

122

1. This *farman* was issued from Allahabad during the second rebellion of Salim. In order to punish him Akbar set out for Allahabad on 21 August 1604 A.D. but was obliged to return on hearing the news of serious illness of Mariyam Makani, who passed away on 29 August 1604 A.D. Subsequently Salim came to Agra on 9 November 1604 A.D. under the excuse of paying a condolence visit on the death of his grand mother and surrenderred to Akbar who raised the Prince up and embraced him. (Srivastava, *op. cit.*, pp. 476. 478).

2. Bari or Bary, was a *mahal* in the *sarkar* of Lucknow, *suba* Oudh, in the reign of Akbar. But no reference to this is available in the *Uttar Pradesh District Gazetteers*, Lucknow, Vol. XXXVII, Allahabad, 1959.

Places of this name are mentioned in Dholpur, and other states.

123

1. *Hazrat-i Ala* (P). His most exalted Highness or Majesty. (Steingass, *op. cit.*, s.v.).

2. *Shahzada-i alamiyan* (P). Prince of the people of the world. (*Ibid.*, s.v.).

124

1. Rai Rai Singh was the father-in-law of Prince Salim. It was, therefore, natural for the Prince to summon him to the court when he found that the illness of his father had taken a serious turn. As a matter of fact Akbar passed away only a week after the issue of this *nishan*.

125

1. It appears that Jahangir followed *Ilahi* era as his regnal era.

2. Kathuah, or Kathua, an overgrown village in the Jasrota District, Jammu Province, situated on the right bank of the Ravi and between it and the Ujh river. (*Imperial Gazetteer of India, Provincial Series, Kashmir and Jammu*, Calcutta, 1909, p. 115).

3. *Narolisanga*. This village is most probably identical with Naroli or Nakki Naroli situated on the Ravi at a distance of about eight miles from Jakhbar in the north-western direction. (Gowswamy and Grewal, *op. cit.*, p. 87).

4. Parol. A small town, now falling in the Kathua district of Jammu and Kashmir. It is situated at a distance of about six miles from Jakhbar. (*Ibid.*, p. 88).

5. Chander Nath Jogi, his name is mentioned in the list of ten *jogis* on the reverse of the *farman* of Akbar, whose transcription is given by Goswamy, and Grewal. He was probably a disciple of Udwant Nath. According to Goswamy and Grewal, Chandar Nath Jogi appears to have founded a separate branch of the Jakhbar *gaddi* in the Jammu territory. (*Ibid.*, pp. 60 and 87, n. 2).

6. *Daftar* (A). A record, a register, archives; an office in which public records are kept. (Wilson, *op. cit.*, s.v.).

7. *Chela* (H). A servant, a slave, a pupil, a disciple, especially one brought up by a religious mendicant to become a member of his order. (*Ibid.*, s.v.).

8. Bhanda Nath, a disciple of Chander Nath. He appears to have succeeded him to the *gaddi* in the Jammu territory. (Goswamy and

Grewal, *op. cit.*, p. 87, n. 3).

9. *Yunt-il* (T) A year of the horse which is the seventh year of the Turkish duodenary cycle. (Khare, *pp. cit.*, op. 174-202).

10. *Jalkar* literally means water-toll. Profits or rents derived from lakes, ponds or the like upon a tract of country or on estate with the right of fishing and of cultivating the beds, if dry. (Wilson, *op. cit.*, s.v.).

11. *Bankar* or *Vanakar* literally means impost on wood. It was probably a tax related in some way to the woods and forests. (Goswamy and Grewal, *op. cit.*, p. 91).

12. *Baghat* (P). It literally means gardens and orchards and connotes tax levied on orchards which constituted, after the land-revenue, a major source of taxation in an ordinary village. Akbar and Jahangir attempted to abolish this tax, but it was reimposed in the reign of Aurangzeb. (Irfan Habib, *op. cit.*, pp. 226-227, 244-45).

13. *Marifat* (A). Literally it means knowledge, but is used more adverbially to imply 'by means of', 'through' or 'by any medium'. (Wilson, *op. cit.*, s.v.). Under the Mughal a petition was always submitted through some noble.

14. Kesho Das Maru, was a Rajput of the province of Mairtha and was in the royal service. Jahangir promoted him to the rank of 1,500 in his first regnal year. He had a *jagir* in Cuttack (Orissa) and was loyal lieutenant of Hashim Khan, the Mughal Governor of Orissa. Under the pretence of pilgrimage he visited the temple of Jagannath and treacherously seized it with its property estimated at more than two or three crores of rupees. He subjected the Brahman priest to torture in order to extort the hidden wealth. In the 10 year his rank was raised to 2,000 and was dignified with a dress of honour; held the *pargana* of Badnor. (Jahangir, *op. cit.*, pp. 21, 79, 296, 297, 390 and 410; Beni Prasad, *op. cit.*, p. 280).

126

1. Abdur Razzaq, probably he is Abdur Razzaq Mamuri. Jahangir allowed him to retain his office and grant. Subsequently he was promoted as *Bakhshi* at the headquarters. In 1612 A.D. he was sent to Thatta to restore order. (Jahangir, *op. cit.*, Vol. I, pp. 13, 82 ; Beni Prasad, *op. cit.*, pp. 121, 187).

127

1. Haveli, was one of *the mahals* in *sarkar* Korah (Kara), *suba* Allahabad. (Abul Fazl, *op. cit.*, *Ayeen*, p. 485).

128

1. At that time Jahangir lay encamped at Hafizabad on his way to Kabul. (Beni Prasad, *op. cit.*, p. 155).

129

1. *Nishan* of Prince Shahryar as given in the National Register of Private Records (VI, 1) is obviously wrong as the said Prince was hardly one year old at the time of the issue of this document.

2. Jan Beg, when Jahangir was a prince, he had given him the title of *Wazirul Mulk*; on his accession he was appointed *Wazir* of the Mughal dominions, he died on 10 *Zulqada* 1016 A.H. (1607 A.D.) (Jahangir, *op. cit.*, pp. 20, n. 2 and 136).

3. Baroda, under the Mughals was one of the *sarkars* of *suba* Gujarat, presently a city and district in the state of Gujarat. (Abul Fazl, *op. cit.*, *Ayeen*, p. 518).

130

1. Date not forthcoming.

2. Prince Khusrau's revolt soon after the accession of Jahangir encouraged Rai Rai Singh and his son Dalpat Singh to raise an insurrection about Nagore. Jahangir sent a punitive expedition under Raja Jagannath, son of Raja Bharmal, with Muizzul Mulk, the *Bakhshi*, as second in command. The encounter that followed broke the back of the rebels and scattered them. Rai Rai Singh was captured, but after a while, was pardoned and restored to his dignities and estates. (Beni Prasad, *op. cit.*, p. 140).

132

1. *Dharmasala* (S). A building for any legal or pious purpose, as a court of justice, a place where religious persons assemble, a place of accomodation for travellers and pilgrims. (Wilson, *op. cit.*, s.v.).

2. Vijayasena Suri, was born in 1548 at village Nadlal in Marwar. He took *diksha* at Surat in 1557 A.D. and rose to the dignity of an *Acharya* in 1572 A.D. in Ahmedabad. Under his advice, Jain temples were erected at Taranga, Shatrnjaya, Shankheshwar, Panchasar, and several other places. He visited the Mughal court at Lahore in June 1593 A.D. and died in 1615 A.D at village Akbarpur, a suburb of Cambay. (Commissariat, *op. cit.*, Vol. II, p. 236 and n. 18).

3. Vijayadeva Suri, Jain Acharya, was a great pontiff and successor of Vijayasena Suri. His doctrines created a schism among Jain monks. In

January 1617, the Jain monks at a conference held at Ahmadabad deprived him of his position and invested Ramavijaya with the title of *Vijaya Tilak Suri*. Jahangir invited Vijayadeva Suri at his court held at Mandu on 2 October 1617 and bestowed upon him the title of *Jahangiri Maha Tapa*. (Commissariat, *op. cit.*, Vol. II, pp. 143, 264).

4. Nandivijaya was one of the disciples of Vijayasena Suri. Akbar had conferred on him the title of *Khush Faham.* (Excellent in Intelligence) (Commissariat, *op. cit.*, II, p. 236).

5. Shatrunjaya, is a hill and a city of temples, situated about a mile and a half from Palitana in the south-east of Saurashtra, it is the most sacred among the holy places of the Jain community in India, being dedicated to their great Tirthankar Adinath. (Commissariat, *op. cit.*, Vol. II, p. 252).

6. *Nauroz* (P). New year's day. According to the Persian calendar it is on this day that the Sun enters Aries. (Platts, *op. cit.*, s.v.).

7. Vivekharsha was an active Jain leader of the Tapa Gachha. He inspired Bharmal, the Rao of Cutch, to sympathise with Jain religious doctrines. He consecrated an idol at a village named Khakhar in Cutch in 1603 A.D. In Jahangir's reign, he installed several idols at Agra on 10 January 1611. In July 1616, he along with Jayanand presented himself before Jahangir and the *farman* was accordingly issued. (*Ibid* ; pp. 257, n. 6, 263).

8. Parmar was a disciple of Vijayasena Suri. (Commissariat, *op. cit.*, II, p. 257).

133

1. The date 17 Tir 4 *Julus*/5 *Rabi* II, 1018 A.H. as given in the exhibit of the *IHRC*, XXIX (i), p. 174, and the National Register of Private Records (VI, p. 19) is obviously wrong in as much as Jan Beg had passed away on 20 *Zilqada*, 1016 A.H.. (Jahangir, *op. cit.*, I pp. 20 136).

134

1. Jahangir allowed Christians to open a church at Ahmadabad in 1620 A.D. and another at Hooghly. At Lahore and Agra public cemeteries were allowed to be set up. (Sri Ram Sharma, *op. cit.*, p. 73).

135

1. Sarang Dev was one of the intimate courtiers of Jahangir. He was promoted to the *mansab* of 800 *zat* and *sawar* in 1029 A.H./1620 A.D. Two years later he was raised to 1500 *zat* and 600 *sawar*. (Jahangir, *op. cit.*, Vol. II, pp. 182, 250).

136

1. Udaiharsha, Pandit, was one of the disciples of Vijayasena Suri of the Tapa Sect of the Jains in 1610 A.D. He, along with Vivekharsha, Parmanand and others, had led the deputation to the Mughal court and urged prohibition of slaughter of animals. (Commissariat, *op. cit.*, Vol. II, p. 257).

2. Prince Khurram, third son of Jahangir, born at Lahore on 30 *Rabi* I, 1000 A.H. (1591 A.D), was Akbar's favourite. In the 11th year Jahangir had given him the title of *Shah*, and when he joined Jahangir at Mandu, he received the title of Shah Jahan and was made a *Si-hazari* (commander of thirty thousand). (Abul Fazl, *op. cit.*, *Ain*, I, pp. 323-24, 358 and n.)

137

1. Mir Sayyid Muhammad Pir Damaria. According to Sayyid Hasan Askari, Pir Damaria was the title of two distinct personages, father and son, the respective name of the two saints being Sayyid Ahmad, i.e., Pir Damaria I, who died in 972 A.H./1564.A.D. and Sayyid Muhammad surnamed Zainul Abidin, i.e., Pir Damaria II, who died in 1024 A.H./1614 A.D. The tombs of these two saints stand on the northern and southern banks of the Ganges. (*IHRC*, Vol. XXVI, Pt. II, pp. 1, 5 n., 3, 6 n., 4, 7 n., 32). If the above findings are taken as correct, then the *farman* issued on 17 July 1610 should not say that Sayyid Muhammad Pir Damaria (II) died, as, according to Hasan Askari, he died in 1614 A.D..

2. Nagra, it is known as Nagla and is adjacent to Simli. (*Ibid.*, p.7, f.n. 35).

3. Haveli Patna, or Patnah. In the Mughal rule, it was a *mahal* of the *sarkar* and *suba* Bihar. Presently it is the capital of the state of Bihar. (Abul Fazl, *op. cit.*, *Ayeen*, p. 476).

4. Khwaja Jahan Bakshiul Mulk, the title was conferred by Jahangir on Dost Muhammad of Kabul who had served him as *Bakhshi* while Jahangir in his 7th year increased his rank from 2000 to 2500; in the 14th year he was raised to the *mansab* of 5000. He died on Friday 3 *Isfandarmaz* 14 *Julus*. (Jahangir, *op. cit.*, Vol. I., p. 217, Vol. II, pp. 81, 122).

5. Itimadud Daulah. His real name was Mirza Ghiyasud Din Muhammad; also known as Mirza Ghiyas Beg, came to the court of Akbar and served him well. He was the father of Nur Jahan. Soon after his accession, Jahangir bestowed upon him the title of Itimadud Daulah. He was *Wakil-i kul* or Prime Minister, and a commander of 6,000, 3,000 and he died in Rabi I, 1031 A.H./January, 1622. (Abul Fazl, *op. cit.*, *Ain*, I, pp. 571-73).

6. Abul Hasan, Khwaja, Asaf Khan, son of Mirza Ghiyasud Din Muhammad and elder brother of Nur Jahan. In Jahangir's reign he became *Khani Saman* (Chief Steward); in 1611 A.D his daughter Arjumand Bano Begam, popularly known as Mumtaz Mahal, was married to Prince Khurram; in the 9th year he received the title of *Asaf Khan* and gradually obtained the rank of 6,000/6,000 and in the 18th year he was the Governor of Bengal. As a financier and as an administrator, he displayed the highest capacity. Shah Jahan appointed him *wakil* and raised him to the rank of 9,000/9,000. He died in Lahore on 17 Shaban 1051 A.H./ November 1641 A.D. (Shah Nawaz Khan, *op. cit.*, Vol. I, pp. 287-93).

138

1. Haveli Ajmer. In the Mughal period, it was one of the *mahals* having a fort on a hill of *sarkar* and *suba* Ajmer, yielding 62,14,731 *dams*. (Abul Fazl, *op. cit., Ayeen*, p. 522).

2. Mustafa Khan was a Sahfi Sayyid. His name was Mir Ziaud Din Qazwini. He did excellent service to Jahangir during his princehood. Jahangir raised him to the rank of 1000 and appointed him Accountant of the Stables. He was given the title of Mustafa Khan and *pargana* of Malda in Bengal for his support and subsistence as *altamgha*. (Jahangir, *op. cit.*, I, pp. 25, 360-61).

139

1. Ram. Name of the 21st day of the solar Persian month adopted by Akbar. (Bendrey, *op. cit.*, p. 17).

2. He is probably the same Khwaja Nizam who brought pomegranates to Surat from Mocha in 1617 A.D. for the Emperor. (Jahangir; *op. cit.* I, p. 391).

3. Nariman Kaka Masani. Nariman Kaka and Meherji or Mehervan were brothers. Masani is the surname. He is the person who sells articles necessary for funeral ceremonies. (Hodiwala, *op. cit.*, pp. 252-3).

4. Changizkhani Chhapris. The *muhr* is identical with Mamudi or Changizi which was worth about 12 pence. Taking the rupee as 2 shillings 3 pence, the *muhr* would be 12/27 of a rupee. (Hodiwala, *op. cit.*, p. 251).

5. *Ghagharna*. Marriage between widow and widower. (*Ibid.*, p. 250).

6. *Vivah*. Marriage between virgin and bachelor. (*Ibid.*, p. 2).

140

1. Darapur. In the Mughal period it was a village in the jurisdiction of *pargana* Mallanwan, *sarkar*, Lucknow, presently it is a village in *tahsil* Bilgram, District Hardoi, U.P., with an area of 777 acres with a junior basic school. (*Census 1971, Series 21, U.P. District Hardoi,* Pt. XA., p. 160, Code No. 489).

2. Muhammadpur. There is no village of this name but Mohabbatpur in *tahsil* Bilgram, District Hardoi, U.P. with an area of 315 acres. (*Ibid.*, p. 15, Code No. 385).

3. Hasanpur Madho. There is no village of this name in *tahsil* Bilgram, but there is Hasanpur village with an area of 1,111 acres having a junior basic school. (*Ibid.*, p. 138, Code No. 219).

4. Bangarpur. Probably it is Bangalpur in *tahsil* Sandila, Hardoi District, U.P. (*Hardoi District Census Report*, 1971, p. 166).

5. Madhopur. Village in *tahsil* and District Hardoi, with an area of 444 acres. (*Census, op. cit.*, p. 100, Code No. 335).

142

1. *Ganwar* (H). A villager, country man, peasant, rustic; stupid fellow. (Platts, *op. cit.*, s.v.).

2. *Kachhis* (H). A caste of industrious cultivators much employed in market and flower gardens; a caste of gardeners. (*Ibid.*, s.v.).

3. *Chamars* (H). A caste of men who work in leather; a member of that caste; a worker in leather; a shoe-maker; a cobbler; a tanner. (*Ibid.*, s.v.).

4. *Baqqal* (A). In India it is a synonym of *bania*; a grain merchant. (*Ibid.*, s.v.).

5. *Khushnawis* (P). Writing an elegant hand; a fine-writer, a calligraphist; a writing-master. (*Ibid.*, s.v.).

146

1. Jagdishpur, village in Chapra Development Block, situated at a distance of 12 km. from Chapra, Bihar. (*Census 1971, Series 4, Bihar*, Pt. X, A & B, *Saran District*, Patna, 1972, pp. 42-43).

2. Chirand *pargana*, Chirand is a village in the Chapra sub-division, situated six miles east of Chapra, on the river Gogra just above its junction with the Ganges. In the Mughal reign it was one of the *mahals* of *sarkar* Saran, *suba* Bihar, yielding 6,33,270 *dams* and is named as Cheranend. (*Bengal District Gazetteers, Saran*, ed. O'Malley, L.S.S. Calcutta 1908, p. 147; Abul Fazl, *op. cit., Ayeen*, p. 478).

3. Saran, *sarkar*. It is now a district in Bihar. In the reign of Jahangir, it was a *sarkar*. (P.C. Roy Chaudhury, *Saran District Gazetteer*, Patna, 1960, p. 1).

147

1. Paranpur. There is no such village in Bahraich, but there is a village Parampur by name, whose area is 370 acres. (*Census 1971, District Bahraich, U.P. Series* 21 1972, p. 46, n 368).

2. Haveli, *pargana*, was one of the *mahals* having a fort on the banks of the river Sowd (Sot) in District Bahraich, U.P. (Abul Fazl, *op. cit., Ain*, p. 488).

150

1. *Igriz*. Church.

151

1. Chaund, *pargana*. Chand is now a village in Bhabha subdivision on the Bhabna-Chand bus route. It is the headquarters of the police station. Under Jahangir it was a *pargana*. (P.C. Roy, *Shahabad District Gazetteer*, Patna, 1966, p. 816).

2. Rohtas, *sarkar*. Also called Rohtasgarh. It is situated on the outlying spur of the Kaimur hills. In 1539 A.D it passed from the hands of the Hindu ruler to Sher Shah. Abul Fazl refers to its great circuit of fourteen *kos* and states that the enclosed land was cultivated and full of springs and lakes. Man Singh did a lot to beautify Rohtas. (Roy, *op. cit.*, pp. 867-74).

152

1. Shaikh Husain, a descendant of Khawaja Muinud Din Chisti. Jahangir, in his 5th regnal year, bestowed upon him 1,000 rupees. In the *Tuzuk*, his name is given as Khwaja Husain. (Jahangir, *op. cit.*, Vol. I, p. 168).

2. Murtaza Khan, *Umdatul Mulk Madarul Maham*. His name was Shaikh Farid Bukhari, a nobleman, who, in the first year of Jahangir, was raised to the rank of 5,000 with the title of *Murtaza Khan*, and was appointed *Bakhshi* or Paymaster-General of the army. He died in 1616 A.D. (Beni Prasad, *op. cit.*, pp. 123, 139; Beale, *op. cit.*, p. 3).

154

1. This undated *farman* must belong to the post 1021 A.H./1612 A.D. when Suraj Singh succeeded his father Rai Rai Singh to the throne of

Bikaner. (Beale, *op. cit.*, p. 217, Beni Prasad, *op. cit.*, p. 186).

155

1. 14 *Shahriwar*, 3 *Ilahi*/26 August 1608 A.D. as given by Khadgawat is obviously wrong. It was in 1613-14 A.D that Dalpat was driven into revolt on his supersession by his brother, Rai Suraj Singh. The latter commissioned to suppress him, inflicted a heavy defeat on his elder brother and drove him into the southern Punjab. Subsequently, he was captured by Hashim, the *Faujdar* of Khost, sent to the court and punished with death. (Beni Prasad, *op. cit.*, p. 186).

156

1. Bagwan. *Pargana* in Nadia District, Bengal. (J.H.E. Garret, *Bengal District Gazetteers, Nadia*, Calcutta, 15 p. 83).

2. Jahangirpur. Probably Jehangirabad, a *pargan* in Nadia district, Bengal. (*Ibid.* 83).

3. Ukhra, *pargana* in Nadia district, Bengal. (*Ibid*, 85).

4. Nadia, town, *pargana* and district in Bengal. It was called Nabadwip also. (*Ibid.*, pp. 1, 83).

157

1. Devhari, village. Probably Deori *urf* Hadipur, situated in Amroha *tahsil*, District Moradabad, U.P. (*Moradabad District Census Report*, 1961, p. LXXXX).

2. Amroha, North Central *tahsil* of Moradabad District, U.P. Under the Mughals, it was one of the prominent *mahals* in the *sarkar* of Sambhal, *suba* Delhi, yielding 63, 42,000 *dams*. (*Imperial Gazetteer of India*, Vol. V, p. 330, Abul Fazl *op. cit.,Ayeen*, p. 530).

3. Tatar Khan seems to be identical with Tatar Khan *Bakawulbegi* who offered a present of one *lal* (ruby), one *yaqut* (cornelian), a jewelled *takhti*, two rings and some cloth-piece to Jahangir on 9 *Rabi* I 1025 A.H./ 27 March, 1616 A.D. (Jahangir, *op. cit.*, I, p. 318).

158

1. Naqib Khan, original name Mir Ghiyasud Din Ali, the son of Abdul Latif Qazwini, became a personal friend of Akbar under whom he served; in the 26th year he received the title of *Naqib Khan*. He was Akbar's reader and superintended translations from Sanskrit into Persian. On Jahangir's accession, he was made a commander of 1500, he died in the beginning of 1023 A.H./1614 A.D. at Ajmer. (Abul Fazl, *op. cit.*, *Ain*, I, pp. 496-98).

161

1. Man Singh Kachhwaha, son of Raja Bhagwan Das of Jaipur; maternal uncle of Khusrau; was appointed Governor of Kabul by Akbar in 1587 A.D. and next year of Bihar. In 1589 A.D. he was honoured with the title of *Raja* and *mansab* of 7,000 and made Governor of Bengal. He was a great general and contributed considerably to the success of the Mughal arms under Jahangir. He died in July 1614. (Jahangir, *op. cit.*, I, p. 266; Beale, *op. cit.*, p. 242).

162

1. Abid Khan, son of the historian Nizamud Din, was in the Imperial service. In the 11th regnal year he was *Bakhshi* and newswriter at Ahmadabad, as also at the court; later, he espoused the cause of Prince Khurram; he was also *Diwan-i Buyutat*. (Jahangir, *op. cit.*, I, pp. 331 420, Vol. II, 61; Beni Prasad, *op. cit.*, p. 329).

164

1. Khurdad, Khwurdad, Khuwardad (P). Name of the third month of the Persian solar calender adopted by Akbar as *Ilahi* era. Name of one of 32 days of the month adopted in the Ilahi system. (Bendery. *op. cit.*, 17).

2. Phukkar, or Pushkar, seven miles north of Ajmer, is a celebrated place of pilgrimage and sanctity of its lake is equalled by that of Mansarowar; has five principal temples. (*Rajasthan District Gazetteers*, Ajmer, ed., Dhoundiyal, B.N. Alwar, 1966, pp. 736, 738).

3. *Qismatnama* (P). A deed of division. (*Platts, op. cit..*, s.v).

4. *Purohit* (H) A family priest, king's domestic chaplain, priest who conducts all the ceremonies and sacrifices of a family. (*Ibid.*, s.v.).

5. *Pujari* (H). A worshipper, priest who officiates at a shrine and lives upon the offerings made to the diety. (*Ibid.*, s.v.).

6. Ani Rai Singh, (Dalan), original name was Anup Ray. As he saved Jahangir at tiger hunt, he was given the title of *Anirai Singh Dalan*, and his *mansab* was raised to 1500 *zat* and 500 *sawar*. Jahangir in his 14th year further raised his *mansab* to 2000 *zat* and 1600 *sawar*. (Jahangir *op. cit.*, Vol. II, pp. 185-87, 188; *Ibid.*, Vol. II, p. 81).

165

1. Parchhiyar, *pargana*. Probably Gurchhappar, a village in Nakur *tahsil*, District Saharanpur, U.P. (*Saharanpur District Census Report*, 1971, p. 126).

2. Saharanpur, *sarkar*. The town of Saharanpur was founded in the reign of Muhammad bin Tughluq about the year 1340 A.D. and derived its name from a Muslim saint called Shah Haran Chishti whose shrine became an object of attraction to the Muslims. According to *Ain-i Akbari* Saharanpur was a *sarkar* in the *suba* of Delhi and this *sarkar* was divided into four *dasturs* or districts of Deoband, Kairana, Sardhana and Indri. There were 36 *mahals* or *parganas* in it. The *mahal* of Saharanpur paid a revenue of 6,951,545 *dams* on a cultivated area of 212,336 *bighas*. It was a favourite summer resort of the Mughal court and the nobles because of the coolness of the climate and the facilities for sport. Nur Jahan had a palace in the village called Nurnagar. (*Saharanpur District Gazetteer*, Allahabad, 1909, pp. 180-83; *Imperial Gazetteer of India*, Vol. XXI, Oxford, 1908, p. 369).

166

1. This document has been wrongly designated as *hukm* by Goswamy and Grewal.

167

1. Hashim Beg Kharshti. He seems to be identical with Hashim Beg, the *Faujdar* of Khost, who captured Dalpat and sent him to the court. (Beni Prasad, *op. cit.*, p. 186).

172

1. *Qindil* (A). A candle; a candle-stick; a lamp-stand; lantern; chandelier. (Platts op. cit., s.v.).

2. *Sartarashi* (P). Literally it means shaving of the head and is synonymous with *mundan* which connotes a ceremony, performed on the children of both Hindus and Muslims; the former commonly and sometimes the latter, leave a lock of hair on the crown of the head. (Wilson, *op. cit.*, s.v.).

173

1. This undated *farman* must have been issued within a couple of months of the date of the *yad dasht* dated 24 *Mihr*, *Ilahi*, 9/28 September, 1614 A.D.

2. Kania or Kaniya, is a village in *tahsil* Beawar, District Ajmer, having an area of 3,095 acres. (*Census 1971, Rajasthan, Ajmer District, Series* 18, Pts., XA & XB, p. 36).

175

1. *Hujra* (P). A chamber, room, closet, cell, a hut. (Platts, *op. cit.* s.v.).

176

1. Sayyid Ahmad Haqq. He seems to have been the *Sadr* of Jahangir till the appointment of Musavi Khan to that post in the 15th regnal year. We have been told of only two *sadras* under Jahangir, viz. (i) Miran Sadr-i Jahan and (ii) Musavi Khan who held the office from 15th year of Jahangir's reign to the 16th year of Shah Jahan's reign (Ibn Hasan, *op. cit.*, p. 287; Shah Nawaz Khan, *op. cit.*, II, pp. 326-27). The present document, therefore, fills up a gap in the history of the *Sadrs* under Jahangir.

177

1. Kakori was an important and ancient town. It was a *pargana* as early as the time of Akbar. From 1843 it was included in the *chakla* of Sandila in District Hardoi. Today it is in district Lucknow. (*Uttar Pradesh District Gazetteers*, Vol. XXXVI, Lucknow, ed., Sharma, Vinod Chandra, Allahabad, 1956, pp. 386-87).

180

1. Deorai or Daurai, village in *tahsil* and district Ajmer, having an area of 2,789 acres, is at a distance of 9 km. from Ajmer. (*Census 1971, Rajasthan, Ajmer District, Series 18*, Pts. XA and XB, p. 8. Code No. 72).

2. Somalpur, village in *tahsil* and district Ajmer, having a area of 2,789 acres, is at a distance of 9 km. from Ajmer. (*Ibid.*, p. 8 Code No. 71).

3. The shrine of Sayyid Husain *Khing Sawar* is situated at Taragarh near Ajmer. (B.N. Dhoudiyal, *Rajasthan District Gazetteers, Ajmer*, Alwar, 1966, p. 741).

4. Iradat Khan. He seems to be identical with Azim Khan Mir Muhammad Baqir. He belongs to the distinguished family of the Sayyids of Sava. On his arrival in India he was appointed by Mirza Jafar Asaf Khan as *Faujdar* of Sialkot, Gujarat and Punjab and afterwards became his son-in-law thus came in contact with Jahangir from whom he received much favour. In the 15th year he was made Governor of Kashmir. From there he went to the court and became *Mir Bakhshi*. After the death of Jahangir he was confirmed in the appointment of *Mir Bakhshi* by Shah Jahan who subsequently made him his *Wazir*. He died in 1059 A.H./1649 A.D. (Shah Nawaz Khan, *op. cit.*, I, pp. 174-80).

181

1. Nawwab Mucanebxhan. He seems to be identical with Nawwab Muqarrab Khan.

2. Masulipatam or Bandar, headquarters of Kistna District, Madras, seaport and early European settlement. In Hisdustani it was called Machhlipatam or fish-town. (*Imperial Gazetteer of India*, Vol. XVII, Oxford, 1908, pp. 215-17).

3. Xerafins. The term is a corruption of *ashrafi* but in its present form represented a silver coin formerly current at Goa and several other European ports, in value somewhat less than ls. 6d. (Yule and Burnell, *op.cit.*, s.v.).

4. Ormuz. Also called Ormus, Hormuz, or Hurmus a famous city on the shores of the Gulf. It was visited more than once by Ibn Batuta. Abdur Razzaq, the envoy of Shah Rukh, on his way to the court of Vijayanagar was in Hormuz in 1442 A.D. and was then frequented by the merchants of all the countries of Asia, more important among them being China, Java, Bengal, Tenasserim, Siam and the Maldives. In September 1507 A.D., the king of Hormuz became a tributary to Portugal and for more than a century Ormuz remained in the dominions of Portugal. (*Encyclopaedia Britannica*, Vol. XVII, Edinburgh, MDCCL XXX IV pp. 856-7).

5. Goga or Gogha, town in Dhandhuka taluk, in the peninsula of Kathiawar on the gulf of Cambay, 193 miles north-west to Bombay city. (*Imperial Gazetteer of India*, Vol. XII, Oxford, 1908, pp. 301-02).

6. Diu, an island forming former portion of the Portuguese possessions in Western India and separated from the peninsula of Kathiawar. The town of Diu was once a famous centre of commerce and had magnificent buildings. (*Imperial Gazetteer of India*, Vol. XI, Oxford, 1908, pp. 362-64.) Now, Daman and Diu form the union territory of India.

7. Jero Xavier. In 1613 A.D. the Portuguese seized four Mughal ships which carried a huge treasure in the vicinity of Surat. The Mughal forces besieged Daman. Most of the Portuguese living in the Mughal empire were arrested. Even Father Jerome Xavier was put in the custody of Muqarrab Khan, the Governor of Surat. All the favours and concessions extended to the Portuguese missionaries were withdrawn. Their religion and worship were interdicted. Thus compelled the Portuguese made peace with the Mughals. During the remainder of Jahangir's reign, there was no war between the Mughals and the Portuguese (Beni Prasad, *op. cit.*, pp. 187-8).

182

1. Suket, *pargana*. The correct name is Sakit, a town and *pargana* in Etah District, U.P.

183

1.*Nazul* (A). Literally it means descent but in revenue language it connotes an escheated property in gardens and houses, any property that is considered to have lapsed to the state; on office for investigating lapsed claims. (Wilson, *op. cit.* s.v.).

186

1. Baghdad or Bagdad, capital of Iraq, on the Tigris. Once it was famous centre of Arabic learning and literature and formed an important trade route between India and Persia. (T.C. Collocott and J.O. Thorne, *Chamber's World Gazetter,* London, 1954, p. 60).

187

1. This undated document must have been issued before 1616 A.D. because it was till that year that *Khan-i Khanan* held supreme command of the Deccan. (Beni Prasad, *op. cit.*, p. 246).

188

1. The correct name seems to be Vivekharshn.

2. *Ghusalkhana* (P). A bath-room. The apartment so called was used by some of the Great Mughals as a place of private audience. (Yule and Burnell, *op. cit.*, s.v.).

3. *Jamaat* (A). A company, body, party, troop, group, congregated or collective body, assembly, congregation, society, class, order. (Platts, *op. cit.*, s.v.).

4. *Yazdan prasti* (P). Divine-worship.

5. Diyanat Khan. His name was Qasim Ali and his title was Diyanat Khan which was given to him by Jahangir. He was an old servant of Akbar and was promoted to the rank of 500 *zat* and 200 *sawar*. He served in Udaipur under Prince Khurram for some time. He was confined in Gwalior for his misconduct towards Ittimadud Daulah. He was afterwards pardoned, released and his property restored to him. In 1615 A.D. he was appointed *Arz-i Mukarrar* by Jahangir but in 1618 A.D. he was removed and sent to the Deccan with Prince Khurram. (Jahangir, *op. cit.*, I, pp. 123, 260, 265, 278-79, 303, 306, 318 331, 333, 335; Jahangir, *op. cit.*, II, 250; Shah Nawaz Khan, *op. cit.*, II, pp. 8-9).

197

1. *Qaum* (A). A people, nation, tribe, race, family sect, caste. (Platts, *op. cit.*, s.v).

198

1. Pahlodi, *pargana*. Phalaudi, Sirsa and Hansi formed part of the Bikaner State and were held by Raja Sur Singhji (Rai Suraj Singh). The fort and territory of Phalaudi were wrested by Bikaner from the Jodhpur State. The fort of Phalaudi, which was strongly built, possessed a great strategic value. It has since reverted to Jodhpur. (Alakh Dhari, *op. cit.*, pp. 102-103).

199

1. Kaiter, village. Perhaps Kotra, a village in Ajmer *tahsil*, District Ajmer, Rajasthan (*Ajmer District Census Report*, 1961, p. 243).

200

1. *Mazar* (A). A shrine; tomb, sepulchre; grave. (Platts, *op. cit.*, s.v.).
2. *Rozina* (P). Daily pay or wages, daily allowance, daily food, stipend, pension. (*Ibid.*, s.v.).

201

1. Fakharpur, *pargana*. In the Mughal period it was one of the *mahals* having a brick fort, in *sarkar* Bahraich, U.P., yielding a revenue of 31,57,376 *dams*. It lies along the banks of the river Ghagra. Today it is in *tahsil* Kaisarganj, District Bahraich, U.P. having an area of 202 acres and is at a distance of 17 miles from Bahraich. (*Census 1971, Series 21, Bahraich District*, Pt. XA, p. 88 Code No. 221).
2. Bibi Sandal. She was the foster-sister of Akbar. When Jahangir ascended the throne, he asked her to bring to him such women as deserved to be presented with land and money. (Jahangir, *op. cit.*, I, p. 46).

203

1. Wazir Khan. He seems to be identical with Wazir Khan who was appointed *Diwan* of Bengal by Jahangir shortly after his accession. (Beni Prasad, *op. cit.*, p. 113).

206

1. This undated *farman* must have been issued some time after 17 *Bahman*, 12 Ilahi the date of the *yad dasht*.

2. *Maqbara* (A). A tomb, mausoleum. (Platts, *op. cit.*, s.v.).

3. Hasan Beg. He seems to be identical with Hasan Beg Badakhashi Umari who was sent against the ruler of Pakhli in Kashmir by Akbar in the 35th year of his reign. In the following year he did good service in Bangash and was promoted to the rank of 2500. In the end of Akbar's reign, he obtained Rohtas in fief and was directed to guard Kabul. In the first year of Jahangir's reign he joined Prince Khusrau in his rebellion but when the rebellion was suppressed Hasan Beg was done to death in 1015 A.D. / 1605 A.D. (Shah Nawaz Khan, *op. cit*., I, pp. 565-68).

4. Bir, or Beer, village in *tahsil* and district Ajmer, having an area of 6,208 acres, is at a distance of 18 km. from Ajmer. (*Census 1971, Rajasthan, Ajmer District*, Series 18, Pt. XA & XB, p. 10, Code No. 112).

5. Kankiniadas. Its name is Kakaniyawas. It is a village in *tahsil* Kishangarh, district Ajmer, having an area of 2,605 acres. (*Ibid.*, p.18, Code No. 74).

6. Bandhan Sundari. Its name is Bandar Sindhri, village in *tahsil* Kishangarh, district Ajmer, having an area of 9,375 acres. In the Mughal period it was a *mahal* of *sarkar* Ajmer yielding revenue of 4,35,664 *dams*. (*Ibid.*, p. 18 Code No. 79; and Abul Fazl, *op. cit., Ayeen*, p. 522).

7. Mutamid Khan. He seems to be identical with the author of *Iqbal Nama*. He was promoted as *Bakhshi* in the 10th year of Jahangir. (Jahangir, *op. cit.*, I, p. 330).

207

1. *Aqil Khan*. He seems to be identical with Aqil Khwaja who was made *Bakhshi* by Jahangir soon after his accession. In the 10th year an increase of *zat* and *sawar* was made to his *mansab* totalling 1200 *zat* and 600 *sawar*. Two years later, he was made *Khan* and came to be known as Aqil Khan. (Jahangir, *op. cit.*, I, pp. 71, 297, 439).

208

1. Inayat Khan. He seems to be identical with Inayatullah who was given the title of *Inayat Khan* in the 4th year of Jahangir. (Jahangir, *op. cit.*, I, p. 160).

209

1. *Gujar*. It is derived from *Gau Char* and connotes a numerous class in the north-west, chiefly engaged in agriculture, though formerly notorious for their martial and predatory character. They profess to descend from Rajput fathers and women of inferior castes. (Wilson, *op. cit.*, s.v.).

2. Danta, village in *tahsil* and district of Ajmer, having an area of 2,149 acres, is 12 km. from Ajmer. (*Census 1971, Rajasthan, Ajmer District Series 18,* Pts. XA & XB, p. 10, Code No. 113).

3. *Marwarid* (P) A pearl. (Platts *op. cit.*, s.v.).

4. *Masha* (H) A jeweller's or goldsmith's weight, equal to 8 *rattis.* (*Ibid.*, s.v.).

5. *Ratti* (H). The seed of the *Abrus precatorius* used as the basis of weights for gold, silver and drugs. The seed varies, but from various trials appears to average about 21/16th of a grain; the artificial weight has been found to average nearly 9/4 grains, being 1/8th of a *masha.* (Wilson, *op.cit.*, s.v.).

6. *Sarraf* (A). A money-changer; a banker; one who knows and distinguishes the relative excellence or superiority of pieces of money. (Platts, *op. cit.,* s.v.).

210

1. Asad Khan. He seems to be identical with Asad Khan Mamuri, the younger brother of Muzaffar Khan Mamuri. Asad Khan was first the Governor of Qandhar in Jahangir's time. He was subsequently made *Bakhshi* of Gujarat when Prince Parvez went to the Deccan in pursuit of Prince Shah Jahan, Asad Khan was one of the auxiliaries. Mahabat Khan, after coming to Burhanpur, put him in change of Ilichpur. In the beginning of Shah Jahan's reign he was removed from office but was subsequently made *Faujdar* of Lakhi Jangal in Sind. He died in 1041 A.H./ 1632 A.D. (Shah Nawaz Khan, *op. cit.*, I, pp. 140-42).

211

1. *Nankar* (P). Connotes an allowance for service. It appears that such allowance remitted to the *chaudhuri* out of the revenue, was not very substantial. (Irfan Habib, *op. cit.*, pp. 146, 2194).

2. Madsudan. His real name seems to be Madhu Sudan.

212

1. This undated *farman* seems to have been issued some time after 16 *Mihr*, 13 *Ilahi*, the date of the *yad dasht*.

2. *Roshnai* (P). Light, brightness, splendour, ink. (Platts, *op. cit.*, s.v.).

3. *Fuqra* (A). Plural of *faqir*, the poor; religious mendicants, *dervishes.* (*Ibid.* s.v.).

4. *Takiadars* (P). One who leans against a cushion; a *faqir*; a *dervish.* (*Ibid.*, s.v.).

5. *Asar* (A). Plural of *sar* which is the Arabicised form of Hindi *seer*; *seers*. (*Ibid.*, s.v.).

213

1. Jai Singh Mirza Raja, was the great grandson of Raja Man Singh and son of Raja Maha Singh. After the death of his father, in the 12th year of Jahangir's reign, when he was 12 year old, he was promoted to 1000 *zat* with 500 *sawar*; appointed to the Deccan along with Sultan Parvez. After Jahangir's death, he served under Shah Jahan and in 1664 A.D. he was recalled to court and died at Burhanpur on 20 July 1667. (Shah Nawaz Khan, *op. cit.*, III, pp. 568-77).

219

1. Khwaja Ibrahim Husain. He is probably identical with Ibrahim Husain, the *Mir Bahr* and *Bakhashi* of *ahadis* in 1017 A.H./1608 A.D. In the 8th *Ilahi*/1613-14 A.D. he proceeded against Azam Khan Azam while Jahangir was at Ajmer. (Jahangir, *op. cit.*,I pp. 149, 257-58).

220

1. Itibar Khan. He was a *Khwajasara* and a confidant of Jahangir. In the 2nd year the *haveli* of Gwalior was assigned to him as his salary. In the 5th year he got a *mansab* of 4000 *zat* with 1000 *sawar*. He made rapid progress and in the 17th year he held the rank of 5000 *zat* with 4000 *sawar*. When he was very old he got the charge of *suba* Agra, the fort and the treasury. In the 18th year he received the rank of 6000 *zat* with 5000 *sawar*. (Shah Nawaz Khan, *op. cit.* I, pp. 134-35).

221

1. Dera, *pargana*. There is no such place given in *District Gazetteer*, Lucknow, most probably it is a misreading of Dewa, which during the Mughal period, was a *mahal* in the *sarkar* of Lucknow. Now it is a *pargana* in *tahsil* Nawabaganj, district Barabanki, U.P. having an area of 242 acres. In Akbar's reign, the town was the headquarters of the *pargana* and a well-known centre of Islamic learning. It is a place of pilgrimage as the *dargah* of Hajji Waris Ali Shah stands here magnificiently. (*Uttar Pradesh District Gazetteers, Barabanki*, ed., Joshi, Esha Basanti, Allahabad, 1964, pp. 30, 267-68).

2. Nur Jahan. Mehrun Nisa, daughter of Mirza Ghiyas Beg, was married to Jahangir in 1611 A.D. and subsequently she was styled *Nur Mahal* (Light of the Palace) and *Nur Jahan* (Light of the World). She exercised considerable influence on the court during the last years of Jahangir. (Beni Prasad, *op. cit.*, pp. 159-84).

222

1. Daryabad, an old town and *pargana* in Barabanki District, U.P. In the Mughal period it was a *pargana* of *sarkar* and *suba* of Avadh. It had a brick fort and yielded 53,69,528 *dams* as revenue. (*Uttar Pradesh District Gazetteers, Barabanki*, ed., Joshi, Esha Basanti, Allahabad, 1964, p. 266, and Abul Fazl, *op. cit.*, *Ayeen*, pp. 486-87).

2. *Mahd uliyya* (A). It literally means cradle of sublimity and refers to Nur Jahan.

225

1. Sipara. Village in *pargana* Sanda, Patna District, Bihar. (*Census 1961, Bihar District Census Handbook, Patna, Bihar,* 1961, p. 189).

2. Sanda is one of the twenty *parganas* of Patna District, Bihar. (L.S.S.O. Malley, *Bengal District Gazetteers, Patna,* Calcutta, 1907, p. 156).

3. Jahangir Quli Khan, eldest son of Aziz Koka. His name was Shamsud Din Khan. He got title of *Jahangir Quli Khan* and a rank of 2,000 *zat* and 1000 *sawar*; was sent to Gujarat as his father's deputy and to Bihar in the 13th year. His tyranny in the *suba* of Bihar was reported and was replaced by Maqarrub Khan. Generally he was always in favour from the time of Akbar to Shah Jahan. Lastly he was made Governor of Sorath and Junagarh and died there in 1631-32. (Jahangir, *op. cit.*, I, pp.144, 153, 373; II, 38; and Shah Nawaz Khan, *op. cit.* Vol. I, pp. 729-30).

4. Afzal Khan. He seems to be identical with Shukrullah Shirazi, the *Mir-i-Adl* of Prince Shah Jahan. It was through his good counsel that peace was made with the Rana of Mewar. Subsequently his reputation increased and he was made the *Diwan* of the Prince. It was on the latter's recommendations that Jahangir conferred on him the title of *Afzal Khan*. He remained loyal to Prince Shah Jhan during his revolt. When Shah Jahan ascended the throne Afzal Khan was made *Mir-i-Saman* and thereafter *Diwan-i-Kul.* He died on 7 January 1639 A.D. (Shah Nawaz Khan, *op.cit.*, I, pp. 145-51).

232

1. *Chakbast* (P). Having an estate marked out, having the fields of a village marked out in a village. (Platts, *op. cit.*, s.v.).

233

1. Exact date of writing of the *farman* is not available. Only the words 'Ilahi 15' are forthcoming. But from the following *'Hasbul hukm'* (234) whose date of writing is 22 *Farwardin*, *Ilahi* 15, and which is of the same tenor and subject as the present *farman* it is evident that the *farman*, must have been written before the *Hasbul hukm* and therefore the *farman* is calendared just before it.

2. Kasmar is misreading of Kachmar, which is now a village in Siswan Development Block, District Saran, Bihar. Under the Mughals, it was a *mahal* by the name of Kusmeer of *sarkar* Saran, *suba* Bihar yielding revenue of 13,14,539 *dams*. Today it has a population of more than 5,000. (*Census 1971*, *Series 4*, *Bihar*, *Saran District*, Pt. XB, p. 196; Abul Fazl, *op. cit. Ayeen*, p. 478).

3. *Hauz* (A). Reservoir, pond, tank, pool, cistern. (Platts, *op. cit.*, s.v.).

235

1. Hakim Masihuz Zaman, whose name was Hakim Sadra, was the son of Hakim Mirza Muhammad. He was honoured with the title of *Musihuz Zaman* (Messiah of the Age), and a rank of 500 *zat* and 30 *sawar* in the year 1017 A.H. 1609 A.D. He was a leading physician of Persia and had come to India from Persia in the reign of Akbar. Jahangir gave him a higher status and position than other court physicians. In 1621 A.D., when Jahangir fell ill, he refused to treat the king and proceeded on pilgrimage to Mecca. Jahangir gave Rs. 20,000 to him to meet the expenses of the journey. (Jahangir, *op. cit.*, Vol. I, p. 155; Vol. II, pp. 11, 213, 217).

238

1. Sayyid Hashim, was the son of Mir Fathullah, a *rais* of his *qaum* and as such he was a distinguished person. The Government was very considerate to him and held him in high esteem. For some time he was a *mutawalli* of the shrine of Khawaja Muinud Din Chishti. Sayyid Hashim could not possess a very high position among the personages of his time, as he fell a victim to the intrigues of his relations. (Maani, *op. cit.* p. 69).

240

1. *Ijara* means lease or farm of land held at a defined revenue or rent, whether from Government direct or from an intermediate payer of public revenue (Wilson, *op.cit.* s.v.). The revenue-farming generally lay under official disapproval but in fact the revenue officials did some time farm out the revenue of individual villages. The practice of giving the revenue of the whole *pargana* or large areas on farm seems to have been very rare or at least the exception in the *Khalisa.* (Irfan Habib, *op. cit.*, pp. 234, 277).

2. Amber. Ancient but now decayed capital of the Kachwaha Rajputs of the former State of Jaipur. It is situated about 7 miles north-east of Jaipur Railway Station. Its picturesque situation has attracted admiration of travellers. (*Rajputana Gazetteer*, Calcutta, 1908, p. 255).

3. *Zimn* (A). Endorsement of a grant giving an abstract of its contents (Wilson, *op. cit.*, s.v.). The *Sahib-i Tawjih* or Military Accountant kept the *taliqa* with himself and wrote the *zimn* on the *farman*. (Abul Fazl, *op. cit., Ain* I, p. 272).

4. *Tamassuk* (A). Bond, note of hand, written acknowledgement or engagement. (Wilson, *op. cit.*, s.v.).

244

1. Chambal. Well-known river in Madhya Pradesh.

2. Ujjain. Town and district in Madhya Pradesh.

3. Burhanpur. Town and *tahsil* in Nimar District of former Central Provinces now Madhya Pradesh. (R. V. Russell, *Nimar District Gazetteer*, Allahabad, 1908, pp. 208-22).

246

1. Darab Khan. He was the second son of Mirza Abdur Rahim *Khanan-i Khanan*. When his elder brother Shah Nawaz Khan died in 14th year of Jahangir, he received the rank of 5000 *zat* and *sawar* and was made Governor of Berar and Ahmadnagar. He distinguished himself in the famous battle of Khirki and remained loyal to Prince Shah Jahan during his revolt. He was killed in 1034 A.H./1625 A.D. (Shah Nawaz Khan, *op.cit.*, II pp. 14-17).

247

1. *Pargana* Haveli was one of the 11 *mahals* in *sarkar* Bahraich, *suba* Avadh, yielding a revenue of 91,37,141 *dams*. (Abul Fazl *op.cit., Ayeen* p. 488).

2. Shahida is probably a misreading of Shiv Daha, quite a big village in *tahsil* Bahraich, U.P., having an area of 2,314 acres, a junior basic school and irrigation facilities. (*Census 1971, Series 21, District Bahraich*, p. 153, Code No. 261).

3. Panyanhari appears to be a misreading of Baniahari, a village in *tahsil* Bahraich, U.P., having an area of 822 acres, a junior basic school and irrigation facilities. (*Ibid.*, p. 140, Code No. 123).

249

1. Parvez Sultan, second son of Jahangir, born of Sahib-i Jamal on 2 October 1589 at Kabul. In 1608, he was appointed in the Deccan with Asaf Khan as his guardian to the supreme command. In his twenties he was full of pride and ambition and fell a prey to intemperance while never displaying any military or administrative capacity. Jahangir gave him Khandesh and Berar and Asir. In his 16th year he was given Bihar and in the 18th his *mansab* was raised to 40,000 *zat* and 30,000 *sawar*. He was married to the sister of Raja Gaj Singh. He died on 28 October 1626 at Burhanpur. (Jahangir, *op. cit.*, I, pp. 18-19, 156-57; II, pp. 200, 259, 295; and Beni Prasad *op. cit.*, p. 393).

252

1. *Sazawal* (A). A native collector of revenue; an officer, specially appointed to take charge and collect the revenue of an estate from the management of which the owner or farmer has been removed; a land-steward, a bailiff, an agent appointed by a landowner or lessor to compel payment of rent by tenants or lease holders. (Wilson, *op. cit.*, s.v.).

253

1. *Thana* (H). A station, military post, police-station; garrison, a place, sometimes with a small fort, where a petty officer, with a small irregular force, was posted to protect the country. (Wilson, *op. cit.*, s.v.).

256

1. Maner, is a large village of historical antiquities, situated in the extreme north-west of Danapur sub-division 17 miles west of Patna. In the Mughal period, it was one of the *mahals* of *sarkar* and *suba* of Bihar. (*Bihar District Gazetteers*, Patna, ed., Kumar, N., Patna, 1970, pp. 643-44).

2. Mustafapur. Village in *pargana* Maner, district Patna, Bihar. (*Census, 1961, Bihar District Census Handbook*, I, Patna, Bihar, 1961, p. 194).

3. Dilwar Khan. His name was Ibrahim. He distinguished himself in Jahangir's presence in the affair of Akhiraj and Abhiraj and received several wounds. This service was the cause of his advancement and he

was given a suitable rank. In the beginning of Jahangir's reign, he was sent off to act as Governor of Lahore. He strengthened the bastions of Lahore city and when Khusrau came there he found the gates closed. Dilawar was suitably rewarded for his loyal services. In the 8th year he accompanied Prince Shah Jahan against the Rana of Mewar. In 1027 A.H./ 1618 A.D. he was made Governor of Kashmir and conquered Kishtawar. For this victory Dilawar received various favours and was made an officer of 4000 *zat* with 3500 *sawar*. He also received a present of a lakh of rupees, being the revenue of conquered territory for one year. He died in 1620 A.D. (Shah Nawaz Khan, *op. cit.* II, pp. 9-14; Jahangir, *op. cit.*, II, p. 167).

257

1. This undated *farman* seems to have been issued after 24 March 1622 A.D., when Prince Shah Jahan rose in revolt against his father and refused to march to Qandhar. (Beni Prasad, *op. cit.*, p. 321).

259

1. Jan Beg. Jahangir divided the *wizarat* of his kingdom in the proportions of half and half between Jan Beg to whom Jahangir in the days of his princehood had given the title of *Wazirul Mulk*, and Wazir Khan (Muqim). Jan Beg had served Jahangir before his accession to the throne, and was *Diwan* of Jahangir's establishment. In 1015 A.H. / 1607 A.D. Jan Beg died of diarrhoea. (Jahangir, *op. cit.*, Vol. I, pp. 20, 136).

263

1. Panipat. Town in Karnal district of Haryana. (*Karnal District Gazetteer*, Lahore, 1912, pp. 210-13).

264

1. Chak Saleha. Saleh Chak is a *mauza* in Patna District in Bihar. (*Census 1961, Bihar District Census Handbook, I, Patna*, Bihar, 1961, p. 191).

266

1. Girdhar Nagar Bahadur. Probably Raja Girdhar, son of Raja Sal Darbari. In 1027 A.H./1618 A.D. Jahangir raised him to the *mansab* of 1000 *zat* and 800 *sawar*. In 1031 A.H./ 1622 A.D. Girdhar came from the Deccan and paid his respects to the Emperor who promoted him to the rank of 2000 *zat* and 1500 *sawar*, honoured him with a *khilat* and the title of Raja. In May 1623 A.D. an army of 40,000 horse, armed with a large park of

artillery, was sent under the command of distinguished officers Khan Alam, Maharaja Gaj Singh, Raja Girdhar, etc., to down Shah Jahan. Raja Girdhar was killed in a strife by the Sayyids in the Deccan in the same year. (Jahangir, *op. cit.*, Vol. II, pp. 44, 252, 282-83; Beni Prasad, *op. cit.*, p. 333).

269

1. Wali Nimat Begam appears to be the name of one of the wives of Akbar, who according to the seal on this document was the mother of Jahangir. She also enjoyed the other covetous title of *Maryam Zamani* as is evident from the *unwan* of this *hukm*. While Jahangir refers to his mother as *Maryam Zamani*. (Jahangir, *op. cit.*, I pp. 76, 78, 81, 145, 230, 401), Sujan Rai Bhandari states that Jahangir was born of the daughter of Raja Bhara Mal Kachwaha (*Khulasatut Tawarikh*, Delhi, 1918, p. 374). It appears that Wali Nimat Begam was the name given to the daughter of Raja Bhara Mal after her marriage with Akbar and it was probably after the birth of Prince Salim. (later on Jahangir) that the honorific of *Maryam Zamani* was conferred on her.

2. Probably, Chaupla modern Moradabad, was included in the *sarkar* of Sambhal in the *subah* of Delhi. (*Morabadad District Gazetteer*, ed., N.R. Nevil, Allahabad, 1911, p. 150).

3. *Fulus* (A). The *dams* and half *dams* (*adhelas*) are *fulus* on their inscriptions. It was a copper coin. (Stanely Lanepoole, *Catalogue of Indian Coins in British Musseum, The Mughal Emperors*, London, 1892 pl., xxvi).

4. *Jital* (H). It is a very old Indian coin and its currency can be traced back to the very dawn of the Delhi Sultanate. In 1340 A.D. the *Jital* was worth 4 *fals* and the *dirham sultani* 3 *fals*. Under Akbar *Jital* was equi valent to 1/25 of *dam* which was divided for purposes of calculation but this division was used only by accountants. (Abul Fazl, *op. cit.*, *Ain* I p. 32; Yule and Burnell, *op. cit.*, p. 457).

271

1. Ahmad Beg. He was the nephew of Ibrahim Khan Fath Jang. When his uncle was Governor of Bengal, Ahmad Beg was Governor of Orissa. In the 19th year of Jahangir, he was sent against the *zamindar* of Kokra but was forced to abandon his expedition when the news came that Prince Shah Jahan was proceeding towards Bengal. He, therefore, joined his uncle Ibrahim Khan. When Ibrahim Khan was killed in the battle, Ahmad Beg went to the Deccan. Subsequently, when Shah Jahan ascended the throne Ahmad Beg received the rank of 2000 *zat* with 1500 *sawar* and in the 25th year he was made *Faujdar* of Baiswara in Avadh. (Shah Nawaz Khan, *op. cit.*, I, pp. 195-96).

273

1. Saif Khan. His full name was Muhammad Shafi Khan. He was appointed *Diwan* and *Bakhshi* of Gujarat in 1616 A.D. and played an important part during Prince Shah Jahan's revolt in 1622-23 A.D. Later on he became the *subadar* of the province but was displaced from that office when Shah Jahan came to the throne. Subsequently he was pardoned and remained *subadar* of Bihar 1628 to 1632 A.D. Three years latter he was sent again to his old province of Gujarat but was displaced by Azam Khan in 1636 A.D. Four year later he passed away at Ahmadabad. (Commissariat, *op. cit.*, II pp. 54, 61, 107-08, 112).

276

1. Rampur is a village in Hajipur Development Block of Muzaffarpur District of Bihar. (*Muzaffarpur District Census Handbook, 1971*, p. 13).

277

1. *Bidualat*, means wretch or a person of dark fortune. Jahangir gave this nick-name to Prince Khurram when he revolted against his father. (Jahangir, *op. cit.*,II p. 248).

279

1. *Khan-i Jahan*. His name was Pir Khan Lodi and was the second son of Daulat Khan Lodi, a famous warrior of Akbar's reign. He fell out with his father in early manhood and served successfully under Raja Man Singh, Prince Daniyal and Prince Salim. His martial talents soon established his reputation. In the second year of Jahangir's reign, he received the rank of 3000 *zat* and 1500 *sawar*, the title of *Salabat Khan* and the distinction of *Farzand* (son). In 1608 A.D. he was styled *Khan-i Jahan* and promoted to 5000 *zat*. On the death of Khan Azam Koka, he was appointed Governor of Gujarat. When Mahabat Khan was removed from the guardianship of Prince Parvez, he was appointed in his place and joined the Prince in Burhanpur. (Jahangir, *op.cit.* I p. 87; Shah Nawaz Khan, *op. cit.*, I, pp. 716-21).

283

1. Fidai Khan's name was Hidayatullah. In Jahangir's reign he was *Mir Bahr*. He became *wakil* of Mahabat Khan, who patronised him. He supported him against the Emperor and risked his life, but was pardoned.

He was appointed Governor of Bengal in 1627 A.D. He also served under Shah Jahan and in the 13th year he got the title of *Jan Nisar Khan*. He got Gorakhpur as his fief. He died in the 19th year of Shah Jahan. (Shah Nawaz Khan, *op. cit.*, Vol. III, pp. 12-18).

290

1. Fazil Khan. His name was Agha Afzal and came from Ispahan in Iran. He joined the service of Shaikh Farid Murtaza Khan on a fixed allowance of a lakh of rupees per annum. When Murtaza Khan was appointed Governor of the Punjab, Agha Afzal was his deputy, who continued to hold the post even under Itimadud Daulah. Subsequently, he was made *Diwan* of Prince Parvez and got a *mansab* and the title of *Fazil Khan*. When Prince Parvez, was appointed to pursue Prince Shah Jahan, Fazil Khan was made *Bakhshi* and recorder of his army. In the 20th year he received the rank of 1500 *zat* with 500 *sawar* and was made *Diwan* of the Deccan. When Shah Jahan ascended the throne, Fazil Khan was summoned and deprived of his office. Subsequently, he was given the fief of Baroda. In the 9th year he received the title of Itimad Khan and the *Diwani* of the Deccan. In the 15th year he was appointed *Diwan* of Bengal where six years later he passed away. (Shah Nawaz Khan, *op. cit.*, III, pp. 18-21).

2. *Hububat* (A). These were the exactions and perquisites appropriated by officials personally and by *zamindars*, etc., and, accordingly, excluded from the *jama*. These were also known as *faruat, abwab-imalba,* and *ikhrajat.* (Irfan Habib, *op. cit.*, p. 243).

3. *Kah Charai* (H). It seems to be an exaction imposed upon herds driven into public pastures. This exaction was forbidden by Dara Shukoh from the herds of cows attached to the *devala* of Govardhan Nath which used to be brought to the pastures in a village. From some of our authorities it would appear that Aurangzeb had abolished both *gau-shumari* and *kah Charai* but in the case of the latter we have a *'Hasbul hukm'* exhorting local officials to collect it according to regulations. (*Ibid.*, p. 244).

298

1. Raja Kalyan. He seems to be identical with Raja Kalyan, son of Todar Mal, who was Governor of Orissa in 1611 A.D. (Beni Prasad, *op. cit.*, p. 281).

302

1. Haveli Bihar, was one of the 46 *mahals* of *sarkar* and *suba* Bihar yielding a revenue of 55,34,151 *dams*. It had a fort of brick and stone.

(Abul Fazl, *op. cit.*, *Ayeen*, p. 476).

304

1. The reference obviously is to Malik Ambar, the celebrated noble of the Deccan, who gave up the places taken from the Mughals to Prince Shah Jahan to whose interest he became attached and continued to be loyal till his death in 1035 A.H./1626 A.D. (Beale, *op. cit.* p. 67).

2. This refers to Prince Shah Jahan's reconciliation with his father in June 1626 A.D. when the former's two sons, Dara and Aurangzeb, arrived at the court in Lahore where they were placed under the care of Nur Jahan. (Beni Prasad, *op. cit.*, p. 363).

306

1. Dawar Bakhsh. He was the son of Prince Khusrau. When Jahangir passed away in 1627 A.D. Asad Khan, who was determined to support Shah Jahan, released Dawar Bakhsh from prison and proclaimed him king as a stop-gap. He was put to death when Shah Jahan ascended the throne. (Beale, *op. cit.*, pp. 80-81).

2. The reference obviously is to Prince Khusrau's death which is reported to have been manipulated by Prince Shah Jahan. (Beni Prasad, *op. cit.*, pp. 308-12).

314

1. 16 *Rabi* II 1036 A.H./ 25 December, 1626 A.D. as given by Khadgawat (*DLFMN*, p. 29) and 21 *Rabi* I, 22 *Julus*/ 1037 A.H./ 20 November 1627 A.D. as stated by Mathur (*JIH*, XXXVII, Pts. 1-3, p. 271) do not tally with the Ilahi dates recorded in the original *hukm*.

316

1. This incomplete *farman* seems to have been issued some time in 1015 A.H./ 1626 A.D. in as much as Asaf Khan was the *wakil* of the empire for a short time in that year. (Shah Nawaz Khan, *op. cit.*, I p. 110).

2. Shantidas Jawahari was the Jain magnate of Ahmedabad who flourished during the reigns of Jahangir and Shah Jahan. In 1625, he built the great temple of Chintamani Parsvanath at Saraspur. He died at Ahmadabad on 5 October 1659. (Commissariat, *op. cit.*, Vol. II, pp. 140-142, 148).

3. Nizamud Din Asaf Khan seems to be the scribe's error for Qiwamud Din Jafar Beg Asaf Khan, brother of Nur Jahan. In 1626 A.D. he was *wakil* of the empire for a shortwhile, and for 14 years in the reign of Shah Jahan.

(Shah Nawaz Khan, *op. cit.*, I, pp. 207-15).

317

1. *Mir-i Adl* (A) An Officer of Justice, a superintendent of the courts who revised the decisions of the *Qazis* and judges, passed sentence and ordered punishment. (Wilson, *op. cit.*, s.v.).

2. Qiam or Kamdin was the son or grandson of Meherji Rana. (Hodivala, *op. cit.*, p. 174).

319

1. Sher Khan was the title of Nahar Khan who joined the service of Akbar when the latter conquered Asir. The Emperor raised him to a suitable *mansab* and gave him in *jagir* the *pargana* of Muhammadpur in Malwa. Under Jahangir he made rapid progress. When the Emperor was at Ahmadabad he waited on him on the bank of Kankariya tank. Thereafter he was promoted to the *mansab* of 1500 *zat* and 100 *sawar* and was presented with an elephant. He remained loyal to the royal cause during the revolt of Prince Shah Jahan and was consequently raised to the *mansab* of 3000 *zat* and 2000 *sawar* and was given a horse and an elephant alongwith the title of Sher Khan on 22 Rajab 1032 A.H./ 12 May 1623 A.D. when the Emperor was at Ajmer. (Jahangir, *op. cit.*, II, pp. 8, 22, 267-68).

2. Hakim Ruhullah hailed from Broach. He joined the service of Abdur Rahim *Khan-i Khanan*. Subsequently, he was included among the physicians of Akbar's court. After Akbar's death, he joined the service of Jahangir. He successfully treated the Emperor and the Empress, when they were in Gujarat. As a reward he was given three villages in his native land. (Abdul Baqi, *Maasir-i-Rahimi* III, Calcutta, 1927, pp. 43; Shah Nawaz Khan, *op. cit.*, II, p. 13; Abul Fazl, *op. cit.*, *Ain* I, p. 613).

320

1. Haibatpur, village, in Siswan Development Block as also in Raghunathpur Development Block, there is no such village. Under the Mughals, Andar or Inder was *mahal* in *sarkar* Saran, *suba* Bihar; probably Siswan and Raghunathpur were included in *pargana* Andar these days. (*Census 1971, Series 4, Bihar*, *Saran District*, Pt. X-B, pp. 204, S. No. 10, 210 S. No. 14, Abul Fazl, *op. cit.*, *Ayeen* p. 478).

333

1. Dakhdar or Dikhdar is a *mahal* in Jullundur district of Punjab. It owes its name to a natural characteristic. There is no reason to doubt the

local derivation from *dhak* or *Butea frondosa*, a tree largely found in this tract (*Jullundur District Gazetteer*, Lahore, 1908, p. 246; Abdul Qadir Bedaoni, *Munthakhabut tawarikh*, II, Eng. tr. W.H. Lowe, Calcutta, 1924, p. 34).

336

1. Islam Shah was the younger son of Sher Shah. On the death of his father he ascended the throne of Delhi in 952 A.H./ 1545 A.D. and reigned for nine years till his death in 961 A.H./ 1554 A.D. (Beale, op. *cit.*, *p.* 348.)

2. Soraon, a village, *tahsil* and *pargana* in Allahabad district of U.P. (E.B. Joshi, *Allahabad District Gazetteer*, Allahabad, 1968, p. 396).

338

1. *Dang* (P) A small denomination of money, the sixth part of a *dinar*; a weight, the fourth part of a drachm; a sixth part of anything, side or quarter. (Platts, *op. cit.*, s.v.).

339

1. *Mahr* (A) Dower, marriage-gift or portion settled upon a wife before marriage; it may be either *muajil*, i.e. prompt, immediate or *muwajil*, i.e. deferred to some specified time; the written contract of a dower or marriage settlement. (Wilson, *op. cit.*, s.v.).

340

1. Zafar Hasan is of the view that this document belongs to the period prior to the establishment of the Mughal rule (*AIOC*, X p. 465). This view cannot be accepted in as much as Sambhal was given as fief to Prince Askari by Humayun in 937 A.H./ 1530 A.D. (Ishwari Prasad, *op. cit.*, p. 81-82). Sambhal, however, appears to have ceased to be the fief of Prince Askari. After Humayun's defeat at the battle of Chausa on 26 June 1539 A.D. Mughals were driven out of Sambhal. (Brijendra Mohan, Sambhal-*A Historical Survey*, New Delhi, 1971, p.44). This fact casts doubt on the authenticity of this document.

2. The *unwan* refers to this document as *hukm* though according to the documentation practices of the Mughal chancellery the princely order was invariably designated as *nishan*.

3. Muhammad Askari, son of Babur and Gul-rukh, received Humayun's old *jagir* of Sambhal on the latter's accession to the throne of Agra on 5 *Jumada* I, 937 A.H./26 December 1530 A.D. Shortly afterwards he was transferred to Gujarat. (Ishwari Prasad, *op. cit.*, pp. 81-82, Babur,

op. cit., pp. 708-79; in *Safar* 946 A.H./ July 1539 A.D.). Humayun reached Agra and was joined by Askari and his other brothers. (Banerji, *op. cit.*, Calcutta 1938, p. 236).

341

1. About this time Humayun was at Rohri where he arrived on 28 *Ramazan* 947 A.H. / 26 January 1541 A.D. and it was after full forty days' amorous discussions that he married Hamida Banu at Pat on 2 *Jumada* I, 948 A.H./ 21 August 1541 A.D. (Avasthi, *op. cit.*, pp. 398-405).

2. Bohra, a trader or a man of affairs. There are two classes of Bohras belonging to different sects of the Shiis, Bohras are towns people and congregate in Surat, Burhanpur, Ujjain, etc., they are traders and money lenders; their original seat was in Gujarat; they are akin in character to the Ismaili sect; the Sunni Bohras are numerous in northern Konkan and Gujarat. They are thriving trading community. (Yule and Burnell, *op. cit.*, pp. 105b, 106a and b).

3. Humayun left Bhakkar for Jodhpur on 21 Muharram 949 A.H.. and arrived at Phalodi in Marwar on 18 Rabi II 949 A.H. (Avasthi, *op. cit.*, p. 415). Thus Humayun entered Marwar about one full year after the date of the issue of the document.

4. Bairam Khan joined Humayun on his exile at Jun in Sind on 7 Muharram 950 A.H. a little less than two years after the date of drafting of the present document. (Shah Nawaz Khan, *op. cit.*, I, 371).

5. The word *Ghazi* in the seal is engraved with *zal* and not *zay*. This adds to the doubts already raised about the authenticity of the document.

6. The *sarnama* found on the *farmans* of Humayun is *Huwal Ghani* and not *Huwa* as is the case with this document.

342

1. On 27 *Zilqada* 960 A.H. Humayun was not in Agra but he was in the Gakhar territory. Thereafter he was in Kabul and on 7 *Ramazan* 960 A.H. he ordered that Mirza Kamran be blinded. He ascended the throne of Delhi on 4 Ramazan 962 A.H. From the above it is rather doubtful if the Emperor or his ministers issued any *farman* from Agra. (Avasthi, *op. cit.*, pp. 477, 480).

2. Machhiwara. Important ancient town 25 miles east of Ludhiana which was held by Sikandar Sur on the eve of Humayun's return from exile. (*Ludhiana District and Malerkotla State Gazetteer*, Lahore, 1907, p. 16). The decisive battle of Machhiwara took place on 2 *Rabi* II 962 A.H./24 February 1555 A.D. after Humayun's return from exile. After the

battle of Machhiwara, Bairam Khan occupied Sirhind and this so delighted Humayun that he honoured Bairam Khan with the title of *Khan-i Khanan* and *Yar-i Wafadar*. (Avasthi, *op. cit.*, pp. 185-86).

3. *Sijillat* (A). Plural of *sijill* ; written statements or contracts; registers, records or decrees of *Qazi;* judicial records; seals of *qazis*; written attestations of a notary. (Platts, *op. cit.*, s.v).

4. The *sarnama 'Allahu Akbar'* was introduced as invocation by Akbar in 992 A.H./ 1584 A.D. (Abul Fazl, *op. cit.*, *Ain* I, p. 212) more than three decades after the date of issue of this *farman*. This makes us doubt the authenticity of this document.

343

1. The *karori* system of revenue collection was introduced by Akbar in the 19th year of his reign, i.e. 1575 A.D. (Irfan Habib, *op. cit.*, p. 275) while this *farman* is reported to have been issued on 27 *Jumada I*, 968 A.H./ 13 February 1561 A.D. This discrepancy casts a shadow of doubt on the authenticity of the document.

2. Gurgaon, a district in Haryana, formerly the southern most of the seven districts of the Delhi division. In the reign of Akbar, it was contained in the *subas* of Delhi and Agra. (*Punjab District Gazetteers, Gurgaon District,* Vol. IV A, Lahore 1911, pp. 1, 19).

3. Sohna, *qasba*, a thriving town, 15 miles on the main road from Gurgaon. The tomb of Shah Najmul Haq is situated at Sohna. It is remarkable for the hot water springs situated in the rock. (*Ibid.*, pp. 245-46).

4. *Shab chiragh* (P). Expenses of lighting lamp at a shrine.

5. Najmul Haq, Hazrat Shah. His *dargah* with a picturesque tomb and a mosque of red and buff sand-stone bearing the date 1481 A.D. is a place of interest at Sohna. This tomb was visited by Gen. Cunningham in 1882 (*ASR*, Vol XX. p. 136) and the *farman* of Akbar and other interesting documents seen by him. These are still in possession of the managers of the mosque. (*Punjab District Gazetteers, Gurgaon District*, p. 27).

6. *Saliana* (P). Annual pension; annuity; land taken up for the whole year. (Platts *op. cit.*, s.v.).

7. *Yaumiya* (P). Daily-pay or allowance; daily food or provisions; daily allowance to pensioners of any kind. (Platts, *op.cit.* s.v.).

344

1. Instead of *Julus,* this *farman* bears Ilahi era which was introduced by Akbar in 1585 A.D. (Bendrey, *op. cit.*, p. 4). The date of this *farman* is, therefore, astonishing.

2. As stated earlier the *karori* experiment was introduced by Akbar in the 19th year of his reign, i.e. 1575 A.D. (Irfan Habib, *op. cit.*, p. 275). How could this *farman* issued nine years earlier refer to *karoris* who did not then exist? This makes us doubt the authenticity of this document.

3. *Khartal* (H). Hard, harsh, formidable. (Platts, *op. cit.*, s.v.).

345

1. This document, though designated as *farman,* must have been a *parwana* in as much as Man Singh had issued it while he was Governor of Bihar. (Prasad, *op. cit.*, p. 76).

2. Sayyid Ahmad was the maternal uncle of Sayyid Muhammad and they together were traditionally known as Mamu Bhanja whose mausoleum is situated in Jaruha quarter of Hajipur town. (*Ibid.*, p. 171).

3. The disparity between the two versions in respect of dates and phraseology is astonishing.

4. Absence of any seal adds to the doubts regarding the authenticity of this otherwise very interesting document.

346

1. Jatipura, lies in Lat. 27° 29' N and long. 77° 26' E, 27.4 km. from Mathura and 3.2 km. south-west of Govardhan. During the reign of Akbar, his mother bestowed it on Gosain Girdharji '*Jati*'. It is an important halting place for the pilgrims. (*Abul Fazl, op. cit., Ayeen)*

2. *Kharak* (H). Cow-house, cow-shed; sheep-pen; pound for cattle. (Platts, *op. cit.*, s.v.).

3. *Karkhana* (P). An office or place where business is carried on; but it is in use more especially applied to places where mechanical work is performed; a workshop, manufactory, an arsenal. (Wilson, *op. cit.*, s.v.).

4. This *farman* dated 9 *Khurdad*, 38 *Ilahi* bears two invocations. viz. '*Allahu Akbar*' and '*Huwal Ghani*' but another *farman* dated 11 *Khurdad*, 38 *Ilahi*, 38 bears only the former invocation (Jhaveri, *op cit.*, No. IV A). It is significant to note in this connection that Akbar had ordered employment of the invocation '*Allahu Akbar*' on all his documents from 992 A.H./1584-85 A.D. (Abul Fazl, *op.cit.*, *Ain*, I, p. 212). This is corraborated by the documents calendared in this book. This makes us doubt the authenticity of this document.

5. The above doubt finds support from the fact that the reverse of the document bears an endorsement of Munim Khan who had passed away in 1575 A D. eighteen years before this *farman* was issued. Vithal Rai, the grantee, himself is reported to have been dead latest by Samvat 1642/

1585 A.D. (Jhaveri, *op. cit.*) eight years prior to the date of issue of this *farman*.

347

1. The Ilahi month of *Dai* is followed by the Hijra year 1004 A.H./1595 A.D. though Akbar employed Ilahi era in all his transactions from 992 A.H./ 1585 A.D. onwards. This naturally makes us doubt the authenticity of this *farman*.

2. *Jamaat* and *millat* did not perhaps connote in the time of Akbar what they purport to do in the context of the present *farman*.

3. What adds to our doubt is the fact that the formula *'Allahu Akbar'* initiates the text though it was adopted by Akbar as superscription since 992 A.H./1584-85 A.D. (Abul Fazl, *op. cit. Ain*, I, p. 212).

348

1. Though designated as *farman* this document issued by Madhav Singh, brother of Man Singh, must have been a *parwana*.

2. *Thakurdwara* (H). An idol-temple and synonymous with *thakurbari*. (Platts, *op. cit.* s.v.).

3. *Bhog* (H). Enjoyment; satisfaction, gratification; any object of enjoyment that which is eaten, food, victuals, food offered to an idol. (*Ibid.*, s.v.).

4. *Urad (H)*. A kind of pulse, *Dolichos Pilosus*. (*Ibid.*, s.v.).

5. *Dal* (G). Split-pea; split-pulse; pulse, lentils, vetches. (*Ibid.*, s.v.).

6. *Ghee* (H). Clarified butter or butter which has been boiled gently and stained and allowed to cool. It is much used in cooking and is highly esteemed by Hindus both in food and for religious purposes. (*Ibid.*, s.v.).

7. Absence of seal raises doubts about the authenticity of this document.

349

1. The grant of 4,000 *bighas* as *madad-i maash* seems to be some what unusual.

2. It is astonishing to note that the *farman* exempts Sayyid Mubariz from *jizya* which he was not required to pay according to the *Sharia*.

3. What is more surprising is the fact that the superscription *'Allahu Akbar'* is appended to the end of the text instead of appearing at the top of the *farman* as was the practice in the reign of Akbar. All these points make us doubt the authenticity of this document.

350

1. Jahangir usually dated all his *farmans* in *Ilahi* calendar and not in *Hijri* era. This casts a shadow of doubt on the authenticity of the document.

2. Absence of a seal on the imperial *farman* adds to the doubt raised above.

BIBLIOGRAPHY

PRIMARY SOURCES

Abul Fazl, *Ain-i Akbari* I tr., H. Blockman, Calcutta, 1927.

-------------, *Ayeen Akbery* tr. Gladwin, Calcutta, 1783

Ahmad, Bashirud Din, *Faramin-i Salatin*, Delhi, 1926.

Ali Muhammad Khan, *Mirat-i Ahmadi*, I, ed., Syed Navab Ali, Baroda, 1927.

Amir Khusrau, *Ijaz-i Khusraui*, Lucknow, 1875-76.

Ambashthya, B.P. *Contributions on Akbar and the Parsees*, Patna, 1976.

Ansari, M.A., *Administrative Documents of Mughal India*, Delhi, 1984.

Babur, Zahirud Din Muhammad. *Baburnamah*, I, tr., A.S. Beveridge, New Delhi, 1979.

Barani, Ziaud Din, *Tarikh-i Firuzshahi*, Calcutta, 1891.

Commissariat, M.S., *Imperial Mughal Farmans in Gujarat*, Bombay, 1940.

Dalal Chimanlal & Shrigodekar, Gajanan K. ed., *Lekhapaddhati, Baroda, 1925.*

Dutta, K.K., *Some Farmans, Sanads and Parwanas.* Patna, 1962.

Erskine, W, *A History of India under the Two First Sovereigns of the Houses of Babar and Humayun,* London, 1854.

Goswamy, B.N. and Grewal, J.S., *The Mughals and Jogis of Jakhhar*, Calcutta, 1969.

Imadud Din Mahmud, Khwaja Jahan, *Riyazul Insha*, ed., Shaikh Chand, Hyderabad, 1948.

Jahangir, Nurud Din, *Tuzuk-i Jahangiri* I-II, tr., Rogers and Beveridge, New Delhi, 1978.

Jhaveri, K.M., *Imperial Farmans (A.D. 1579 to A.D. 1805) granted to the Ancestors of His Holiness the Tilkayat Maharaj,* Bombay, 1928.

Juvayni, Ata Malik, *Tarikh-i Jahangushay,* II, tr., J A. Boyles, Manchester, 1958.

Khadgawat, N.R., *Descriptive List of Farmans, Manshurs and Nishans,* Bikaner, 1962.

Khan, Shah Nawaz, *Maasirul Umara,* I-III. Calcutta, 1888-91.

Khan, Yusuf Husain, ed., *Farmans and Sanads of the Deccan Sultans,* Hyderabad, 1963.

-------------, *Selected Documents of Aurangzeb's Reign (1659-1706 A.D.)* Hyderabad,1958.

-------------, *Selected Documents of Shah Jahan's Reign (1634-1658 A.D.)* Hyderabad, 1953.

-------------, *Selected Waqai of the Deccan (1660-1671)*, Hyderabad, 1953.

Kitab-i Daftar-i Diwani wa Mal wa Mulki-i Sarkar-i Alyee, Hyderabad, 1933.

Mahru, Ainud Din, *Insha-i Mahru*, ed., Shaikh Abdur Rashid, Lahore, 1965.

Maani, Abdul Bari, *Asanidus Sanadid*, Ajmer, 1952.

Minhaj Siraj, *Tabaqat-i Nasiri*, tr., C. Raverty, London, 1881.

Mir Khurd, *Siyarul Auliya*, Delhi, 1302 A.H.

Modi, J.J., *The Parsees at the Court of Akbar and Dastur Meherji Rana*, Bombay, 1903.

Navai, Abdul Hossain, *Asnad wa Makatibat-i Tarikh-i Iran*, Tehran, 1977.

Nayeem, M.A., *Mughal Documents: Catalogue of Aurangzeb's Reign (1658-1663 A.D.)* Vol. I (Part I) Hyderabad, 1980.

Nichola, Manuchi *Storia Do Mongar (1653-1708)*, II, tr., W. Irvine, London, 1907.

Rashid, S.A., *A Calendar of Oriental Records, II* Allahabad, 1956.

Saksena, B.P., *Calendar of Oriental Records, I.* Allahabad, 1955.

Saqi Mustaid Khan, *Maasiri Alamgiri, tr.*, J.N. Sarkar, Calcutta, 1947.

Shakeb, M.Z.A., *Mughal Archives*, I, Delhi, 1979.

Srivastava, K.P., *Mughal Farmans*, Lucknow, 1974.

Sarkar, Benoy Kumar, *The Sukramiti*, New Delhi, 1973.

Tirmizi, S.A.I., ed., *Ajmer Through Inscriptions*, Delhi, 1968.

-------------, *Calendar of Acquired Documents (1402-1719)*, New Delhi, 1982.

-------------, *Edicts From the Mughal Harem*, New Delhi, 1979.

Watters, Thomas, *On Yuan Chwang Travels in India 629-645*, London, 1904-06.

SECONDARY SOURCES

Abbasi, Mahmud Ahmad, *Tazkiratul Kiram* alias *Tarikh-i Amroha*, Delhi.

Aga Mahdi Hasan, *The Tughlaq Dynasty*, New Delhi, 1976.

Alakh Chari, *Raja Rai Singh of Bikaner*, Bikaner, 1935.

Ashraf, K.M., *Life and Conditions of the People of Hindustan,* New Delhi, 1970.

Barthold, V.V., *Four Studies in the History of Central Asia,* Leiden, 1958.

Bendre, V.S., *Tarikh-i Ilahi*, Poona, 1933.

Bilgirami, Muhammad Mahmud, *Tanqihul Kalam fi Tarikh-i Bilgiram.* Aligarh, 1937

Buhler, George, *Indian Paleography,* New Delhi, 1980.

Habibullah, A.D.M., *Foundation of Muslim Rule in India,* Allahabad, 1971.

Hodivala, S.H., *Studies in Parsi History,* Bombay, 1930.

Ibn Hasan, *Central Structure of the Mughal Empire*, New Delhi, 1970.

Irfan Habib, *The Agrarian System of Mughal India*, Bombay, 1963.

Lambton, A.K.S., *Landlord and Peasant in Persia,* Oxford, 1953.

Momin, Mohiuddin, *The Chancellary and Persian Epistolography under the Mughals,* Calcutta, 1971.

Moreland, W.H., *The Agrarian System of Muslim India*, Delhi 1929.

Nizami, K.A., *Some Aspects of Religion and Politics in the Thirteenth Century,* Aligarh, 1961.

Prasad, R.N., *Raja Mansingh of Amber*, Calcutta, 1966.

Qureshi, Ishtiaq Husain, *The Administration of the Mughal* Empire. Patna, 1979.

Saran, P., *The Provincial Government of Mughals 1526-1658,* Bombay, 1973.

Sarkar, J.N., *Mughal Administration,* Calcutta 1952.

Sastri, Nilkanta, K.A., *The Colas,* Madras, 1925.

Sen, S.N., *India Through Chinese Eyes,* 1956.

Siddiqui, Numan Ahmad, *Land Revenue Administration Under the Mughals 1700-1750,* Bombay, 1960.

Sircar, D.C., *Indian Epigraphy,* Delhi, 1965.

Srivastava A.L. *Akbar-The Great.* I-II, Agra, 1962, 1967.

Tirmizi, S.A.I., *Index to Titles,* Calcutta 1979.

Tripathi, R.P., *Some Aspects of Muslim Administration,* Allahabad, 1956.

Wahid Mirza, *The Life and Works of Amir Khusrau,* Delhi, 1974.

PERIODICALS, PROCEEDINGS & CATALOGUES

All Indian Oriental Conference X, 1940.

Catalogue of the Delhi Museum of Archaeology, Red Fort, Calcutta.

Epigraphia-Indica, XXXIII.

Idara-i Maarif-i Islami, Lahore, 1936.

Indian Economic and Social History Review, IV 1967.

Indian Historical Records Commission, VI, VIII, IX, XVXII, XVIII, XXII, XXIV, XXVI, XXIX, XXXII, XXXIV, XXXVI, XLIV, XLVII.

Indian History Congress, XIII (1938), XV (1940), XXI (1944), XXX (1967), XXXXIII (1982).

Islamic Culture, XLVII.

Journal of Asiatic Society of Bengal, Calcutta, 1923.

Journal of Bombay Branch of the Royal Asiatic Society, XXI, 1900-1904, XXV.

Journal of Bihar Research Society, XLIII, Pt. III.

Journal of Indian History XXXVI, Pts. I-III.

Journal of Punjab History Society, II,V.

Journal of the University of Bombay, XX.

Medieval India-A Miscellany,1969.

National Register of Private Records, Vol.VI.

New Indian Antiquary, II, 1939.

Oriental College Magazine, May 1939.

Persian Catalogue, ed., C.V. Joshi, Baroda.

Studies in Islam Vol., XV 1978

DICTIONARIES AND CENSUS REPORTS

Gurdaspur District, Punjab, Census 1971 Series 17, No. 384.

Gurdaspur District Punjab Census Handbook, No. 94.

Platts J.T., *A Distionary of Urdu, Classical Hindi and English*, London, 1884.

Steingass, A, *Comprehensive Persian English Dictionary*, London, 1930.

Wilson, H.H., *A Glossary of Judical and Revenue Terms*, London 1855.

ANNEXURE 1

PERSIAN AND HIJRA MONTHS

	Persian		Hijra
1.	Farwardin	1.	Muharram
2.	Ardibinisht	2.	Safar
3.	Khurdad	3.	Rabiul awwal
4.	Tir	4.	Rabius sani
5.	Amardad	5.	Jamadiul awwal
6.	Shahriwar	6.	Jamadius sani
7.	Mihr	7.	Rajab
8.	Aban	8.	Shaban
9.	Azar	9.	Ramazan
10.	Dai	10.	Shawwal
11.	Bahman	11.	Zil 'qa' dah
12.	Isfandarmaz	12.	Zilhijja

ANNEXURE 2

DAYS OF THE PERSIAN MONTH

1. Ormuz , Ormuzd
2. Bahman
3. Ardibihisht
4. Shahri-war
5. Isfandarmaz
6. Khurdad
7. Amardad
8. Dai
9. Azar
10. Aban
11. Khwur
12. Mah
13. Tir
14. Gosh
15. Dai
16. Mihr
17. Sarosh
18. Rashn
19. Farwardin
20. Bahram
21. Ram
22. Bad
23. Dai
24. Din
25. Arad
26. Astad
27. Asman
28. Zamyad, Ramyad
29. Marispand
30. Aniran
31. Roz
32. Shab

ANNEXURE 3

THE TURKISH DUODENARY CYCLE

1.	Sichqan-i	(The mouse year)
2.	Ud-il	(The cow year)
3.	Pars-il	(The leopard year)
4.	Tawishaqan-il	(The hare year)
5.	Lui-il	(The crocodile year)
6.	Ilan-il	(The snake year)
7.	Yunt-il	(The horse year)
8.	Qui-il	(The sheep year)
9.	Bichi-il	(The monkey year)
10.	Takhaqui-il	(The fowl year)
11.	It-il	(The dog year)
12.	Tanguz-il	(The hog year)

ANNEXURE 4

SEALS

Owner	Shape	Legend
Hamida Banu	Flower with eight petals	*Hamida Banu bint-i Ali Akbar*
Maryam Zamani	Pitcher	*Wali Nimat Bagam Walidah-i Jahangir Badshah*
Nur Jahan	(a) Lozenge	*Ze mehr-i Shah-i Jahangir shud chun mah furuzan; nigin-i muhr-i Nur Jahan Badshah Begam-i dauran* 1029. By the light of the Sun of Emperor *Jahangir* ; the bezel of the seal of *Nur Jahan* has become resplendant like the Moon.
	(b) Rose with six petals	*Allahu Akbar.* *Ze nuri mehr-i Jahangir Badshah-i jahahban 1033; nigin-i Nur- Jahan Badshah gasht furuzan 19 Julus.* By the light of the Sun of *Jahangir*, the world protecting monarch 1033; the bezel of Empress *Nur Jahan* became resplendant 19 Regnal year.

ANNEXURE 5

TUGHRAS AND UNWANS

Owner	Status	Tughra	Unwan
Babur	Emperor		*Farman-i Zahirud Din Muhammad Babur Badshah Ghazi*
Humayun	Emperor	*Farman-i Muhammad Humayun Badshah Ghazi*	
Akbar	Emperor	*Farman-i Jalalud Din Muhammad Akbar Badshah Ghazi.*	
Jahangir	Emperor	*Farman-i Abul Muzaffar Nurud Din Muhmmad Jahangir Badshah Ghazi*	
Hamida Banu	Queen Mother		*Hukm-i Hamida Banu*
Maryam Zamini	Queen Mother		*Hukm-i Maryam Zamani*
Nur Jahan	Queen Consort	*Hukm-i uliya i aliya mahd uliya Nur Jahan Badshah Begam*	

ANNEXURE 6

TAKID AND TAHID

(a) *Bayad ke hasbul hukm amal namuda ba taqdim rasanand* (it is incumbent upon them to obey the order and act accordingly).

(b) *Az farmuda takhaluf wa inhiraf na warzand* (they should not act contrary to and deviate from the order).

(c) *Dar in bab qadghan wa takid tamanm lazim danista* (taking every care and considering this matter imperative).

(d) *Az farmuda dar naghuzrand* (they should not do anything contrary to the command).

(e) *Dar uhda shinasad* (this should be considered premptory).

(f) *Husbul mastur amal numayand* (they should act according to what has been written).

(g) *Muzahim wa mutarriz nabashand* (they should not importune and molest).

(h) *Mujaddad natalaband* (they should not demand renewal).

ANNEXURE 7

Official	Endorsement
Wakil-i Mutlaq	*Manzur darand* (May be sanctioned)
Pishdast (Personal Assistant) of Wakil-i Mutlaq	*Alimtu* (I have noted)
Diwan	*Sabt numayand* (May be recorded)
Pishdast-i Diwan	*Sabt shud* (It has been recorded)
Diwan-i Buyutat	*Naql bi dahand* (Copy be given)
Pishdast-i Diwan-i Buyutat	*Waqif shud* (Noted)
Khan-i Saman	*Qalami numayand* (Let it be recorded)
Pishdast-i Khan-i Saman	*Ittalatu alaih* (I have been informed)
Bakhshi	*Biguzarand* (Let it be submitted)
Pishdast-i Bakhshi	*Waqaftu alaih* (I have been intimated)
Mustaufi	*Mulahiza numayand* (Let it be perused)
Pishdast-i Mustaufi	*Muttala shud* (Has been informed)

Index